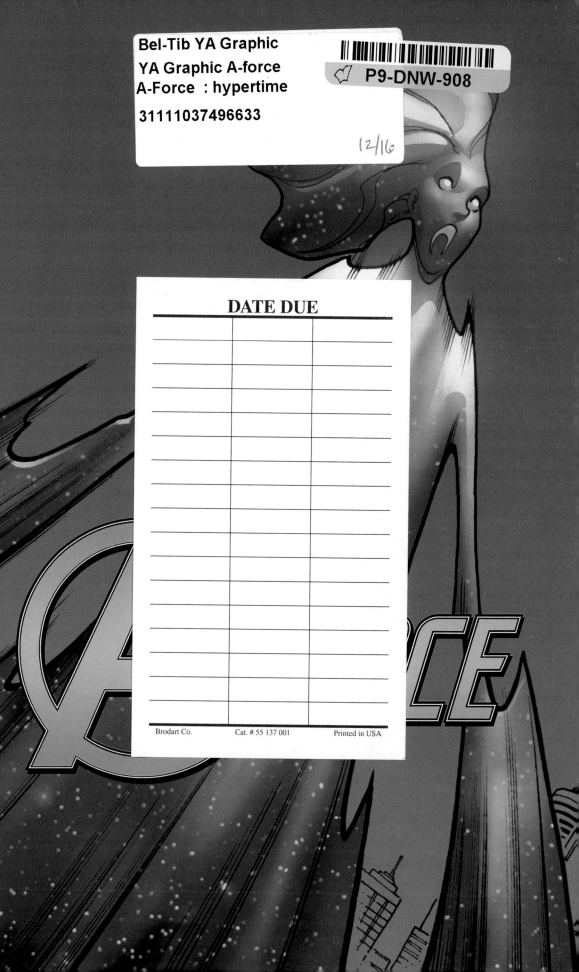

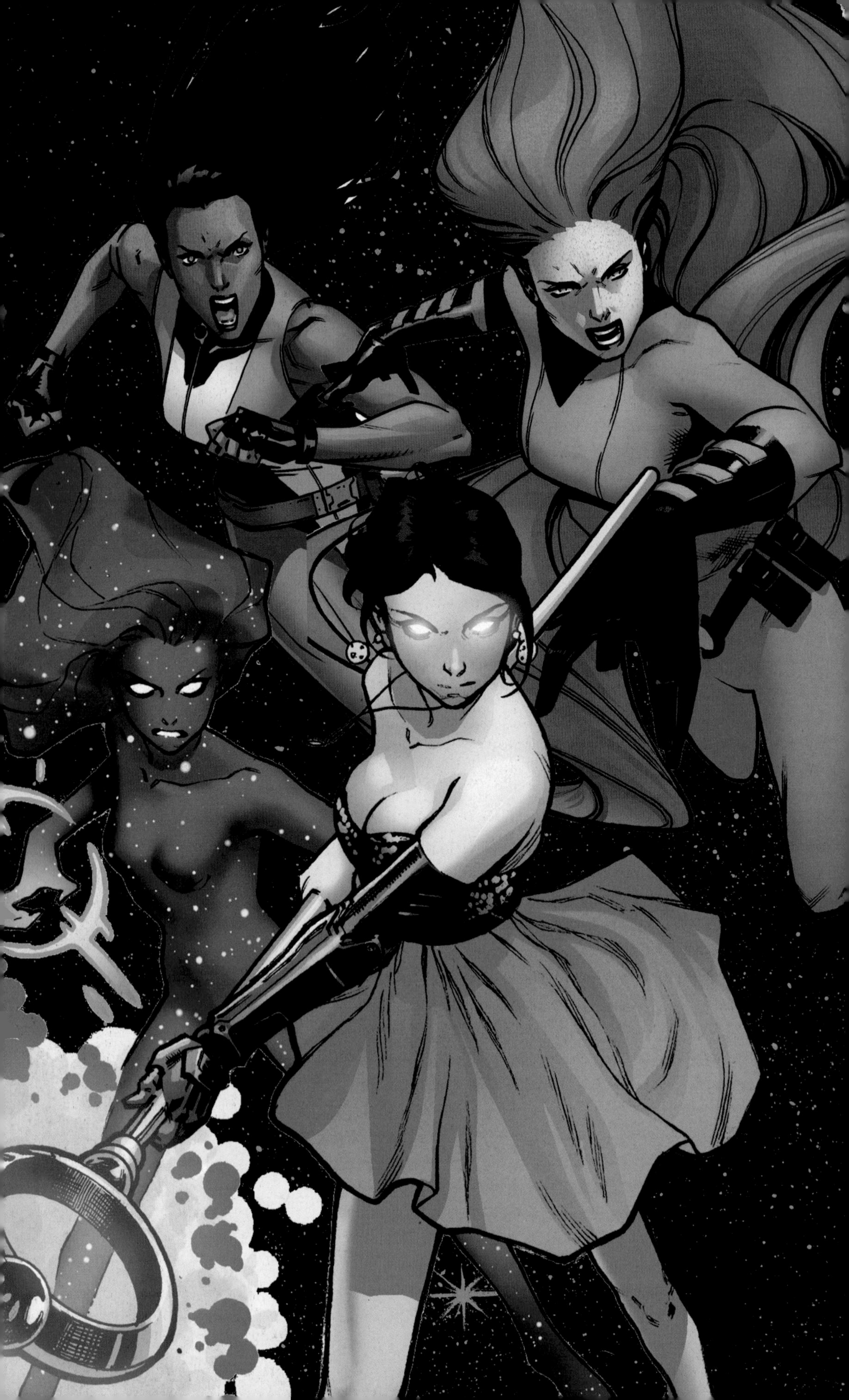

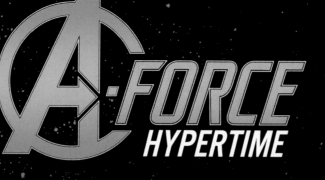

A-FORCE
HYPERTIME

"IN THE BEGINNING" (FROM *AVENGERS #0*)

WRITER
G. WILLOW WILSON

ARTIST
VICTOR IBAÑEZ

COLOR ARTIST
LAURA MARTIN

LETTERER
VC'S CORY PETIT

EDITORS
DANIEL KETCHUM & ALANNA SMITH

A-FORCE #1-4

WRITERS
G. WILLOW WILSON & KELLY THOMPSON

ARTIST
JORGE MOLINA

COLOR ARTISTS
LAURA MARTIN (#1-2, #4) & MATT MILLA (#3)

LETTERER
VC'S CORY PETIT

COVER ART
JORGE MOLINA

ASSISTANT EDITOR
ALANNA SMITH

EDITORS
KATIE KUBERT WITH DANIEL KETCHUM

COLLECTION EDITOR
JENNIFER GRÜNWALD

ASSOCIATE EDITOR
SARAH BRUNSTAD

ASSOCIATE MANAGING EDITOR
ALEX STARBUCK

EDITOR, SPECIAL PROJECTS
MARK D. BEAZLEY

VP, PRODUCTION & SPECIAL PROJECTS
JEFF YOUNGQUIST

SVP PRINT, SALES & MARKETING
DAVID GABRIEL

BOOK DESIGNER
JAY BOWEN

EDITOR IN CHIEF
AXEL ALONSO

CHIEF CREATIVE OFFICER
JOE QUESADA

PUBLISHER
DAN BUCKLEY

EXECUTIVE PRODUCER
ALAN FINE

RCE VOL. 1: HYPERTIME. Contains material originally published in magazine form as A-FORCE (2016) #1-4, AVENGERS #0, AVENGERS #83 and A-FORCE (2015) #1. First printing 2016. ISBN# 978-0-7851-9605-1. Published by MARVEL .DWIDE, INC., a subsidiary of MARVEL ENTERTAINMENT, LLC. OFFICE OF PUBLICATION: 135 West 50th Street, New York, NY 10020. **Printed in the U.S.A.** ALAN FINE, President, Marvel Entertainment; DAN BUCKLEY, dent, TV, Publishing & Brand Management; JOE QUESADA, Chief Creative Officer; TOM BREVOORT, SVP of Publishing; DAVID BOGART, SVP of Business Affairs & Operations, Publishing & Partnership; C.B. CEBULSKI, VP of Brand Management velopment, Asia; DAVID GABRIEL, SVP of Sales & Marketing, Publishing; JEFF YOUNGQUIST, VP of Production & Special Projects; DAN CARR, Executive Director of Publishing Technology; ALEX MORALES, Director of Publishing Operations; N CRESPI, Production Manager; STAN LEE, Chairman Emeritus. For information regarding advertising in Marvel Comics or on Marvel.com, please contact Vit DeBellis, Integrated Sales Manager, at vdebellis@marvel.com. For Marvel ription inquiries, please call 888-511-5480. **Manufactured between 5/13/2016 and 6/20/2016 by R.R. DONNELLEY, INC., SALEM, VA, USA.**

37654321

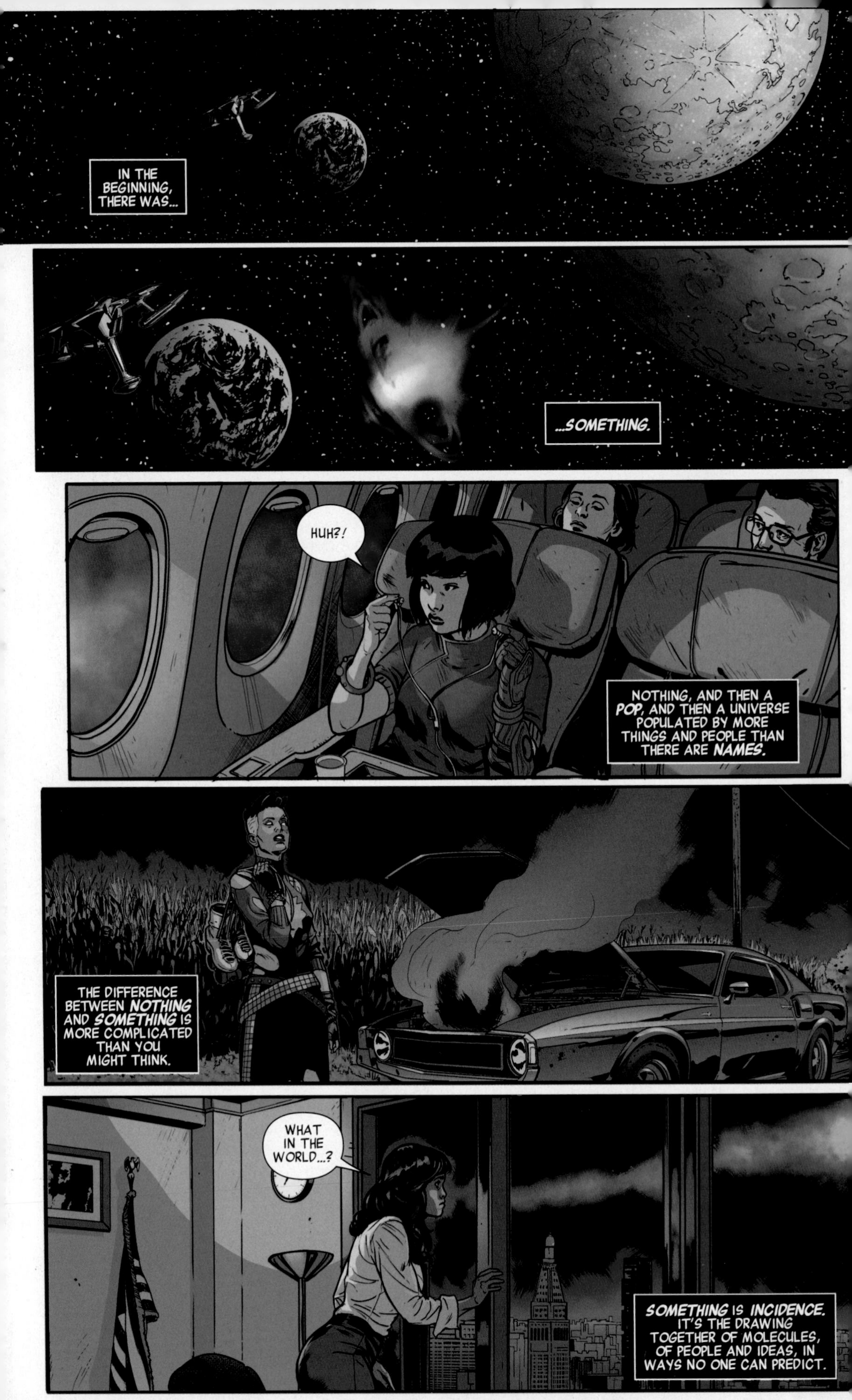
IN THE BEGINNING, THERE WAS...
...SOMETHING.
HUH?!
NOTHING, AND THEN A POP, AND THEN A UNIVERSE POPULATED BY MORE THINGS AND PEOPLE THAN THERE ARE NAMES.
THE DIFFERENCE BETWEEN NOTHING AND SOMETHING IS MORE COMPLICATED THAN YOU MIGHT THINK.
WHAT IN THE WORLD...?
SOMETHING IS INCIDENCE. IT'S THE DRAWING TOGETHER OF MOLECULES, OF PEOPLE AND IDEAS, IN WAYS NO ONE CAN PREDICT.

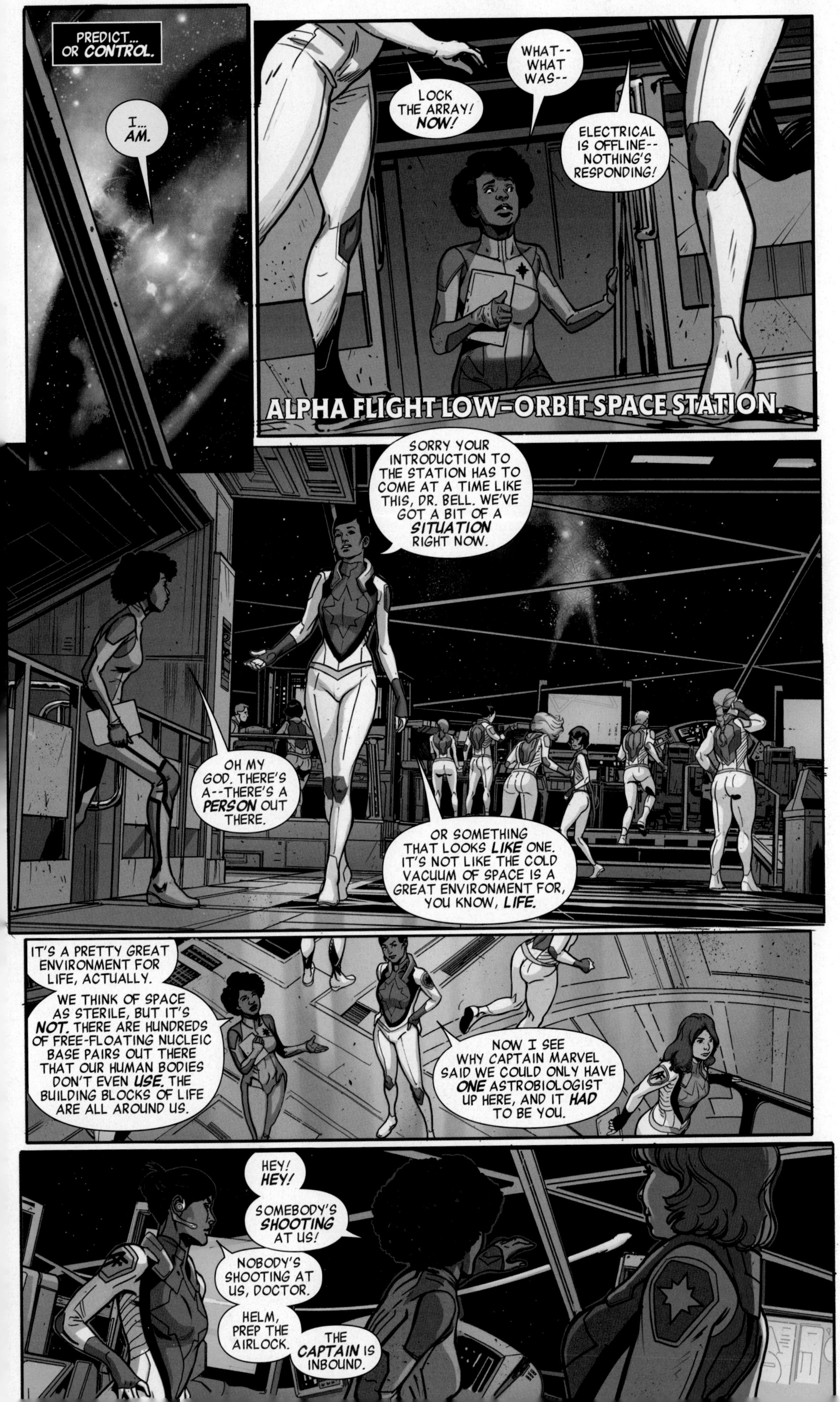
PREDICT... OR CONTROL.
I... AM.
LOCK THE ARRAY! NOW!
WHAT-- WHAT WAS--
ELECTRICAL IS OFFLINE-- NOTHING'S RESPONDING!
ALPHA FLIGHT LOW-ORBIT SPACE STATION.
SORRY YOUR INTRODUCTION TO THE STATION HAS TO COME AT A TIME LIKE THIS, DR. BELL. WE'VE GOT A BIT OF A SITUATION RIGHT NOW.
OH MY GOD. THERE'S A--THERE'S A PERSON OUT THERE.
OR SOMETHING THAT LOOKS LIKE ONE. IT'S NOT LIKE THE COLD VACUUM OF SPACE IS A GREAT ENVIRONMENT FOR, YOU KNOW, LIFE.
IT'S A PRETTY GREAT ENVIRONMENT FOR LIFE, ACTUALLY.
WE THINK OF SPACE AS STERILE, BUT IT'S NOT. THERE ARE HUNDREDS OF FREE-FLOATING NUCLEIC BASE PAIRS OUT THERE THAT OUR HUMAN BODIES DON'T EVEN USE. THE BUILDING BLOCKS OF LIFE ARE ALL AROUND US.
NOW I SEE WHY CAPTAIN MARVEL SAID WE COULD ONLY HAVE ONE ASTROBIOLOGIST UP HERE, AND IT HAD TO BE YOU.
HEY! HEY!
SOMEBODY'S SHOOTING AT US!
NOBODY'S SHOOTING AT US, DOCTOR.
HELM, PREP THE AIRLOCK.
THE CAPTAIN IS INBOUND.

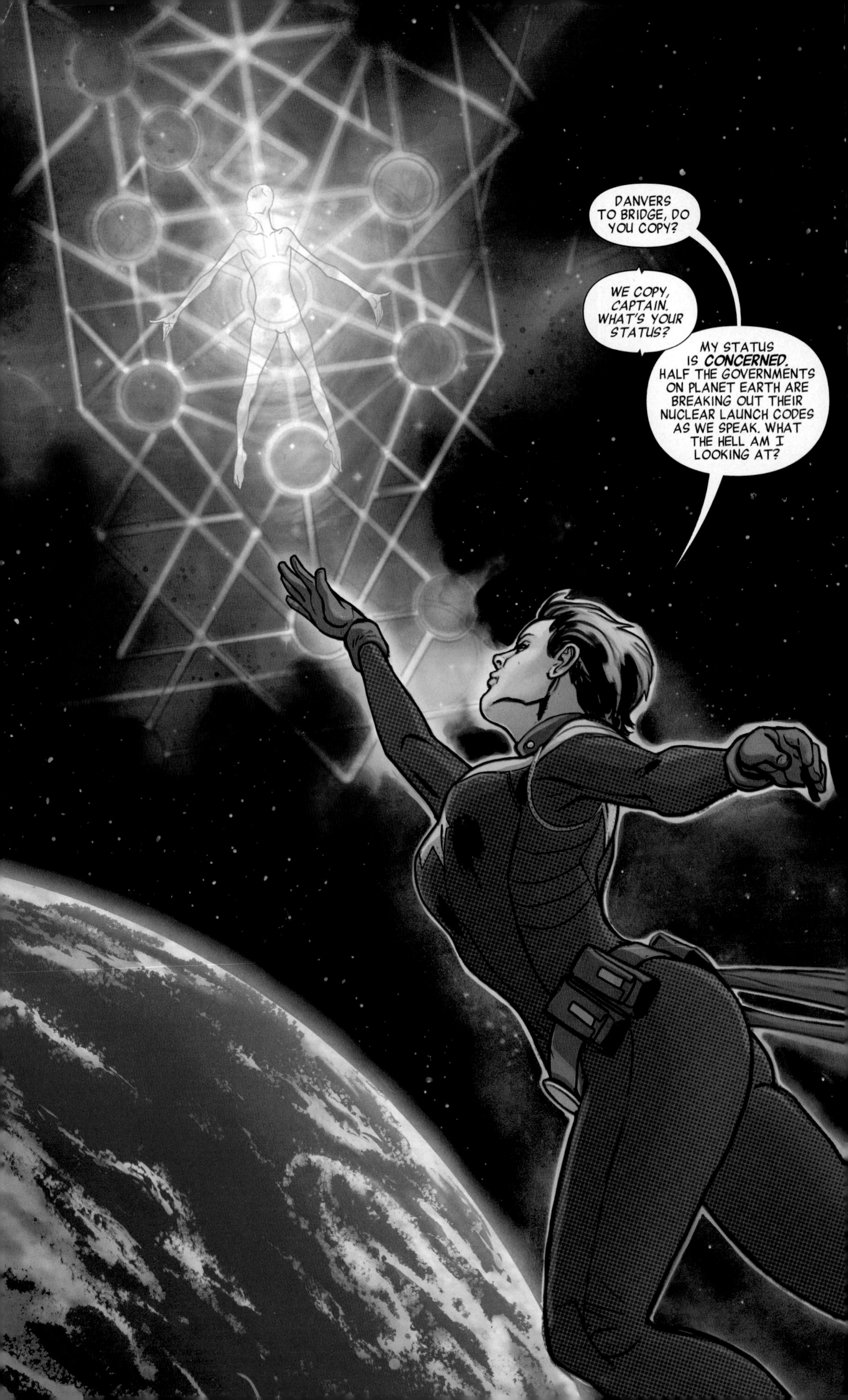
DANVERS TO BRIDGE, DO YOU COPY?
WE COPY, CAPTAIN. WHAT'S YOUR STATUS?
MY STATUS IS **CONCERNED.** HALF THE GOVERNMENTS ON PLANET EARTH ARE BREAKING OUT THEIR NUCLEAR LAUNCH CODES AS WE SPEAK. WHAT THE HELL AM I LOOKING AT?

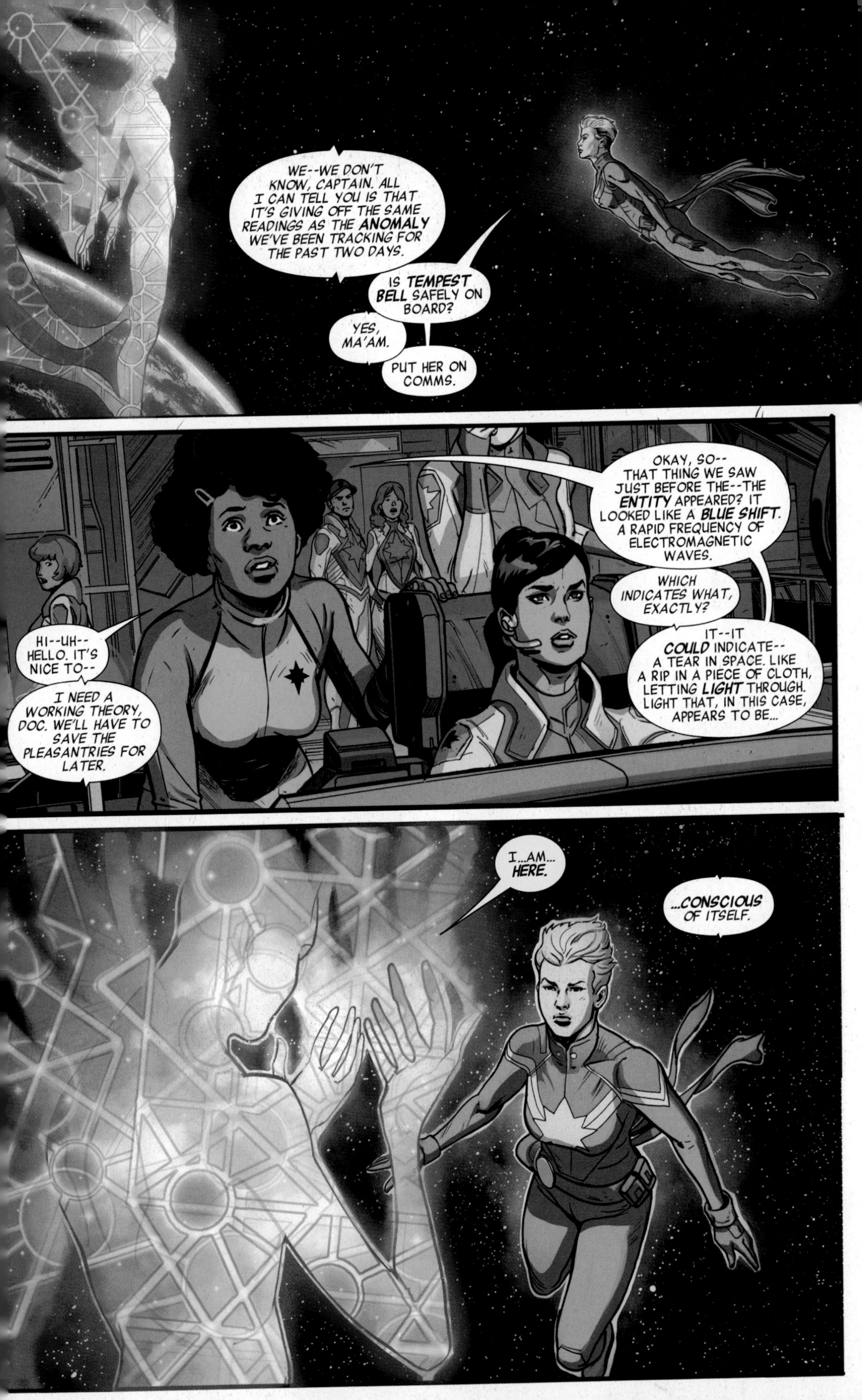
WE--WE DON'T KNOW, CAPTAIN. ALL I CAN TELL YOU IS THAT IT'S GIVING OFF THE SAME READINGS AS THE ANOMALY WE'VE BEEN TRACKING FOR THE PAST TWO DAYS.
IS TEMPEST BELL SAFELY ON BOARD?
YES, MA'AM.
PUT HER ON COMMS.
HI--UH--HELLO. IT'S NICE TO--
I NEED A WORKING THEORY, DOC. WE'LL HAVE TO SAVE THE PLEASANTRIES FOR LATER.
OKAY, SO-- THAT THING WE SAW JUST BEFORE THE--THE ENTITY APPEARED? IT LOOKED LIKE A BLUE SHIFT. A RAPID FREQUENCY OF ELECTROMAGNETIC WAVES.
WHICH INDICATES WHAT, EXACTLY?
IT--IT COULD INDICATE-- A TEAR IN SPACE. LIKE A RIP IN A PIECE OF CLOTH, LETTING LIGHT THROUGH. LIGHT THAT, IN THIS CASE, APPEARS TO BE...
I...AM... HERE.
...CONSCIOUS OF ITSELF.

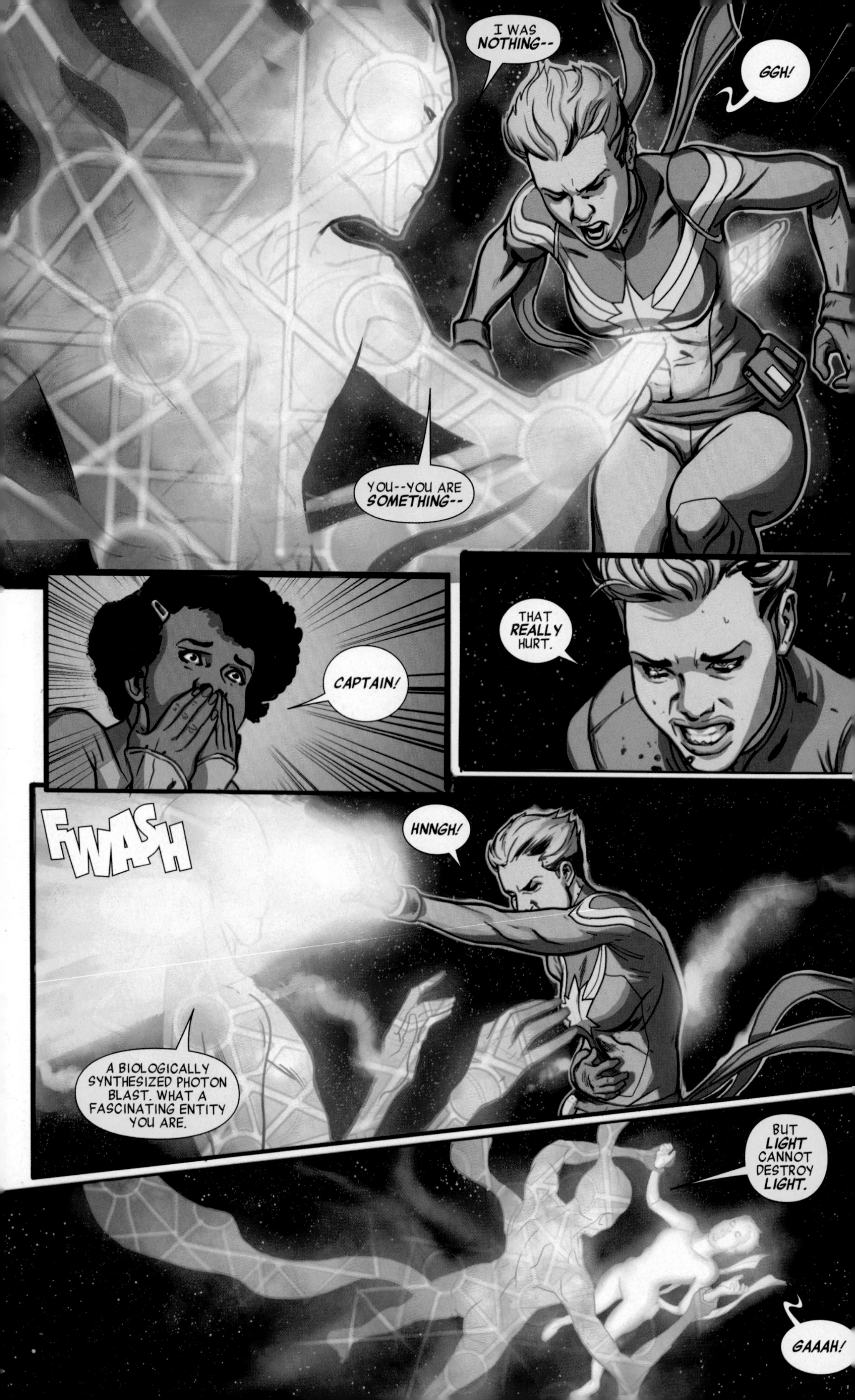
I WAS NOTHING--
GGH!
YOU--YOU ARE SOMETHING--
CAPTAIN!
THAT REALLY HURT.
FWASH
HNNGH!
A BIOLOGICALLY SYNTHESIZED PHOTON BLAST. WHAT A FASCINATING ENTITY YOU ARE.
BUT LIGHT CANNOT DESTROY LIGHT.
GAAAH!

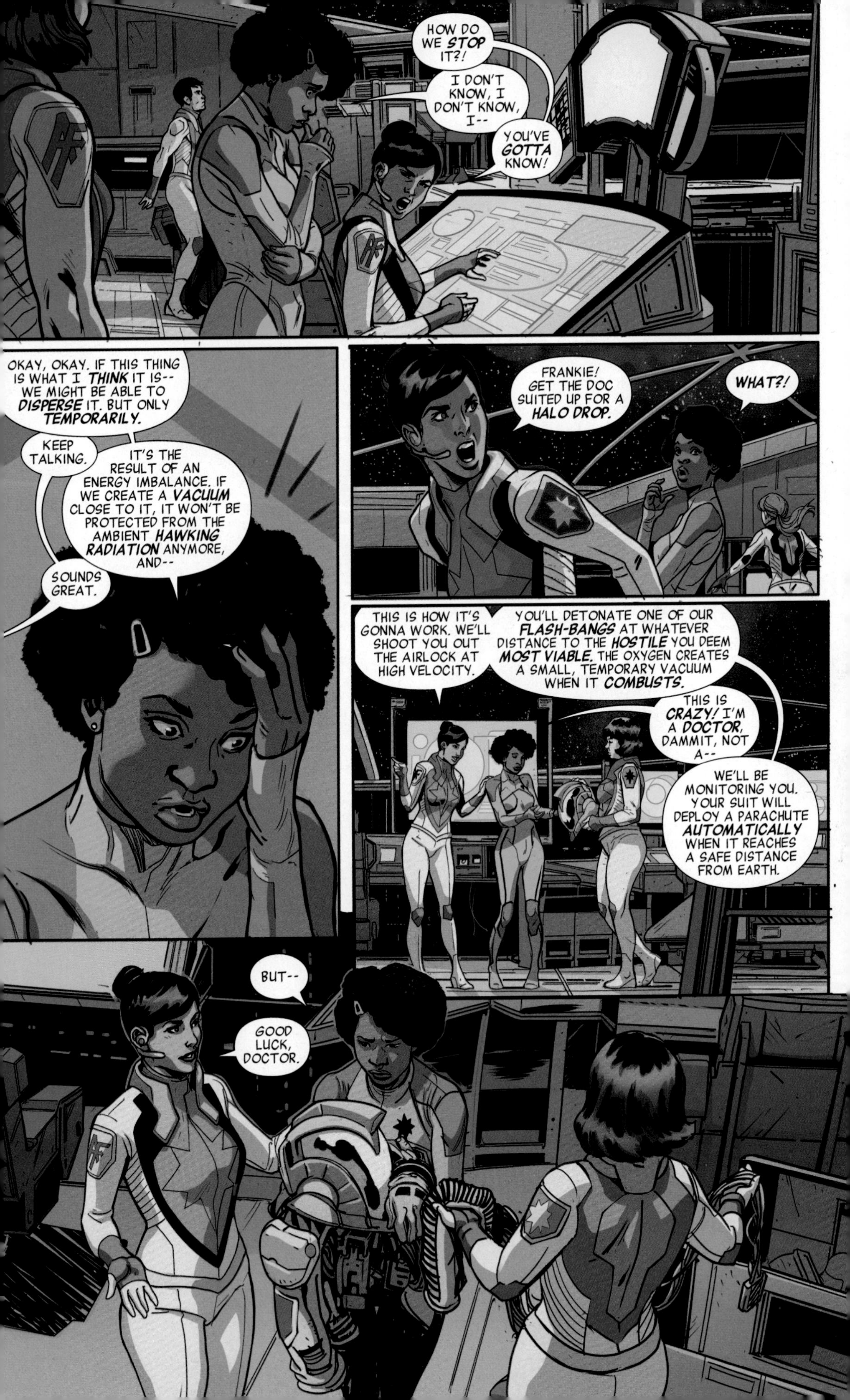
HOW DO WE STOP IT?!
I DON'T KNOW, I DON'T KNOW, I--
YOU'VE GOTTA KNOW!
OKAY, OKAY. IF THIS THING IS WHAT I THINK IT IS-- WE MIGHT BE ABLE TO DISPERSE IT. BUT ONLY TEMPORARILY.
KEEP TALKING.
IT'S THE RESULT OF AN ENERGY IMBALANCE. IF WE CREATE A VACUUM CLOSE TO IT, IT WON'T BE PROTECTED FROM THE AMBIENT HAWKING RADIATION ANYMORE, AND--
SOUNDS GREAT.
FRANKIE! GET THE DOC SUITED UP FOR A HALO DROP.
WHAT?!
THIS IS HOW IT'S GONNA WORK. WE'LL SHOOT YOU OUT THE AIRLOCK AT HIGH VELOCITY.
YOU'LL DETONATE ONE OF OUR FLASH-BANGS AT WHATEVER DISTANCE TO THE HOSTILE YOU DEEM MOST VIABLE. THE OXYGEN CREATES A SMALL, TEMPORARY VACUUM WHEN IT COMBUSTS.
THIS IS CRAZY! I'M A DOCTOR, DAMMIT, NOT A--
WE'LL BE MONITORING YOU. YOUR SUIT WILL DEPLOY A PARACHUTE AUTOMATICALLY WHEN IT REACHES A SAFE DISTANCE FROM EARTH.
BUT--
GOOD LUCK, DOCTOR.

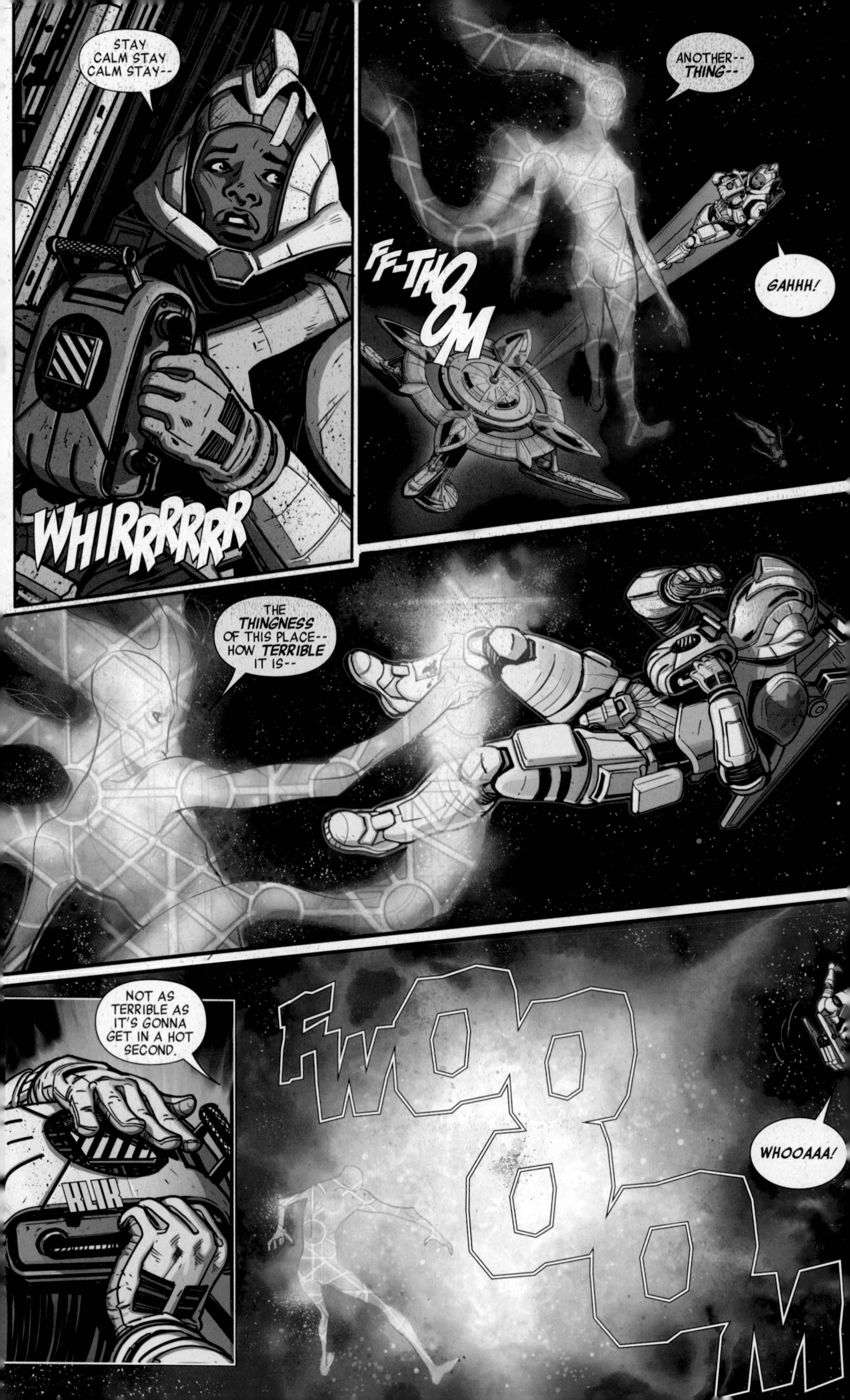
STAY CALM STAY CALM STAY--
WHIRRRRRR
ANOTHER-- THING--
FF-THOOM
GAHHH!
THE THINGNESS OF THIS PLACE-- HOW TERRIBLE IT IS--
NOT AS TERRIBLE AS IT'S GONNA GET IN A HOT SECOND.
KLIK
FWOOOOOM
WHOOAAA!

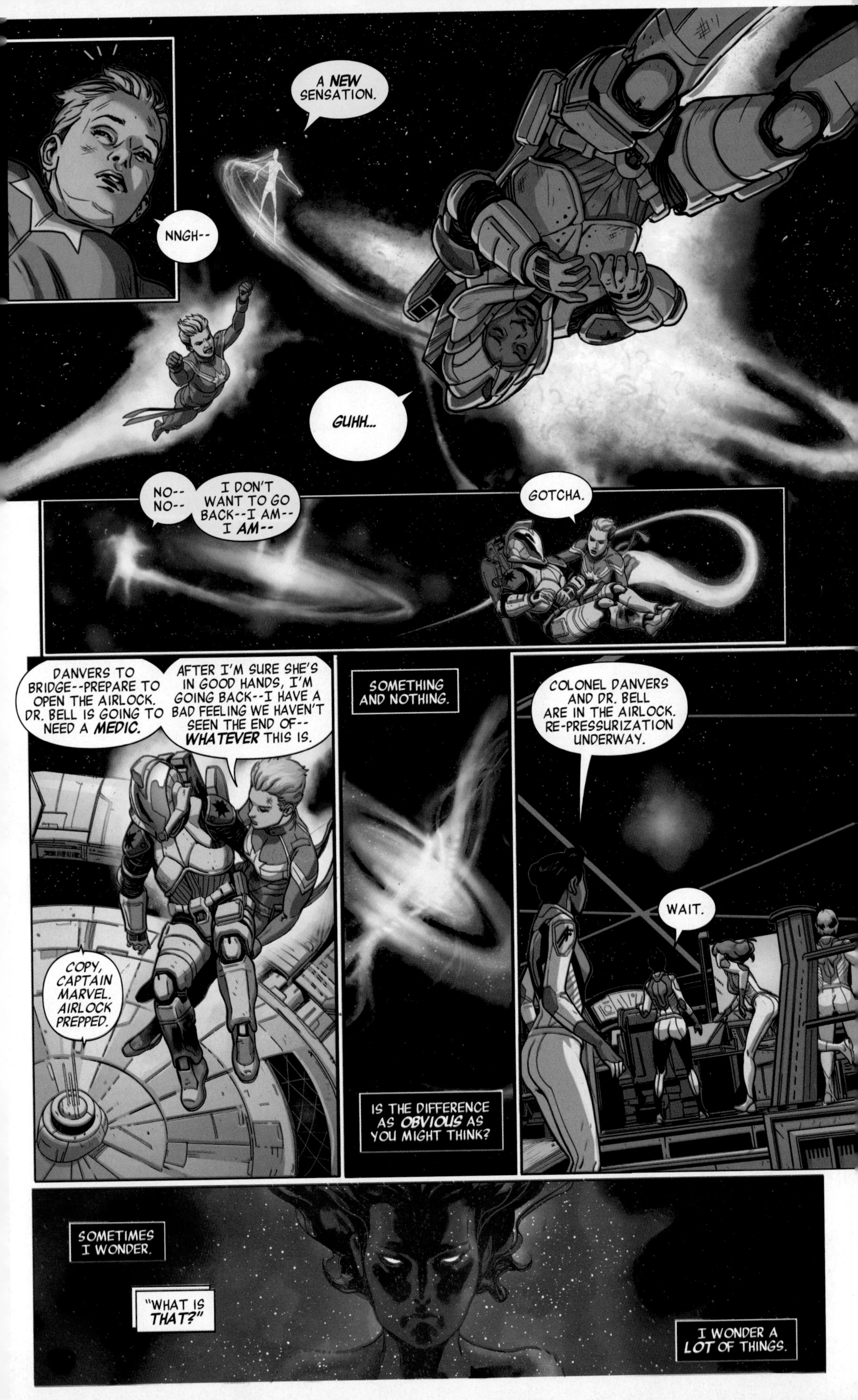
A NEW SENSATION.
NNGH--
GUHH...
NO-- NO--
I DON'T WANT TO GO BACK--I AM-- I AM--
GOTCHA.
DANVERS TO BRIDGE--PREPARE TO OPEN THE AIRLOCK. DR. BELL IS GOING TO NEED A MEDIC.
AFTER I'M SURE SHE'S IN GOOD HANDS, I'M GOING BACK--I HAVE A BAD FEELING WE HAVEN'T SEEN THE END OF-- WHATEVER THIS IS.
COPY, CAPTAIN MARVEL. AIRLOCK PREPPED.
SOMETHING AND NOTHING.
IS THE DIFFERENCE AS OBVIOUS AS YOU MIGHT THINK?
COLONEL DANVERS AND DR. BELL ARE IN THE AIRLOCK. RE-PRESSURIZATION UNDERWAY.
WAIT.
SOMETIMES I WONDER.
"WHAT IS THAT?"
I WONDER A LOT OF THINGS.

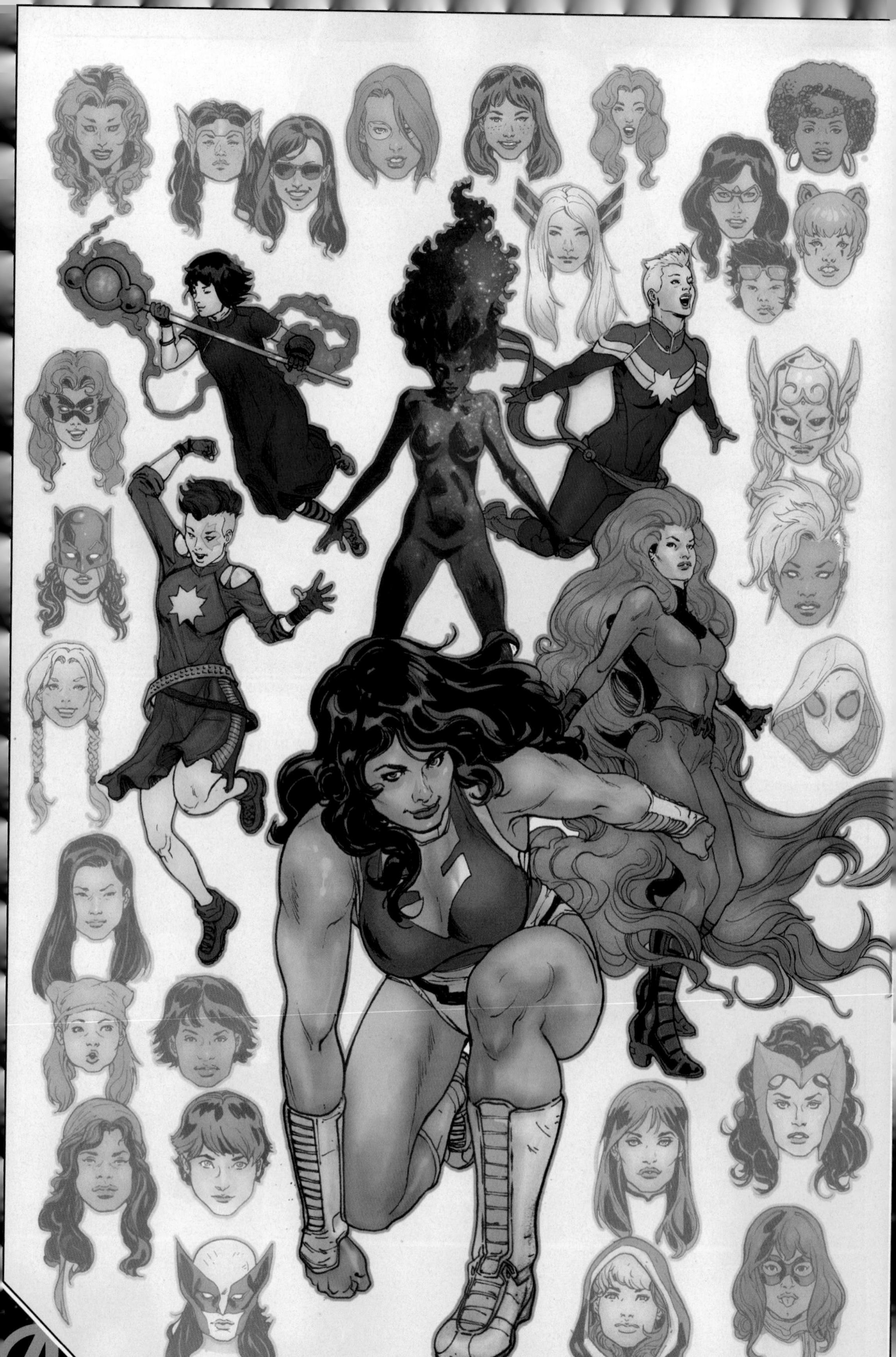

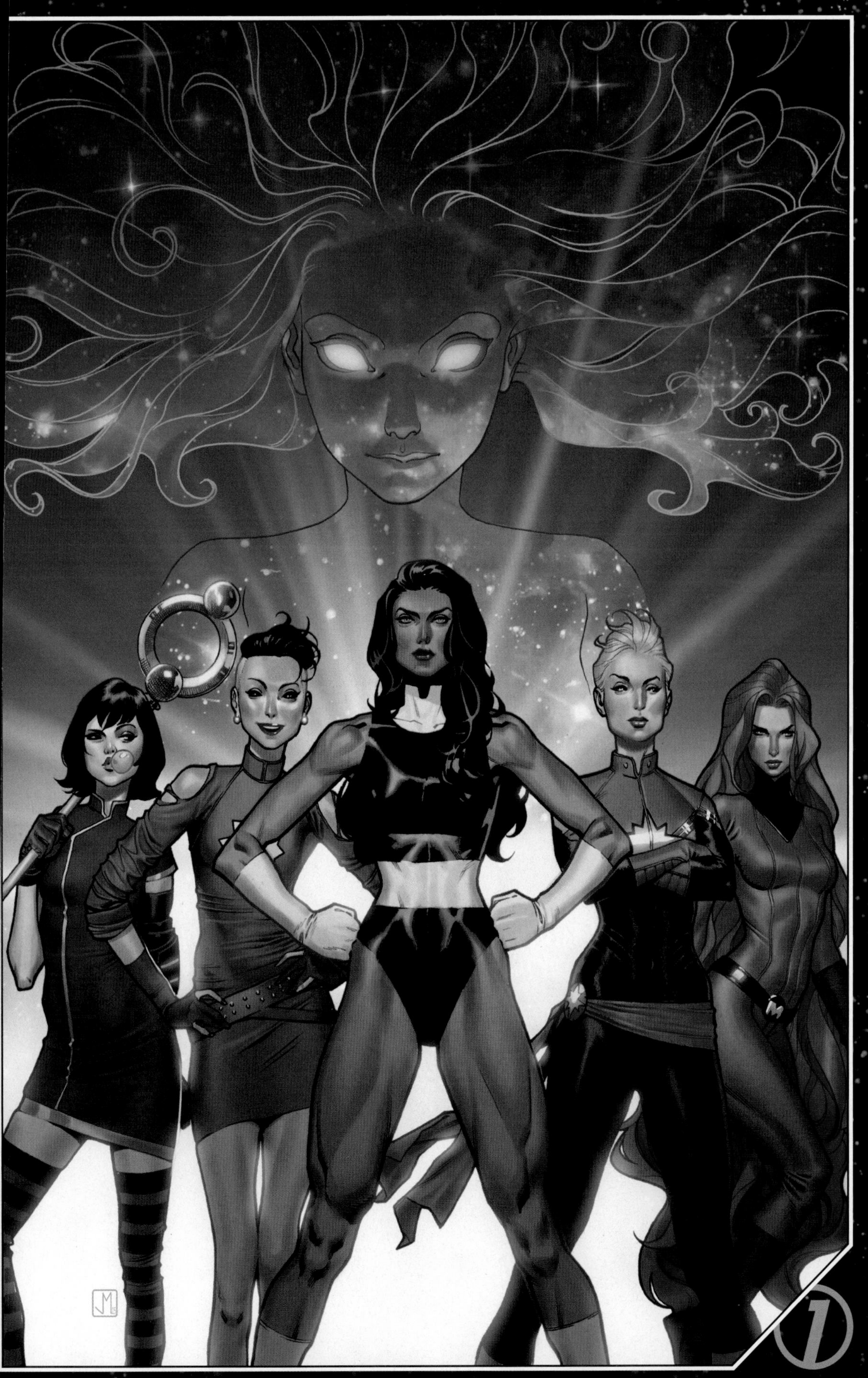
1

MEDUSA

SHE-HULK

SINGULARITY

CAPTAIN MARVEL

NICO MINORU

DAZZLER

A-FORCE

ON BATTLEWORLD, THERE WAS AN ISLAND PARADISE CALLED ARCADIA, PROTECTED BY THE WOMEN OF A-FORCE.

BUT BATTLEWORLD IS GONE, ALONG WITH ALL THE WOMEN WHO FOUGHT TO MAKE IT BETTER.

EXCEPT FOR ONE...

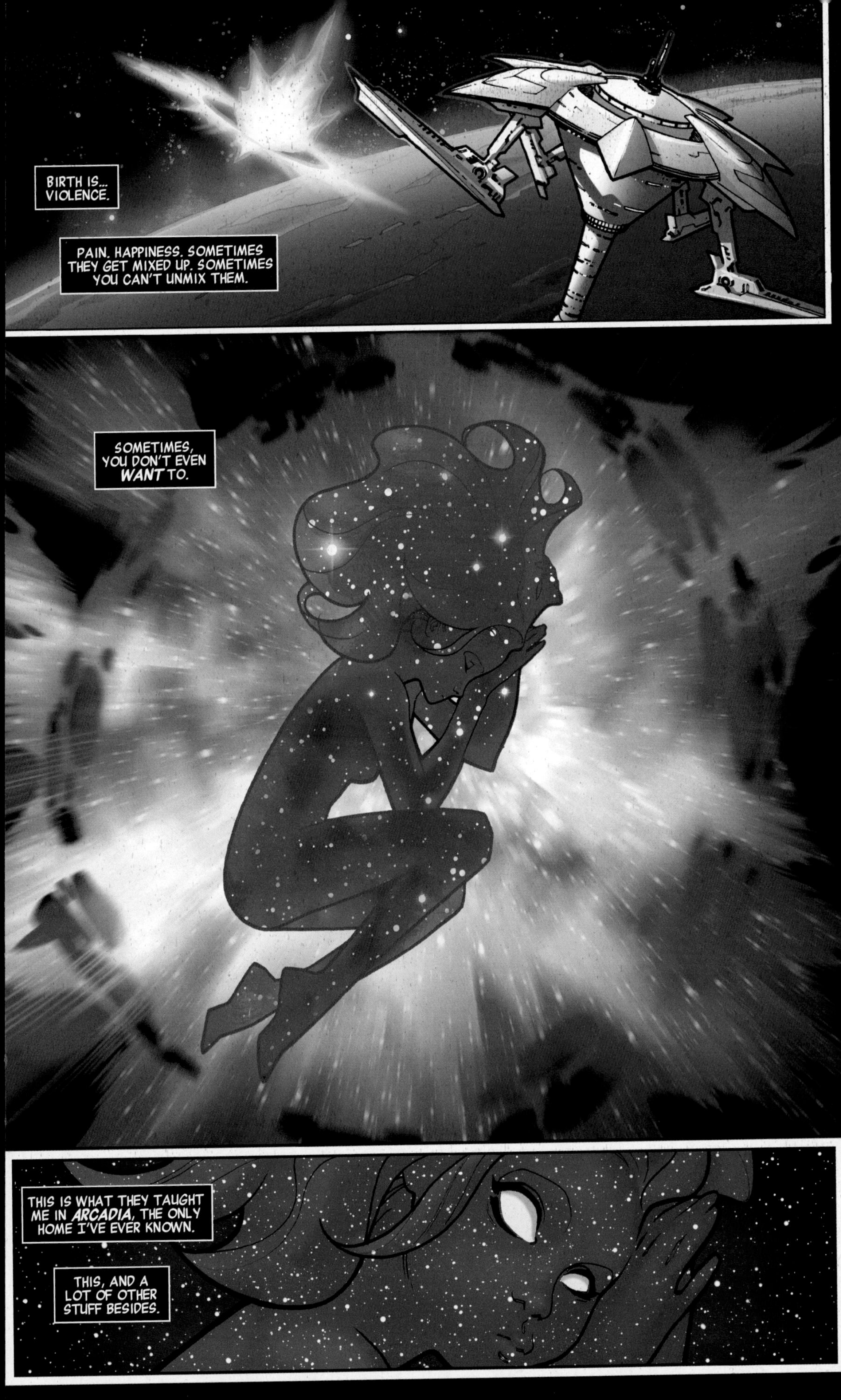
BIRTH IS... VIOLENCE.
PAIN. HAPPINESS. SOMETIMES THEY GET MIXED UP. SOMETIMES YOU CAN'T UNMIX THEM.
SOMETIMES, YOU DON'T EVEN WANT TO.
THIS IS WHAT THEY TAUGHT ME IN ARCADIA, THE ONLY HOME I'VE EVER KNOWN.
THIS, AND A LOT OF OTHER STUFF BESIDES.

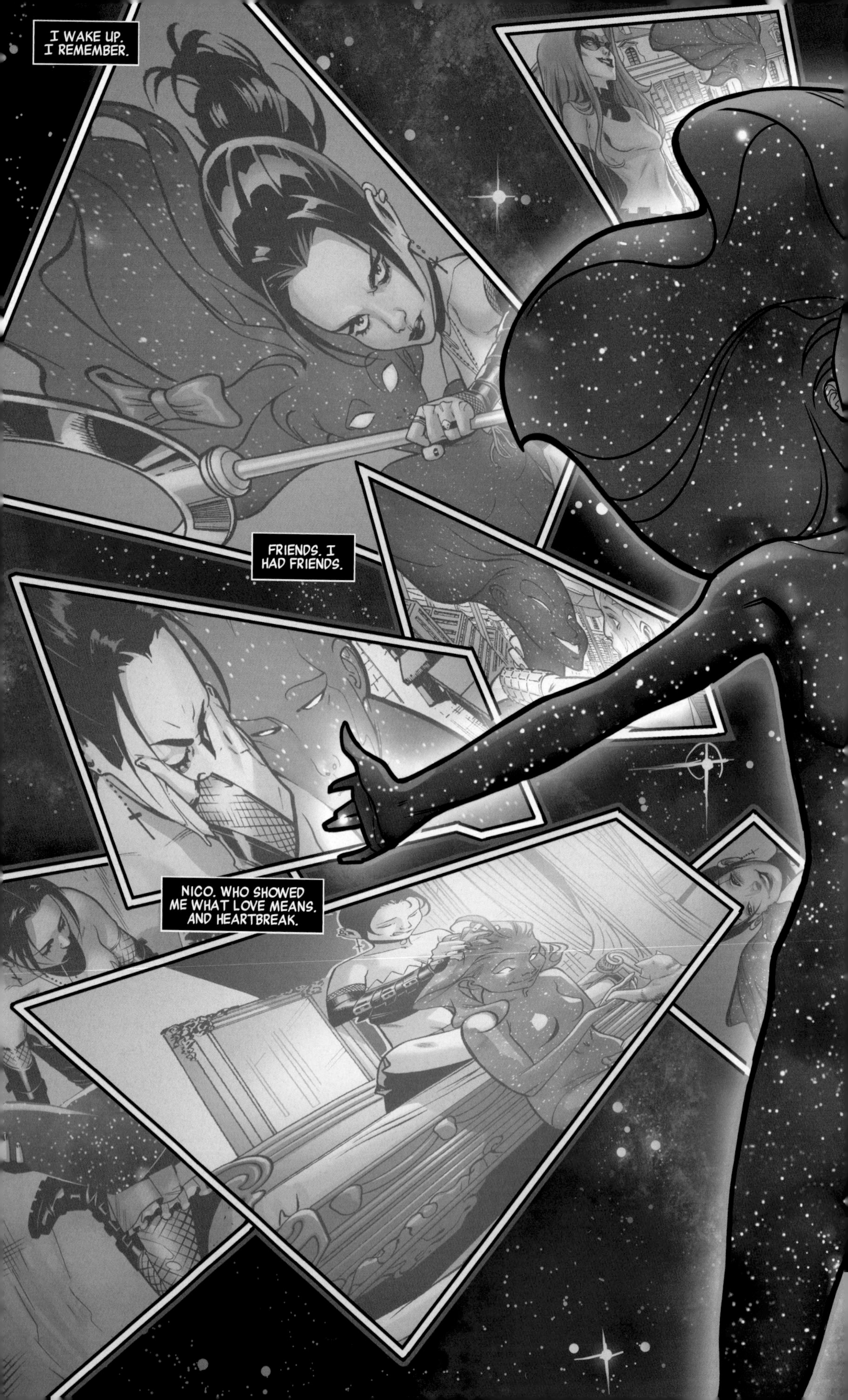
I WAKE UP. I REMEMBER.
FRIENDS. I HAD FRIENDS.
NICO. WHO SHOWED ME WHAT LOVE MEANS. AND HEARTBREAK.

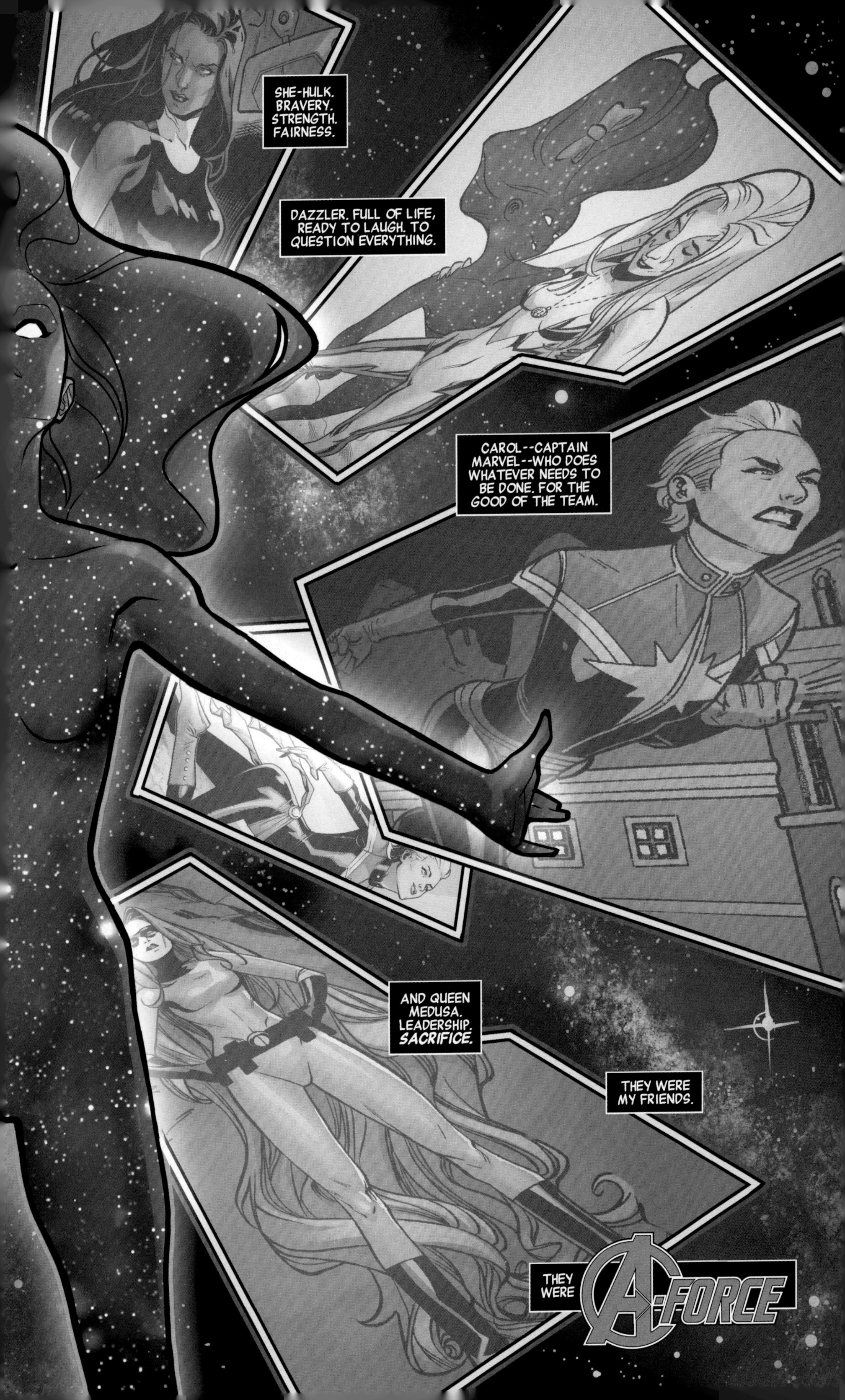
SHE-HULK. BRAVERY. STRENGTH. FAIRNESS.
DAZZLER. FULL OF LIFE, READY TO LAUGH. TO QUESTION EVERYTHING.
CAROL--CAPTAIN MARVEL--WHO DOES WHATEVER NEEDS TO BE DONE. FOR THE GOOD OF THE TEAM.
AND QUEEN MEDUSA. LEADERSHIP. SACRIFICE.
THEY WERE MY FRIENDS.
THEY WERE A-FORCE

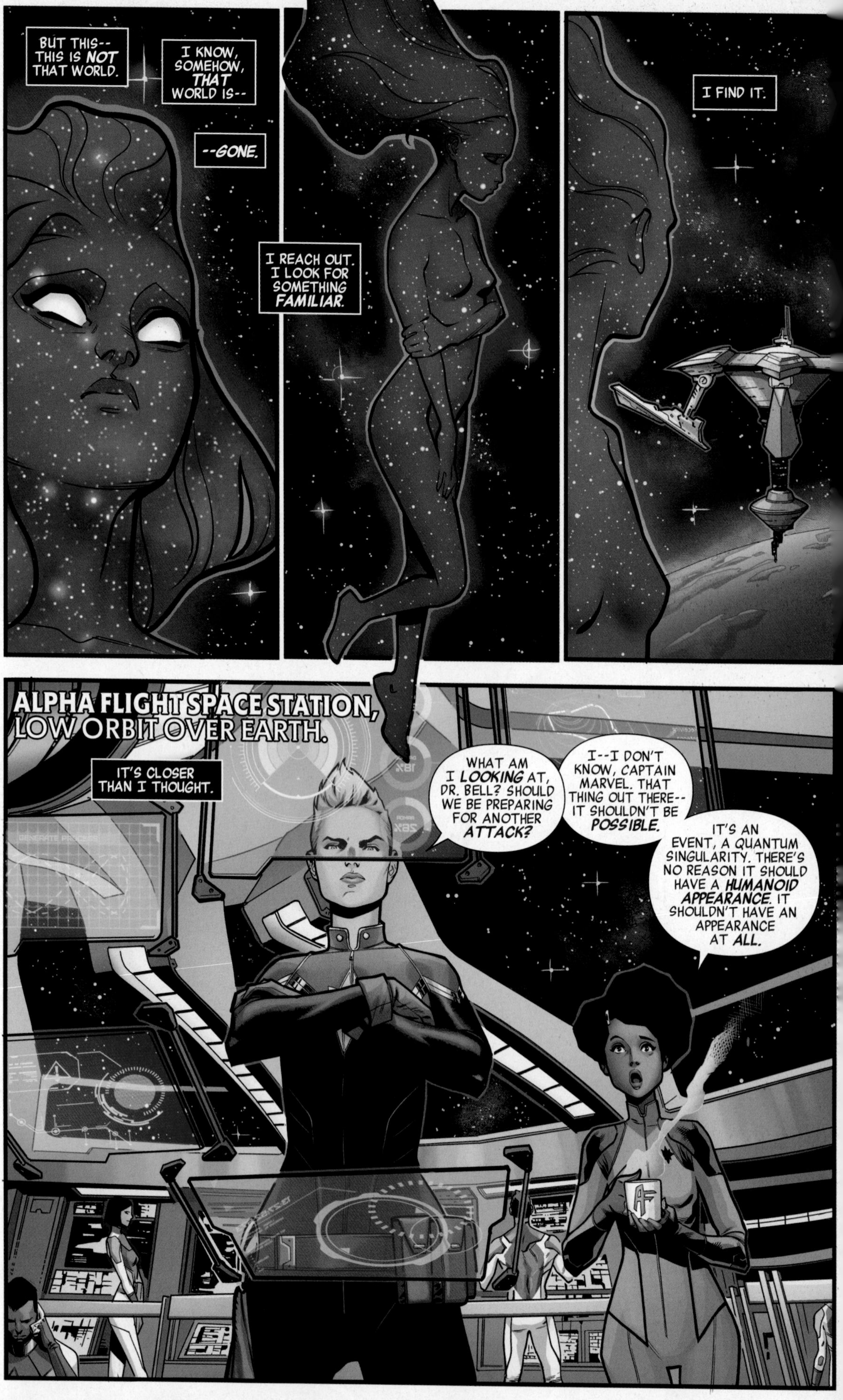
BUT THIS-- THIS IS NOT THAT WORLD.
I KNOW, SOMEHOW, THAT WORLD IS--
--GONE.
I REACH OUT. I LOOK FOR SOMETHING FAMILIAR.
I FIND IT.
ALPHA FLIGHT SPACE STATION, LOW ORBIT OVER EARTH.
IT'S CLOSER THAN I THOUGHT.
WHAT AM I LOOKING AT, DR. BELL? SHOULD WE BE PREPARING FOR ANOTHER ATTACK?
I--I DON'T KNOW, CAPTAIN MARVEL. THAT THING OUT THERE-- IT SHOULDN'T BE POSSIBLE.
IT'S AN EVENT, A QUANTUM SINGULARITY. THERE'S NO REASON IT SHOULD HAVE A HUMANOID APPEARANCE. IT SHOULDN'T HAVE AN APPEARANCE AT ALL.

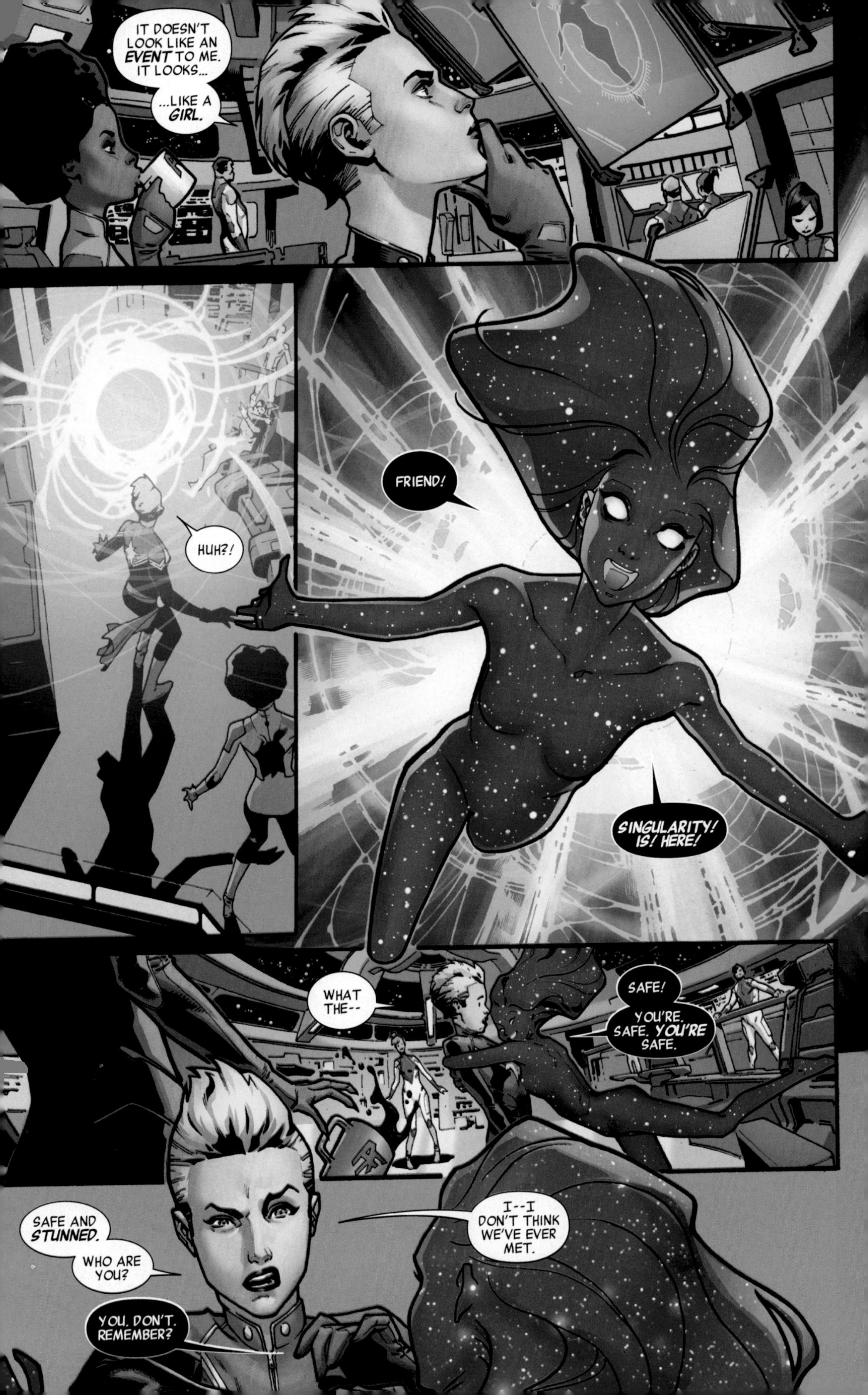
IT DOESN'T LOOK LIKE AN EVENT TO ME. IT LOOKS...
...LIKE A GIRL.
FRIEND!
HUH?!
SINGULARITY! IS! HERE!
WHAT THE--
SAFE!
YOU'RE. SAFE. YOU'RE SAFE.
SAFE AND STUNNED.
WHO ARE YOU?
YOU. DON'T. REMEMBER?
I--I DON'T THINK WE'VE EVER MET.

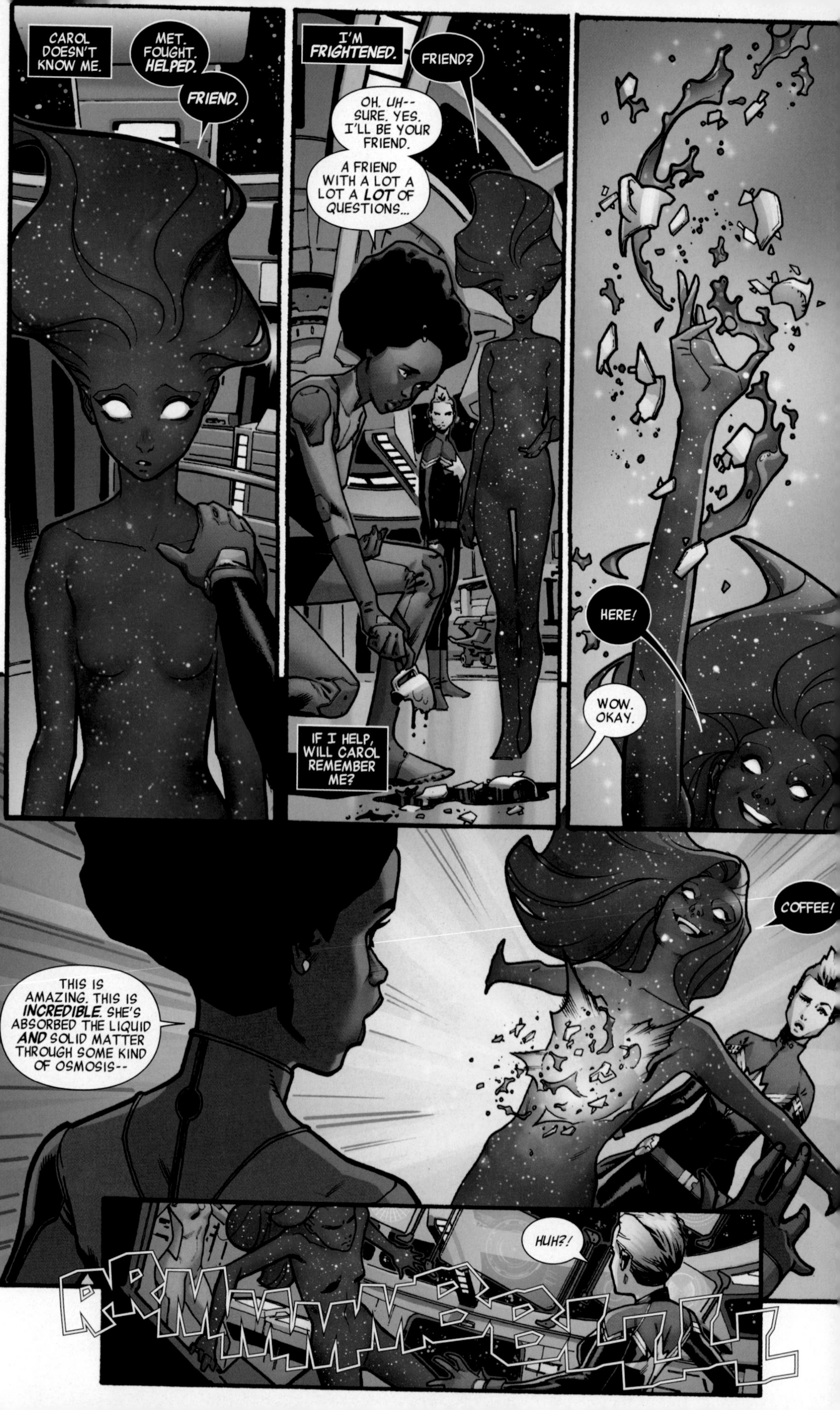
CAROL DOESN'T KNOW ME.
MET. FOUGHT. HELPED.
FRIEND.
I'M FRIGHTENED.
FRIEND?
OH. UH-- SURE. YES. I'LL BE YOUR FRIEND.
A FRIEND WITH A LOT A LOT A LOT OF QUESTIONS...
IF I HELP, WILL CAROL REMEMBER ME?
HERE!
WOW. OKAY.
THIS IS AMAZING. THIS IS INCREDIBLE. SHE'S ABSORBED THE LIQUID AND SOLID MATTER THROUGH SOME KIND OF OSMOSIS--
COFFEE!
HUH?!

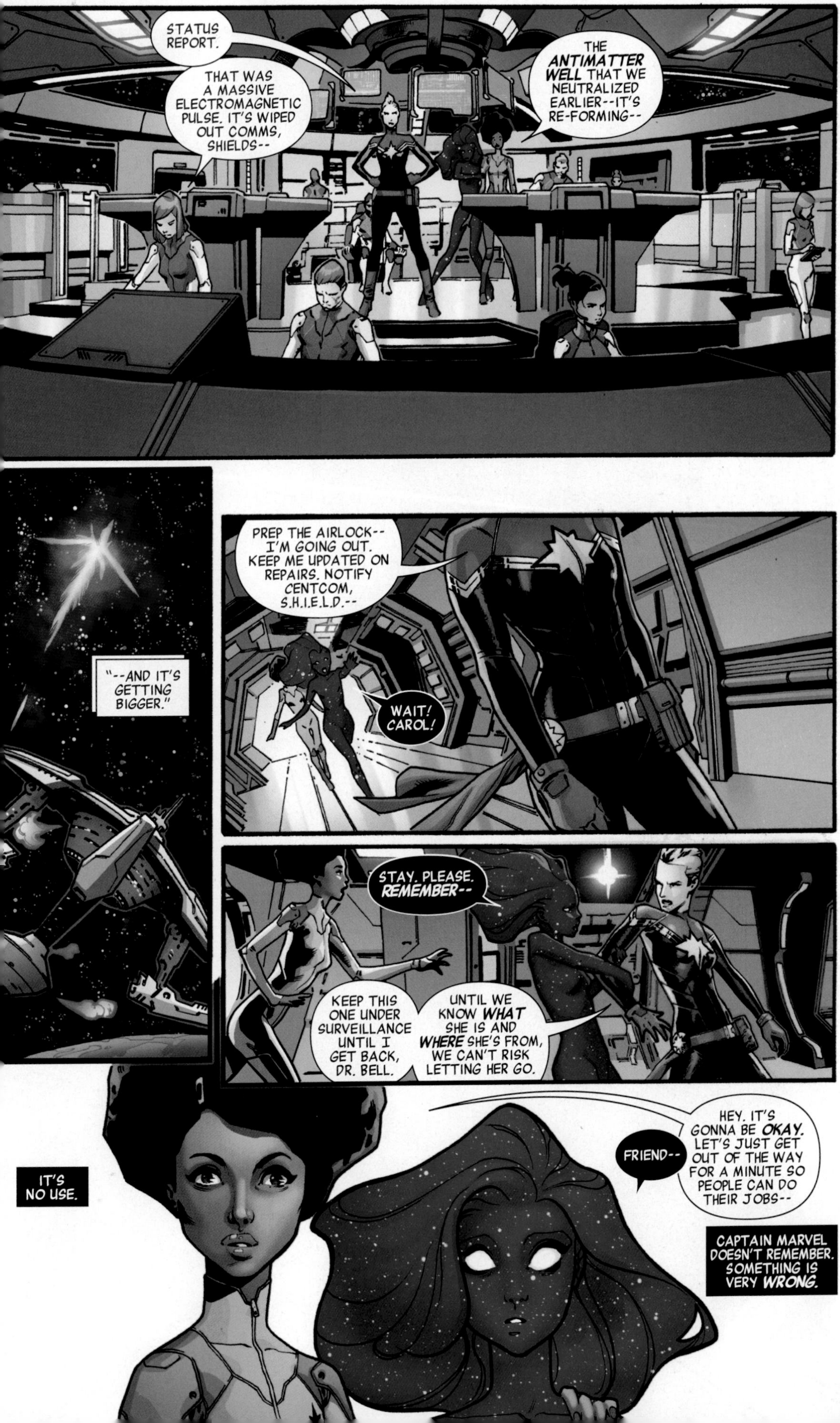
STATUS REPORT.
THAT WAS A MASSIVE ELECTROMAGNETIC PULSE. IT'S WIPED OUT COMMS, SHIELDS--
THE ANTIMATTER WELL THAT WE NEUTRALIZED EARLIER--IT'S RE-FORMING--
"--AND IT'S GETTING BIGGER."
PREP THE AIRLOCK-- I'M GOING OUT. KEEP ME UPDATED ON REPAIRS. NOTIFY CENTCOM, S.H.I.E.L.D.--
WAIT! CAROL!
STAY. PLEASE. REMEMBER--
KEEP THIS ONE UNDER SURVEILLANCE UNTIL I GET BACK, DR. BELL.
UNTIL WE KNOW WHAT SHE IS AND WHERE SHE'S FROM, WE CAN'T RISK LETTING HER GO.
IT'S NO USE.
FRIEND--
HEY. IT'S GONNA BE OKAY. LET'S JUST GET OUT OF THE WAY FOR A MINUTE SO PEOPLE CAN DO THEIR JOBS--
CAPTAIN MARVEL DOESN'T REMEMBER. SOMETHING IS VERY WRONG.

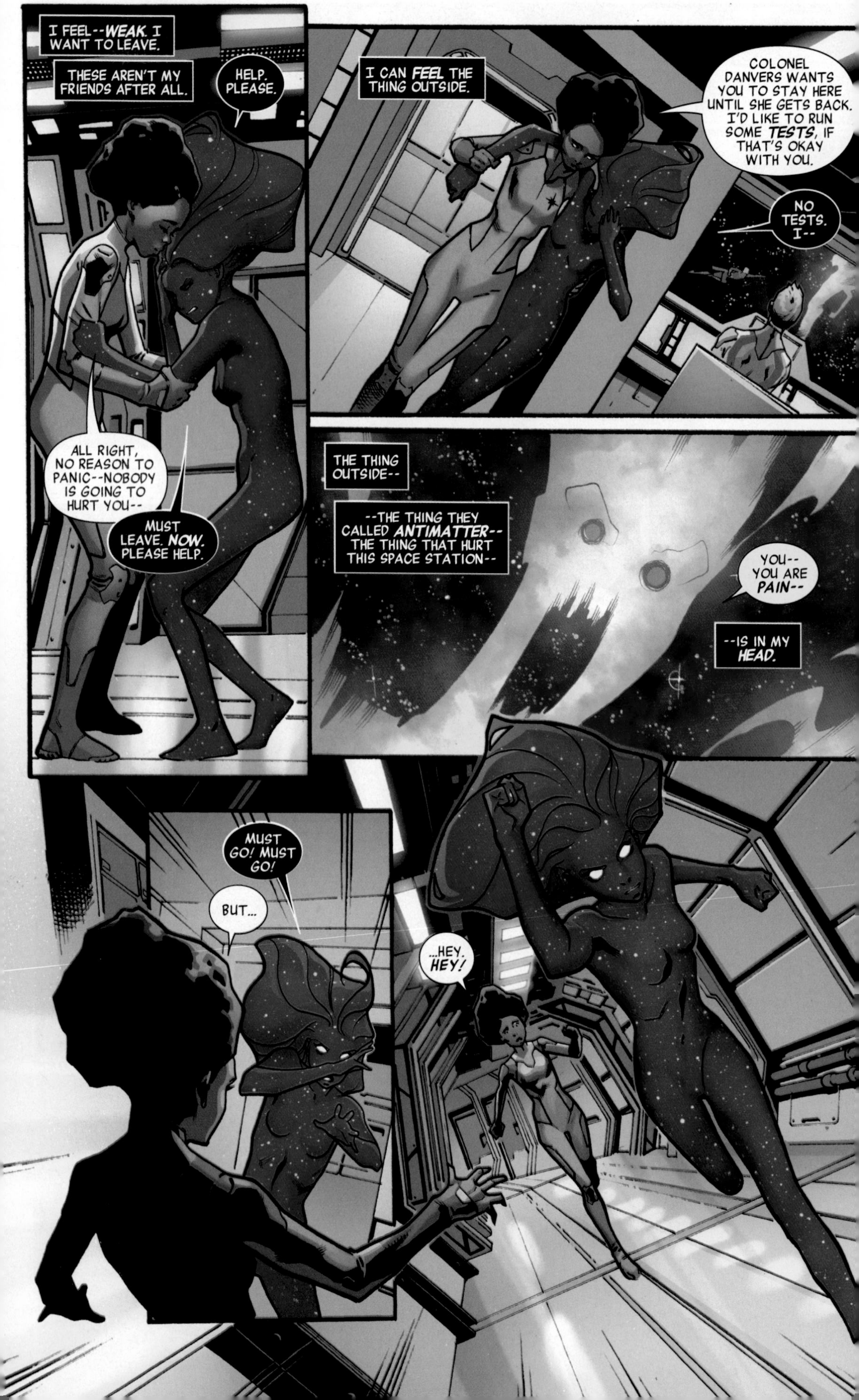

I FEEL--WEAK. I WANT TO LEAVE.
THESE AREN'T MY FRIENDS AFTER ALL.
HELP. PLEASE.
ALL RIGHT, NO REASON TO PANIC--NOBODY IS GOING TO HURT YOU--
MUST LEAVE. NOW. PLEASE HELP.
I CAN FEEL THE THING OUTSIDE.
COLONEL DANVERS WANTS YOU TO STAY HERE UNTIL SHE GETS BACK. I'D LIKE TO RUN SOME TESTS, IF THAT'S OKAY WITH YOU.
NO TESTS. I--
THE THING OUTSIDE--
--THE THING THEY CALLED ANTIMATTER--THE THING THAT HURT THIS SPACE STATION--
YOU--YOU ARE PAIN--
--IS IN MY HEAD.
MUST GO! MUST GO!
BUT...
...HEY. HEY!

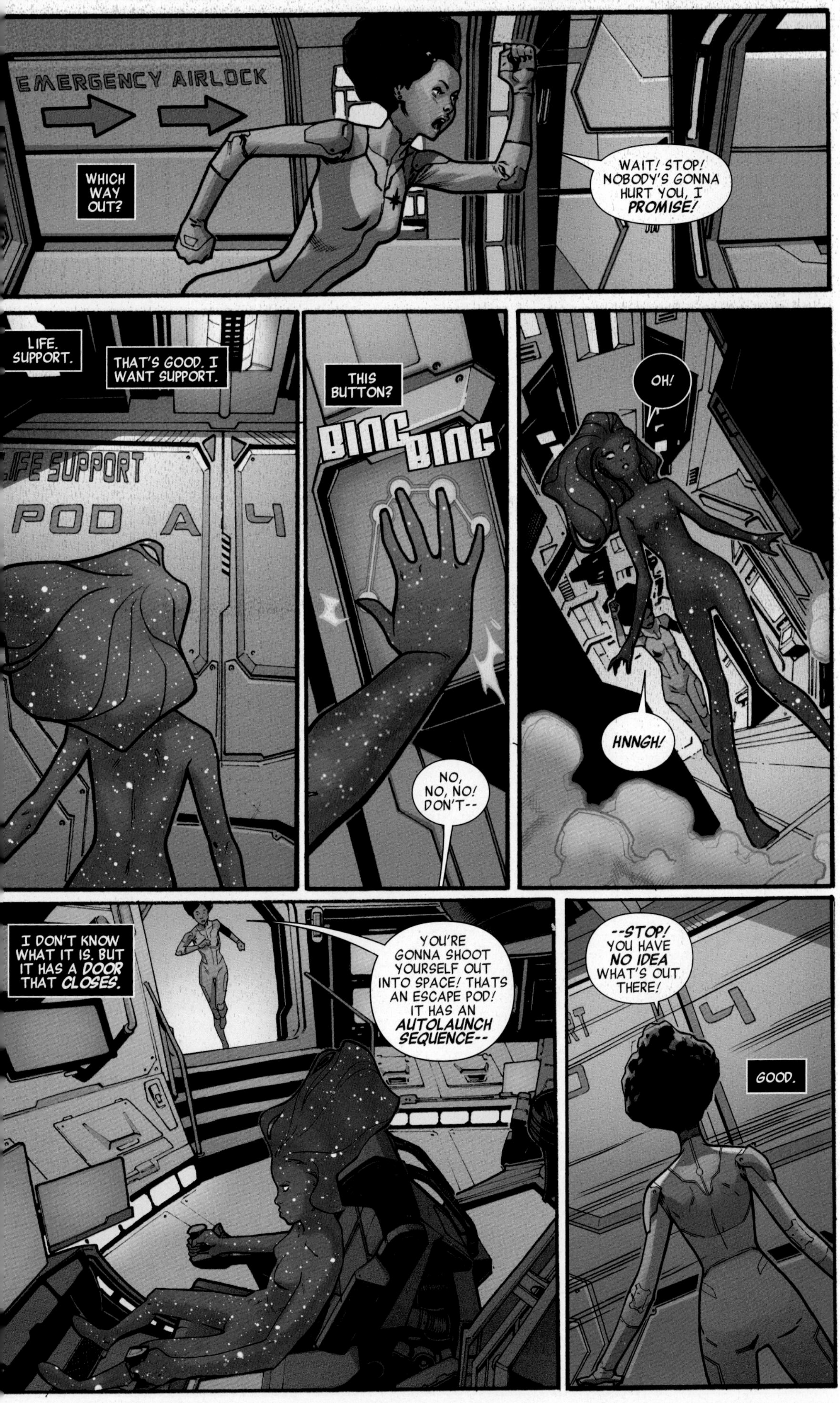
EMERGENCY AIRLOCK
WHICH WAY OUT?
WAIT! STOP! NOBODY'S GONNA HURT YOU, I PROMISE!
LIFE. SUPPORT.
THAT'S GOOD. I WANT SUPPORT.
LIFE SUPPORT
POD A 4
THIS BUTTON?
BING BING
NO, NO, NO! DON'T--
OH!
HNNGH!
I DON'T KNOW WHAT IT IS. BUT IT HAS A DOOR THAT CLOSES.
YOU'RE GONNA SHOOT YOURSELF OUT INTO SPACE! THATS AN ESCAPE POD! IT HAS AN AUTOLAUNCH SEQUENCE--
--STOP! YOU HAVE NO IDEA WHAT'S OUT THERE!
GOOD.

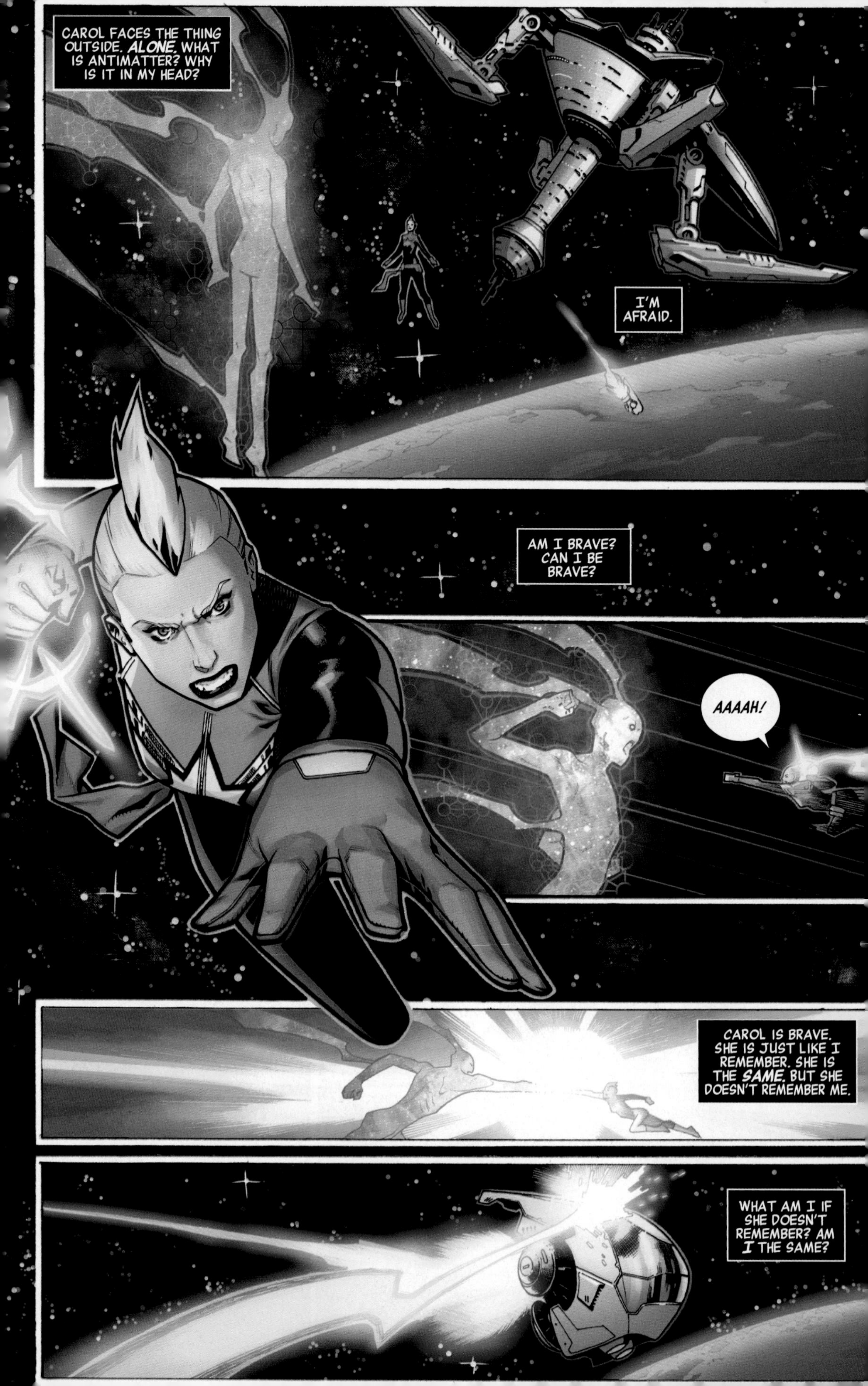

CAROL FACES THE THING OUTSIDE. ALONE. WHAT IS ANTIMATTER? WHY IS IT IN MY HEAD?
I'M AFRAID.
AM I BRAVE? CAN I BE BRAVE?
AAAAH!
CAROL IS BRAVE. SHE IS JUST LIKE I REMEMBER. SHE IS THE SAME. BUT SHE DOESN'T REMEMBER ME.
WHAT AM I IF SHE DOESN'T REMEMBER? AM I THE SAME?

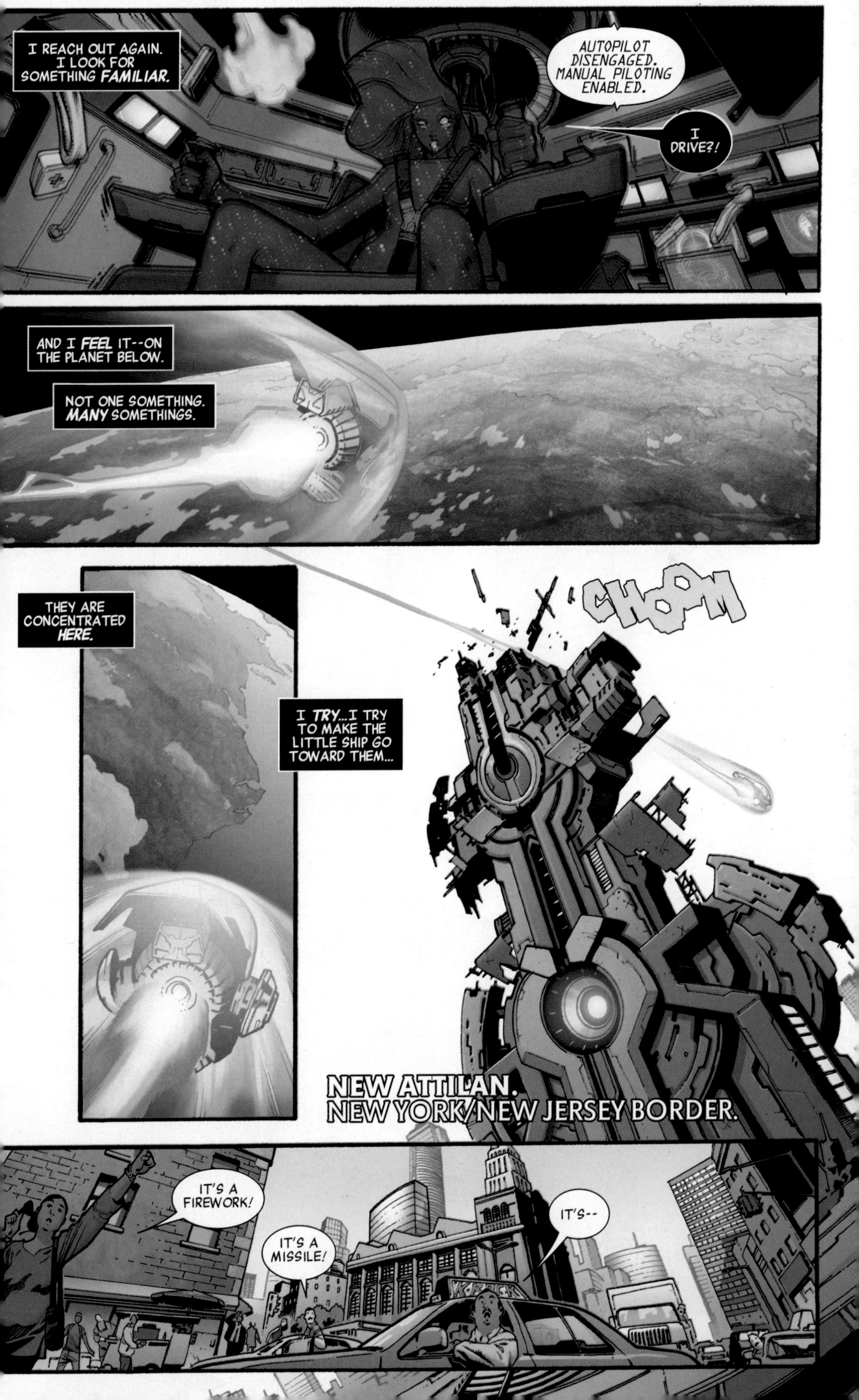
I REACH OUT AGAIN. I LOOK FOR SOMETHING FAMILIAR.
AUTOPILOT DISENGAGED. MANUAL PILOTING ENABLED.
I DRIVE?!
AND I FEEL IT--ON THE PLANET BELOW.
NOT ONE SOMETHING. MANY SOMETHINGS.
THEY ARE CONCENTRATED HERE.
I TRY...I TRY TO MAKE THE LITTLE SHIP GO TOWARD THEM...
CHOOM
NEW ATTILAN.
NEW YORK/NEW JERSEY BORDER.
IT'S A FIREWORK!
IT'S A MISSILE!
IT'S--

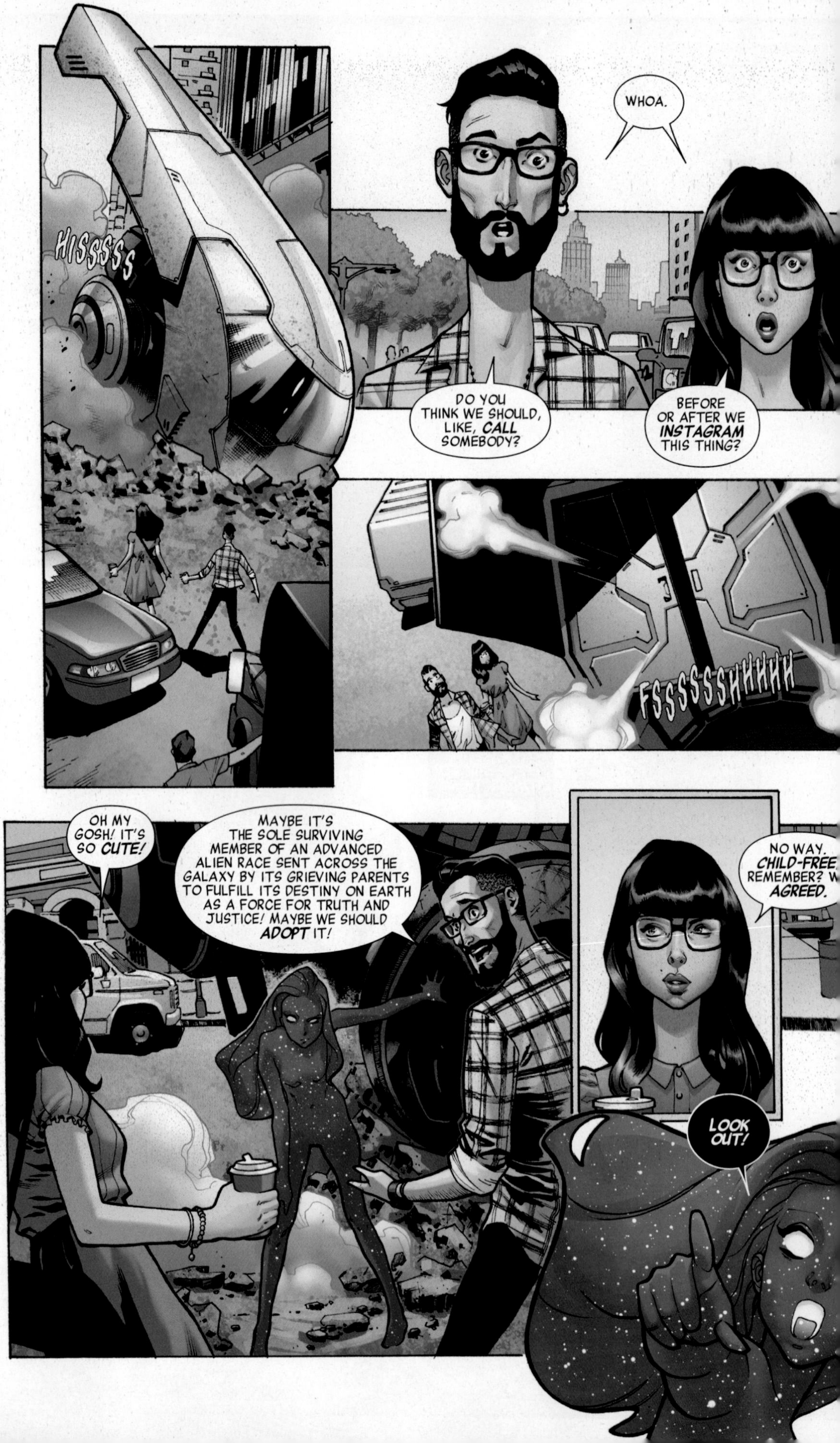
HISSSSS
WHOA.
DO YOU THINK WE SHOULD, LIKE, CALL SOMEBODY?
BEFORE OR AFTER WE INSTAGRAM THIS THING?
FSSSSSSHHHHH
OH MY GOSH! IT'S SO CUTE!
MAYBE IT'S THE SOLE SURVIVING MEMBER OF AN ADVANCED ALIEN RACE SENT ACROSS THE GALAXY BY ITS GRIEVING PARENTS TO FULFILL ITS DESTINY ON EARTH AS A FORCE FOR TRUTH AND JUSTICE! MAYBE WE SHOULD ADOPT IT!
NO WAY. CHILD-FREE, REMEMBER? W AGREED.
LOOK OUT!

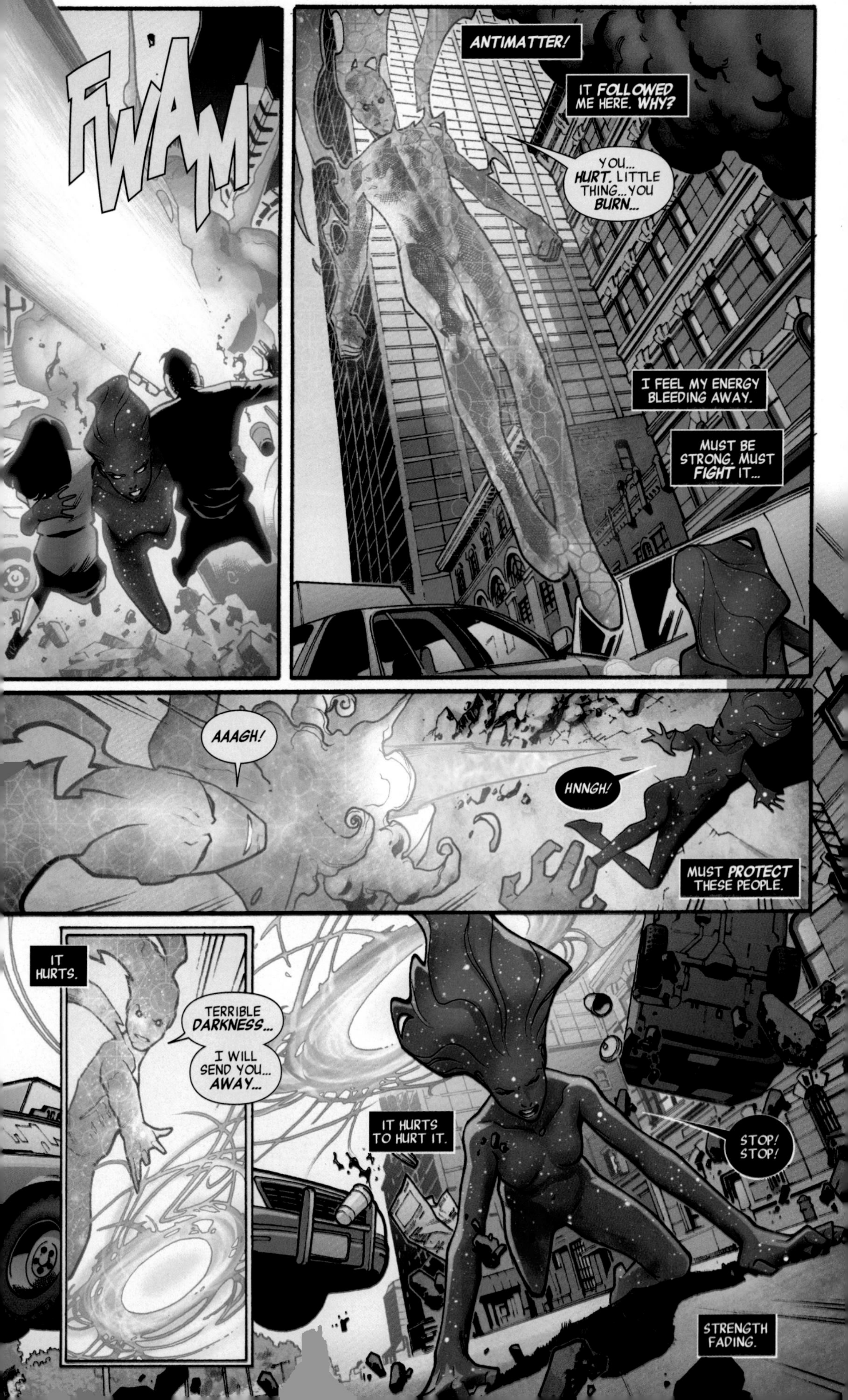
FWAM
ANTIMATTER!
IT FOLLOWED ME HERE. WHY?
YOU... HURT. LITTLE THING...YOU BURN...
I FEEL MY ENERGY BLEEDING AWAY.
MUST BE STRONG. MUST FIGHT IT...
AAAGH!
HNNGH!
MUST PROTECT THESE PEOPLE.
IT HURTS.
TERRIBLE DARKNESS...
I WILL SEND YOU... AWAY...
IT HURTS TO HURT IT.
STOP! STOP!
STRENGTH FADING.

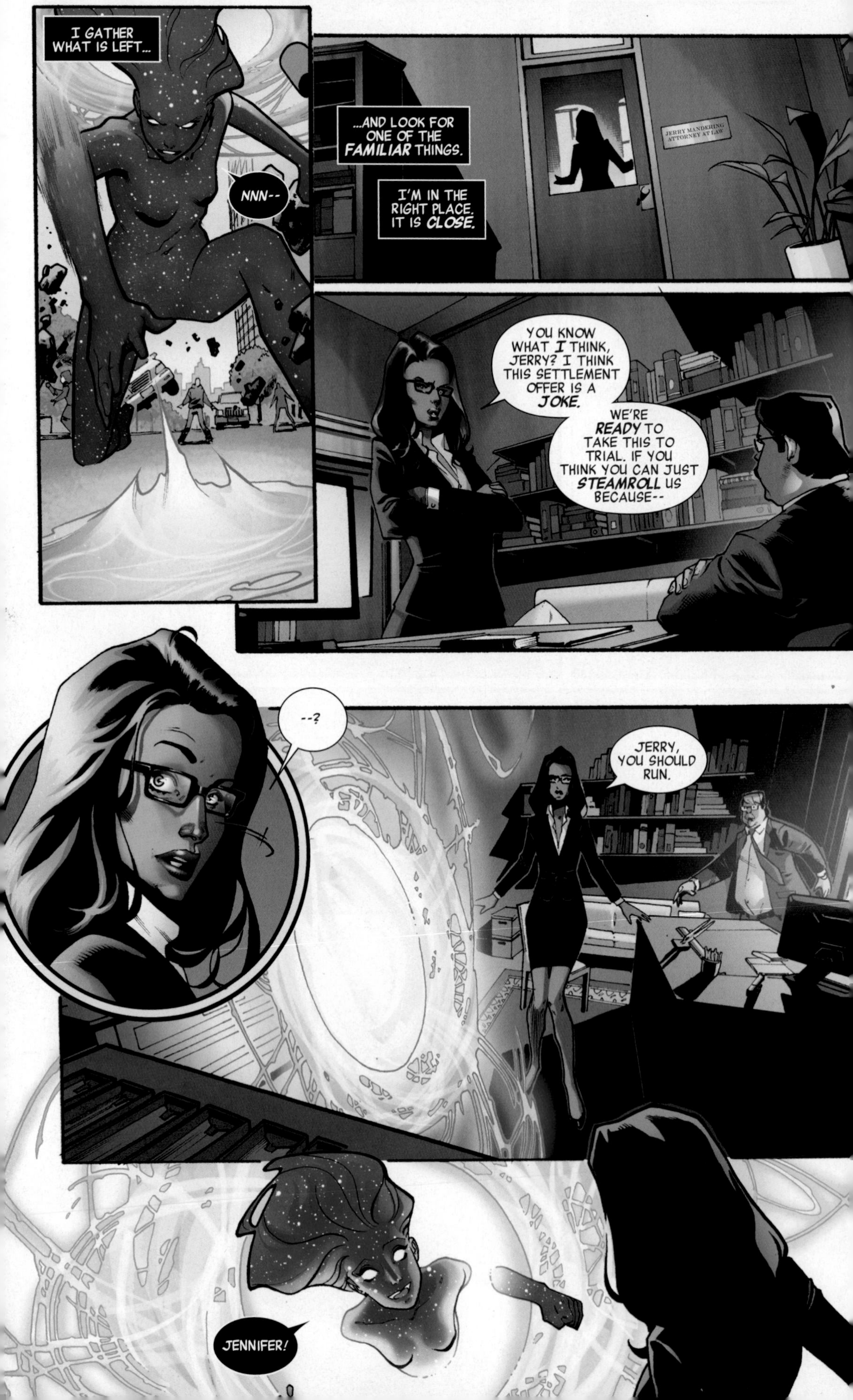
I GATHER WHAT IS LEFT...
NNN--
...AND LOOK FOR ONE OF THE FAMILIAR THINGS.
I'M IN THE RIGHT PLACE. IT IS CLOSE.
JERRY MANDERING ATTORNEY AT LAW
YOU KNOW WHAT I THINK, JERRY? I THINK THIS SETTLEMENT OFFER IS A JOKE.
WE'RE READY TO TAKE THIS TO TRIAL. IF YOU THINK YOU CAN JUST STEAMROLL US BECAUSE--
--?
JERRY, YOU SHOULD RUN.
JENNIFER!

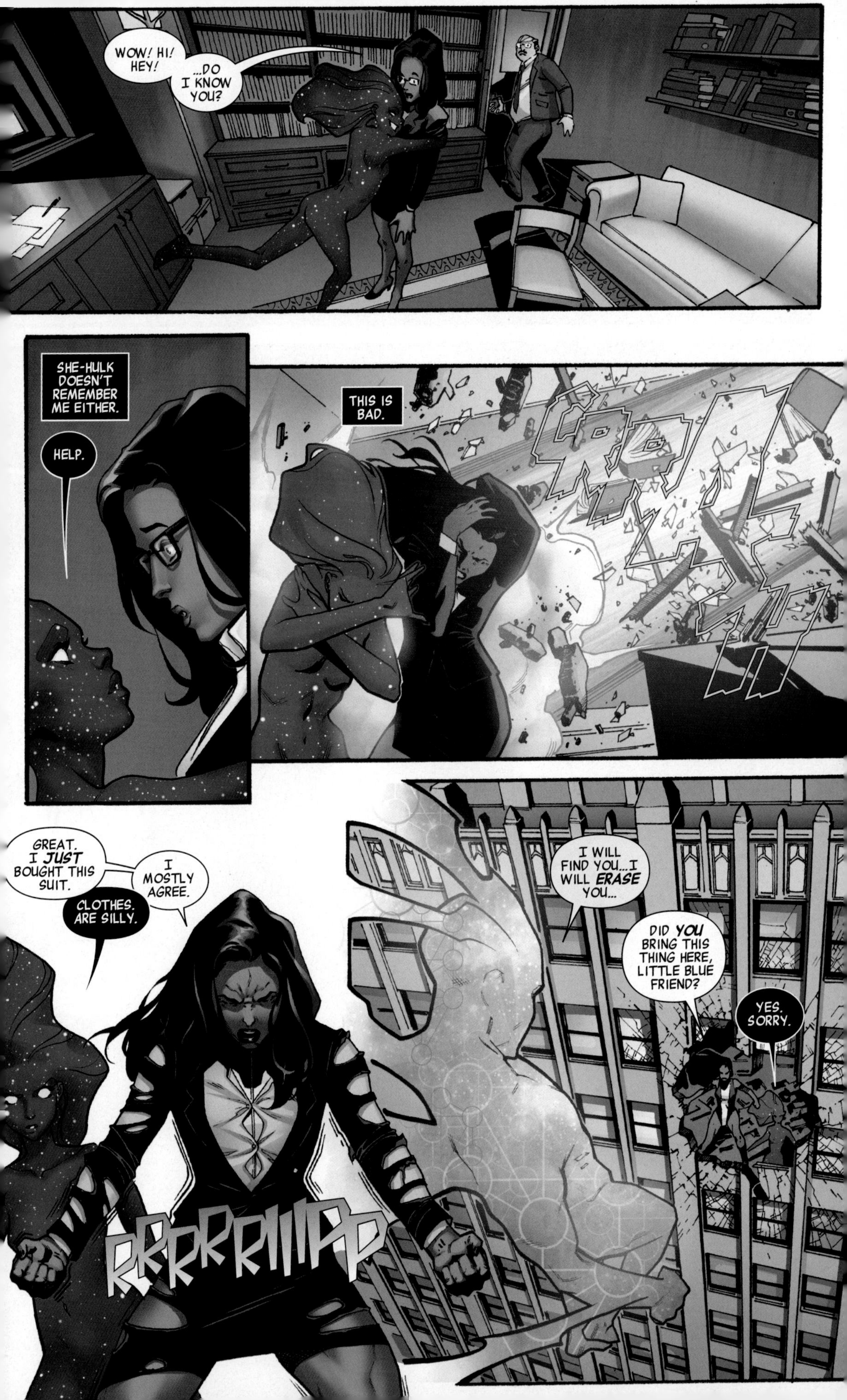

WOW! HI! HEY!
...DO I KNOW YOU?
SHE-HULK DOESN'T REMEMBER ME EITHER.
HELP.
THIS IS BAD.
GREAT. I JUST BOUGHT THIS SUIT.
I MOSTLY AGREE.
CLOTHES. ARE SILLY.
RRRRRIIIPP
I WILL FIND YOU...I WILL ERASE YOU...
DID YOU BRING THIS THING HERE, LITTLE BLUE FRIEND?
YES. SORRY.

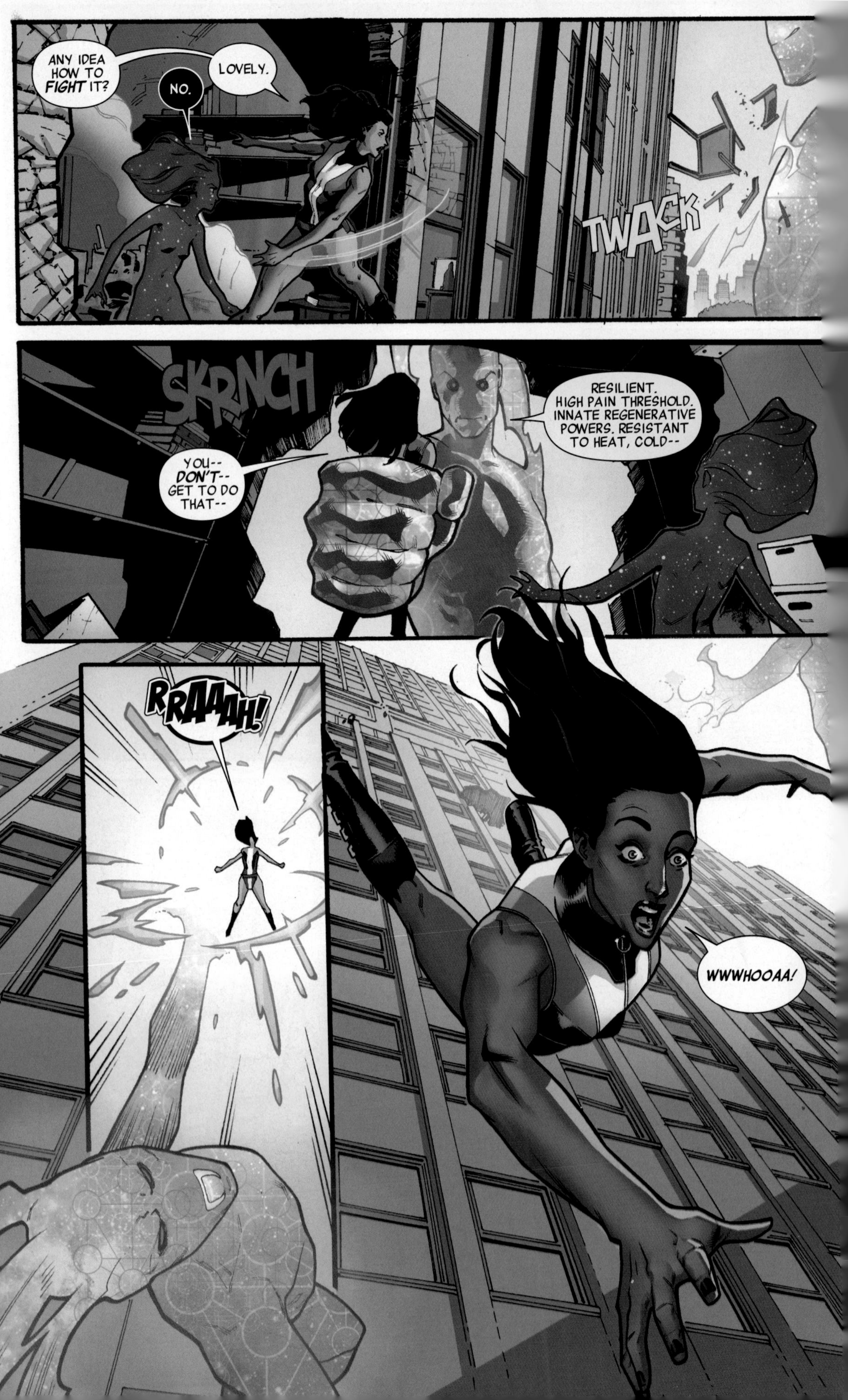
ANY IDEA HOW TO FIGHT IT?
NO.
LOVELY.
TWACK
SKRNCH
RESILIENT. HIGH PAIN THRESHOLD. INNATE REGENERATIVE POWERS. RESISTANT TO HEAT, COLD--
YOU-- DON'T-- GET TO DO THAT--
RRAAAAH!
WWWHOOAA!

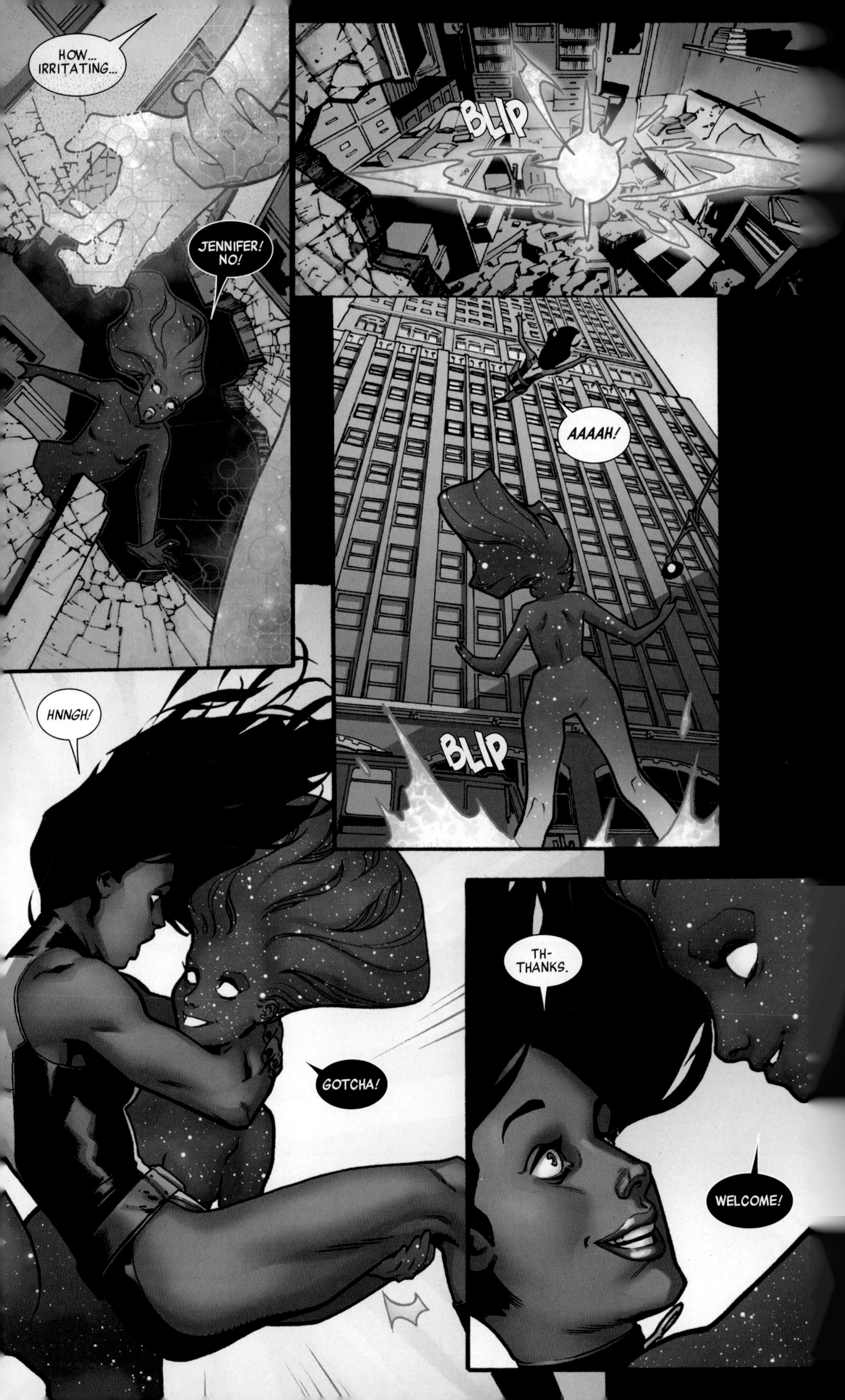
HOW... IRRITATING...
JENNIFER! NO!
BLIP
AAAAH!
BLIP
HNNGH!
GOTCHA!
TH-THANKS.
WELCOME!

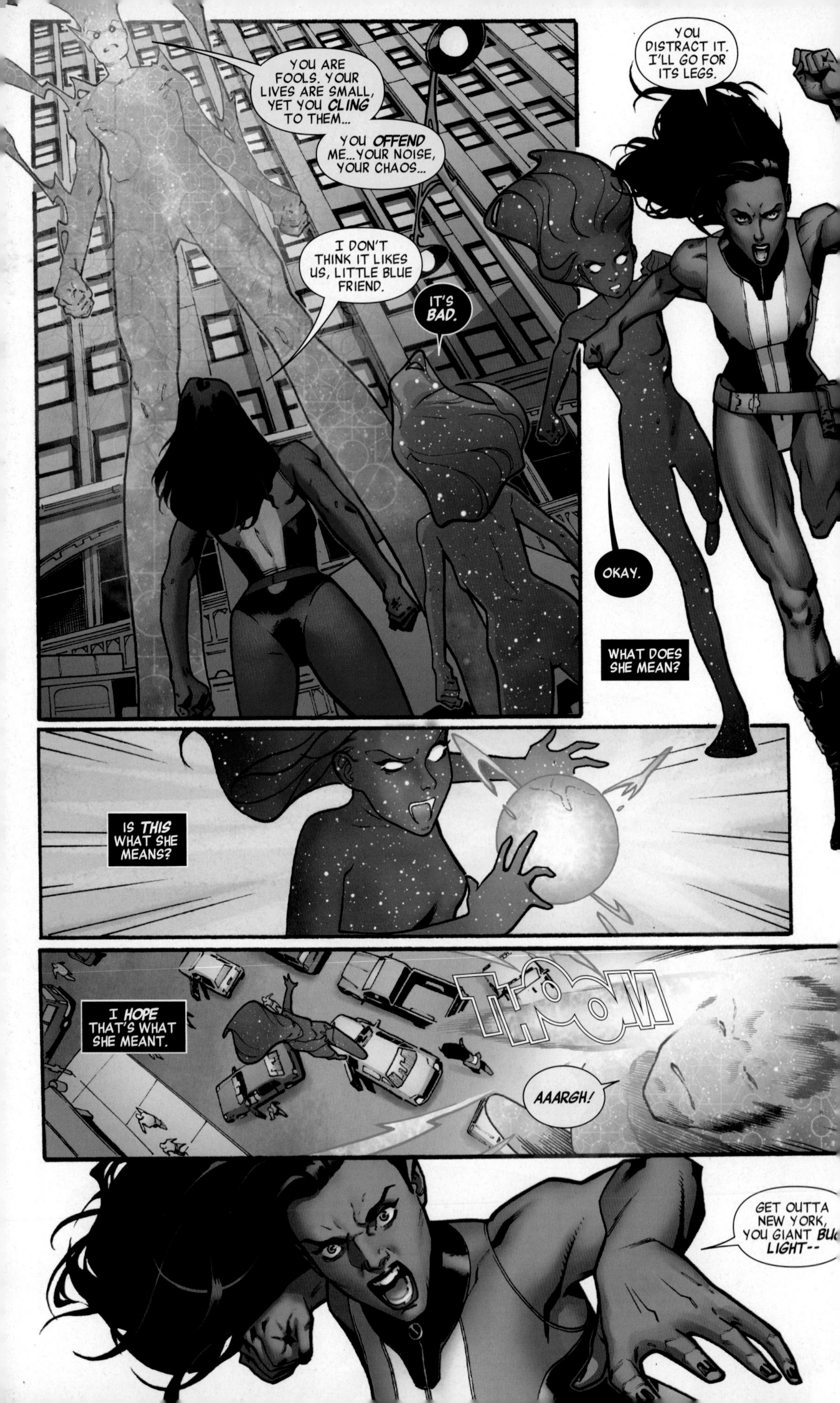

YOU ARE FOOLS. YOUR LIVES ARE SMALL, YET YOU CLING TO THEM...
YOU OFFEND ME...YOUR NOISE, YOUR CHAOS...
YOU DISTRACT IT. I'LL GO FOR ITS LEGS.
I DON'T THINK IT LIKES US, LITTLE BLUE FRIEND.
IT'S BAD.
OKAY.
WHAT DOES SHE MEAN?
IS THIS WHAT SHE MEANS?
I HOPE THAT'S WHAT SHE MEANT.
THOOM
AAARGH!
GET OUTTA NEW YORK, YOU GIANT BU
LIGHT--

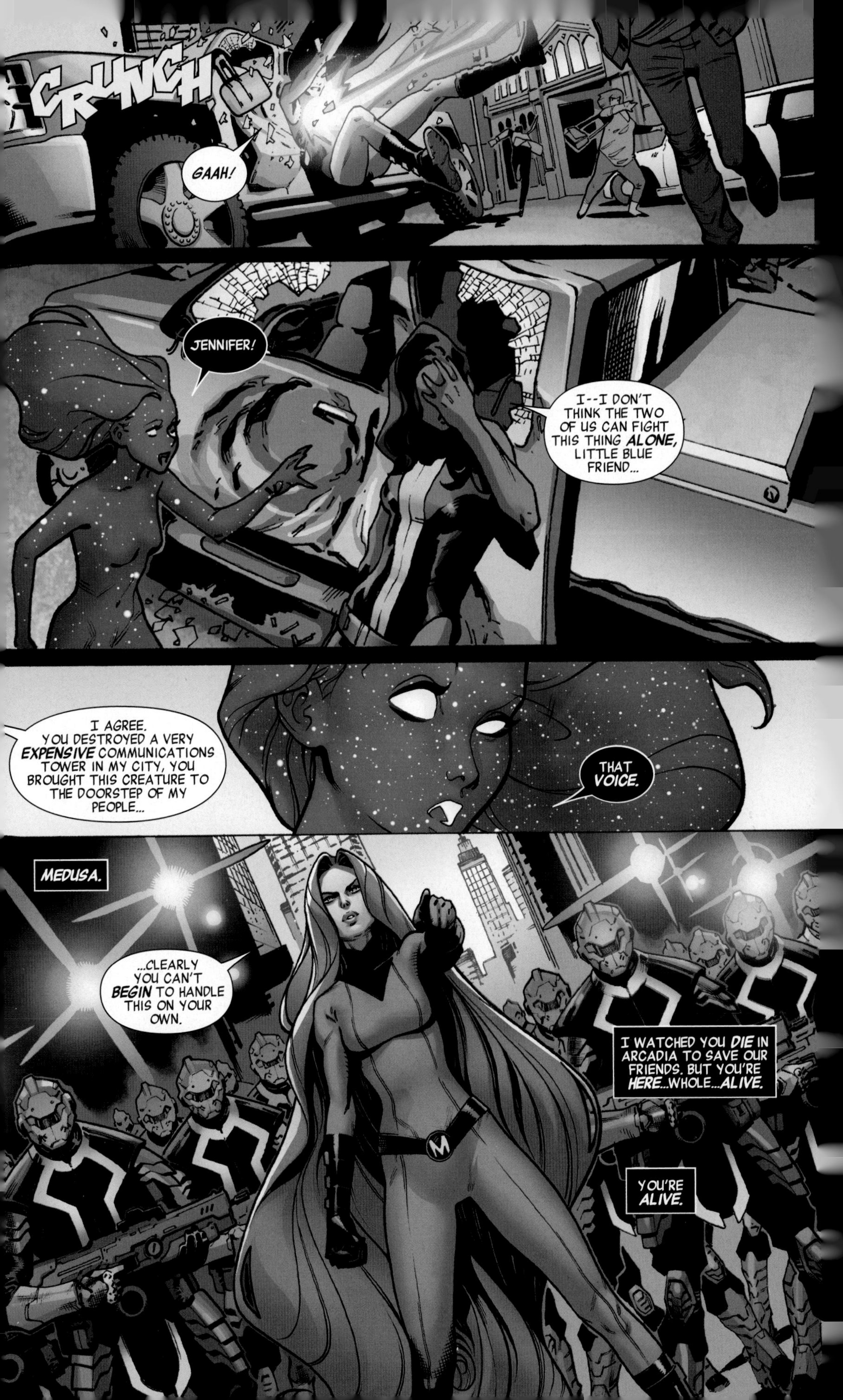
CRUNCH
GAAH!
JENNIFER!
I--I DON'T THINK THE TWO OF US CAN FIGHT THIS THING ALONE, LITTLE BLUE FRIEND...
I AGREE. YOU DESTROYED A VERY EXPENSIVE COMMUNICATIONS TOWER IN MY CITY, YOU BROUGHT THIS CREATURE TO THE DOORSTEP OF MY PEOPLE...
THAT VOICE.
MEDUSA.
...CLEARLY YOU CAN'T BEGIN TO HANDLE THIS ON YOUR OWN.
I WATCHED YOU DIE IN ARCADIA TO SAVE OUR FRIENDS. BUT YOU'RE HERE...WHOLE...ALIVE.
YOU'RE ALIVE.

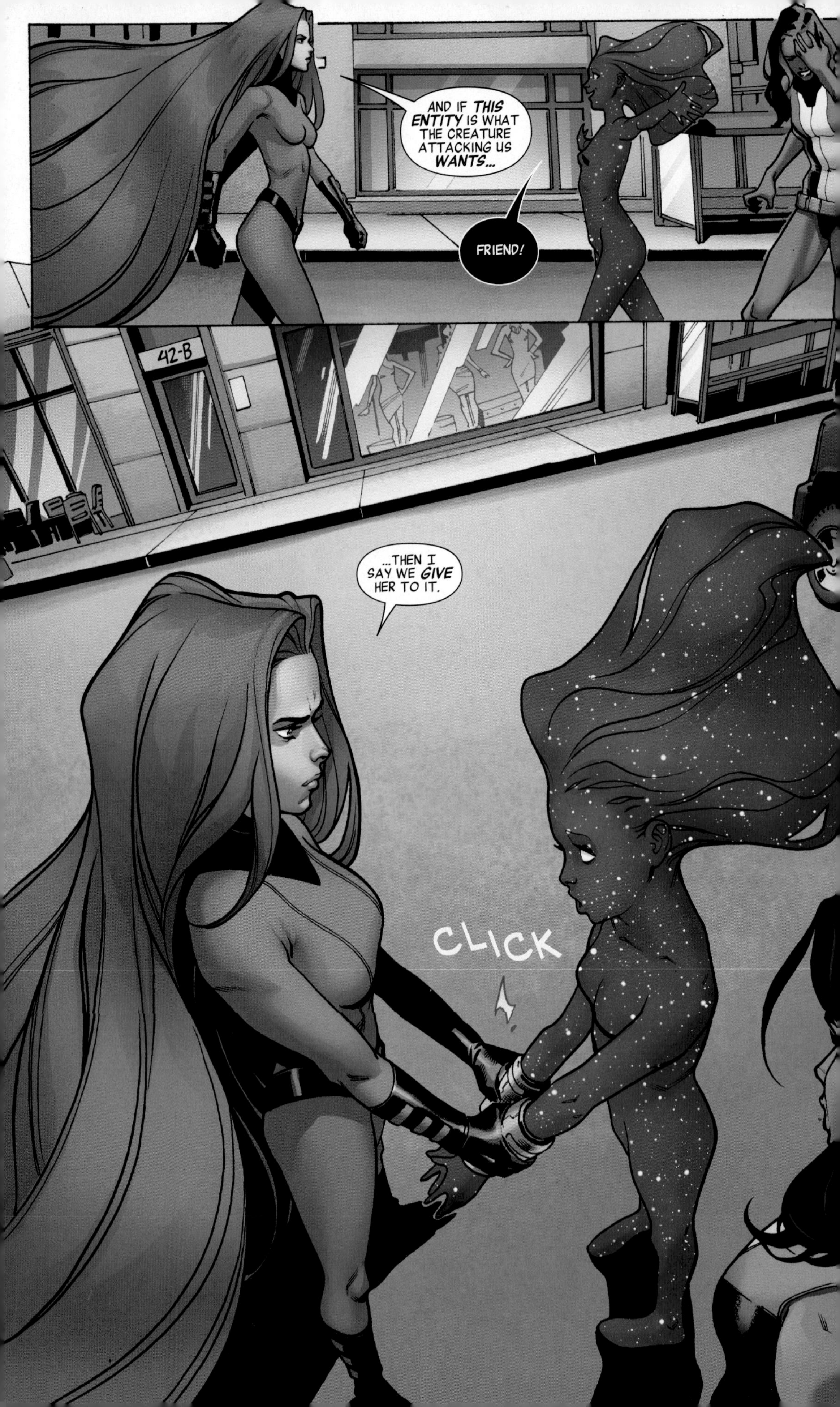

AND IF THIS ENTITY IS WHAT THE CREATURE ATTACKING US WANTS...
FRIEND!
42-B
...THEN I SAY WE GIVE HER TO IT.
CLICK

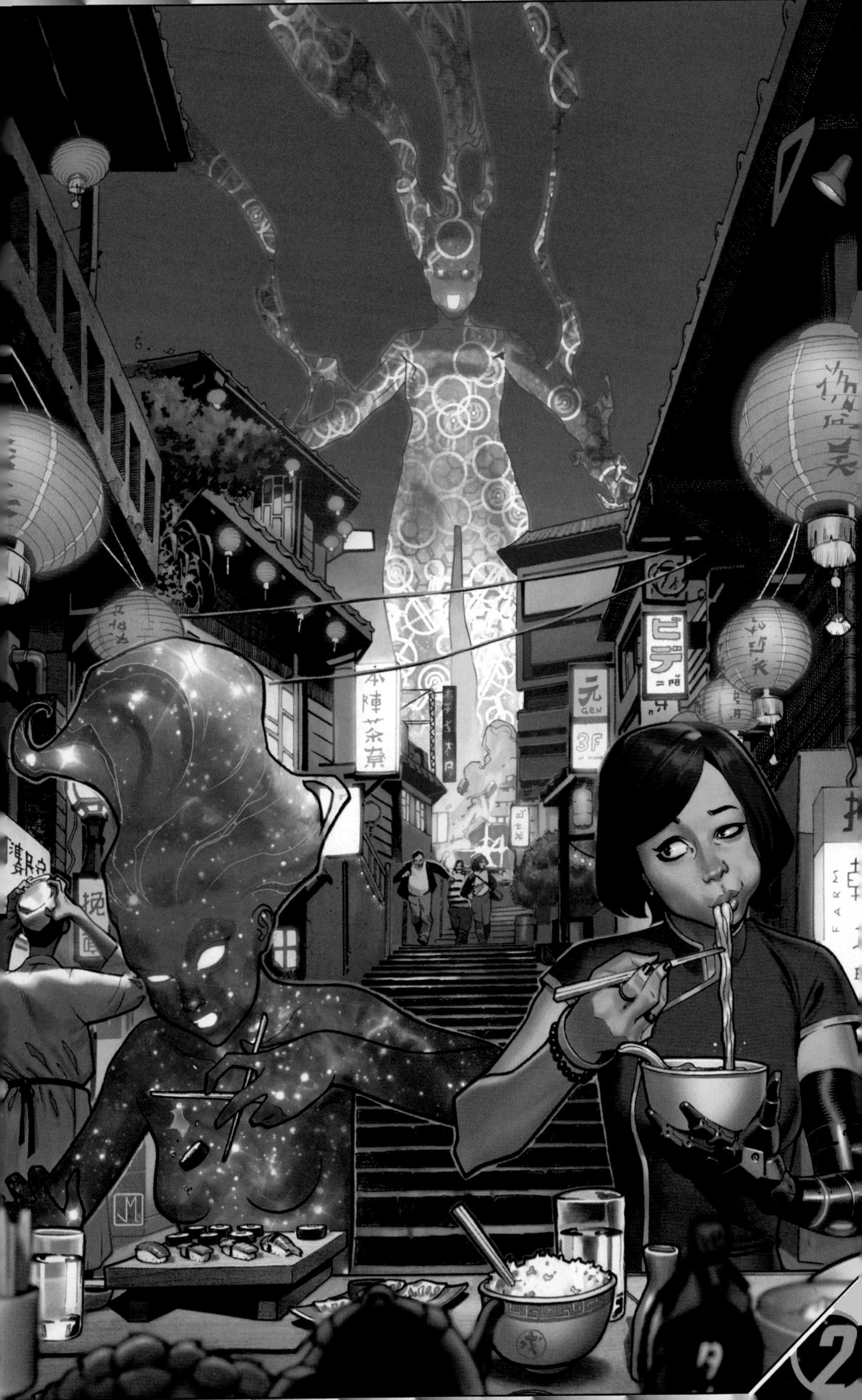

本陣茶寮
ビデ
元
GEN
3F
FARM

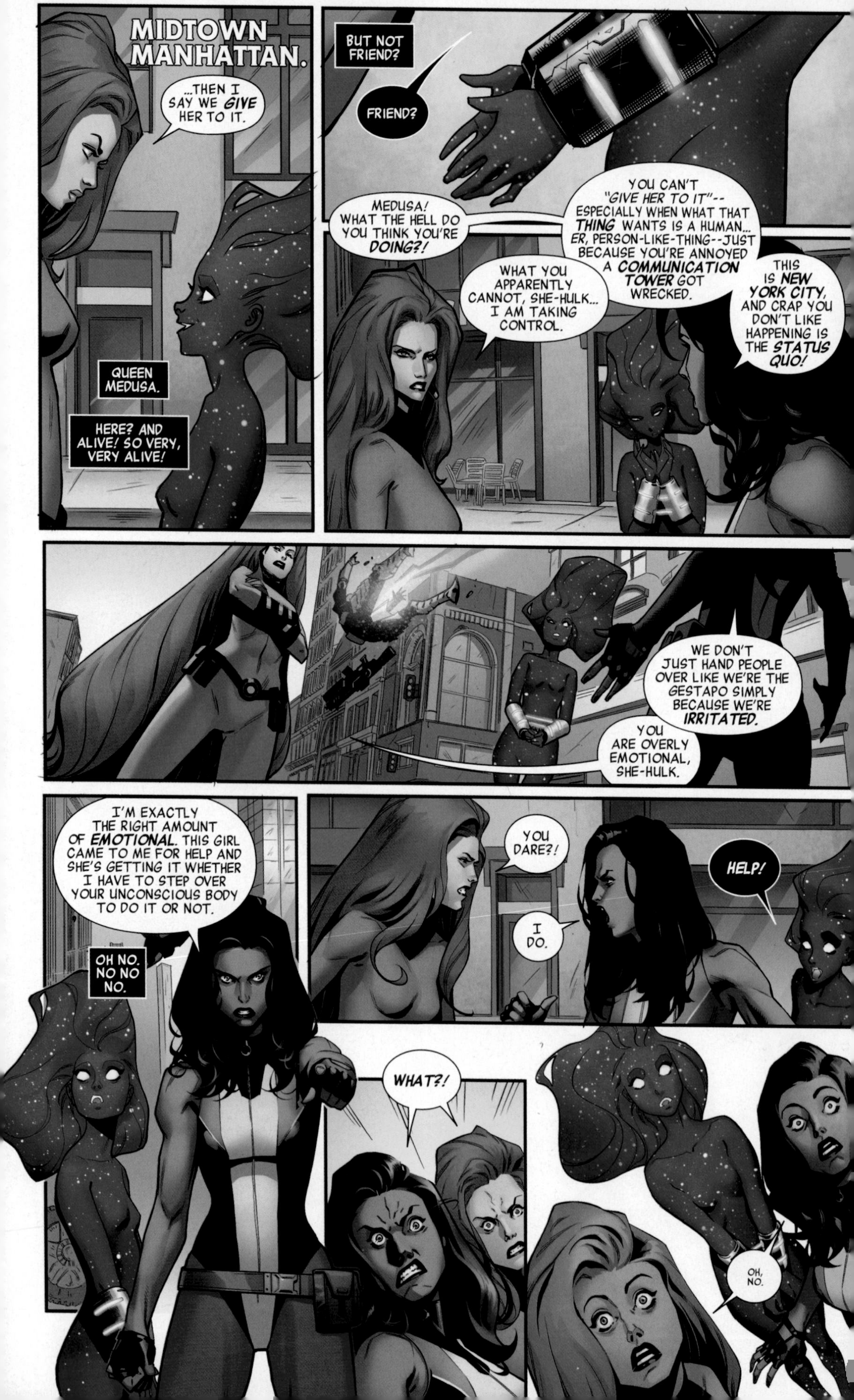
MIDTOWN MANHATTAN.
...THEN I SAY WE GIVE HER TO IT.
QUEEN MEDUSA.
HERE? AND ALIVE! SO VERY, VERY ALIVE!
BUT NOT FRIEND?
FRIEND?
MEDUSA! WHAT THE HELL DO YOU THINK YOU'RE DOING?!
YOU CAN'T "GIVE HER TO IT"-- ESPECIALLY WHEN WHAT THAT THING WANTS IS A HUMAN... ER, PERSON-LIKE-THING--JUST BECAUSE YOU'RE ANNOYED A COMMUNICATION TOWER GOT WRECKED.
THIS IS NEW YORK CITY, AND CRAP YOU DON'T LIKE HAPPENING IS THE STATUS QUO!
WHAT YOU APPARENTLY CANNOT, SHE-HULK... I AM TAKING CONTROL.
WE DON'T JUST HAND PEOPLE OVER LIKE WE'RE THE GESTAPO SIMPLY BECAUSE WE'RE IRRITATED.
YOU ARE OVERLY EMOTIONAL, SHE-HULK.
I'M EXACTLY THE RIGHT AMOUNT OF EMOTIONAL. THIS GIRL CAME TO ME FOR HELP AND SHE'S GETTING IT WHETHER I HAVE TO STEP OVER YOUR UNCONSCIOUS BODY TO DO IT OR NOT.
OH NO. NO NO NO.
YOU DARE?!
I DO.
HELP!
WHAT?!
OH, NO.

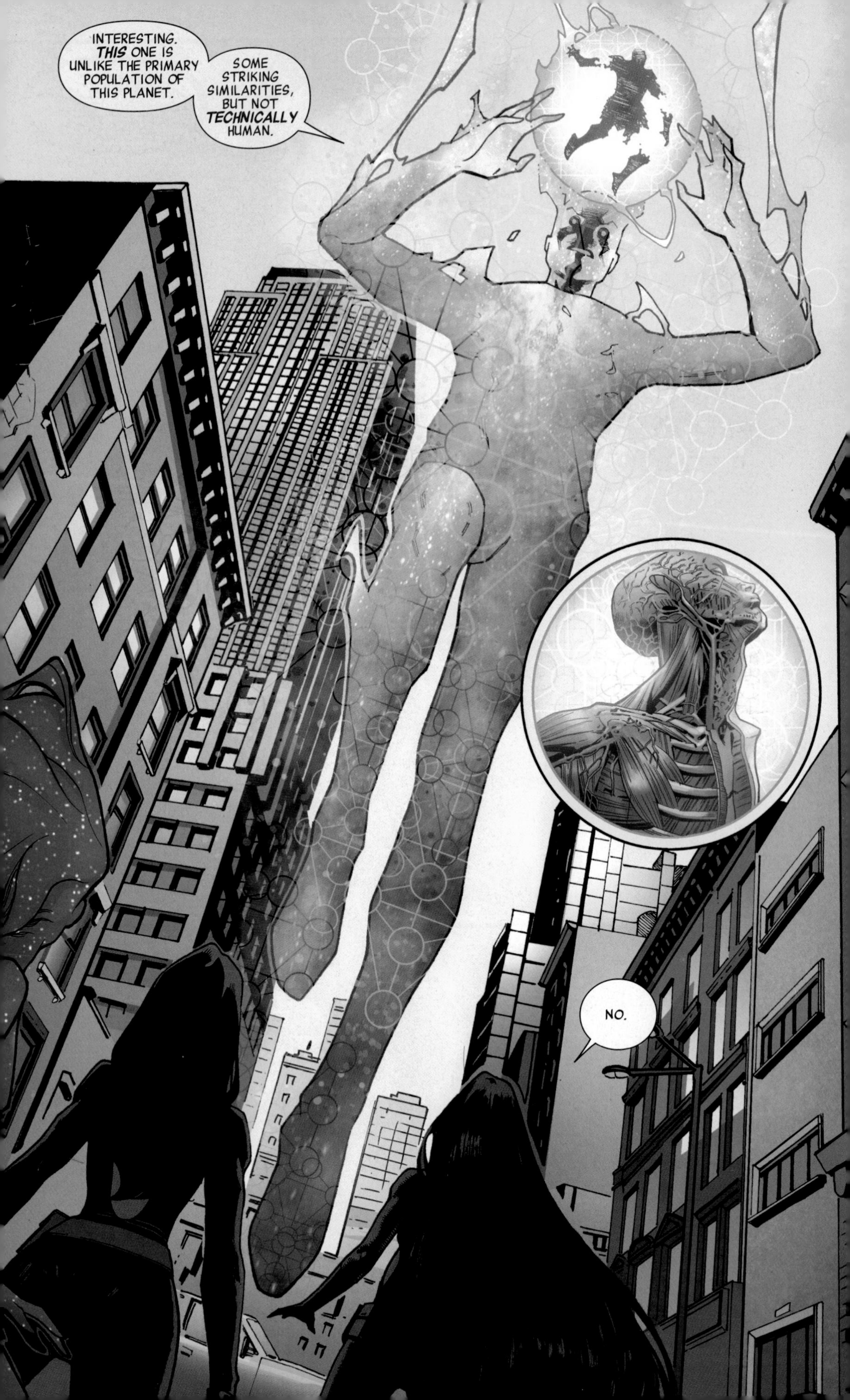
INTERESTING. THIS ONE IS UNLIKE THE PRIMARY POPULATION OF THIS PLANET.
SOME STRIKING SIMILARITIES, BUT NOT TECHNICALLY HUMAN.
NO.

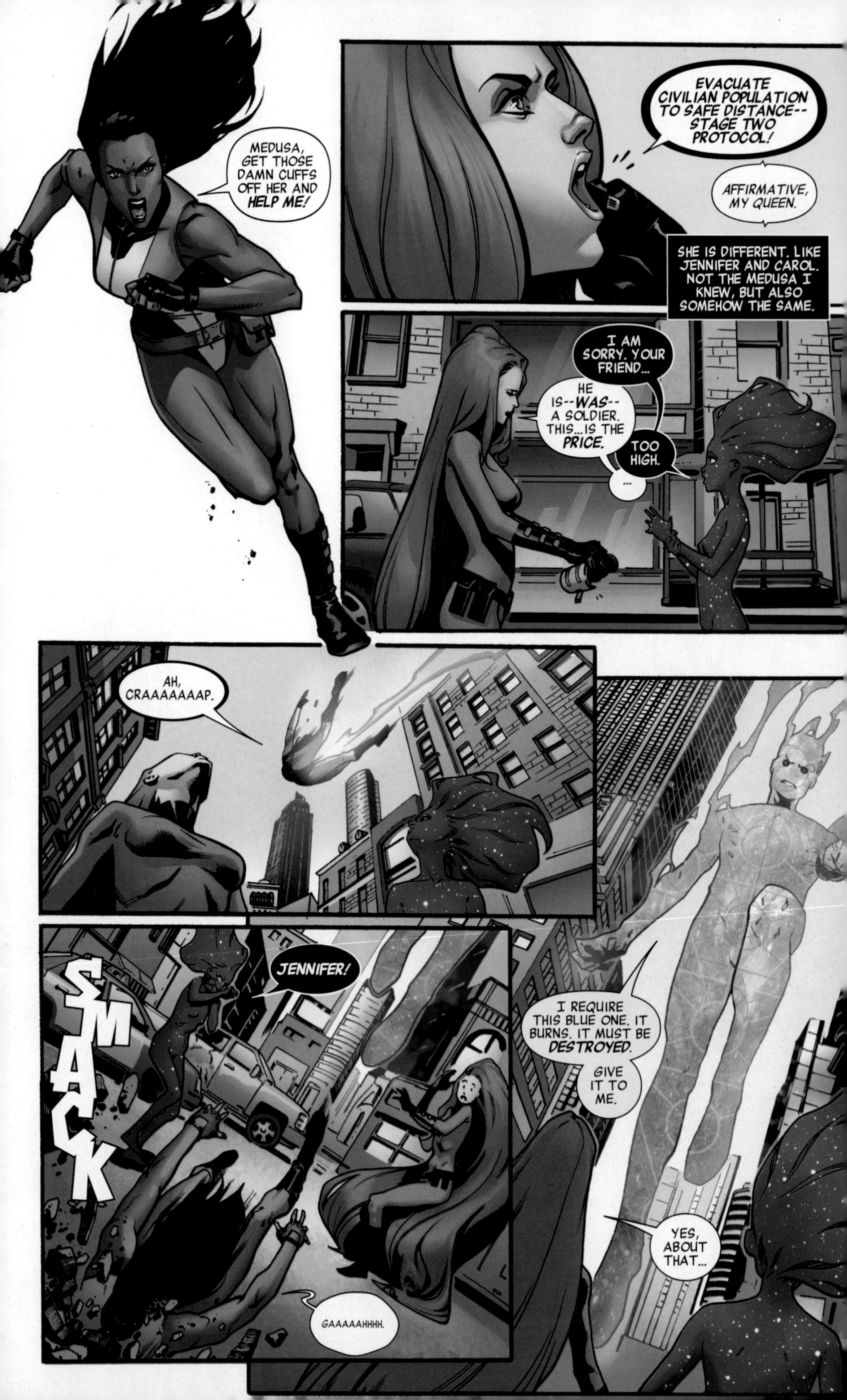
MEDUSA, GET THOSE DAMN CUFFS OFF HER AND HELP ME!
EVACUATE CIVILIAN POPULATION TO SAFE DISTANCE-- STAGE TWO PROTOCOL!
AFFIRMATIVE, MY QUEEN.
SHE IS DIFFERENT. LIKE JENNIFER AND CAROL. NOT THE MEDUSA I KNEW, BUT ALSO SOMEHOW THE SAME.
I AM SORRY. YOUR FRIEND...
HE IS--WAS-- A SOLDIER. THIS...IS THE PRICE.
TOO HIGH.
...
AH, CRAAAAAAAP.
JENNIFER!
SMACK
GAAAAAHHHH.
I REQUIRE THIS BLUE ONE. IT BURNS. IT MUST BE DESTROYED.
GIVE IT TO ME.
YES, ABOUT THAT...

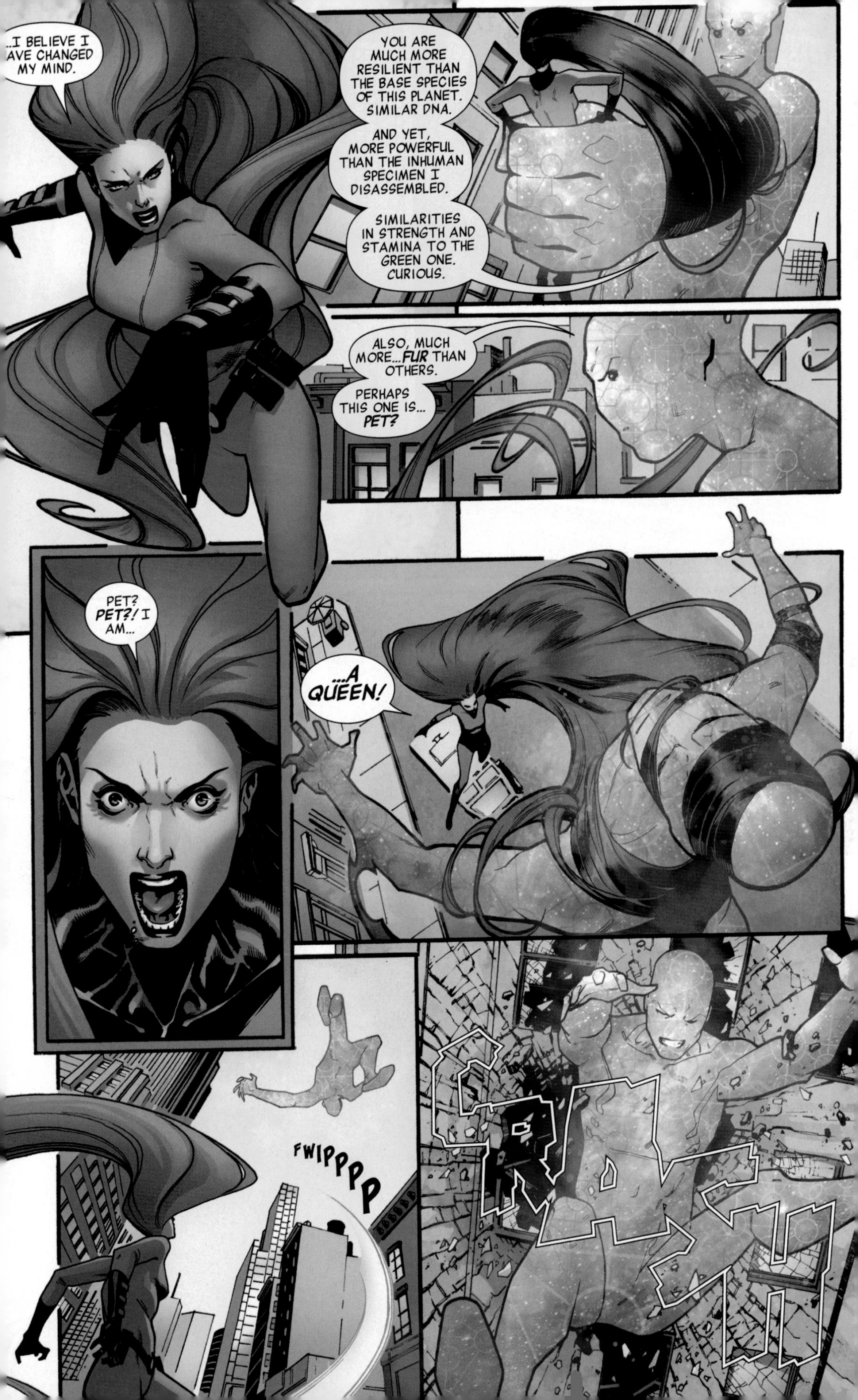
..I BELIEVE I AVE CHANGED MY MIND.
YOU ARE MUCH MORE RESILIENT THAN THE BASE SPECIES OF THIS PLANET. SIMILAR DNA.
AND YET, MORE POWERFUL THAN THE INHUMAN SPECIMEN I DISASSEMBLED.
SIMILARITIES IN STRENGTH AND STAMINA TO THE GREEN ONE. CURIOUS.
ALSO, MUCH MORE... FUR THAN OTHERS.
PERHAPS THIS ONE IS... PET?
PET? PET?! I AM...
...A QUEEN!
FWIPPPPP

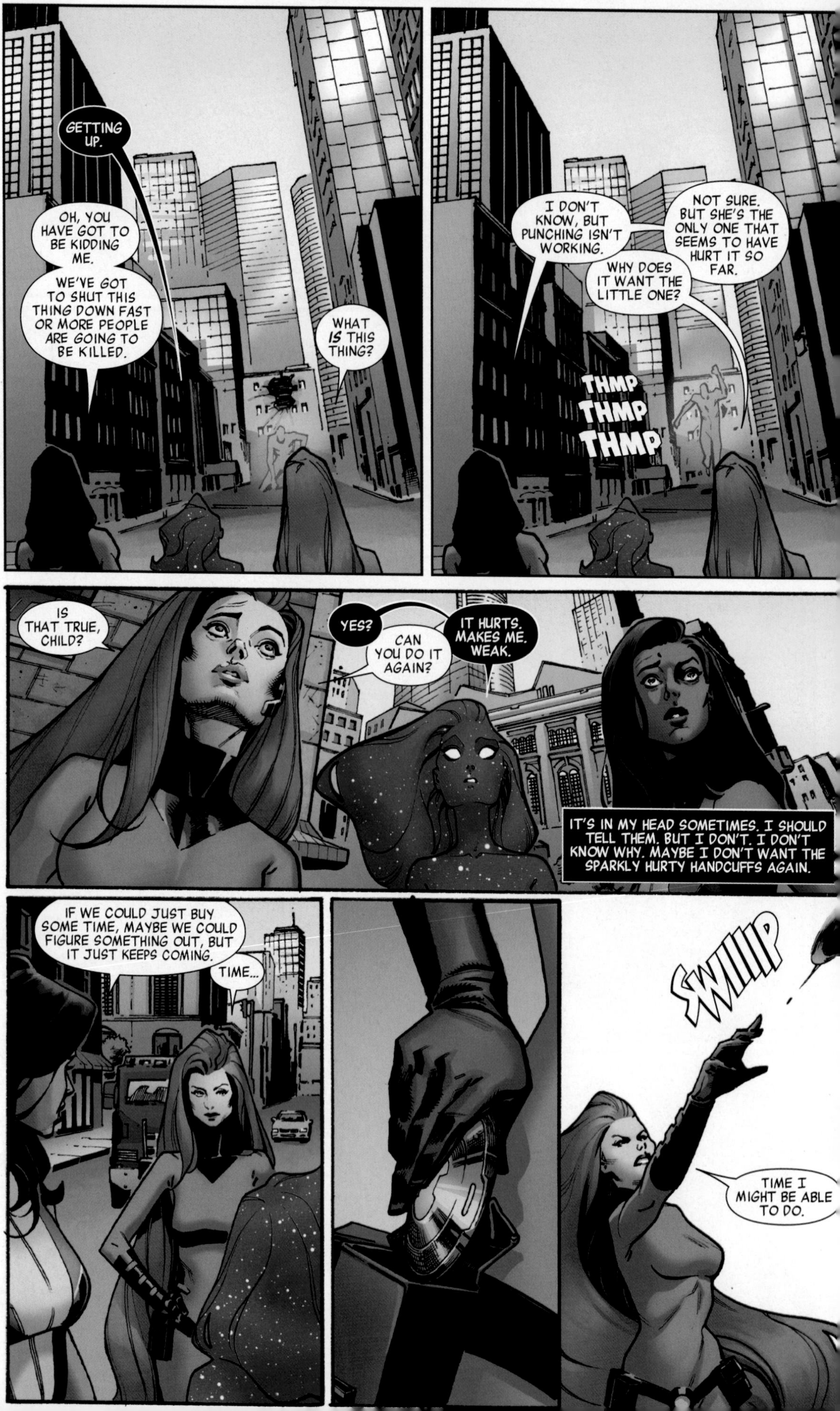
GETTING UP.
OH, YOU HAVE GOT TO BE KIDDING ME.
WE'VE GOT TO SHUT THIS THING DOWN FAST OR MORE PEOPLE ARE GOING TO BE KILLED.
WHAT IS THIS THING?
I DON'T KNOW, BUT PUNCHING ISN'T WORKING.
NOT SURE. BUT SHE'S THE ONLY ONE THAT SEEMS TO HAVE HURT IT SO FAR.
WHY DOES IT WANT THE LITTLE ONE?
THMP THMP THMP
IS THAT TRUE, CHILD?
YES?
CAN YOU DO IT AGAIN?
IT HURTS. MAKES ME. WEAK.
IT'S IN MY HEAD SOMETIMES. I SHOULD TELL THEM. BUT I DON'T. I DON'T KNOW WHY. MAYBE I DON'T WANT THE SPARKLY HURTY HANDCUFFS AGAIN.
IF WE COULD JUST BUY SOME TIME, MAYBE WE COULD FIGURE SOMETHING OUT, BUT IT JUST KEEPS COMING.
TIME...
SWIIIP
TIME I MIGHT BE ABLE TO DO.

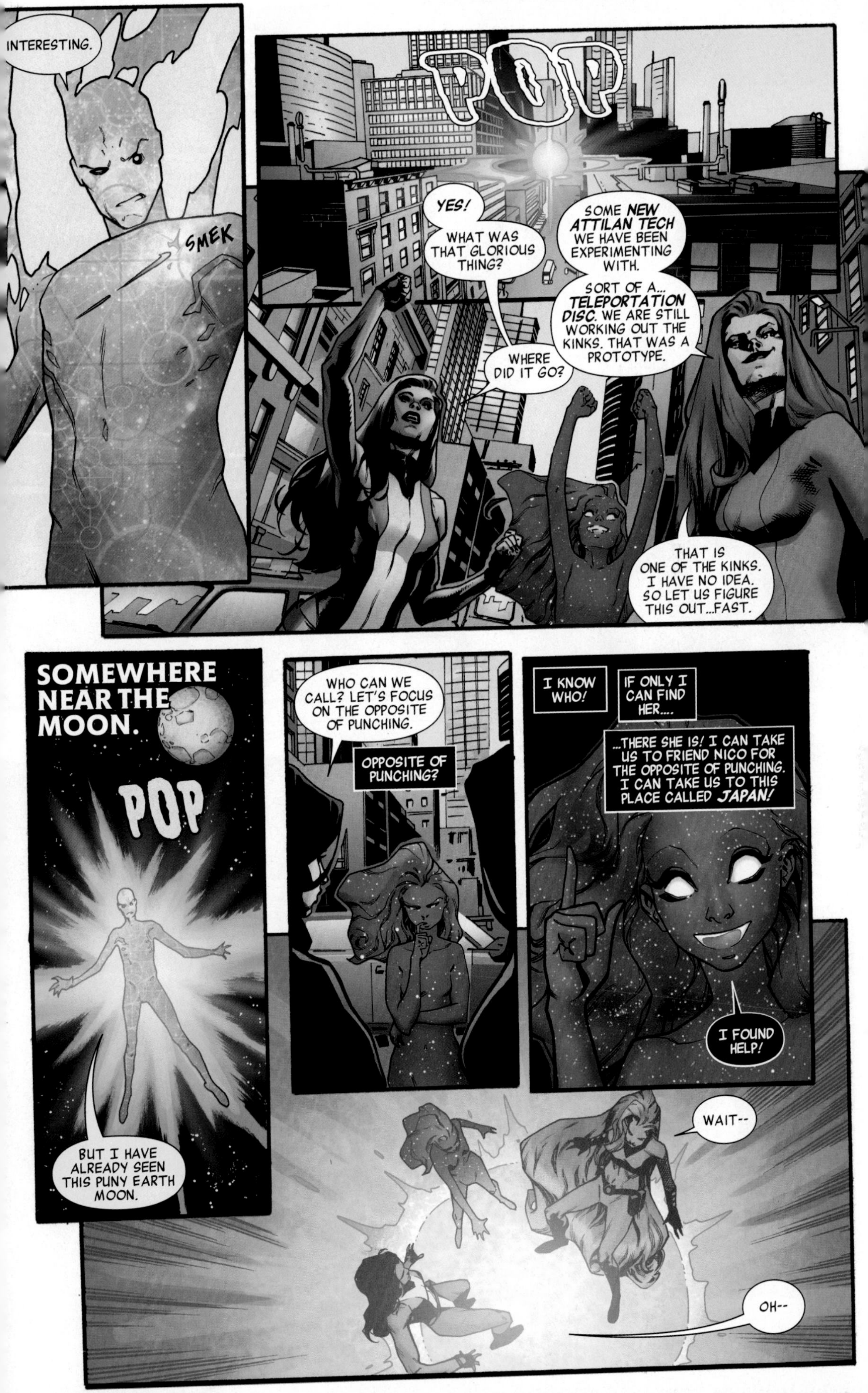
INTERESTING.
SMEK
POP
YES! WHAT WAS THAT GLORIOUS THING?
WHERE DID IT GO?
SOME NEW ATTILAN TECH WE HAVE BEEN EXPERIMENTING WITH.
SORT OF A... TELEPORTATION DISC. WE ARE STILL WORKING OUT THE KINKS. THAT WAS A PROTOTYPE.
THAT IS ONE OF THE KINKS. I HAVE NO IDEA. SO LET US FIGURE THIS OUT...FAST.
SOMEWHERE NEAR THE MOON.
POP
BUT I HAVE ALREADY SEEN THIS PUNY EARTH MOON.
WHO CAN WE CALL? LET'S FOCUS ON THE OPPOSITE OF PUNCHING.
OPPOSITE OF PUNCHING?
I KNOW WHO!
IF ONLY I CAN FIND HER....
...THERE SHE IS! I CAN TAKE US TO FRIEND NICO FOR THE OPPOSITE OF PUNCHING. I CAN TAKE US TO THIS PLACE CALLED JAPAN!
I FOUND HELP!
WAIT--
OH--

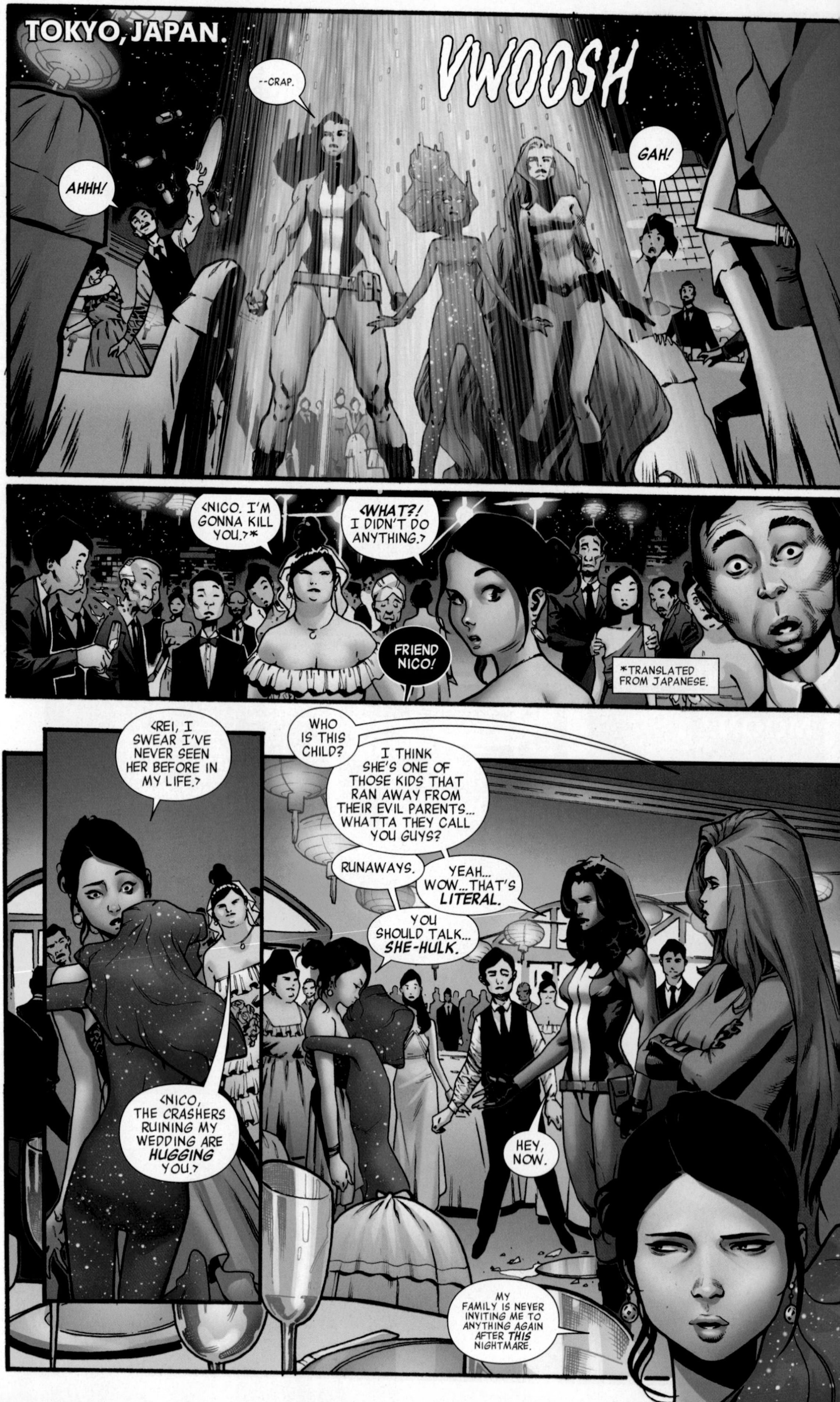

TOKYO, JAPAN.
VWOOSH
--CRAP.
AHHH!
GAH!
<NICO. I'M GONNA KILL YOU.>*
<WHAT?! I DIDN'T DO ANYTHING.>
FRIEND NICO!
*TRANSLATED FROM JAPANESE.
<REI, I SWEAR I'VE NEVER SEEN HER BEFORE IN MY LIFE.>
WHO IS THIS CHILD?
I THINK SHE'S ONE OF THOSE KIDS THAT RAN AWAY FROM THEIR EVIL PARENTS... WHATTA THEY CALL YOU GUYS?
RUNAWAYS.
YEAH... WOW...THAT'S LITERAL.
YOU SHOULD TALK... SHE-HULK.
<NICO, THE CRASHERS RUINING MY WEDDING ARE HUGGING YOU.>
HEY, NOW.
MY FAMILY IS NEVER INVITING ME TO ANYTHING AGAIN AFTER THIS NIGHTMARE.

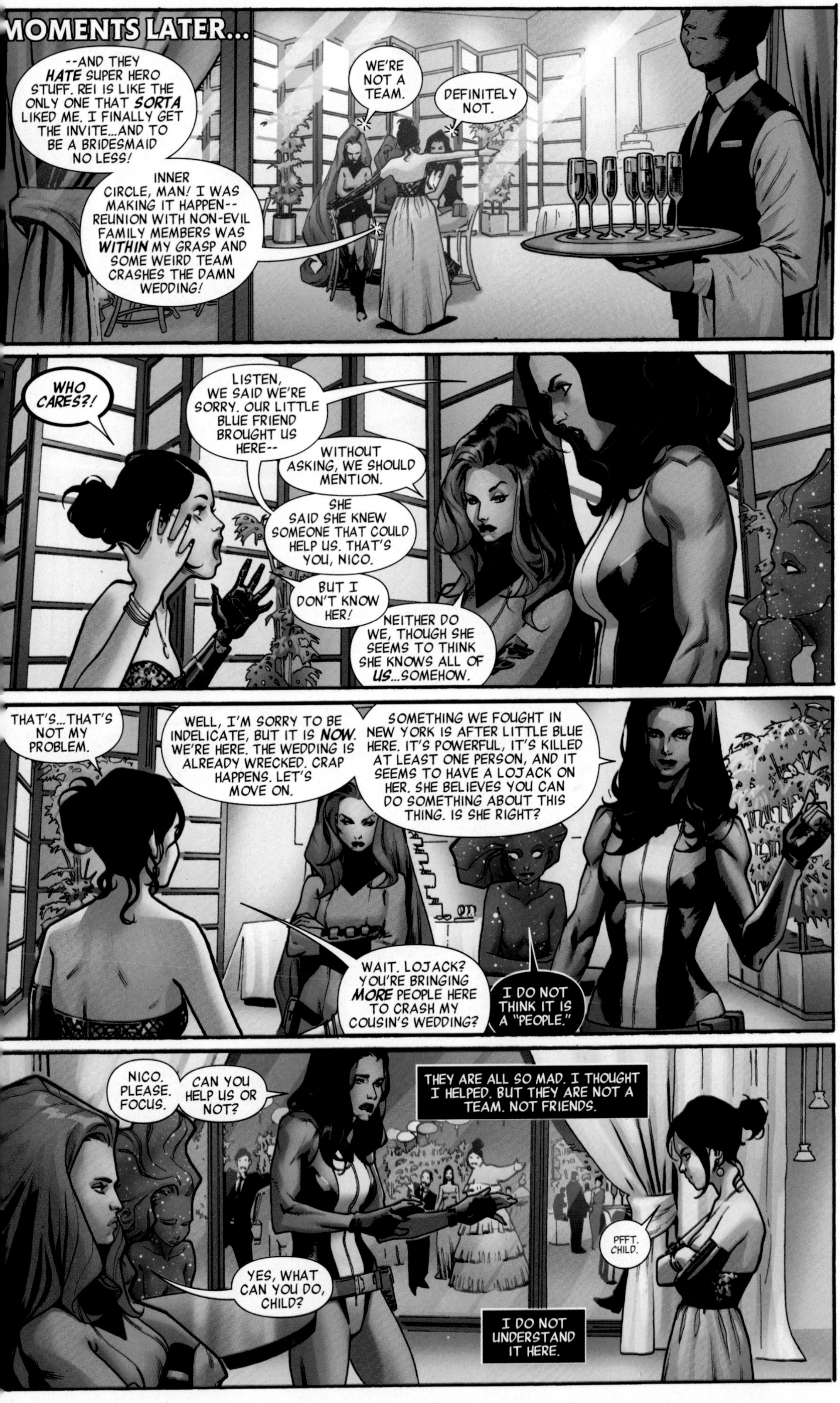
MOMENTS LATER...
--AND THEY HATE SUPER HERO STUFF. REI IS LIKE THE ONLY ONE THAT SORTA LIKED ME. I FINALLY GET THE INVITE...AND TO BE A BRIDESMAID NO LESS!
INNER CIRCLE, MAN! I WAS MAKING IT HAPPEN-- REUNION WITH NON-EVIL FAMILY MEMBERS WAS WITHIN MY GRASP AND SOME WEIRD TEAM CRASHES THE DAMN WEDDING!
WE'RE NOT A TEAM.
DEFINITELY NOT.
WHO CARES?!
LISTEN, WE SAID WE'RE SORRY. OUR LITTLE BLUE FRIEND BROUGHT US HERE--
WITHOUT ASKING, WE SHOULD MENTION.
SHE SAID SHE KNEW SOMEONE THAT COULD HELP US. THAT'S YOU, NICO.
BUT I DON'T KNOW HER!
NEITHER DO WE, THOUGH SHE SEEMS TO THINK SHE KNOWS ALL OF US...SOMEHOW.
THAT'S...THAT'S NOT MY PROBLEM.
WELL, I'M SORRY TO BE INDELICATE, BUT IT IS NOW. WE'RE HERE. THE WEDDING IS ALREADY WRECKED. CRAP HAPPENS. LET'S MOVE ON.
SOMETHING WE FOUGHT IN NEW YORK IS AFTER LITTLE BLUE HERE. IT'S POWERFUL, IT'S KILLED AT LEAST ONE PERSON, AND IT SEEMS TO HAVE A LOJACK ON HER. SHE BELIEVES YOU CAN DO SOMETHING ABOUT THIS THING. IS SHE RIGHT?
WAIT. LOJACK? YOU'RE BRINGING MORE PEOPLE HERE TO CRASH MY COUSIN'S WEDDING?
I DO NOT THINK IT IS A "PEOPLE."
NICO. PLEASE. FOCUS.
CAN YOU HELP US OR NOT?
THEY ARE ALL SO MAD. I THOUGHT I HELPED. BUT THEY ARE NOT A TEAM. NOT FRIENDS.
YES, WHAT CAN YOU DO, CHILD?
PFFT. CHILD.
I DO NOT UNDERSTAND IT HERE.

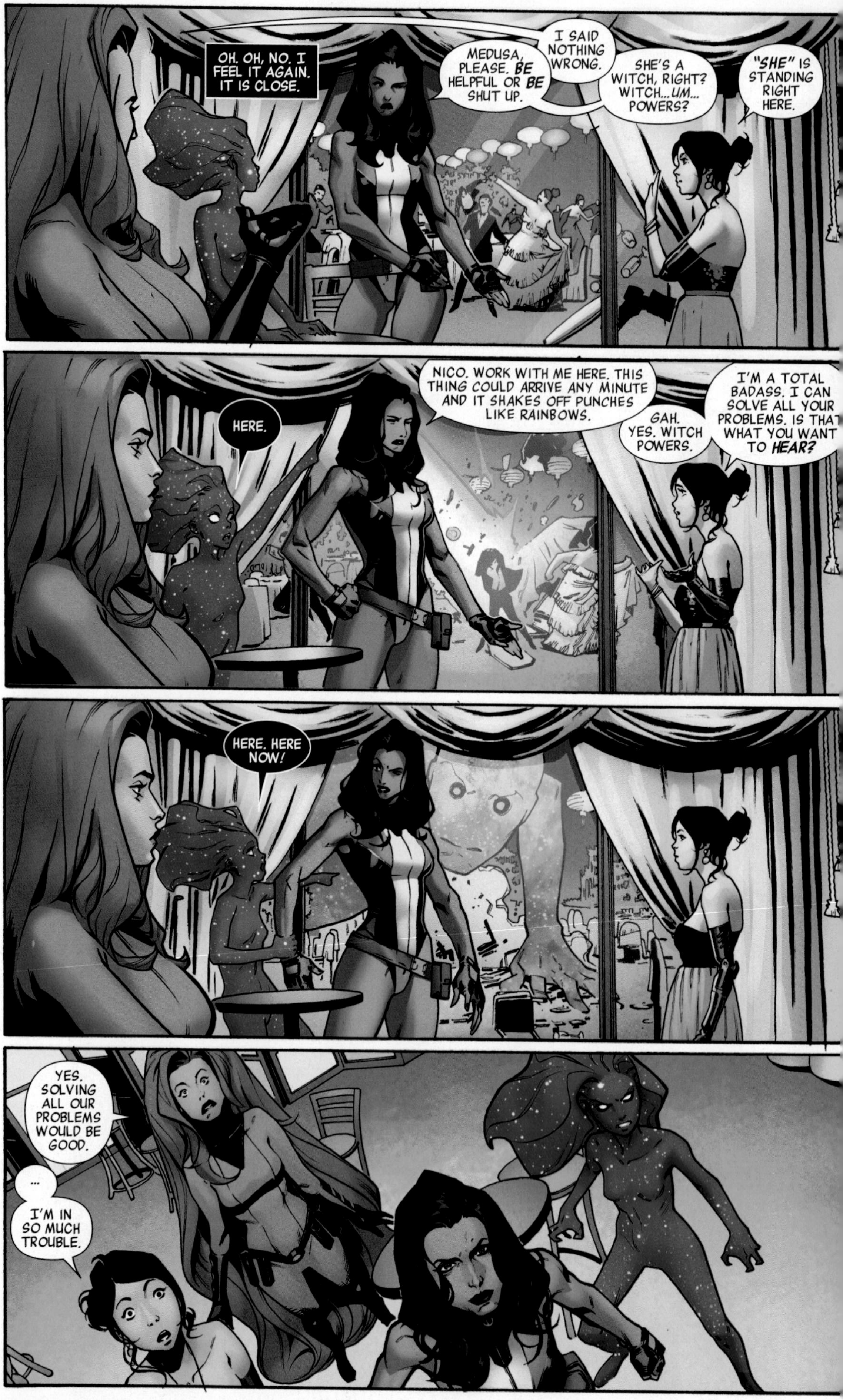

OH. OH, NO. I FEEL IT AGAIN. IT IS CLOSE.
MEDUSA, PLEASE. BE HELPFUL OR BE SHUT UP.
I SAID NOTHING WRONG.
SHE'S A WITCH, RIGHT? WITCH...UM... POWERS?
"SHE" IS STANDING RIGHT HERE.
HERE.
NICO. WORK WITH ME HERE. THIS THING COULD ARRIVE ANY MINUTE AND IT SHAKES OFF PUNCHES LIKE RAINBOWS.
GAH. YES. WITCH POWERS.
I'M A TOTAL BADASS. I CAN SOLVE ALL YOUR PROBLEMS. IS THAT WHAT YOU WANT TO HEAR?
HERE. HERE NOW!
YES. SOLVING ALL OUR PROBLEMS WOULD BE GOOD.
...
I'M IN SO MUCH TROUBLE.

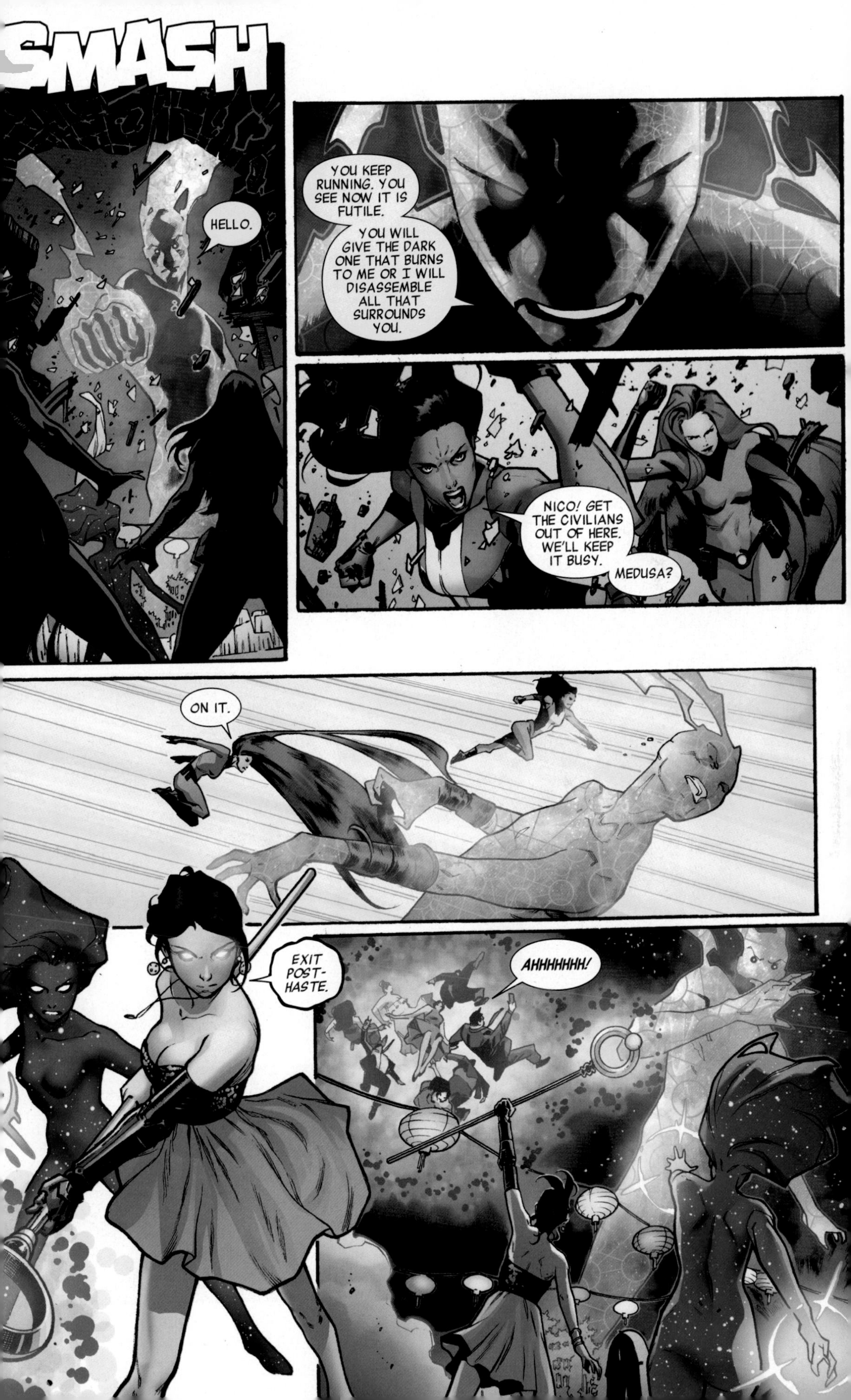
SMASH
HELLO.
YOU KEEP RUNNING. YOU SEE NOW IT IS FUTILE.
YOU WILL GIVE THE DARK ONE THAT BURNS TO ME OR I WILL DISASSEMBLE ALL THAT SURROUNDS YOU.
NICO! GET THE CIVILIANS OUT OF HERE. WE'LL KEEP IT BUSY.
MEDUSA?
ON IT.
EXIT POST-HASTE.
AHHHHHHH!

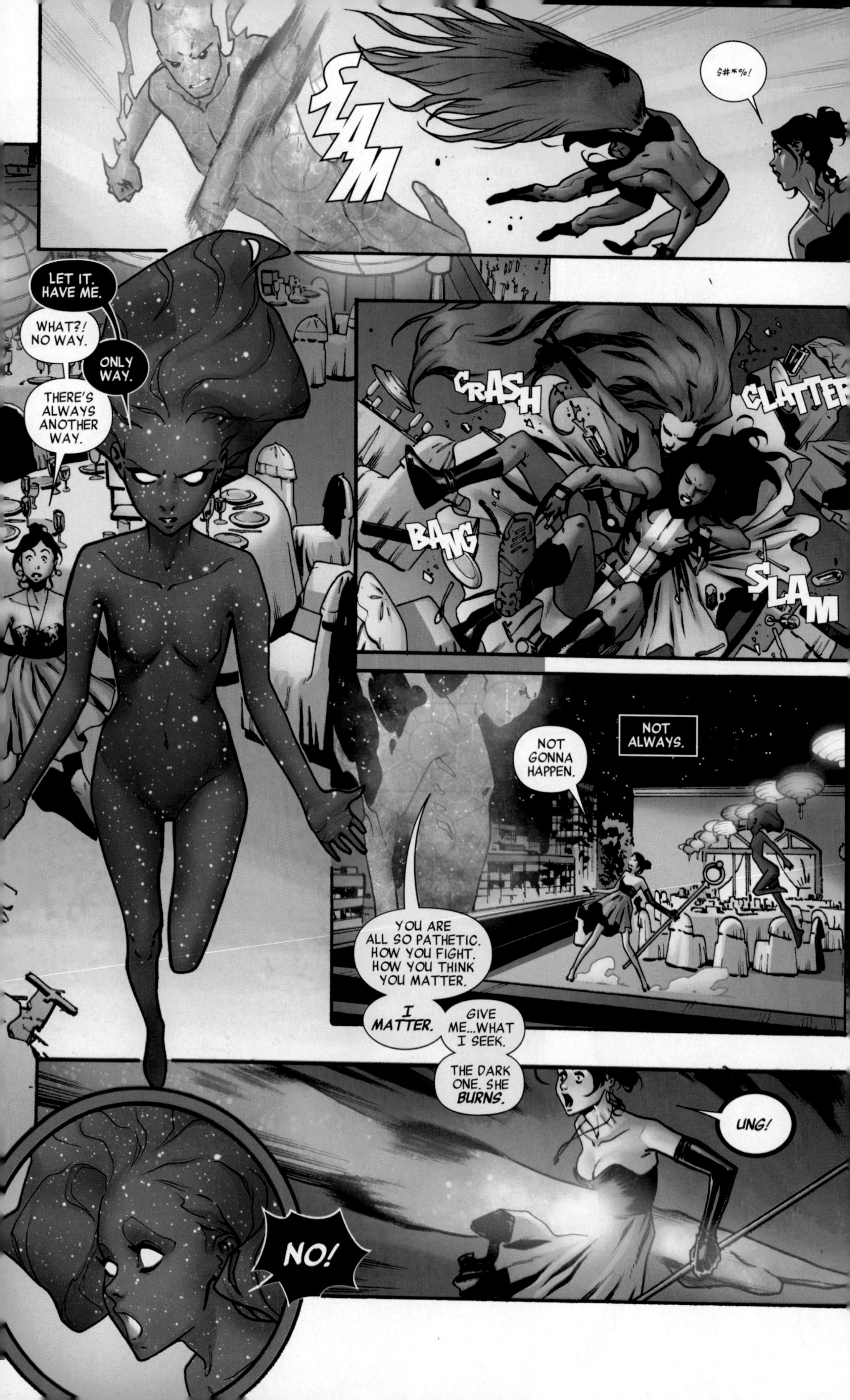
SLAM
$#*%!
LET IT. HAVE ME.
WHAT?! NO WAY.
ONLY WAY.
THERE'S ALWAYS ANOTHER WAY.
CRASH
CLATTER
BANG
SLAM
NOT ALWAYS.
NOT GONNA HAPPEN.
YOU ARE ALL SO PATHETIC. HOW YOU FIGHT. HOW YOU THINK YOU MATTER.
I MATTER.
GIVE ME...WHAT I SEEK.
THE DARK ONE. SHE BURNS.
UNG!
NO!

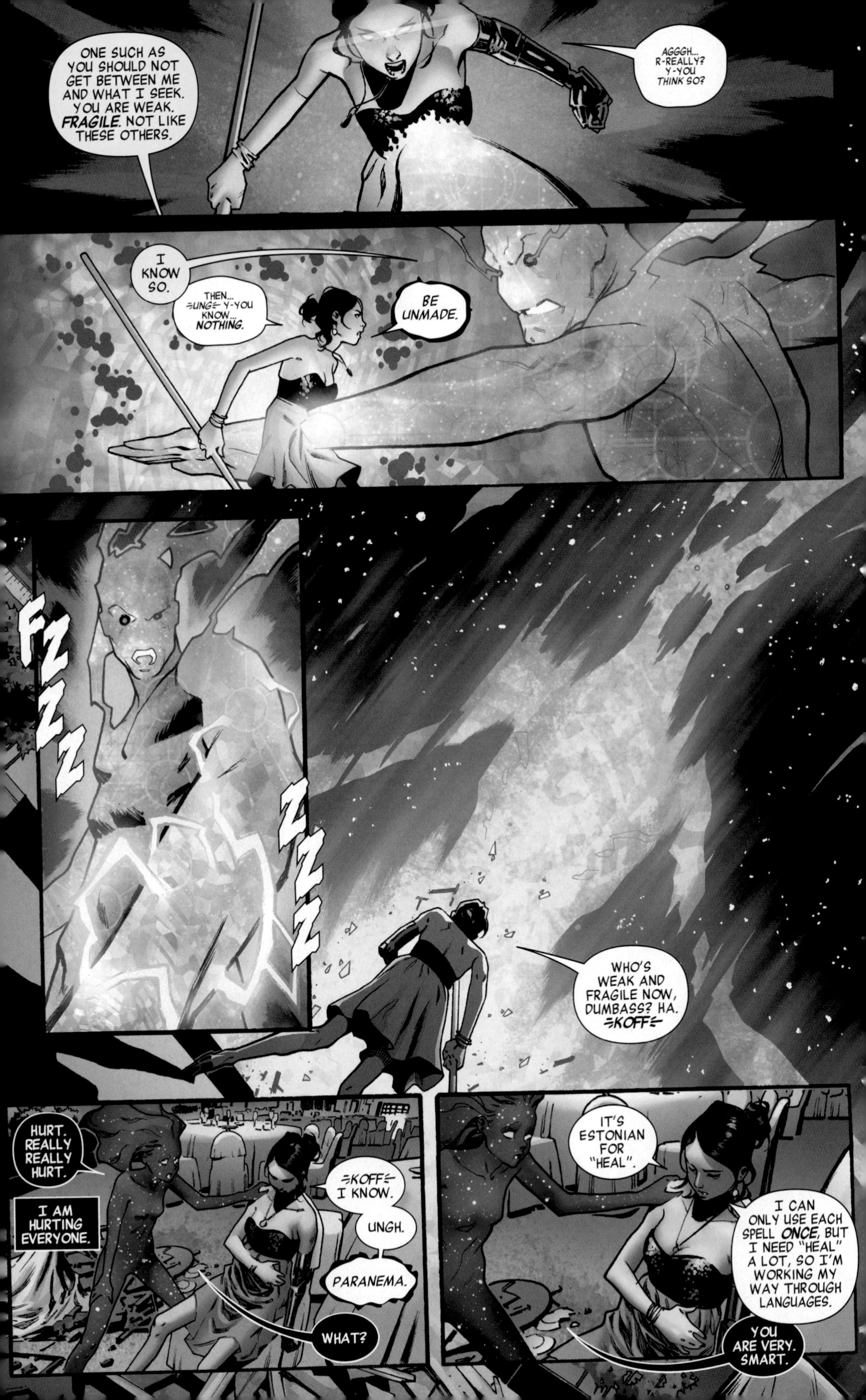
ONE SUCH AS YOU SHOULD NOT GET BETWEEN ME AND WHAT I SEEK. YOU ARE WEAK. FRAGILE. NOT LIKE THESE OTHERS.
AGGGH... R-REALLY? Y-YOU THINK SO?
I KNOW SO.
THEN... UNG Y-YOU KNOW... NOTHING.
BE UNMADE.
FZZZZ
ZZZZ
WHO'S WEAK AND FRAGILE NOW, DUMBASS? HA. KOFF
HURT. REALLY REALLY HURT.
I AM HURTING EVERYONE.
KOFF I KNOW.
UNGH.
PARANEMA.
WHAT?
IT'S ESTONIAN FOR "HEAL".
I CAN ONLY USE EACH SPELL ONCE, BUT I NEED "HEAL" A LOT, SO I'M WORKING MY WAY THROUGH LANGUAGES.
YOU ARE VERY. SMART.

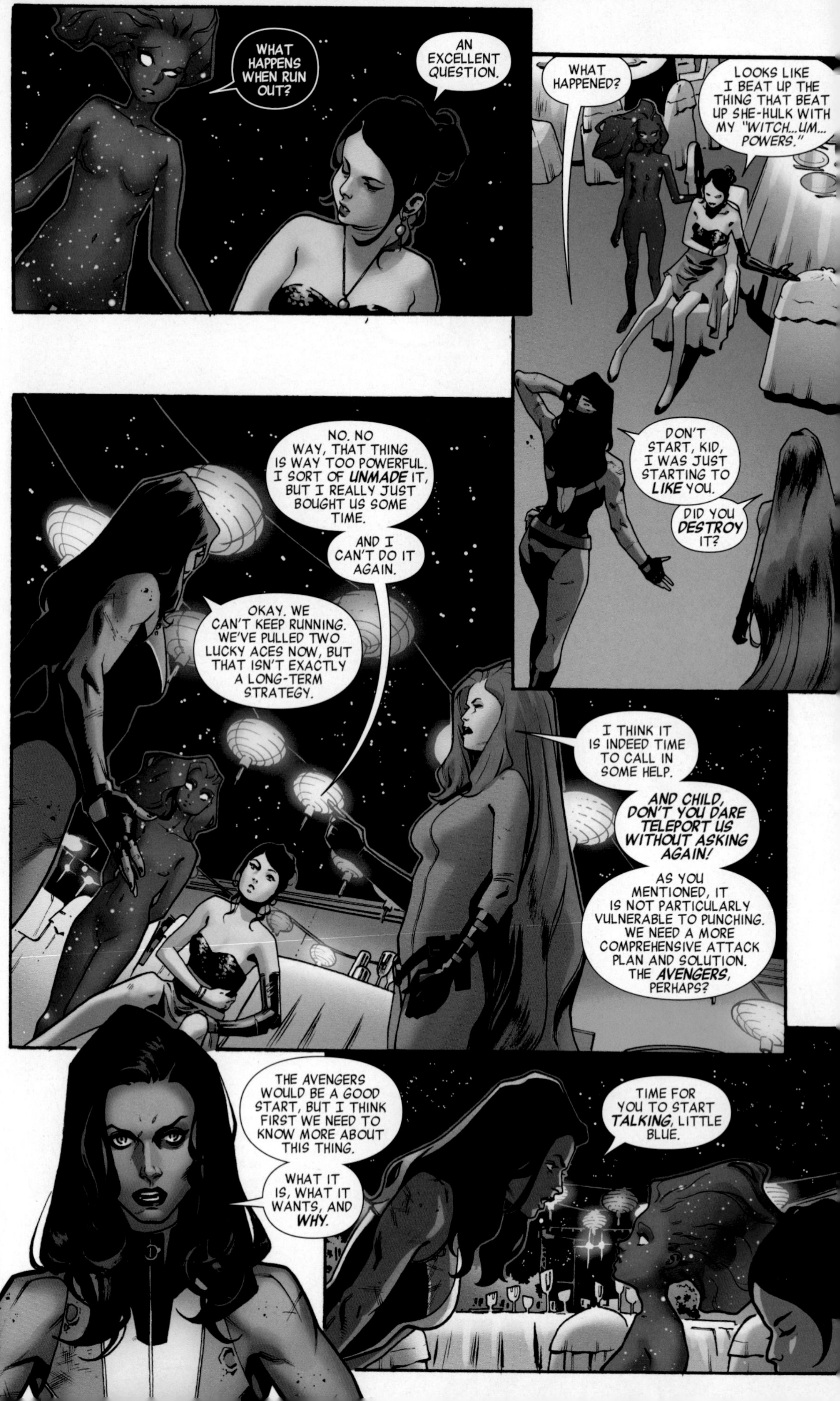

WHAT HAPPENS WHEN RUN OUT?
AN EXCELLENT QUESTION.
WHAT HAPPENED?
LOOKS LIKE I BEAT UP THE THING THAT BEAT UP SHE-HULK WITH MY "WITCH...UM... POWERS."
DON'T START, KID, I WAS JUST STARTING TO LIKE YOU.
DID YOU DESTROY IT?
NO. NO WAY, THAT THING IS WAY TOO POWERFUL. I SORT OF UNMADE IT, BUT I REALLY JUST BOUGHT US SOME TIME.
AND I CAN'T DO IT AGAIN.
OKAY. WE CAN'T KEEP RUNNING. WE'VE PULLED TWO LUCKY ACES NOW, BUT THAT ISN'T EXACTLY A LONG-TERM STRATEGY.
I THINK IT IS INDEED TIME TO CALL IN SOME HELP.
AND CHILD, DON'T YOU DARE TELEPORT US WITHOUT ASKING AGAIN!
AS YOU MENTIONED, IT IS NOT PARTICULARLY VULNERABLE TO PUNCHING. WE NEED A MORE COMPREHENSIVE ATTACK PLAN AND SOLUTION. THE AVENGERS, PERHAPS?
THE AVENGERS WOULD BE A GOOD START, BUT I THINK FIRST WE NEED TO KNOW MORE ABOUT THIS THING.
WHAT IT IS, WHAT IT WANTS, AND WHY.
TIME FOR YOU TO START TALKING, LITTLE BLUE.

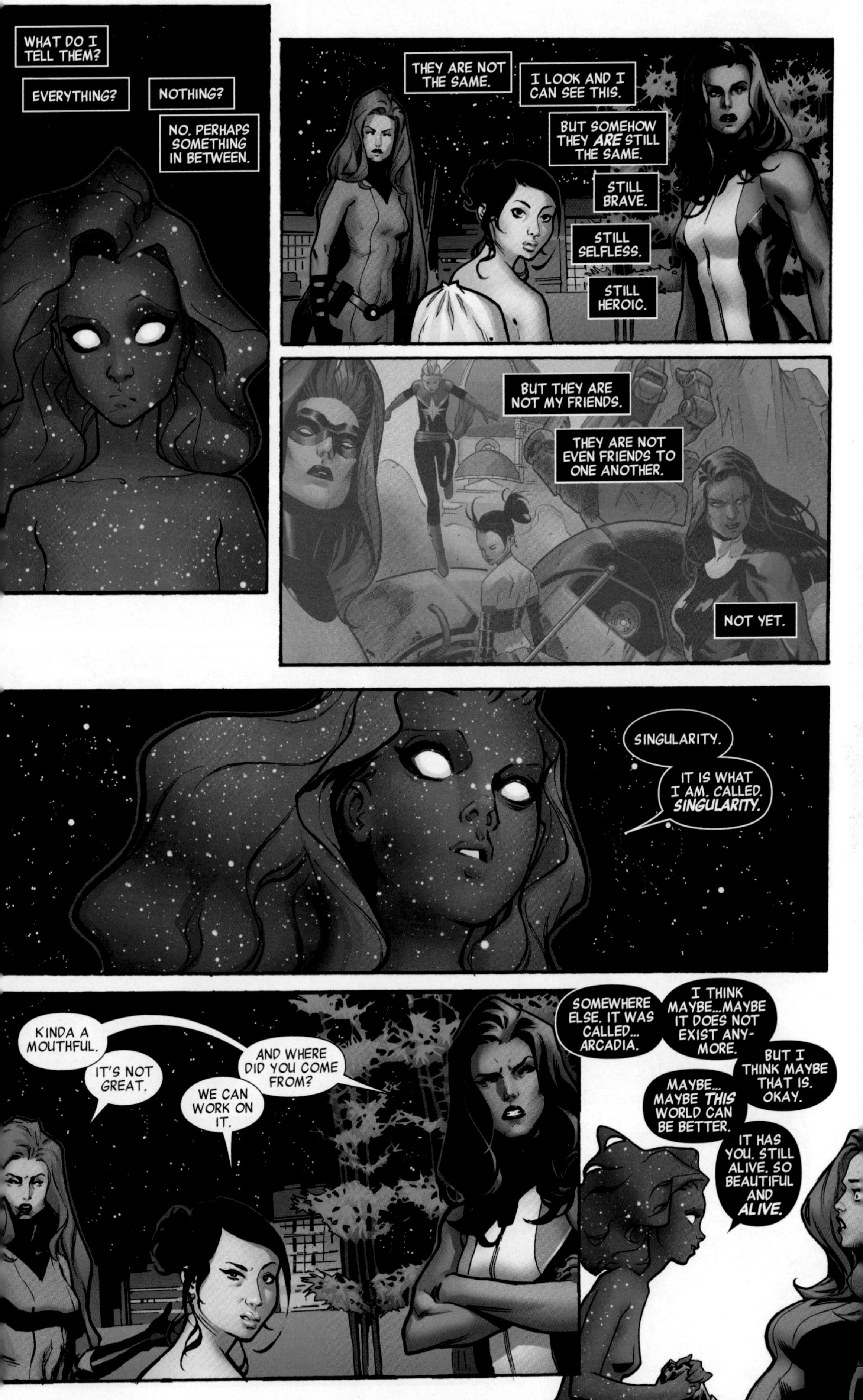
WHAT DO I TELL THEM?
EVERYTHING?
NOTHING?
NO. PERHAPS SOMETHING IN BETWEEN.
THEY ARE NOT THE SAME.
I LOOK AND I CAN SEE THIS.
BUT SOMEHOW THEY ARE STILL THE SAME.
STILL BRAVE.
STILL SELFLESS.
STILL HEROIC.
BUT THEY ARE NOT MY FRIENDS.
THEY ARE NOT EVEN FRIENDS TO ONE ANOTHER.
NOT YET.
SINGULARITY.
IT IS WHAT I AM. CALLED. SINGULARITY.
KINDA A MOUTHFUL.
IT'S NOT GREAT.
WE CAN WORK ON IT.
AND WHERE DID YOU COME FROM?
SOMEWHERE ELSE. IT WAS CALLED... ARCADIA.
I THINK MAYBE...MAYBE IT DOES NOT EXIST ANY-MORE.
BUT I THINK MAYBE THAT IS. OKAY.
MAYBE... MAYBE THIS WORLD CAN BE BETTER.
IT HAS YOU. STILL ALIVE. SO BEAUTIFUL AND ALIVE.

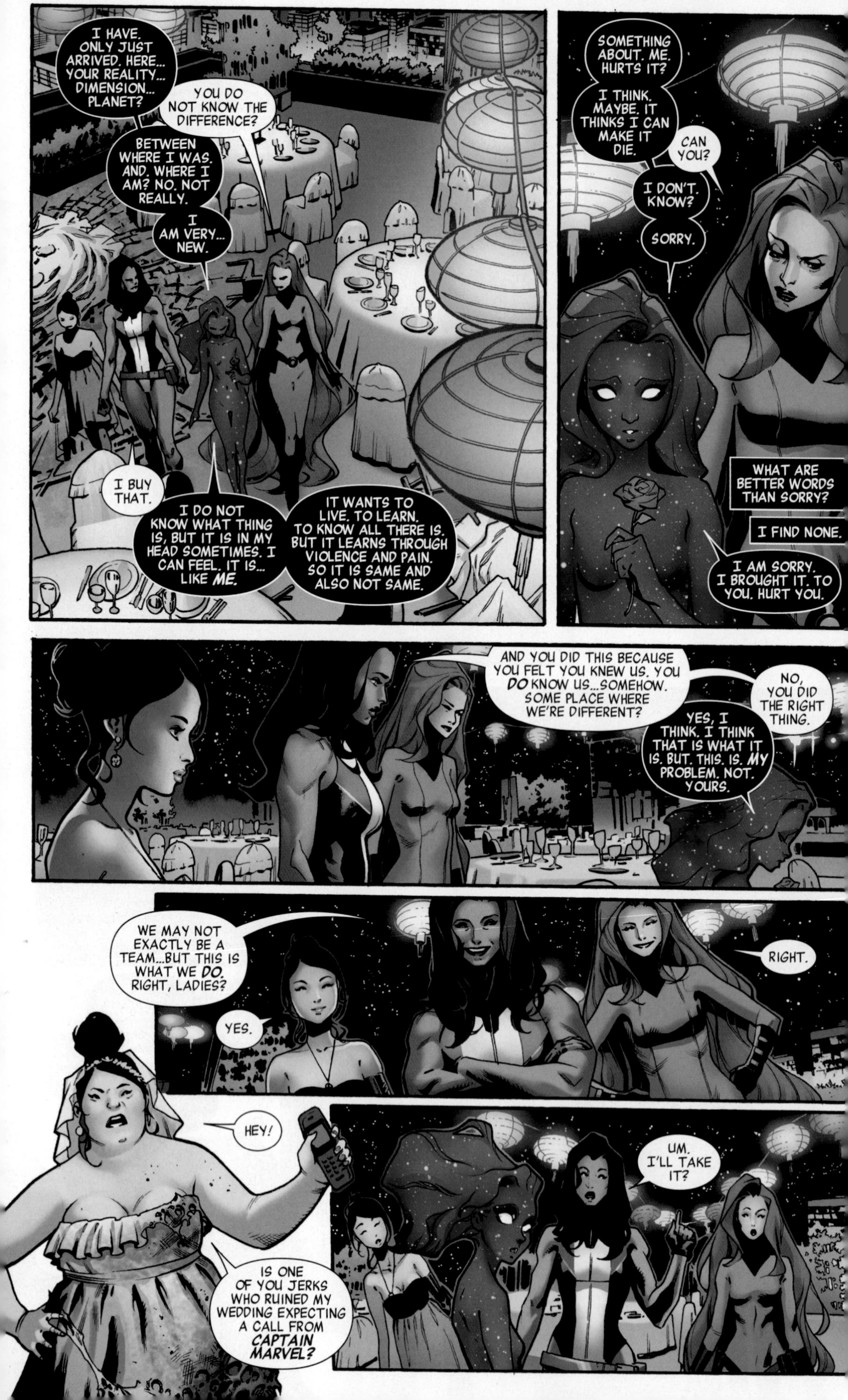
I HAVE. ONLY JUST ARRIVED. HERE... YOUR REALITY... DIMENSION... PLANET?
YOU DO NOT KNOW THE DIFFERENCE?
BETWEEN WHERE I WAS. AND. WHERE I AM? NO. NOT REALLY.
I AM VERY... NEW.
I BUY THAT.
I DO NOT KNOW WHAT THING IS, BUT IT IS IN MY HEAD SOMETIMES. I CAN FEEL. IT IS... LIKE ME.
IT WANTS TO LIVE. TO LEARN. TO KNOW ALL THERE IS. BUT IT LEARNS THROUGH VIOLENCE AND PAIN. SO IT IS SAME AND ALSO NOT SAME.
SOMETHING ABOUT. ME. HURTS IT?
I THINK. MAYBE. IT THINKS I CAN MAKE IT DIE.
CAN YOU?
I DON'T. KNOW?
SORRY.
WHAT ARE BETTER WORDS THAN SORRY?
I FIND NONE.
I AM SORRY. I BROUGHT IT. TO YOU. HURT YOU.
AND YOU DID THIS BECAUSE YOU FELT YOU KNEW US. YOU DO KNOW US...SOMEHOW. SOME PLACE WHERE WE'RE DIFFERENT?
YES, I THINK. I THINK THAT IS WHAT IT IS. BUT. THIS. IS. MY PROBLEM. NOT. YOURS.
NO, YOU DID THE RIGHT THING.
WE MAY NOT EXACTLY BE A TEAM...BUT THIS IS WHAT WE DO. RIGHT, LADIES?
YES.
RIGHT.
HEY!
IS ONE OF YOU JERKS WHO RUINED MY WEDDING EXPECTING A CALL FROM CAPTAIN MARVEL?
UM. I'LL TAKE IT?

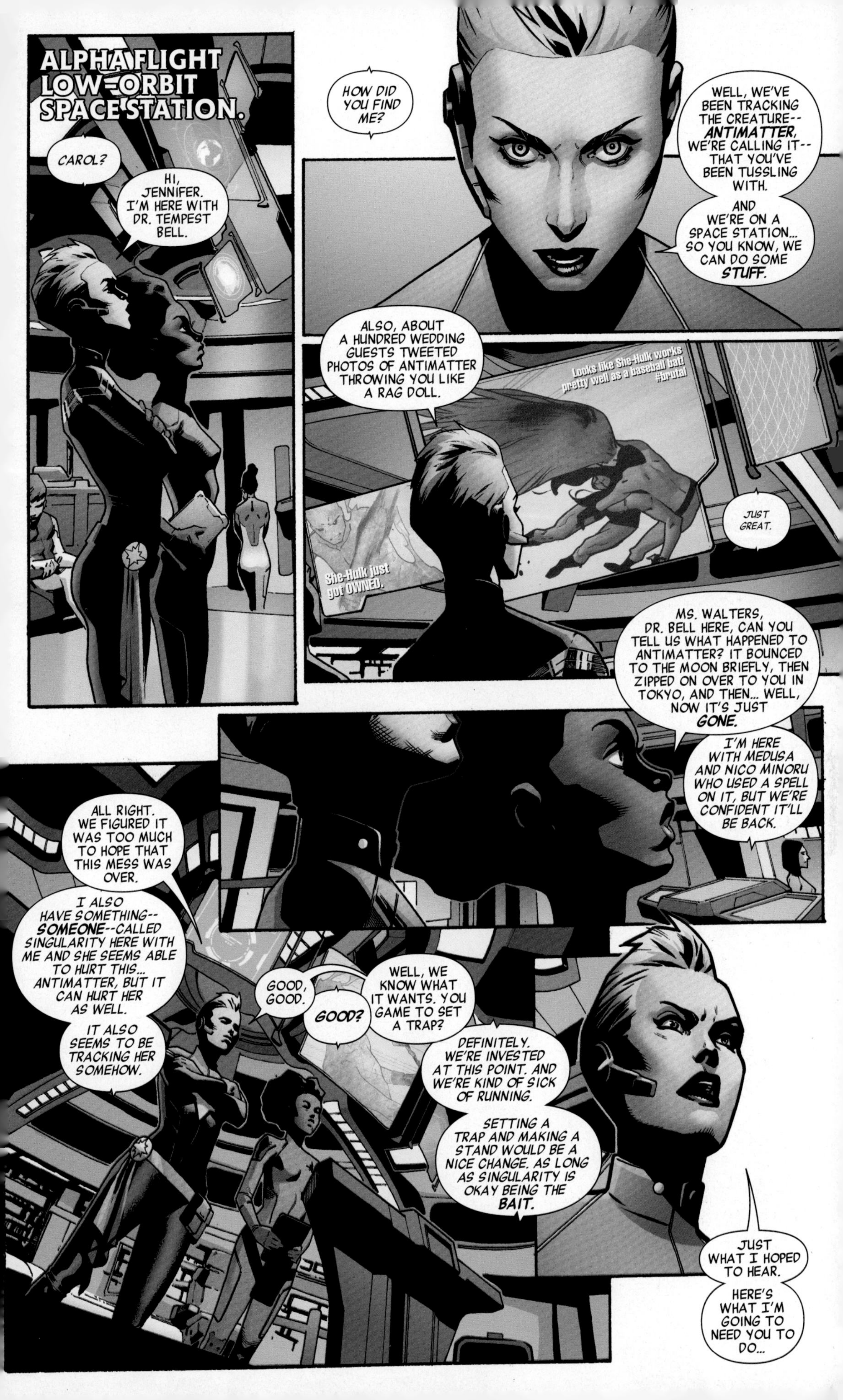

ALPHA FLIGHT LOW-ORBIT SPACE STATION.
CAROL?
HI, JENNIFER. I'M HERE WITH DR. TEMPEST BELL.
HOW DID YOU FIND ME?
WELL, WE'VE BEEN TRACKING THE CREATURE-- ANTIMATTER, WE'RE CALLING IT-- THAT YOU'VE BEEN TUSSLING WITH.
AND WE'RE ON A SPACE STATION... SO YOU KNOW, WE CAN DO SOME STUFF.
ALSO, ABOUT A HUNDRED WEDDING GUESTS TWEETED PHOTOS OF ANTIMATTER THROWING YOU LIKE A RAG DOLL.
Looks like She-Hulk works pretty well as a baseball bat! #brutal
She-Hulk just got OWNED.
JUST GREAT.
MS. WALTERS, DR. BELL HERE, CAN YOU TELL US WHAT HAPPENED TO ANTIMATTER? IT BOUNCED TO THE MOON BRIEFLY, THEN ZIPPED ON OVER TO YOU IN TOKYO, AND THEN... WELL, NOW IT'S JUST GONE.
I'M HERE WITH MEDUSA AND NICO MINORU WHO USED A SPELL ON IT, BUT WE'RE CONFIDENT IT'LL BE BACK.
ALL RIGHT. WE FIGURED IT WAS TOO MUCH TO HOPE THAT THIS MESS WAS OVER.
I ALSO HAVE SOMETHING-- SOMEONE--CALLED SINGULARITY HERE WITH ME AND SHE SEEMS ABLE TO HURT THIS... ANTIMATTER, BUT IT CAN HURT HER AS WELL.
IT ALSO SEEMS TO BE TRACKING HER SOMEHOW.
GOOD, GOOD.
GOOD?
WELL, WE KNOW WHAT IT WANTS. YOU GAME TO SET A TRAP?
DEFINITELY. WE'RE INVESTED AT THIS POINT. AND WE'RE KIND OF SICK OF RUNNING.
SETTING A TRAP AND MAKING A STAND WOULD BE A NICE CHANGE. AS LONG AS SINGULARITY IS OKAY BEING THE BAIT.
JUST WHAT I HOPED TO HEAR.
HERE'S WHAT I'M GOING TO NEED YOU TO DO...

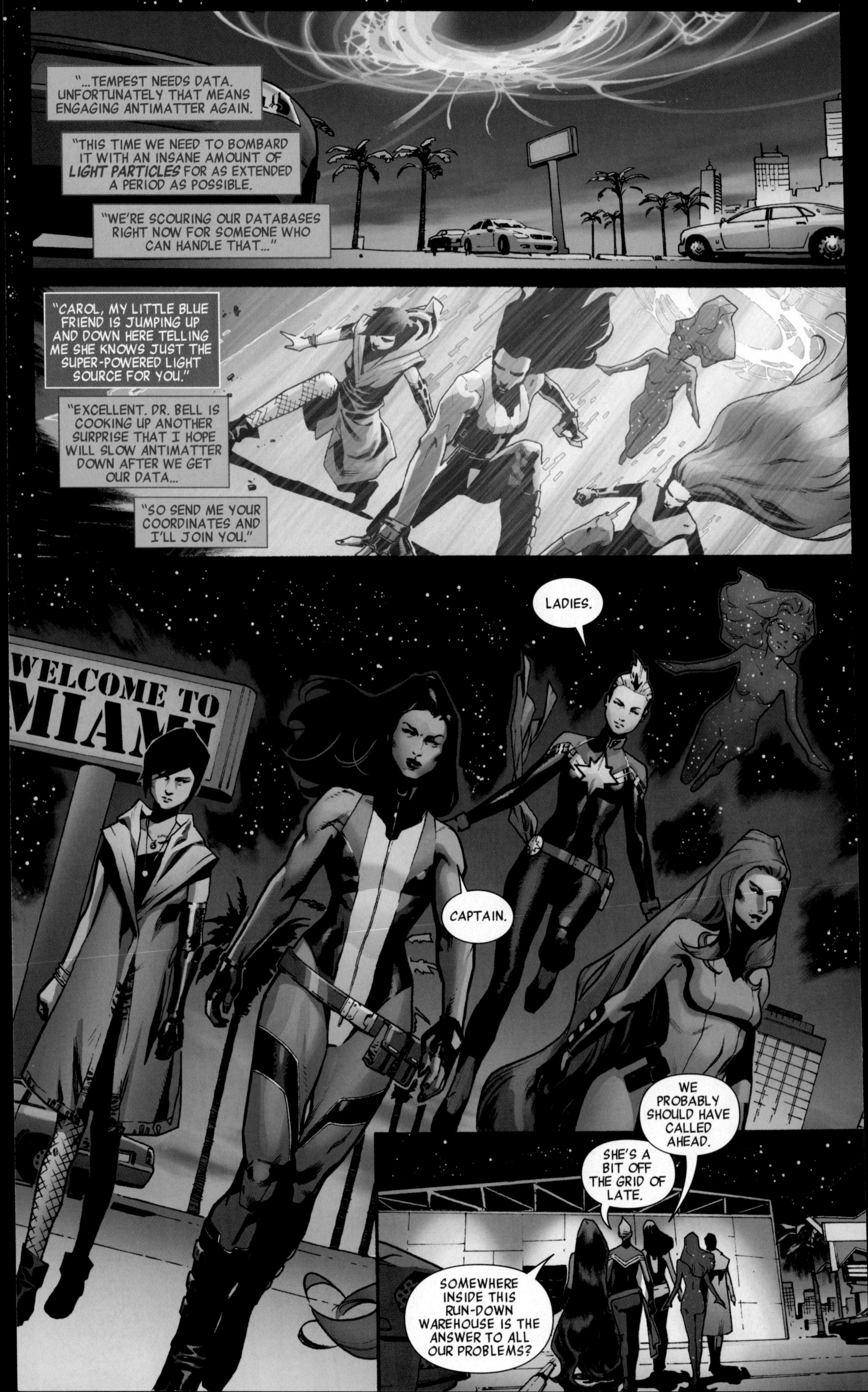
"...TEMPEST NEEDS DATA. UNFORTUNATELY THAT MEANS ENGAGING ANTIMATTER AGAIN.
"THIS TIME WE NEED TO BOMBARD IT WITH AN INSANE AMOUNT OF LIGHT PARTICLES FOR AS EXTENDED A PERIOD AS POSSIBLE.
"WE'RE SCOURING OUR DATABASES RIGHT NOW FOR SOMEONE WHO CAN HANDLE THAT..."
"CAROL, MY LITTLE BLUE FRIEND IS JUMPING UP AND DOWN HERE TELLING ME SHE KNOWS JUST THE SUPER-POWERED LIGHT SOURCE FOR YOU."
"EXCELLENT. DR. BELL IS COOKING UP ANOTHER SURPRISE THAT I HOPE WILL SLOW ANTIMATTER DOWN AFTER WE GET OUR DATA...
"SO SEND ME YOUR COORDINATES AND I'LL JOIN YOU."
LADIES.
CAPTAIN.
WE PROBABLY SHOULD HAVE CALLED AHEAD.
SHE'S A BIT OFF THE GRID OF LATE.
SOMEWHERE INSIDE THIS RUN-DOWN WAREHOUSE IS THE ANSWER TO ALL OUR PROBLEMS?

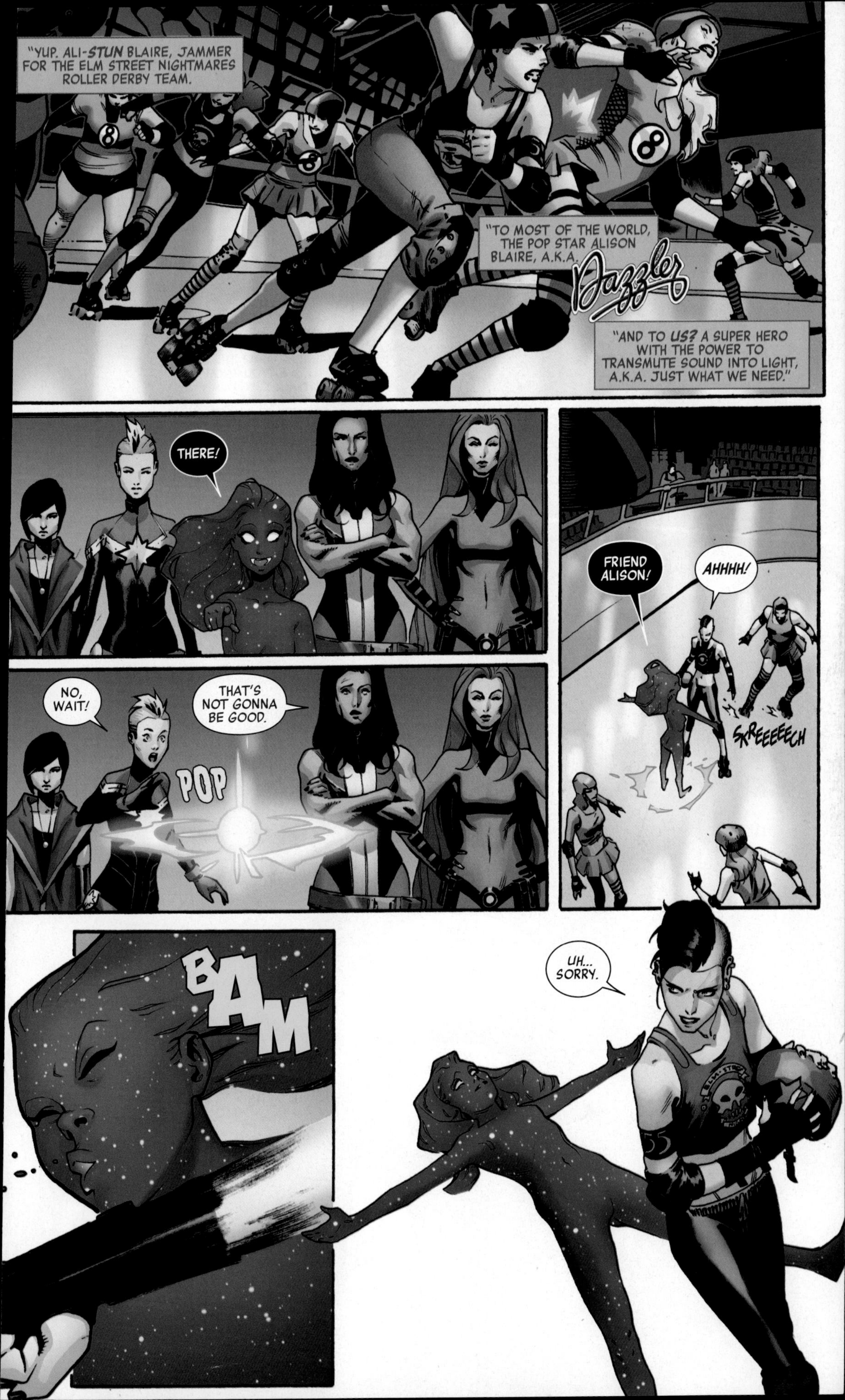
"YUP. ALI-STUN BLAIRE, JAMMER FOR THE ELM STREET NIGHTMARES ROLLER DERBY TEAM.
"TO MOST OF THE WORLD, THE POP STAR ALISON BLAIRE, A.K.A. Dazzler
"AND TO US? A SUPER HERO WITH THE POWER TO TRANSMUTE SOUND INTO LIGHT, A.K.A. JUST WHAT WE NEED."
THERE!
NO, WAIT!
THAT'S NOT GONNA BE GOOD.
POP
FRIEND ALISON!
AHHHH!
SKREEEEECH
BAM
UH... SORRY.

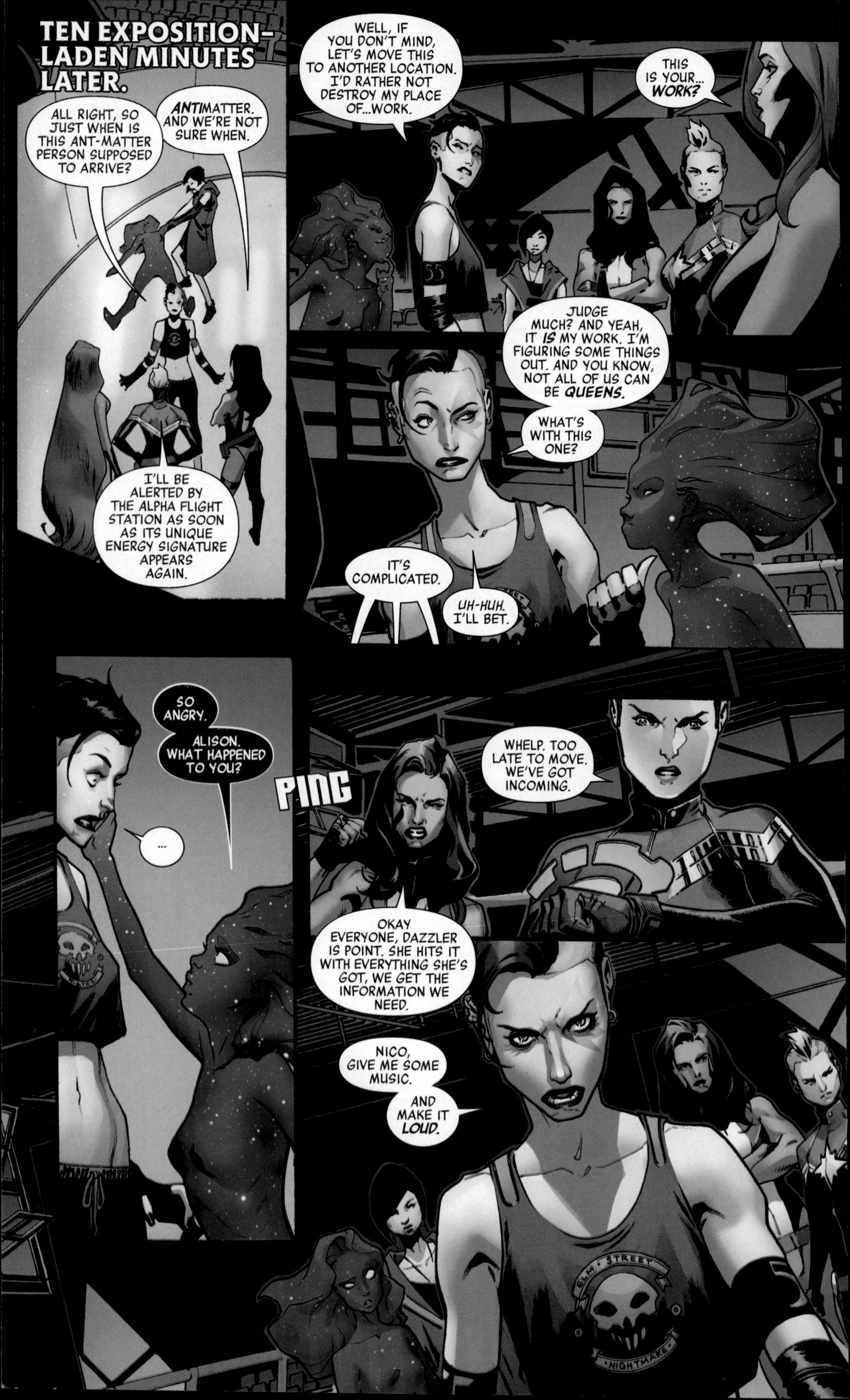

TEN EXPOSITION-LADEN MINUTES LATER.
ALL RIGHT, SO JUST WHEN IS THIS ANT-MATTER PERSON SUPPOSED TO ARRIVE?
ANTIMATTER. AND WE'RE NOT SURE WHEN.
I'LL BE ALERTED BY THE ALPHA FLIGHT STATION AS SOON AS ITS UNIQUE ENERGY SIGNATURE APPEARS AGAIN.
WELL, IF YOU DON'T MIND, LET'S MOVE THIS TO ANOTHER LOCATION. I'D RATHER NOT DESTROY MY PLACE OF...WORK.
THIS IS YOUR... WORK?
JUDGE MUCH? AND YEAH, IT IS MY WORK. I'M FIGURING SOME THINGS OUT. AND YOU KNOW, NOT ALL OF US CAN BE QUEENS.
WHAT'S WITH THIS ONE?
IT'S COMPLICATED.
UH-HUH. I'LL BET.
SO ANGRY.
ALISON. WHAT HAPPENED TO YOU?
...
PING
WHELP. TOO LATE TO MOVE. WE'VE GOT INCOMING.
OKAY EVERYONE, DAZZLER IS POINT. SHE HITS IT WITH EVERYTHING SHE'S GOT, WE GET THE INFORMATION WE NEED.
NICO, GIVE ME SOME MUSIC.
AND MAKE IT LOUD.
ELM STREET
NIGHTMARE

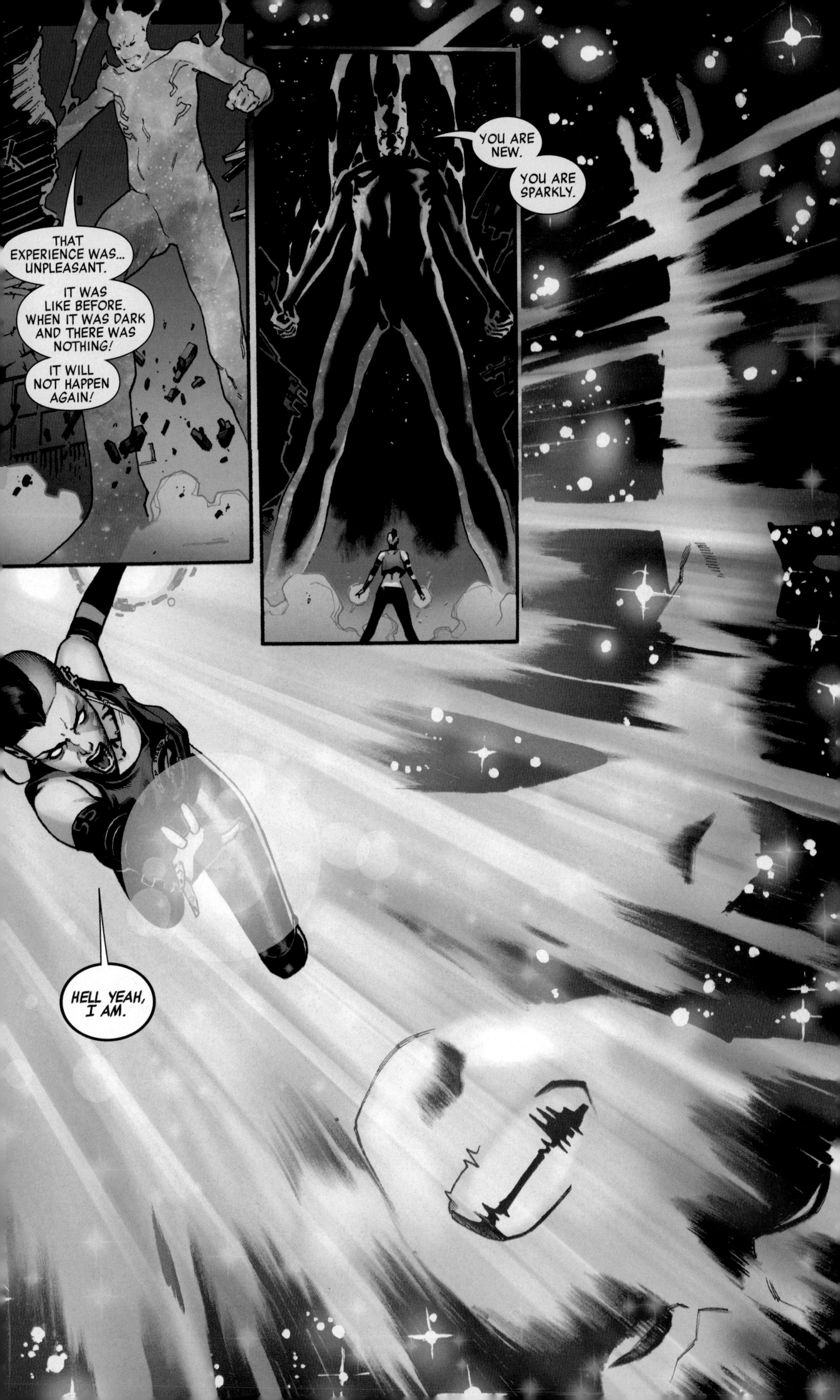

THAT EXPERIENCE WAS... UNPLEASANT.
IT WAS LIKE BEFORE. WHEN IT WAS DARK AND THERE WAS NOTHING!
IT WILL NOT HAPPEN AGAIN!
YOU ARE NEW.
YOU ARE SPARKLY.
HELL YEAH, I AM.

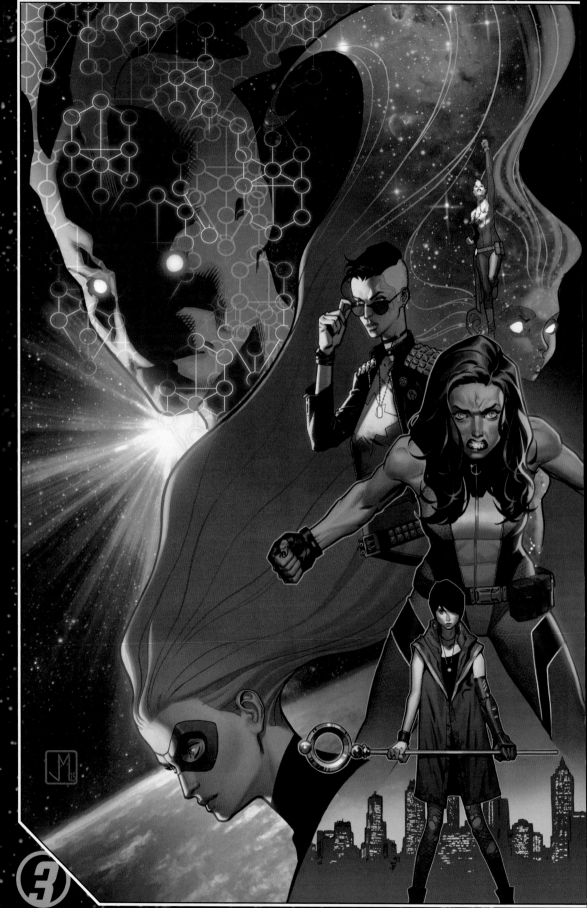

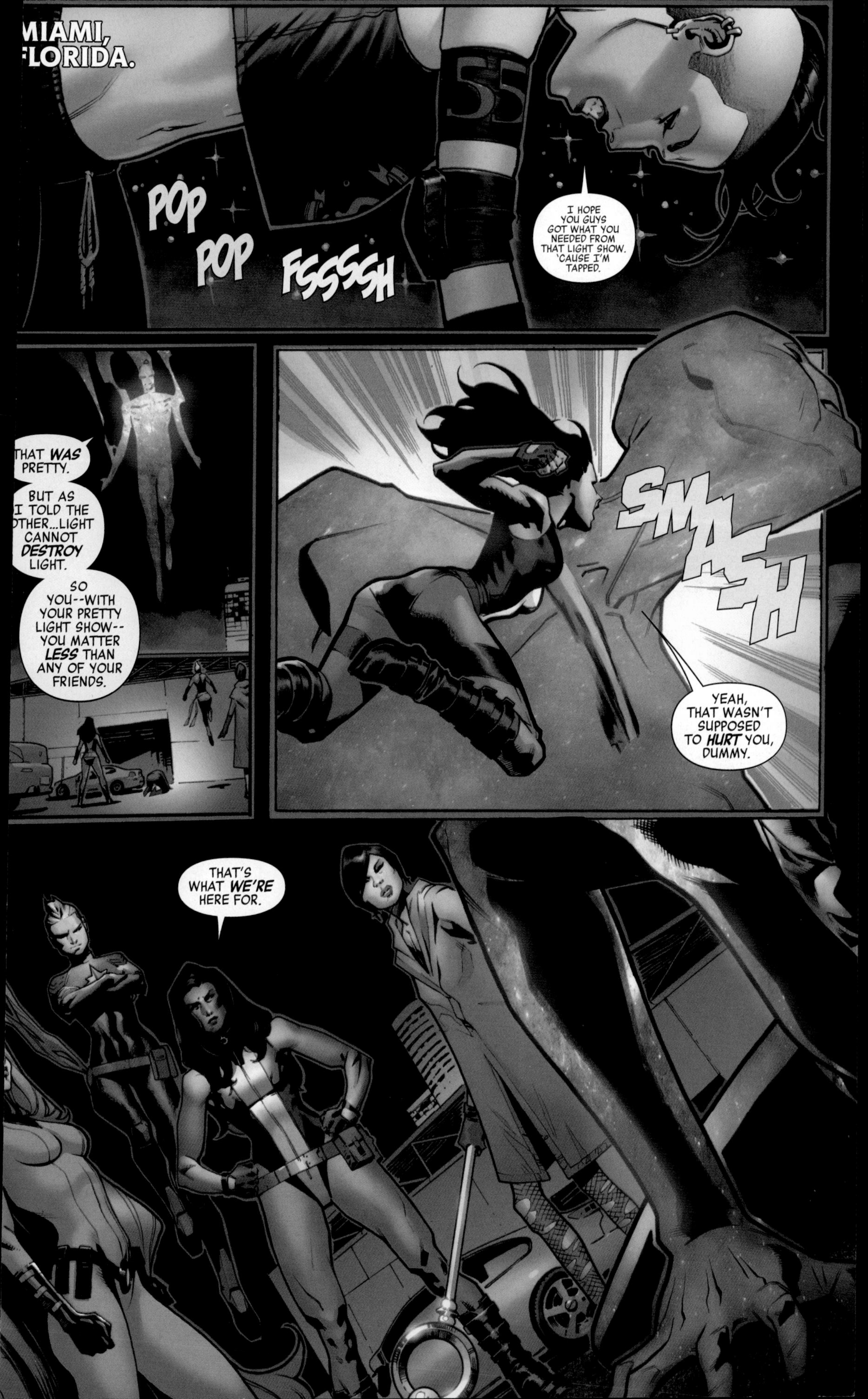
MIAMI, FLORIDA.
POP
POP
FSSSSH
I HOPE YOU GUYS GOT WHAT YOU NEEDED FROM THAT LIGHT SHOW. 'CAUSE I'M TAPPED.
THAT WAS PRETTY.
BUT AS I TOLD THE OTHER...LIGHT CANNOT DESTROY LIGHT.
SO YOU--WITH YOUR PRETTY LIGHT SHOW--YOU MATTER LESS THAN ANY OF YOUR FRIENDS.
SMASH
YEAH, THAT WASN'T SUPPOSED TO HURT YOU, DUMMY.
THAT'S WHAT WE'RE HERE FOR.

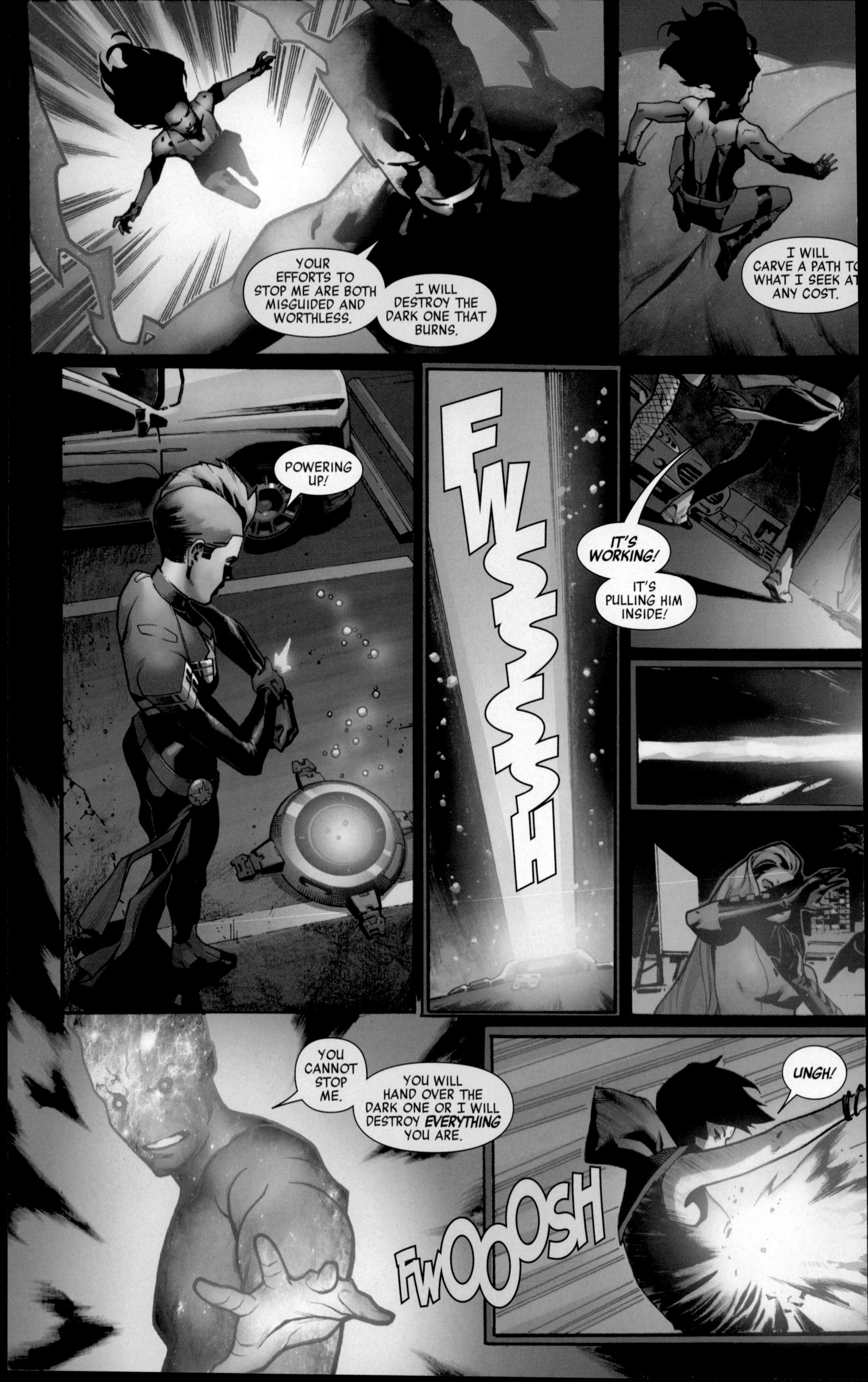
YOUR EFFORTS TO STOP ME ARE BOTH MISGUIDED AND WORTHLESS.
I WILL DESTROY THE DARK ONE THAT BURNS.
I WILL CARVE A PATH TO WHAT I SEEK AT ANY COST.
POWERING UP!
FWSSSSH
IT'S WORKING!
IT'S PULLING HIM INSIDE!
YOU CANNOT STOP ME.
YOU WILL HAND OVER THE DARK ONE OR I WILL DESTROY EVERYTHING YOU ARE.
UNGH!
FWOOOSH

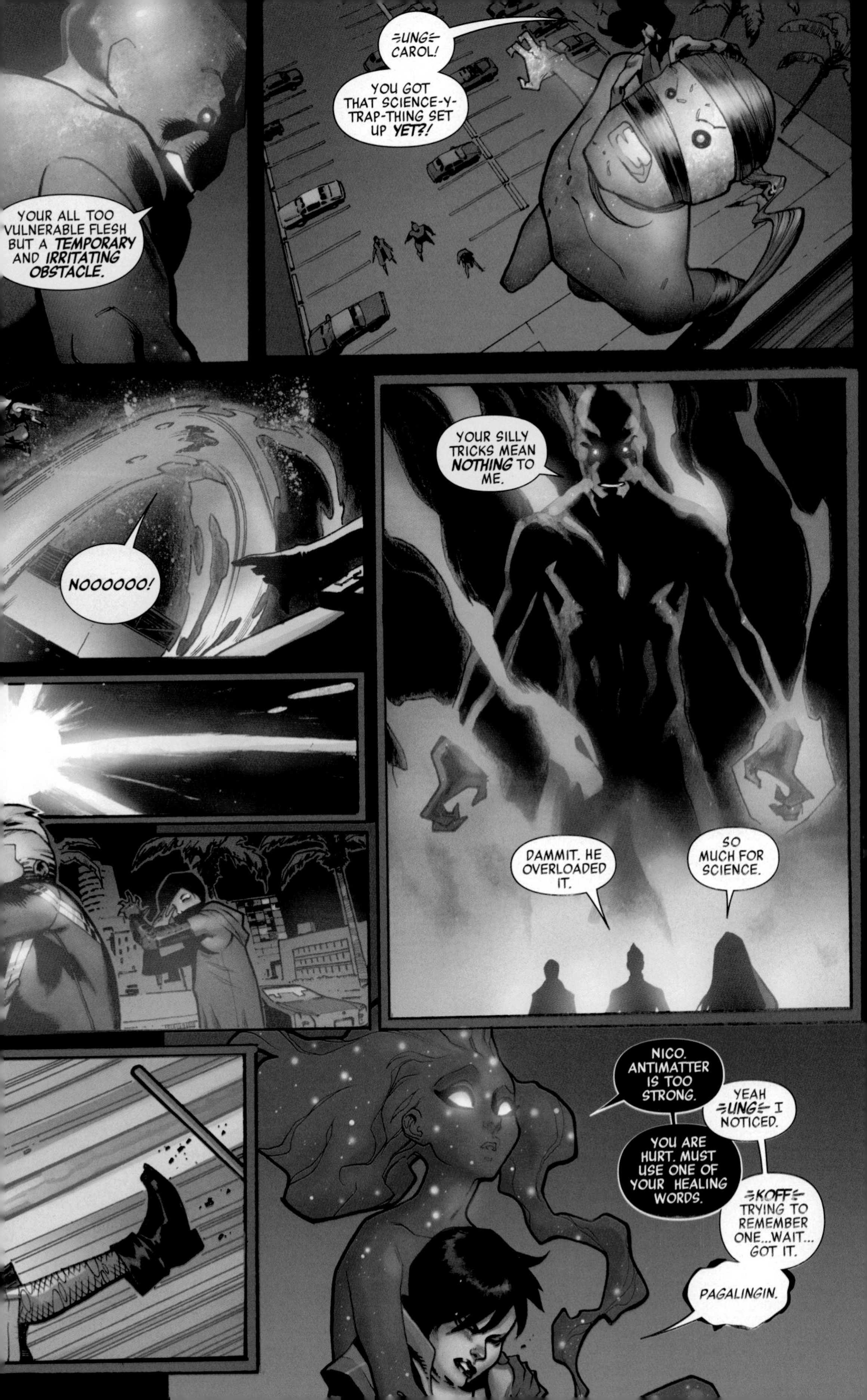
YOUR ALL TOO VULNERABLE FLESH BUT A TEMPORARY AND IRRITATING OBSTACLE.
=UNG= CAROL!
YOU GOT THAT SCIENCE-Y-TRAP-THING SET UP YET?!
NOOOOOO!
YOUR SILLY TRICKS MEAN NOTHING TO ME.
DAMMIT. HE OVERLOADED IT.
SO MUCH FOR SCIENCE.
NICO. ANTIMATTER IS TOO STRONG.
YOU ARE HURT. MUST USE ONE OF YOUR HEALING WORDS.
YEAH =UNG= I NOTICED.
=KOFF= TRYING TO REMEMBER ONE...WAIT... GOT IT.
PAGALINGIN.

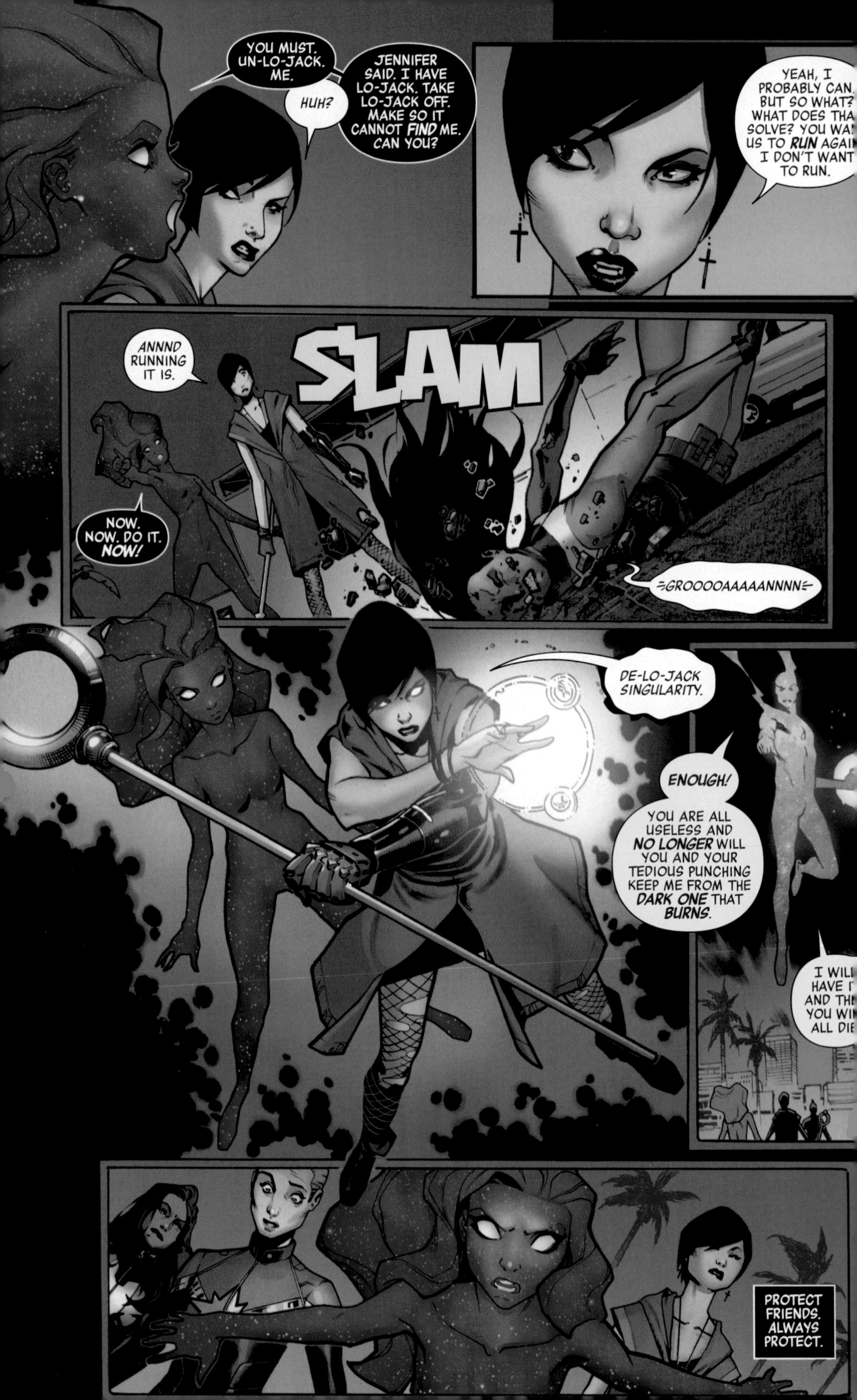
YOU MUST. UN-LO-JACK. ME.
HUH?
JENNIFER SAID. I HAVE LO-JACK. TAKE LO-JACK OFF. MAKE SO IT CANNOT FIND ME. CAN YOU?
YEAH, I PROBABLY CAN. BUT SO WHAT? WHAT DOES THA SOLVE? YOU WA US TO RUN AGAI I DON'T WANT TO RUN.
ANNND RUNNING IT IS.
SLAM
NOW. NOW. DO IT. NOW!
GROOOOAAAAANNNN
DE-LO-JACK SINGULARITY.
ENOUGH!
YOU ARE ALL USELESS AND NO LONGER WILL YOU AND YOUR TEDIOUS PUNCHING KEEP ME FROM THE DARK ONE THAT BURNS.
I WIL HAVE I AND TH YOU WI ALL DI
PROTECT FRIENDS. ALWAYS PROTECT.

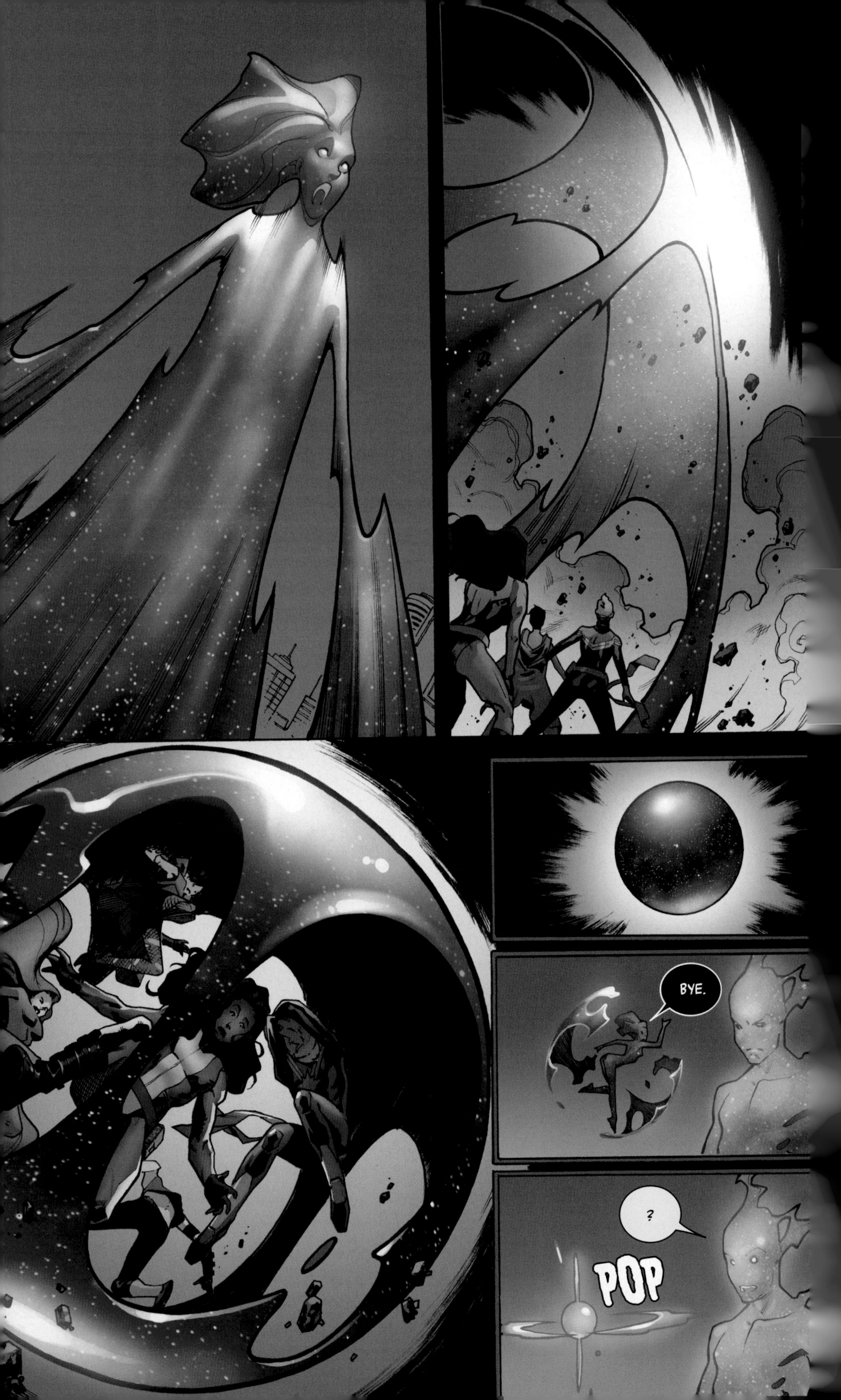
BYE.
?
POP

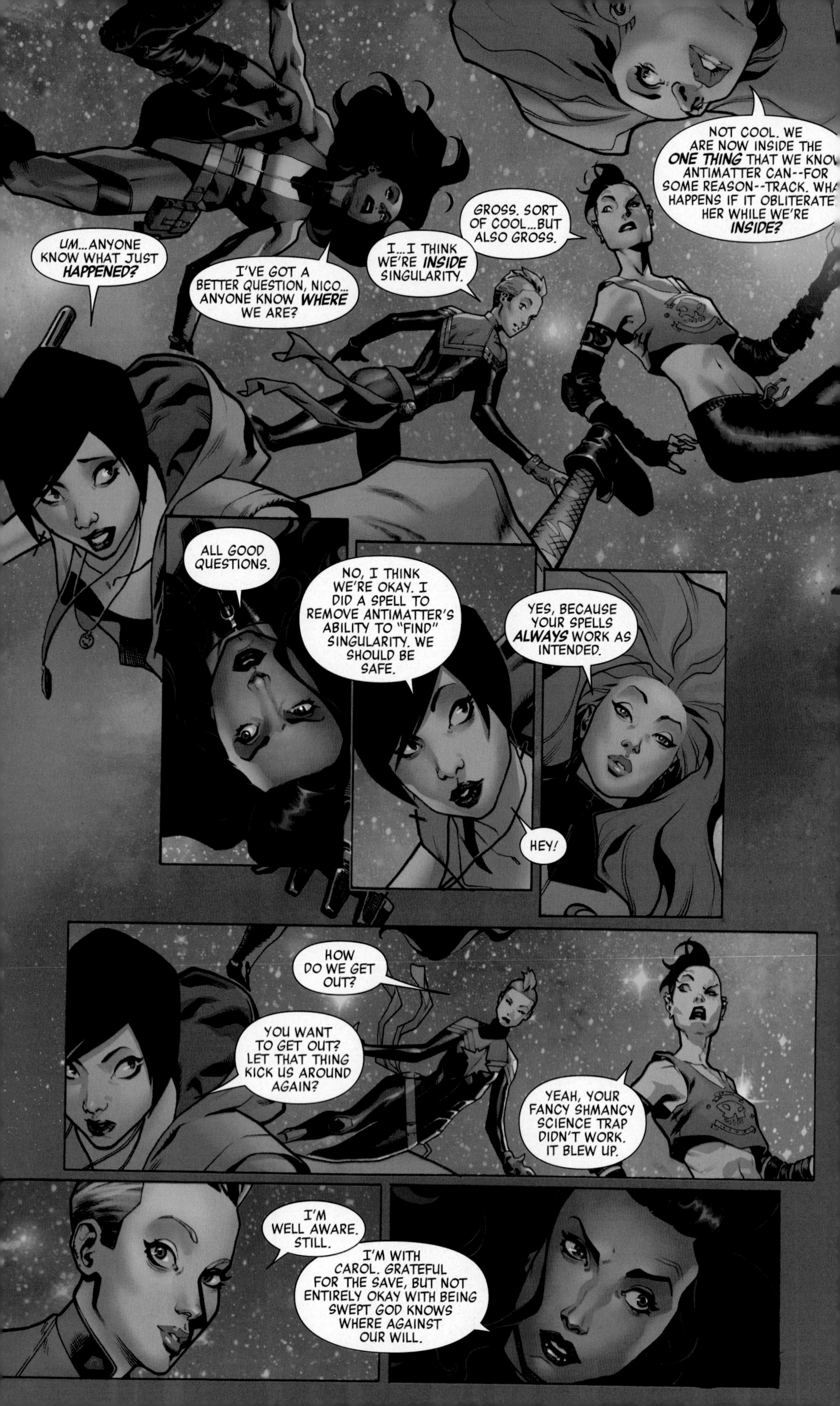
NOT COOL. WE ARE NOW INSIDE THE ONE THING THAT WE KNOW ANTIMATTER CAN--FOR SOME REASON--TRACK. WHA HAPPENS IF IT OBLITERATE HER WHILE WE'RE INSIDE?
UM...ANYONE KNOW WHAT JUST HAPPENED?
I'VE GOT A BETTER QUESTION, NICO... ANYONE KNOW WHERE WE ARE?
I...I THINK WE'RE INSIDE SINGULARITY.
GROSS. SORT OF COOL...BUT ALSO GROSS.
ALL GOOD QUESTIONS.
NO, I THINK WE'RE OKAY. I DID A SPELL TO REMOVE ANTIMATTER'S ABILITY TO "FIND" SINGULARITY. WE SHOULD BE SAFE.
YES, BECAUSE YOUR SPELLS ALWAYS WORK AS INTENDED.
HEY!
HOW DO WE GET OUT?
YOU WANT TO GET OUT? LET THAT THING KICK US AROUND AGAIN?
YEAH, YOUR FANCY SHMANCY SCIENCE TRAP DIDN'T WORK. IT BLEW UP.
I'M WELL AWARE. STILL.
I'M WITH CAROL. GRATEFUL FOR THE SAVE, BUT NOT ENTIRELY OKAY WITH BEING SWEPT GOD KNOWS WHERE AGAINST OUR WILL.

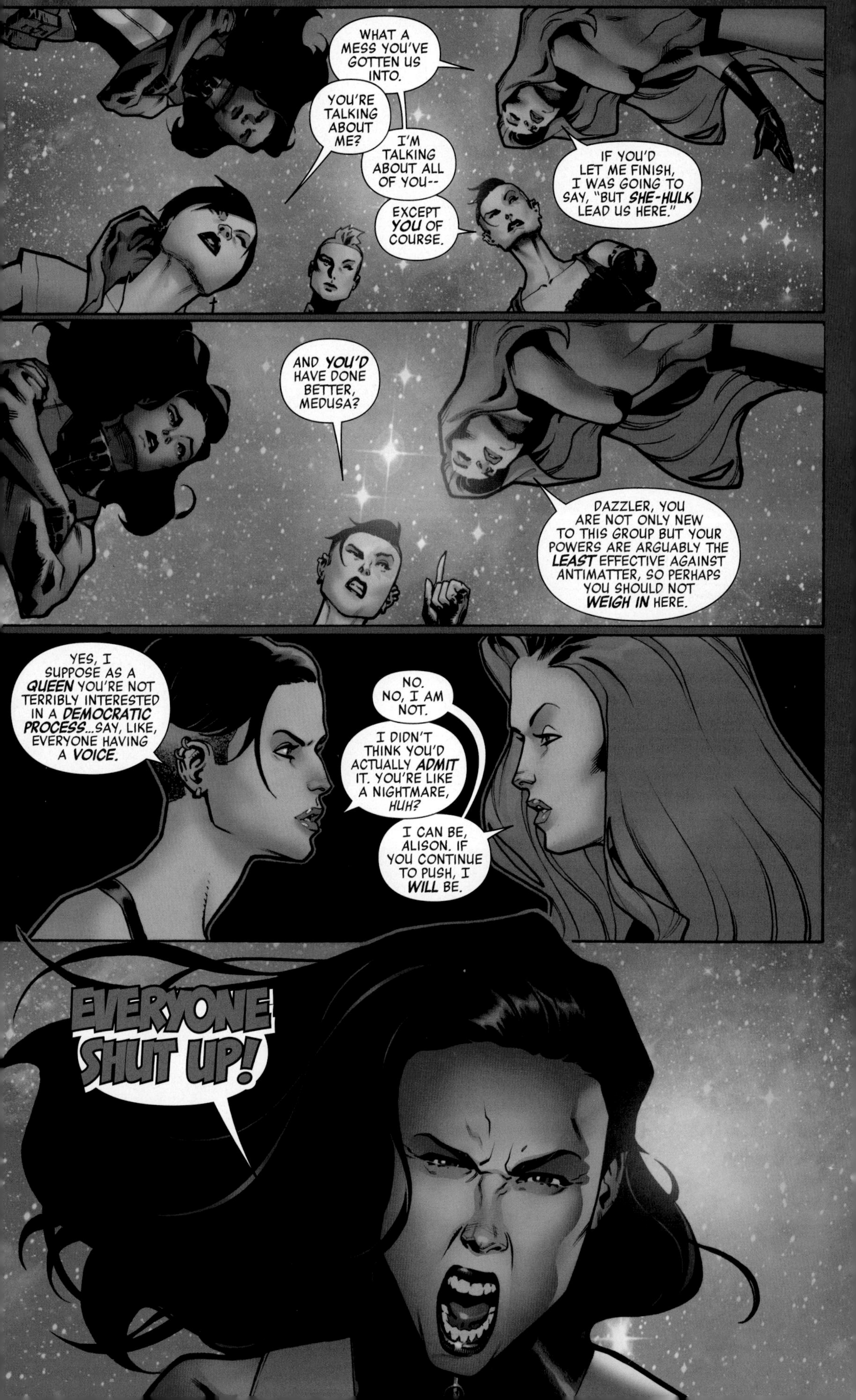

WHAT A MESS YOU'VE GOTTEN US INTO.
YOU'RE TALKING ABOUT ME?
I'M TALKING ABOUT ALL OF YOU--
EXCEPT *YOU* OF COURSE.
IF YOU'D LET ME FINISH, I WAS GOING TO SAY, "BUT *SHE-HULK* LEAD US HERE."
AND *YOU'D* HAVE DONE BETTER, MEDUSA?
DAZZLER, YOU ARE NOT ONLY NEW TO THIS GROUP BUT YOUR POWERS ARE ARGUABLY THE *LEAST* EFFECTIVE AGAINST ANTIMATTER, SO PERHAPS YOU SHOULD NOT *WEIGH IN* HERE.
YES, I SUPPOSE AS A *QUEEN* YOU'RE NOT TERRIBLY INTERESTED IN A *DEMOCRATIC PROCESS*...SAY, LIKE, EVERYONE HAVING A *VOICE.*
NO. NO, I AM NOT.
I DIDN'T THINK YOU'D ACTUALLY *ADMIT* IT. YOU'RE LIKE A NIGHTMARE, *HUH?*
I CAN BE, ALISON. IF YOU CONTINUE TO PUSH, I *WILL* BE.
EVERYONE SHUT UP!

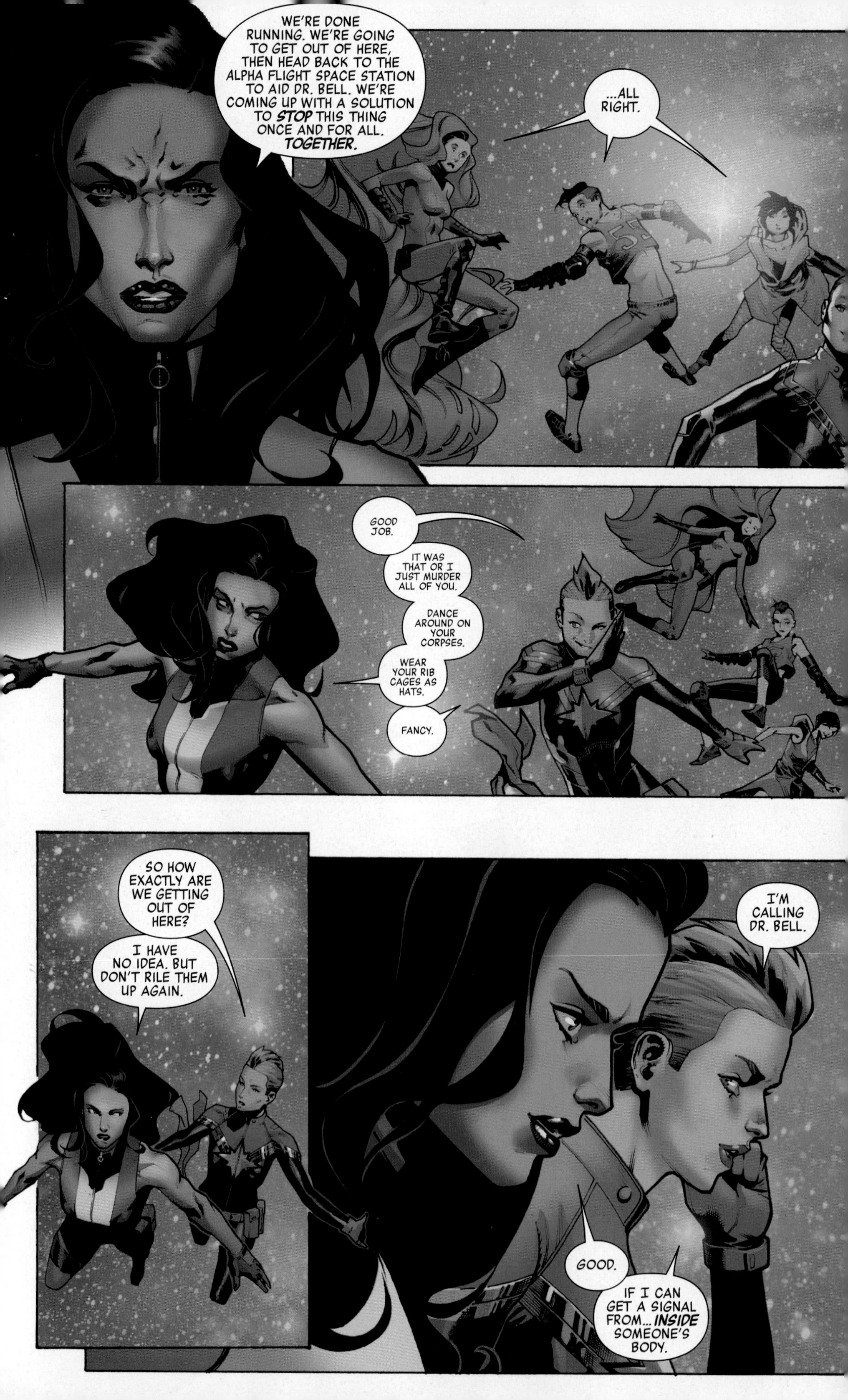
WE'RE DONE RUNNING. WE'RE GOING TO GET OUT OF HERE, THEN HEAD BACK TO THE ALPHA FLIGHT SPACE STATION TO AID DR. BELL. WE'RE COMING UP WITH A SOLUTION TO STOP THIS THING ONCE AND FOR ALL. TOGETHER.
...ALL RIGHT.
GOOD JOB.
IT WAS THAT OR I JUST MURDER ALL OF YOU.
DANCE AROUND ON YOUR CORPSES.
WEAR YOUR RIB CAGES AS HATS.
FANCY.
SO HOW EXACTLY ARE WE GETTING OUT OF HERE?
I HAVE NO IDEA. BUT DON'T RILE THEM UP AGAIN.
I'M CALLING DR. BELL.
GOOD.
IF I CAN GET A SIGNAL FROM... INSIDE SOMEONE'S BODY.

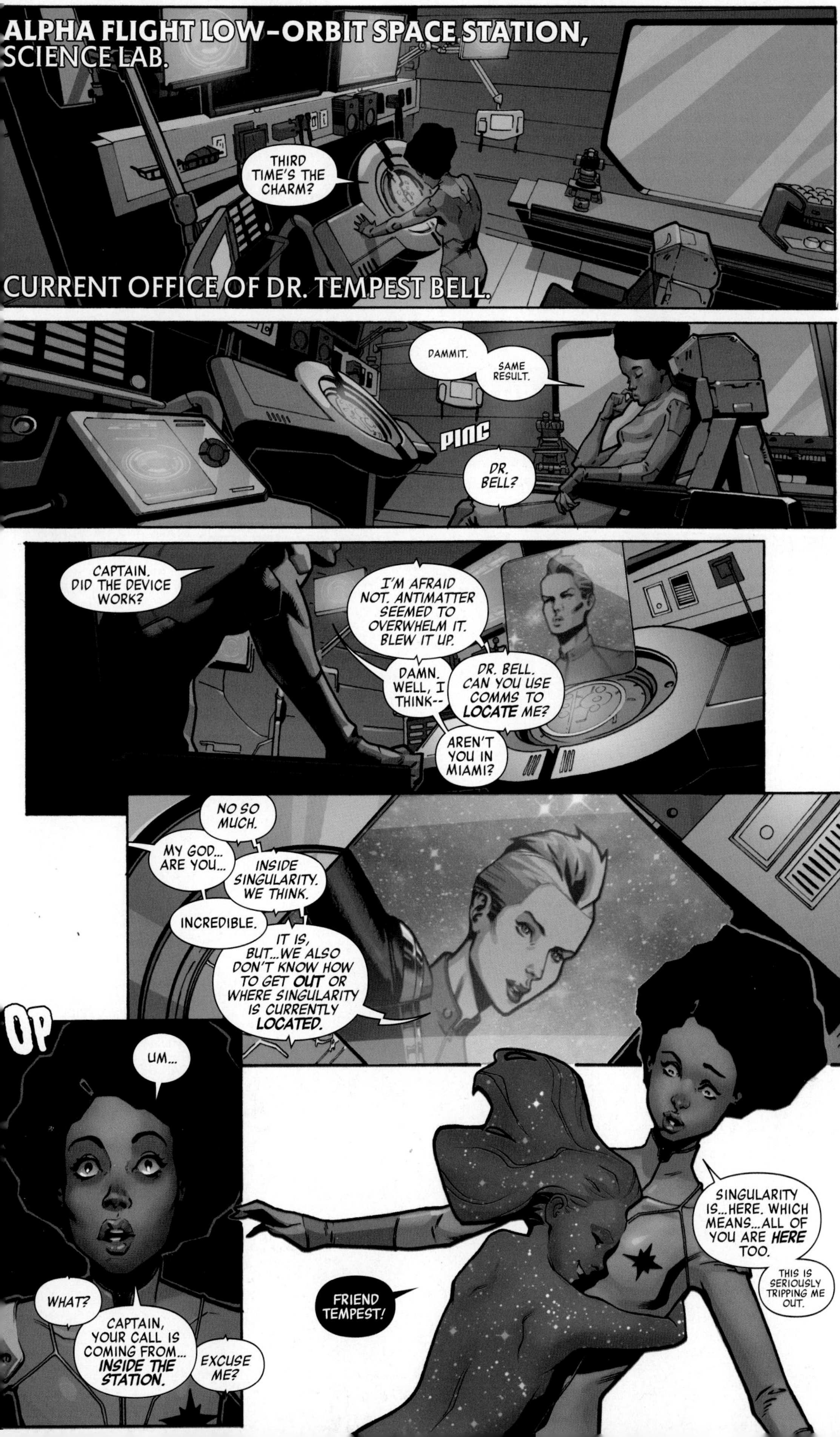

ALPHA FLIGHT LOW-ORBIT SPACE STATION, SCIENCE LAB.
THIRD TIME'S THE CHARM?
CURRENT OFFICE OF DR. TEMPEST BELL.
DAMMIT.
SAME RESULT.
PING
DR. BELL?
CAPTAIN. DID THE DEVICE WORK?
I'M AFRAID NOT. ANTIMATTER SEEMED TO OVERWHELM IT. BLEW IT UP.
DAMN. WELL, I THINK--
DR. BELL. CAN YOU USE COMMS TO LOCATE ME?
AREN'T YOU IN MIAMI?
NO SO MUCH.
MY GOD... ARE YOU...
INSIDE SINGULARITY. WE THINK.
INCREDIBLE.
IT IS, BUT...WE ALSO DON'T KNOW HOW TO GET OUT OR WHERE SINGULARITY IS CURRENTLY LOCATED.
OP
UM...
WHAT?
CAPTAIN, YOUR CALL IS COMING FROM... INSIDE THE STATION.
EXCUSE ME?
FRIEND TEMPEST!
SINGULARITY IS...HERE. WHICH MEANS...ALL OF YOU ARE HERE TOO.
THIS IS SERIOUSLY TRIPPING ME OUT.

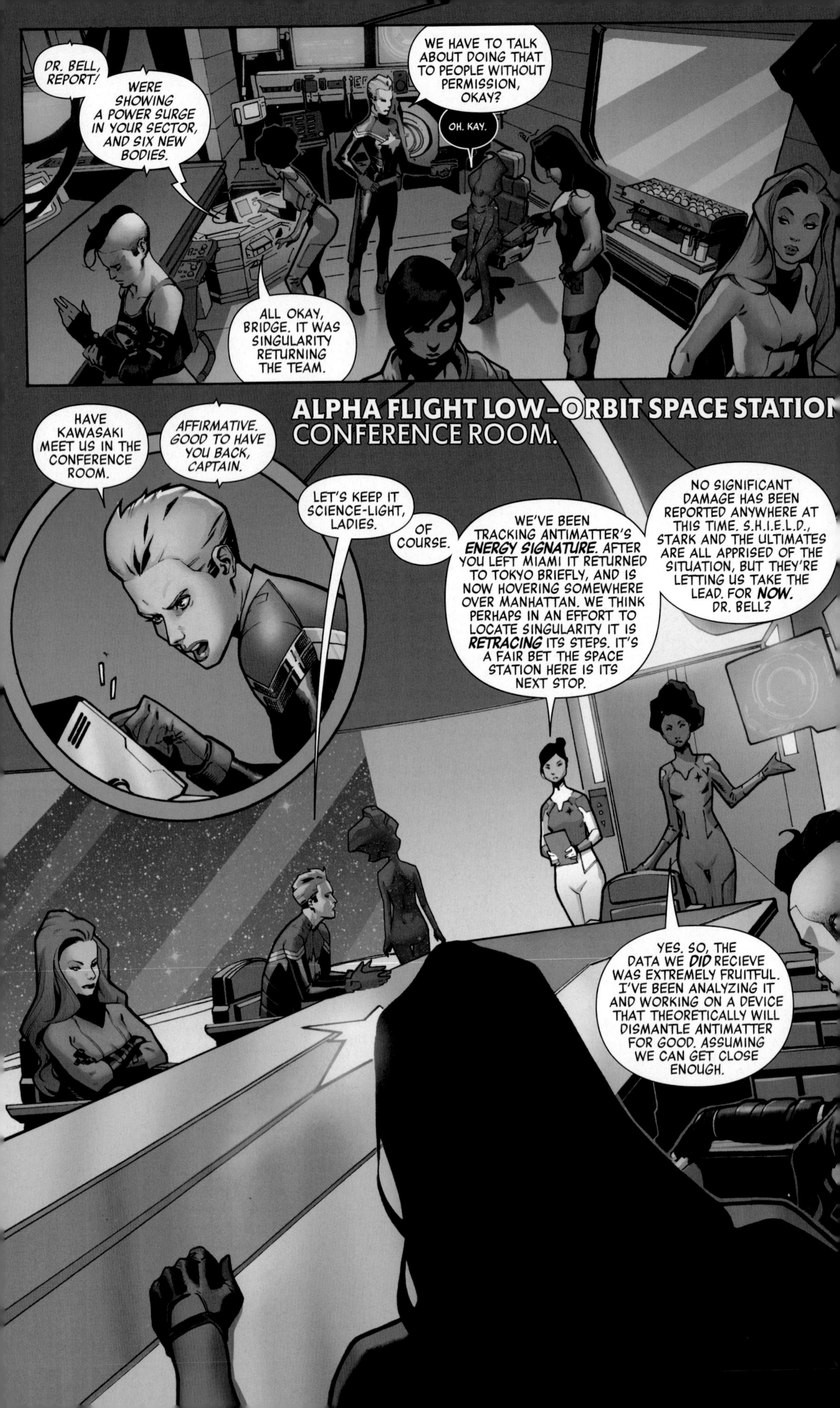

DR. BELL, REPORT!
WERE SHOWING A POWER SURGE IN YOUR SECTOR, AND SIX NEW BODIES.
WE HAVE TO TALK ABOUT DOING THAT TO PEOPLE WITHOUT PERMISSION, OKAY?
OH. KAY.
ALL OKAY, BRIDGE. IT WAS SINGULARITY RETURNING THE TEAM.
ALPHA FLIGHT LOW-ORBIT SPACE STATION CONFERENCE ROOM.
HAVE KAWASAKI MEET US IN THE CONFERENCE ROOM.
AFFIRMATIVE. GOOD TO HAVE YOU BACK, CAPTAIN.
LET'S KEEP IT SCIENCE-LIGHT, LADIES.
OF COURSE.
WE'VE BEEN TRACKING ANTIMATTER'S ENERGY SIGNATURE. AFTER YOU LEFT MIAMI IT RETURNED TO TOKYO BRIEFLY, AND IS NOW HOVERING SOMEWHERE OVER MANHATTAN. WE THINK PERHAPS IN AN EFFORT TO LOCATE SINGULARITY IT IS RETRACING ITS STEPS. IT'S A FAIR BET THE SPACE STATION HERE IS ITS NEXT STOP.
NO SIGNIFICANT DAMAGE HAS BEEN REPORTED ANYWHERE AT THIS TIME. S.H.I.E.L.D., STARK AND THE ULTIMATES ARE ALL APPRISED OF THE SITUATION, BUT THEY'RE LETTING US TAKE THE LEAD. FOR NOW. DR. BELL?
YES. SO, THE DATA WE DID RECIEVE WAS EXTREMELY FRUITFUL. I'VE BEEN ANALYZING IT AND WORKING ON A DEVICE THAT THEORETICALLY WILL DISMANTLE ANTIMATTER FOR GOOD. ASSUMING WE CAN GET CLOSE ENOUGH.

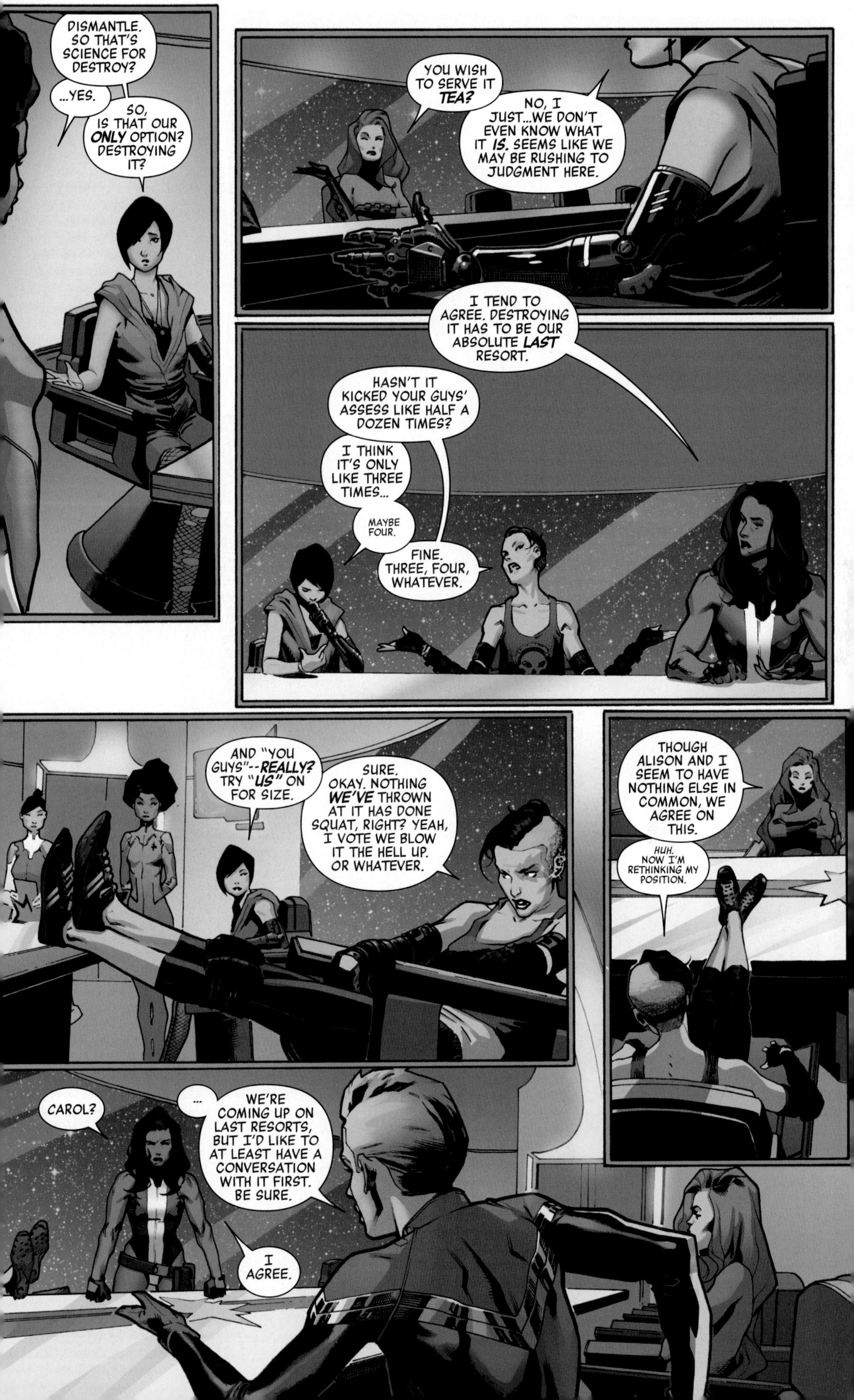

DISMANTLE. SO THAT'S SCIENCE FOR DESTROY?
...YES.
SO, IS THAT OUR ONLY OPTION? DESTROYING IT?
YOU WISH TO SERVE IT TEA?
NO, I JUST...WE DON'T EVEN KNOW WHAT IT IS. SEEMS LIKE WE MAY BE RUSHING TO JUDGMENT HERE.
I TEND TO AGREE. DESTROYING IT HAS TO BE OUR ABSOLUTE LAST RESORT.
HASN'T IT KICKED YOUR GUYS' ASSESS LIKE HALF A DOZEN TIMES?
I THINK IT'S ONLY LIKE THREE TIMES...
MAYBE FOUR.
FINE. THREE, FOUR, WHATEVER.
AND "YOU GUYS"--REALLY? TRY "US" ON FOR SIZE.
SURE. OKAY. NOTHING WE'VE THROWN AT IT HAS DONE SQUAT, RIGHT? YEAH, I VOTE WE BLOW IT THE HELL UP. OR WHATEVER.
THOUGH ALISON AND I SEEM TO HAVE NOTHING ELSE IN COMMON, WE AGREE ON THIS.
HUH. NOW I'M RETHINKING MY POSITION.
CAROL?
...
WE'RE COMING UP ON LAST RESORTS, BUT I'D LIKE TO AT LEAST HAVE A CONVERSATION WITH IT FIRST. BE SURE.
I AGREE.

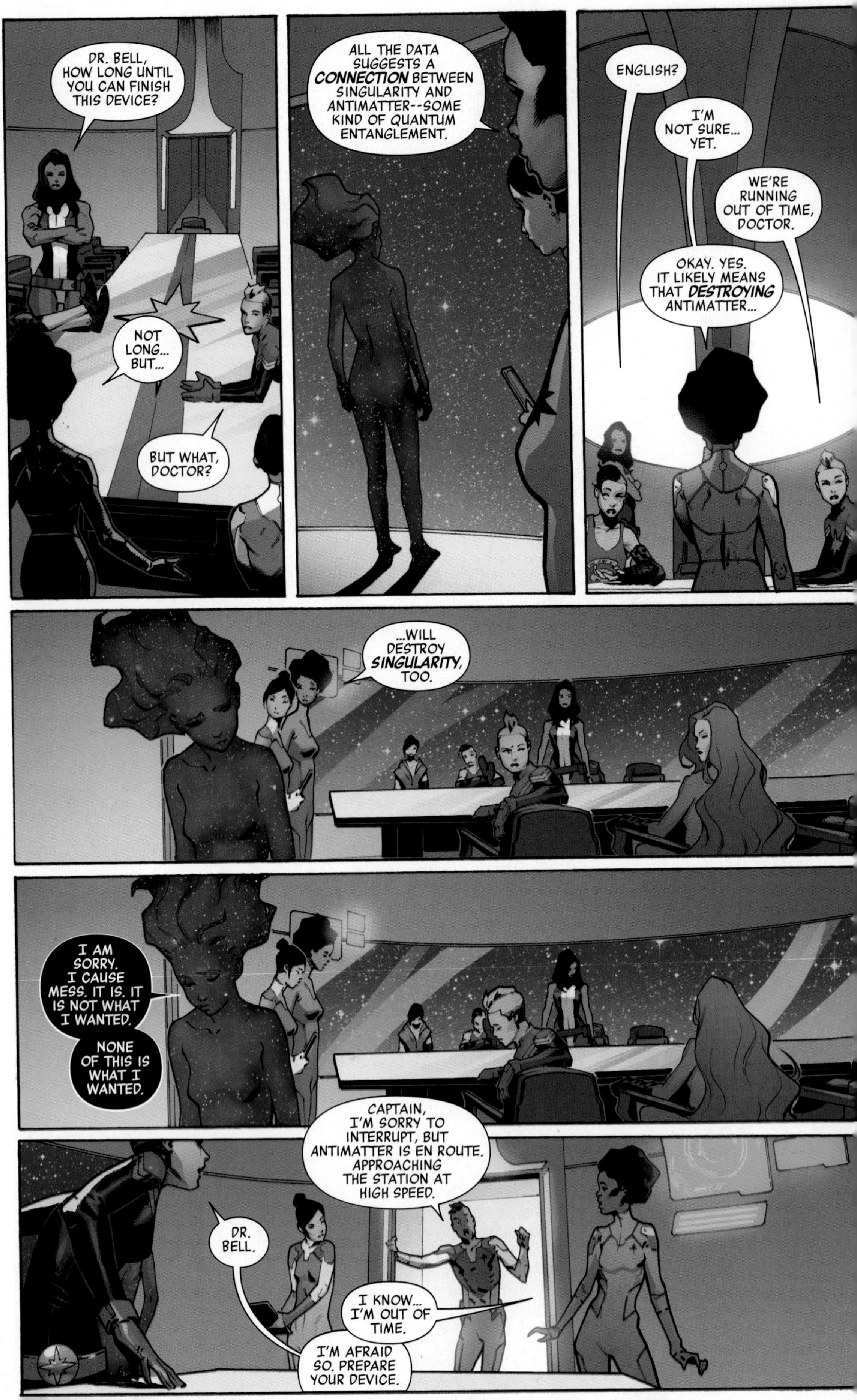
DR. BELL, HOW LONG UNTIL YOU CAN FINISH THIS DEVICE?
NOT LONG... BUT...
BUT WHAT, DOCTOR?
ALL THE DATA SUGGESTS A CONNECTION BETWEEN SINGULARITY AND ANTIMATTER--SOME KIND OF QUANTUM ENTANGLEMENT.
ENGLISH?
I'M NOT SURE... YET.
WE'RE RUNNING OUT OF TIME, DOCTOR.
OKAY. YES. IT LIKELY MEANS THAT DESTROYING ANTIMATTER...
...WILL DESTROY SINGULARITY, TOO.
I AM SORRY. I CAUSE MESS. IT IS. IT IS NOT WHAT I WANTED.
NONE OF THIS IS WHAT I WANTED.
CAPTAIN, I'M SORRY TO INTERRUPT, BUT ANTIMATTER IS EN ROUTE. APPROACHING THE STATION AT HIGH SPEED.
DR. BELL.
I KNOW... I'M OUT OF TIME.
I'M AFRAID SO. PREPARE YOUR DEVICE.

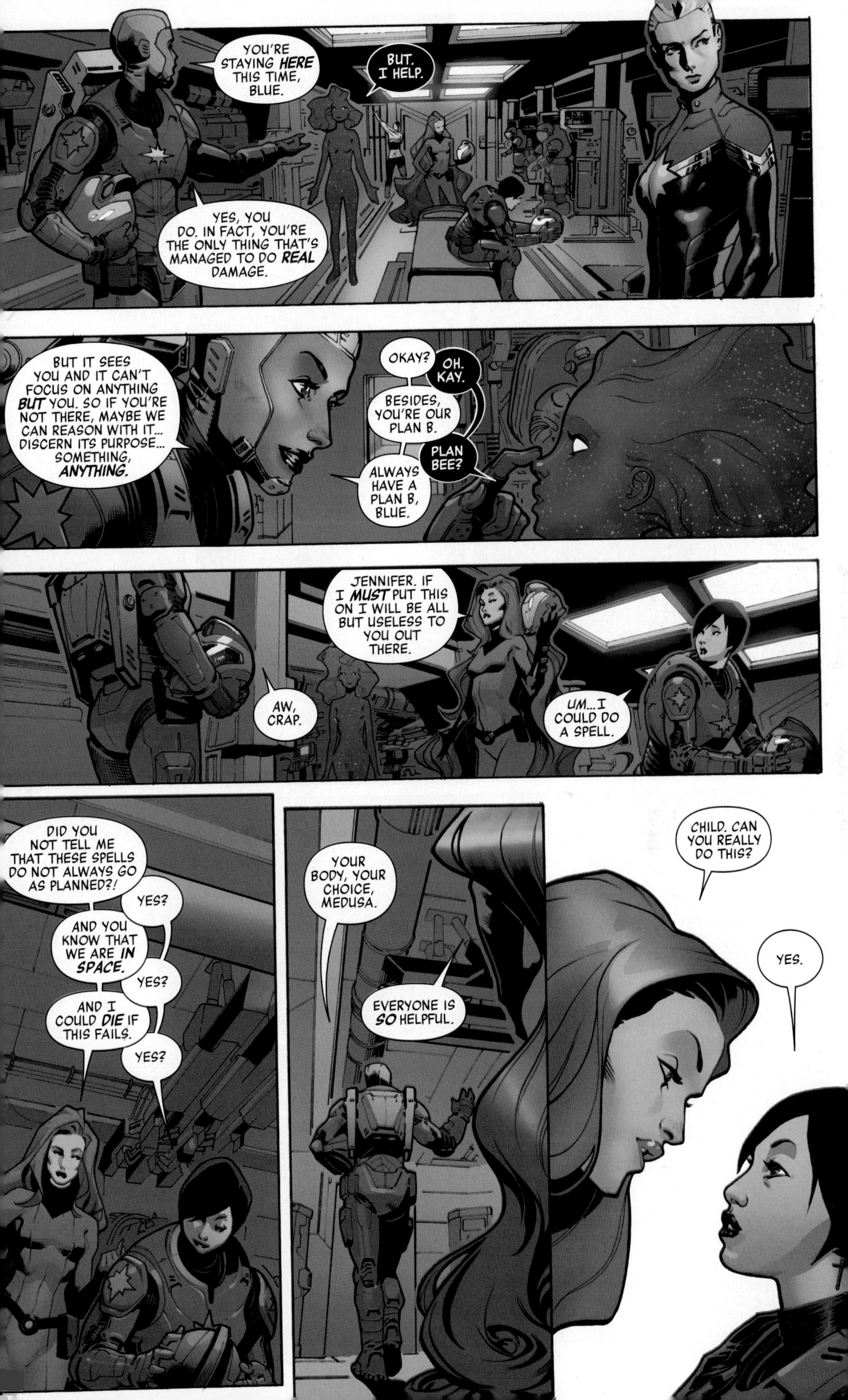
YOU'RE STAYING HERE THIS TIME, BLUE.
BUT. I HELP.
YES, YOU DO. IN FACT, YOU'RE THE ONLY THING THAT'S MANAGED TO DO REAL DAMAGE.
BUT IT SEES YOU AND IT CAN'T FOCUS ON ANYTHING BUT YOU. SO IF YOU'RE NOT THERE, MAYBE WE CAN REASON WITH IT... DISCERN ITS PURPOSE... SOMETHING, ANYTHING.
OKAY?
OH. KAY.
BESIDES, YOU'RE OUR PLAN B.
PLAN BEE?
ALWAYS HAVE A PLAN B, BLUE.
JENNIFER. IF I MUST PUT THIS ON I WILL BE ALL BUT USELESS TO YOU OUT THERE.
AW, CRAP.
UM... I COULD DO A SPELL.
DID YOU NOT TELL ME THAT THESE SPELLS DO NOT ALWAYS GO AS PLANNED?!
YES?
AND YOU KNOW THAT WE ARE IN SPACE.
YES?
AND I COULD DIE IF THIS FAILS.
YES?
YOUR BODY, YOUR CHOICE, MEDUSA.
EVERYONE IS SO HELPFUL.
CHILD. CAN YOU REALLY DO THIS?
YES.

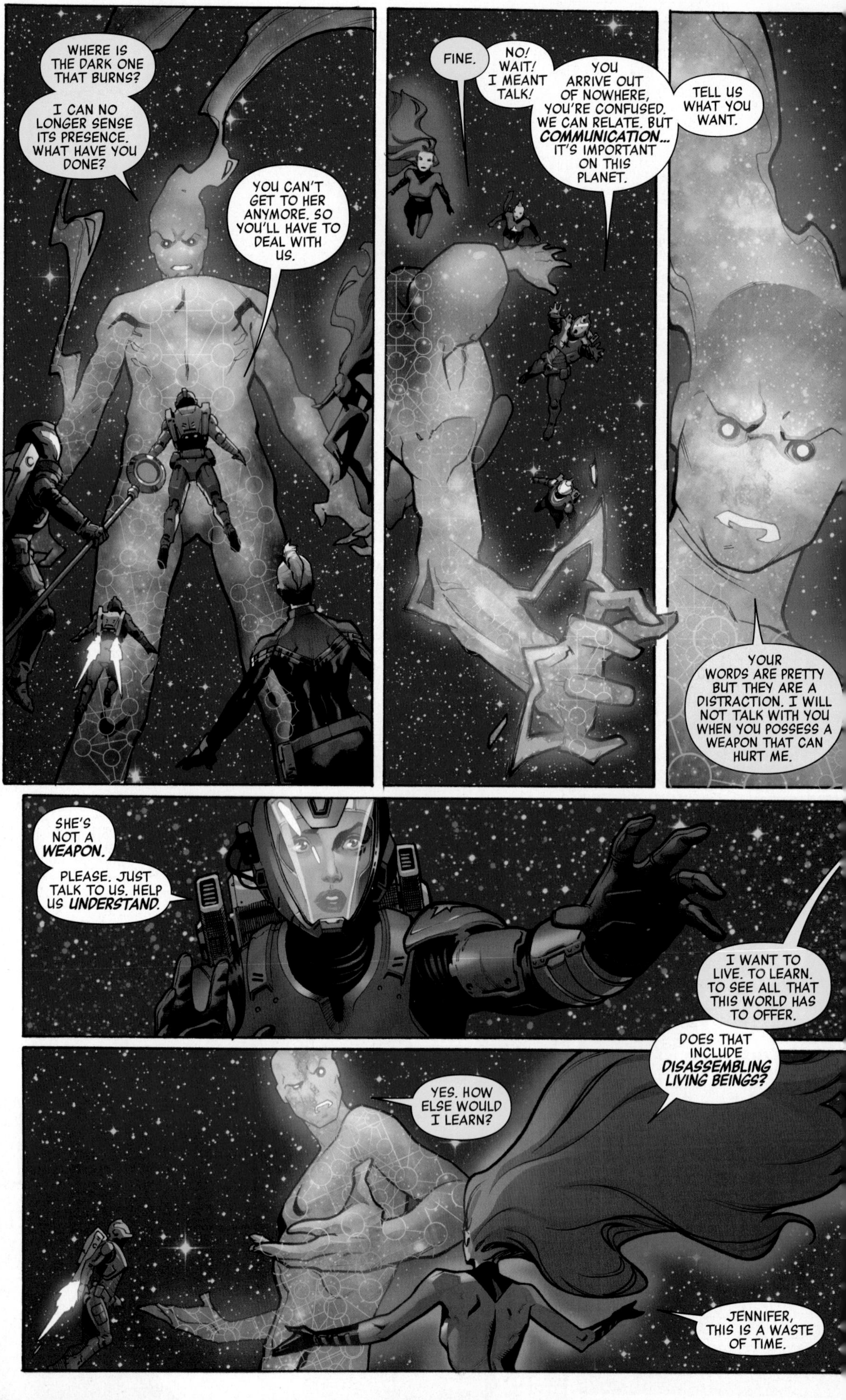
WHERE IS THE DARK ONE THAT BURNS?
I CAN NO LONGER SENSE ITS PRESENCE. WHAT HAVE YOU DONE?
YOU CAN'T GET TO HER ANYMORE. SO YOU'LL HAVE TO DEAL WITH US.
FINE.
NO! WAIT! I MEANT TALK!
YOU ARRIVE OUT OF NOWHERE, YOU'RE CONFUSED. WE CAN RELATE. BUT COMMUNICATION... IT'S IMPORTANT ON THIS PLANET.
TELL US WHAT YOU WANT.
YOUR WORDS ARE PRETTY BUT THEY ARE A DISTRACTION. I WILL NOT TALK WITH YOU WHEN YOU POSSESS A WEAPON THAT CAN HURT ME.
SHE'S NOT A WEAPON.
PLEASE. JUST TALK TO US. HELP US UNDERSTAND.
I WANT TO LIVE. TO LEARN. TO SEE ALL THAT THIS WORLD HAS TO OFFER.
DOES THAT INCLUDE DISASSEMBLING LIVING BEINGS?
YES. HOW ELSE WOULD I LEARN?
JENNIFER, THIS IS A WASTE OF TIME.

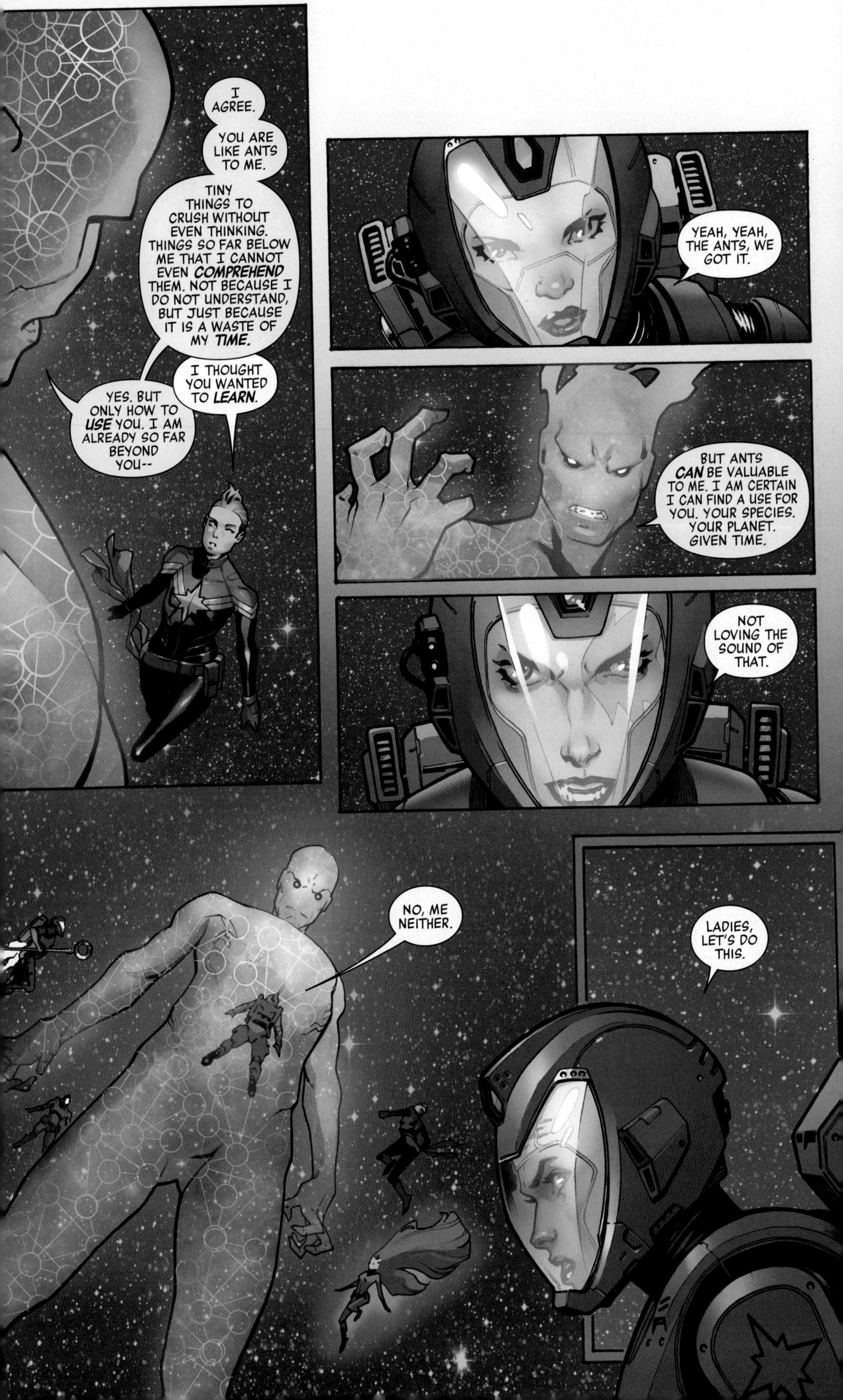
I AGREE.
YOU ARE LIKE ANTS TO ME.
TINY THINGS TO CRUSH WITHOUT EVEN THINKING. THINGS SO FAR BELOW ME THAT I CANNOT EVEN COMPREHEND THEM. NOT BECAUSE I DO NOT UNDERSTAND, BUT JUST BECAUSE IT IS A WASTE OF MY TIME.
I THOUGHT YOU WANTED TO LEARN.
YES. BUT ONLY HOW TO USE YOU. I AM ALREADY SO FAR BEYOND YOU--
YEAH, YEAH, THE ANTS, WE GOT IT.
BUT ANTS CAN BE VALUABLE TO ME. I AM CERTAIN I CAN FIND A USE FOR YOU. YOUR SPECIES. YOUR PLANET. GIVEN TIME.
NOT LOVING THE SOUND OF THAT.
NO, ME NEITHER.
LADIES, LET'S DO THIS.

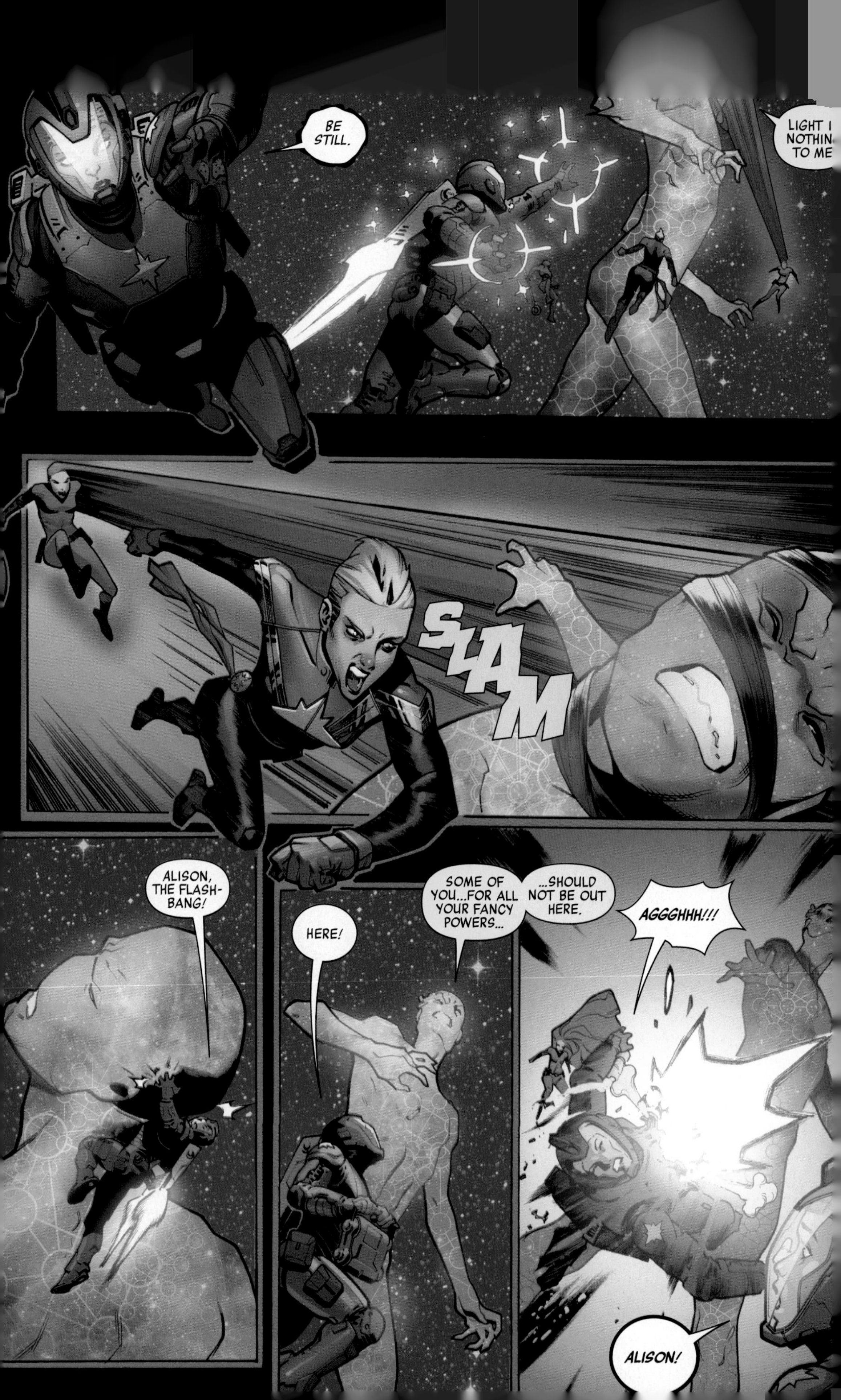
BE STILL.
LIGHT I NOTHIN TO ME
SLAM
ALISON, THE FLASH-BANG!
HERE!
SOME OF YOU...FOR ALL YOUR FANCY POWERS...
...SHOULD NOT BE OUT HERE.
AGGGHHH!!!
ALISON!

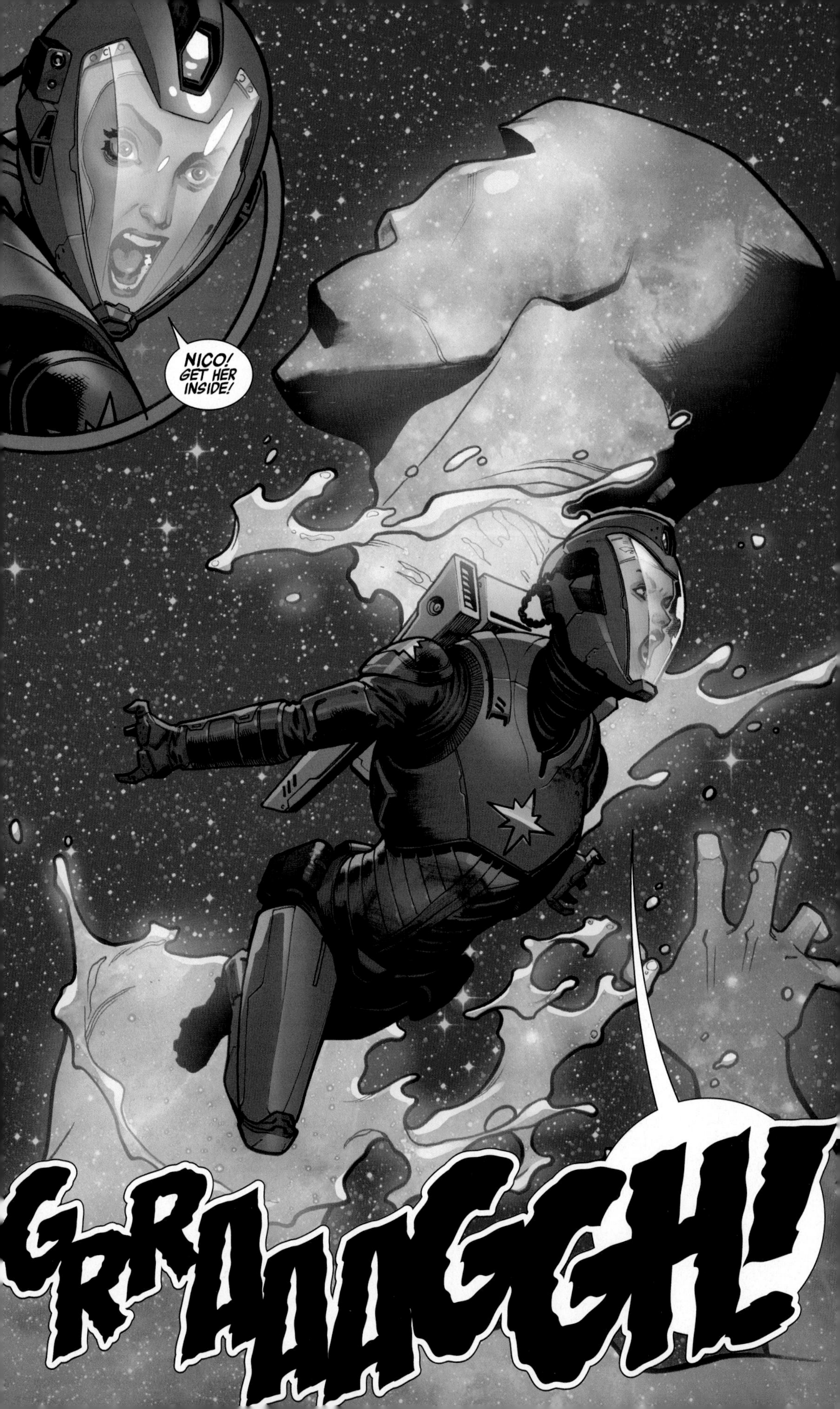
NICO! GET HER INSIDE!
GRRAAAGGH!

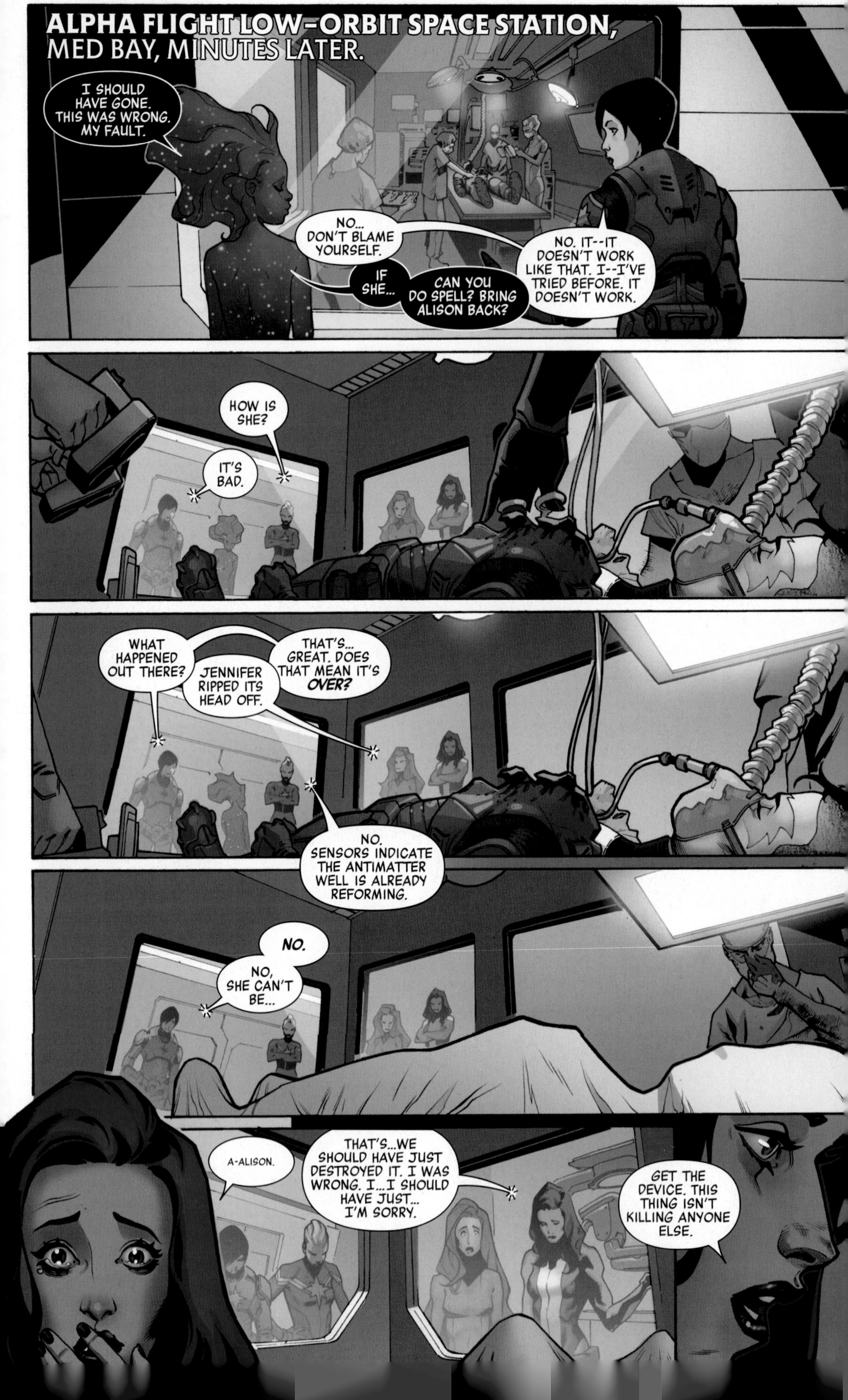

ALPHA FLIGHT LOW-ORBIT SPACE STATION, MED BAY, MINUTES LATER.
I SHOULD HAVE GONE. THIS WAS WRONG. MY FAULT.
NO... DON'T BLAME YOURSELF.
IF SHE...
CAN YOU DO SPELL? BRING ALISON BACK?
NO. IT--IT DOESN'T WORK LIKE THAT. I--I'VE TRIED BEFORE. IT DOESN'T WORK.
HOW IS SHE?
IT'S BAD.
WHAT HAPPENED OUT THERE?
JENNIFER RIPPED ITS HEAD OFF.
THAT'S... GREAT. DOES THAT MEAN IT'S *OVER?*
NO. SENSORS INDICATE THE ANTIMATTER WELL IS ALREADY REFORMING.
NO.
NO, SHE CAN'T BE...
A-ALISON.
THAT'S...WE SHOULD HAVE JUST DESTROYED IT. I WAS WRONG. I...I SHOULD HAVE JUST... I'M SORRY.
GET THE DEVICE. THIS THING ISN'T KILLING ANYONE ELSE.

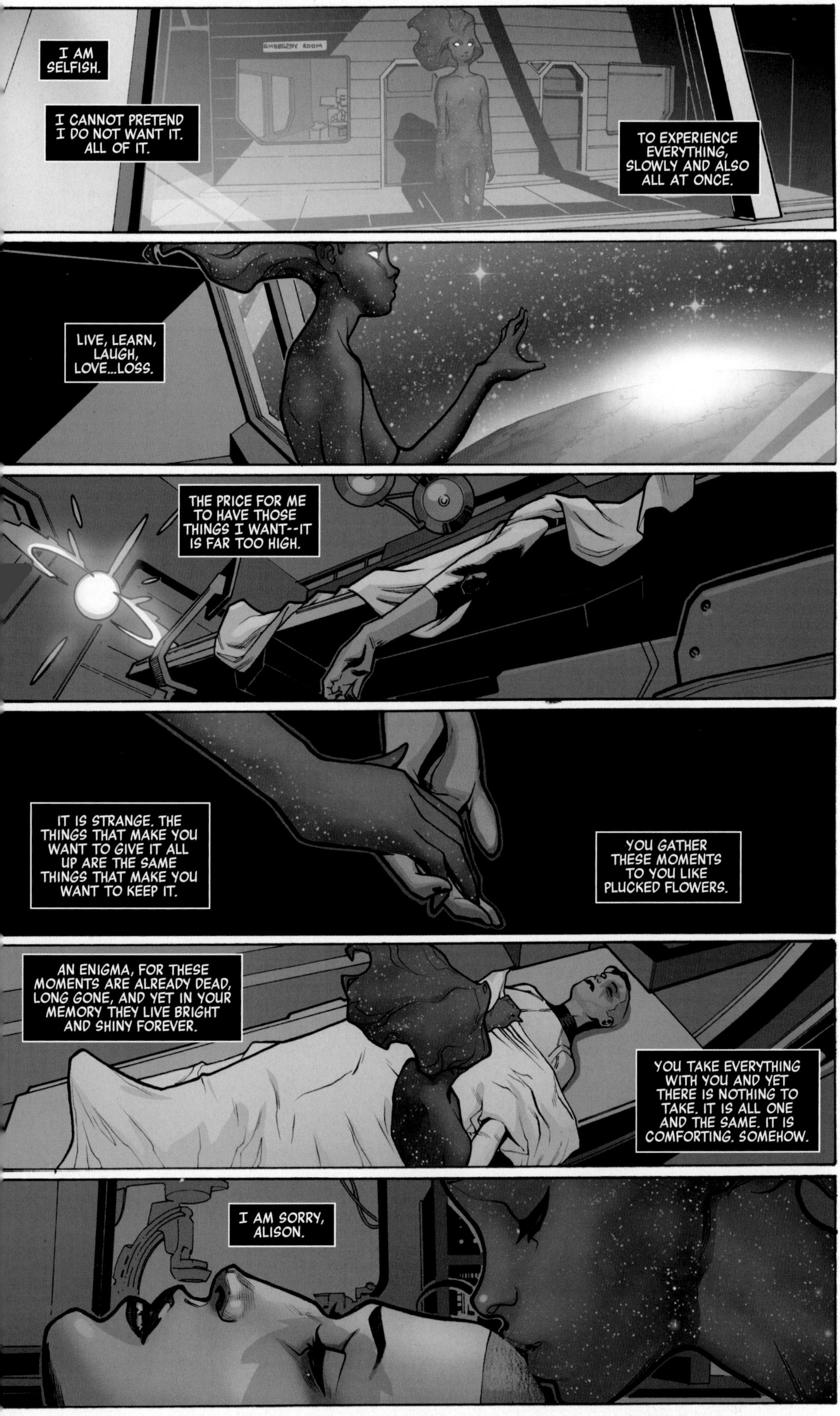
EMERGENCY ROOM
I AM SELFISH.
I CANNOT PRETEND I DO NOT WANT IT. ALL OF IT.
TO EXPERIENCE EVERYTHING, SLOWLY AND ALSO ALL AT ONCE.
LIVE, LEARN, LAUGH, LOVE...LOSS.
THE PRICE FOR ME TO HAVE THOSE THINGS I WANT--IT IS FAR TOO HIGH.
IT IS STRANGE. THE THINGS THAT MAKE YOU WANT TO GIVE IT ALL UP ARE THE SAME THINGS THAT MAKE YOU WANT TO KEEP IT.
YOU GATHER THESE MOMENTS TO YOU LIKE PLUCKED FLOWERS.
AN ENIGMA, FOR THESE MOMENTS ARE ALREADY DEAD, LONG GONE, AND YET IN YOUR MEMORY THEY LIVE BRIGHT AND SHINY FOREVER.
YOU TAKE EVERYTHING WITH YOU AND YET THERE IS NOTHING TO TAKE. IT IS ALL ONE AND THE SAME. IT IS COMFORTING. SOMEHOW.
I AM SORRY, ALISON.

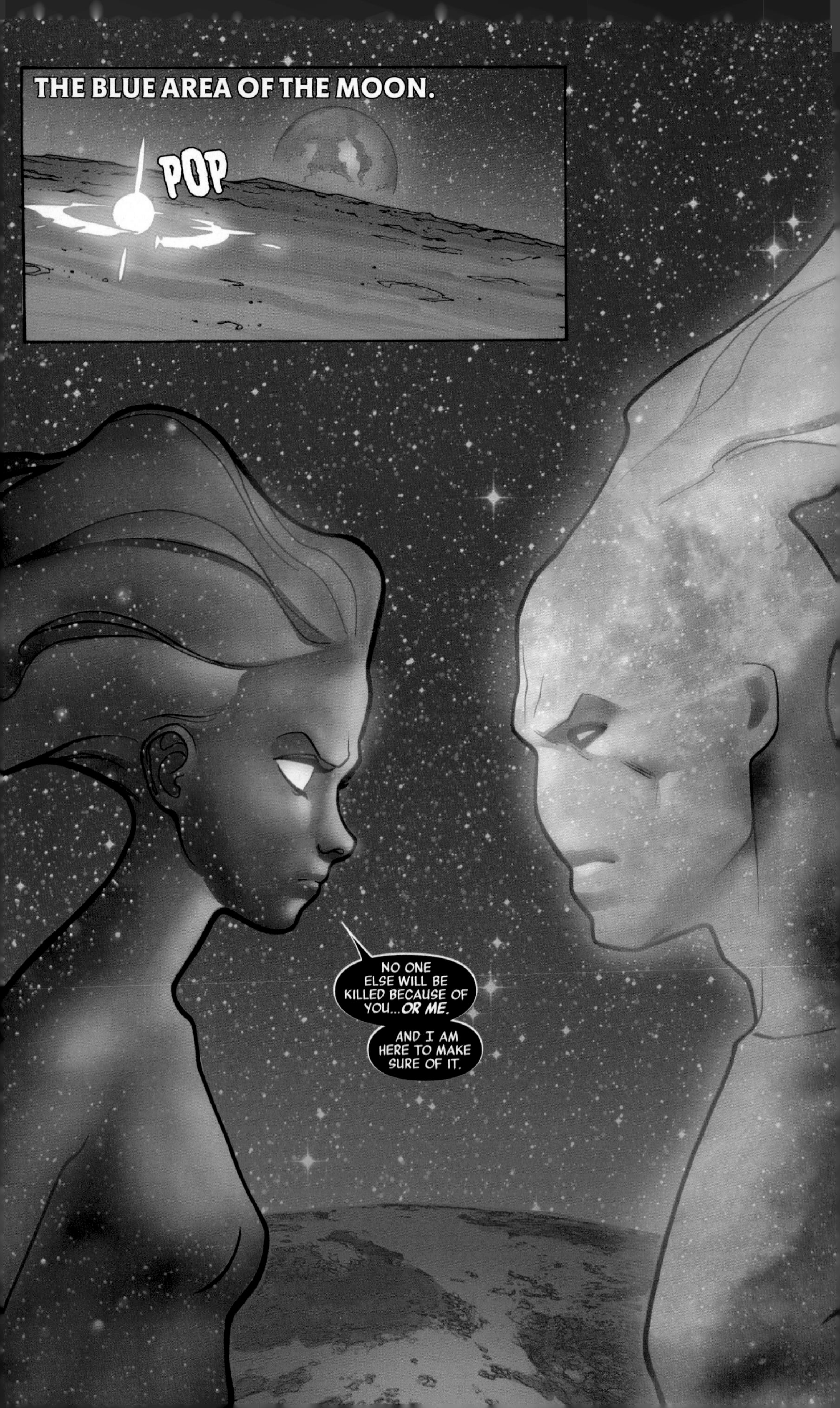
THE BLUE AREA OF THE MOON.
POP
NO ONE ELSE WILL BE KILLED BECAUSE OF YOU...OR ME.
AND I AM HERE TO MAKE SURE OF IT.

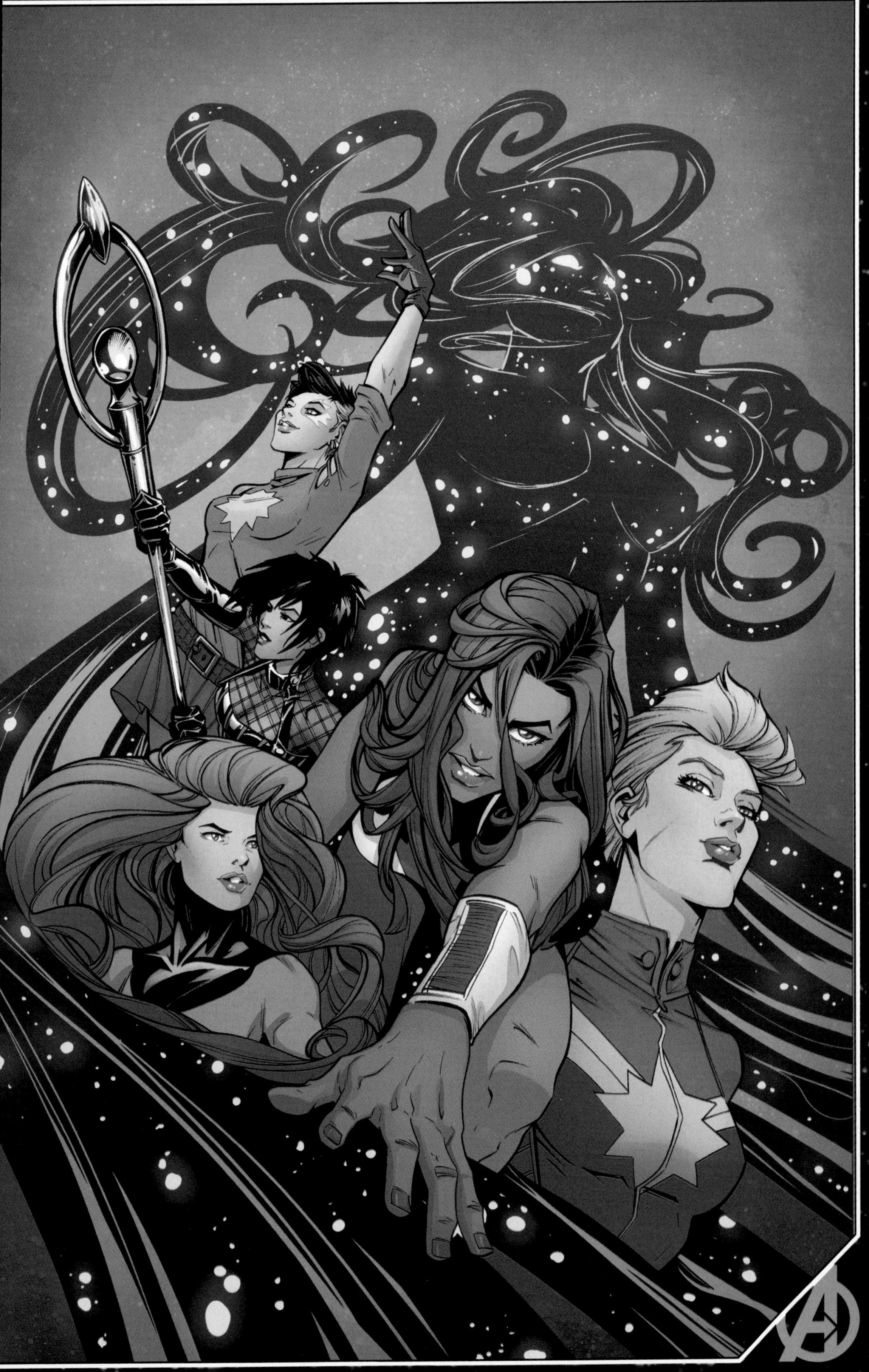

#2 VARIANT BY **JÖELLE JONES & RACHELLE ROSENBERG**

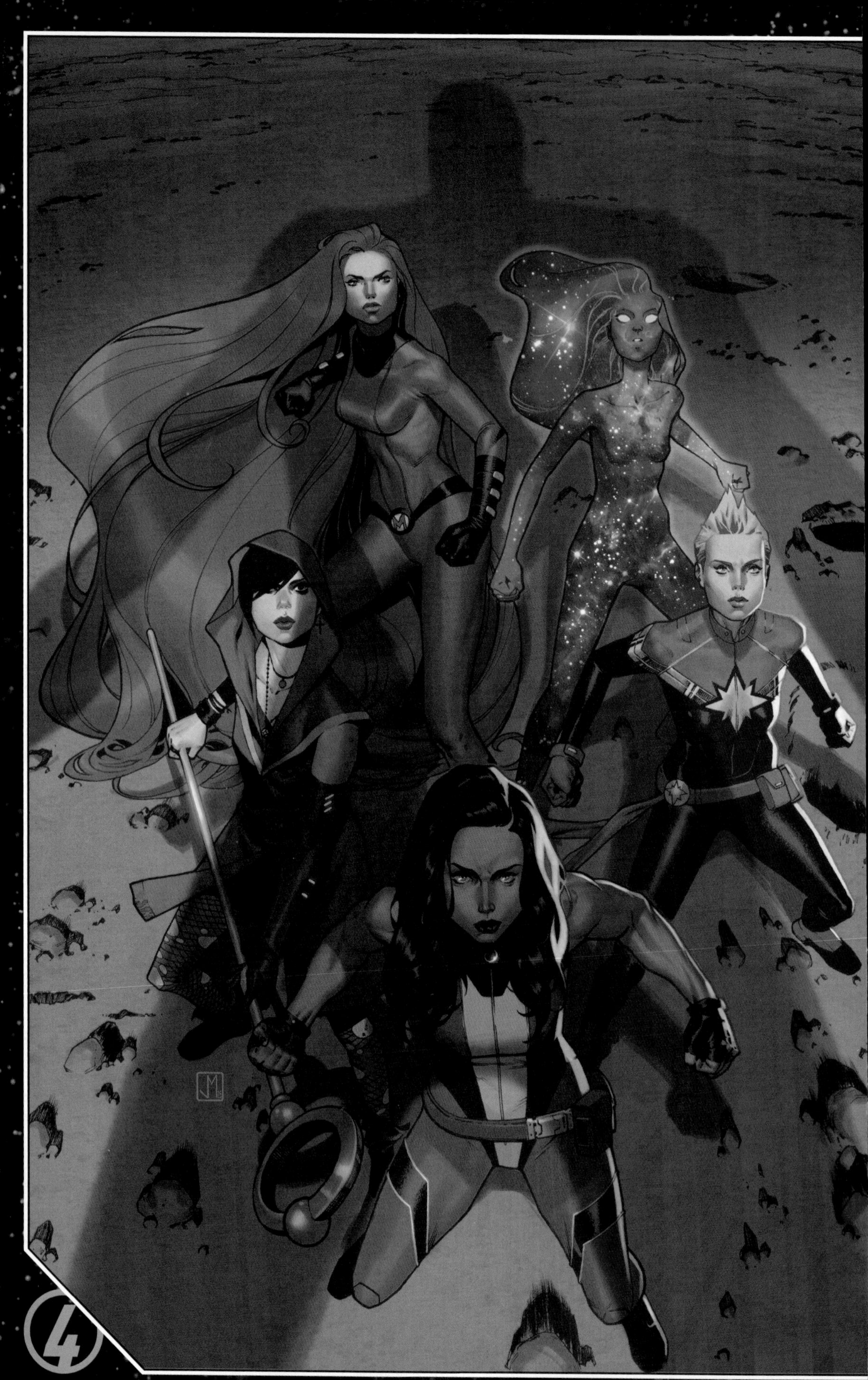

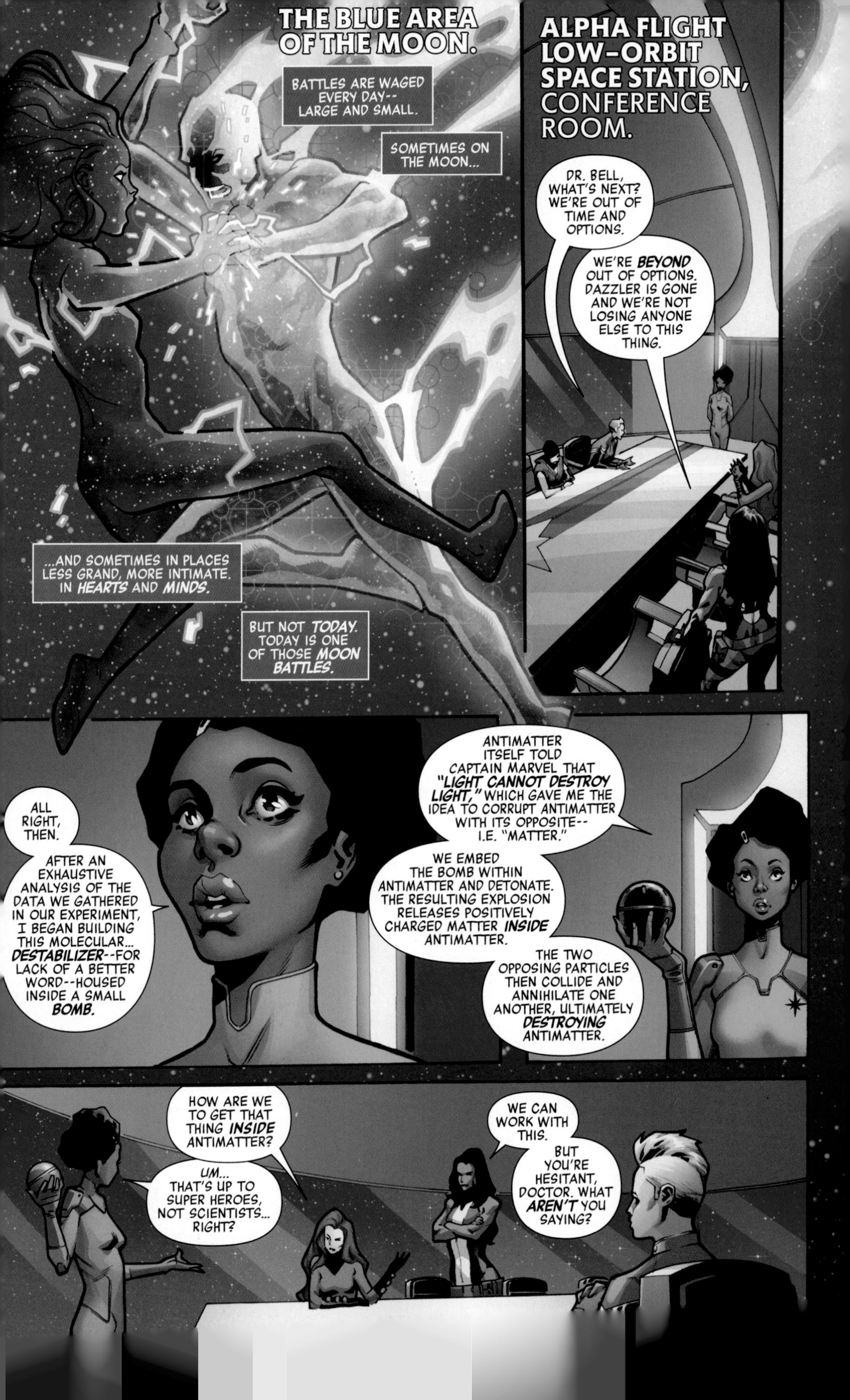
THE BLUE AREA OF THE MOON.
BATTLES ARE WAGED EVERY DAY-- LARGE AND SMALL.
SOMETIMES ON THE MOON...
...AND SOMETIMES IN PLACES LESS GRAND, MORE INTIMATE. IN HEARTS AND MINDS.
BUT NOT TODAY. TODAY IS ONE OF THOSE MOON BATTLES.
ALPHA FLIGHT LOW-ORBIT SPACE STATION, CONFERENCE ROOM.
DR. BELL, WHAT'S NEXT? WE'RE OUT OF TIME AND OPTIONS.
WE'RE BEYOND OUT OF OPTIONS. DAZZLER IS GONE AND WE'RE NOT LOSING ANYONE ELSE TO THIS THING.
ALL RIGHT, THEN.
AFTER AN EXHAUSTIVE ANALYSIS OF THE DATA WE GATHERED IN OUR EXPERIMENT, I BEGAN BUILDING THIS MOLECULAR... DESTABILIZER--FOR LACK OF A BETTER WORD--HOUSED INSIDE A SMALL BOMB.
ANTIMATTER ITSELF TOLD CAPTAIN MARVEL THAT "LIGHT CANNOT DESTROY LIGHT," WHICH GAVE ME THE IDEA TO CORRUPT ANTIMATTER WITH ITS OPPOSITE-- I.E. "MATTER."
WE EMBED THE BOMB WITHIN ANTIMATTER AND DETONATE. THE RESULTING EXPLOSION RELEASES POSITIVELY CHARGED MATTER INSIDE ANTIMATTER.
THE TWO OPPOSING PARTICLES THEN COLLIDE AND ANNIHILATE ONE ANOTHER, ULTIMATELY DESTROYING ANTIMATTER.
HOW ARE WE TO GET THAT THING INSIDE ANTIMATTER?
UM... THAT'S UP TO SUPER HEROES, NOT SCIENTISTS... RIGHT?
WE CAN WORK WITH THIS.
BUT YOU'RE HESITANT, DOCTOR. WHAT AREN'T YOU SAYING?

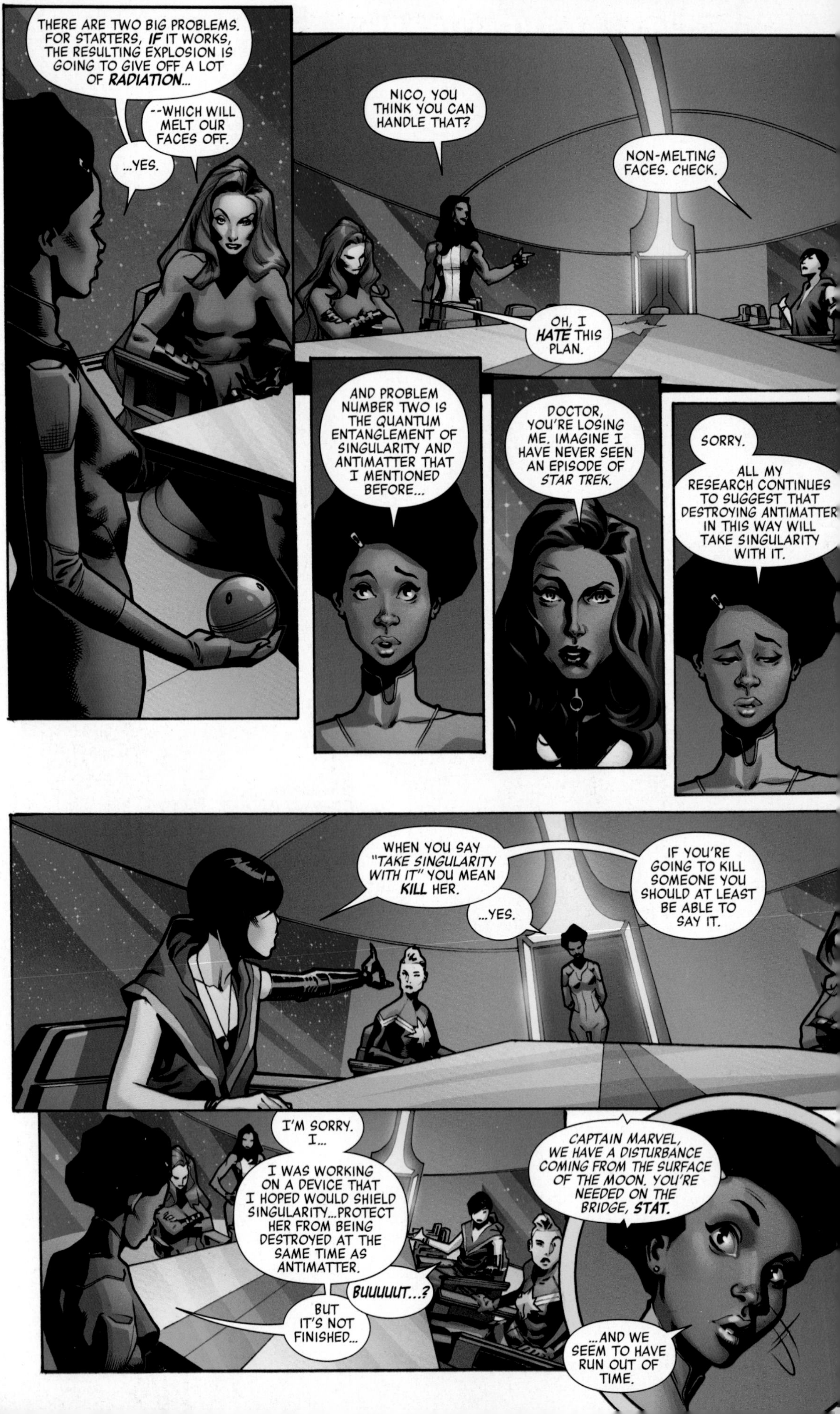
THERE ARE TWO BIG PROBLEMS. FOR STARTERS, IF IT WORKS, THE RESULTING EXPLOSION IS GOING TO GIVE OFF A LOT OF RADIATION...
--WHICH WILL MELT OUR FACES OFF.
...YES.
NICO, YOU THINK YOU CAN HANDLE THAT?
NON-MELTING FACES. CHECK.
OH, I HATE THIS PLAN.
AND PROBLEM NUMBER TWO IS THE QUANTUM ENTANGLEMENT OF SINGULARITY AND ANTIMATTER THAT I MENTIONED BEFORE...
DOCTOR, YOU'RE LOSING ME. IMAGINE I HAVE NEVER SEEN AN EPISODE OF STAR TREK.
SORRY.
ALL MY RESEARCH CONTINUES TO SUGGEST THAT DESTROYING ANTIMATTER IN THIS WAY WILL TAKE SINGULARITY WITH IT.
WHEN YOU SAY "TAKE SINGULARITY WITH IT" YOU MEAN KILL HER.
...YES.
IF YOU'RE GOING TO KILL SOMEONE YOU SHOULD AT LEAST BE ABLE TO SAY IT.
I'M SORRY. I...
I WAS WORKING ON A DEVICE THAT I HOPED WOULD SHIELD SINGULARITY...PROTECT HER FROM BEING DESTROYED AT THE SAME TIME AS ANTIMATTER.
BUUUUUT...?
BUT IT'S NOT FINISHED...
CAPTAIN MARVEL, WE HAVE A DISTURBANCE COMING FROM THE SURFACE OF THE MOON. YOU'RE NEEDED ON THE BRIDGE, STAT.
...AND WE SEEM TO HAVE RUN OUT OF TIME.

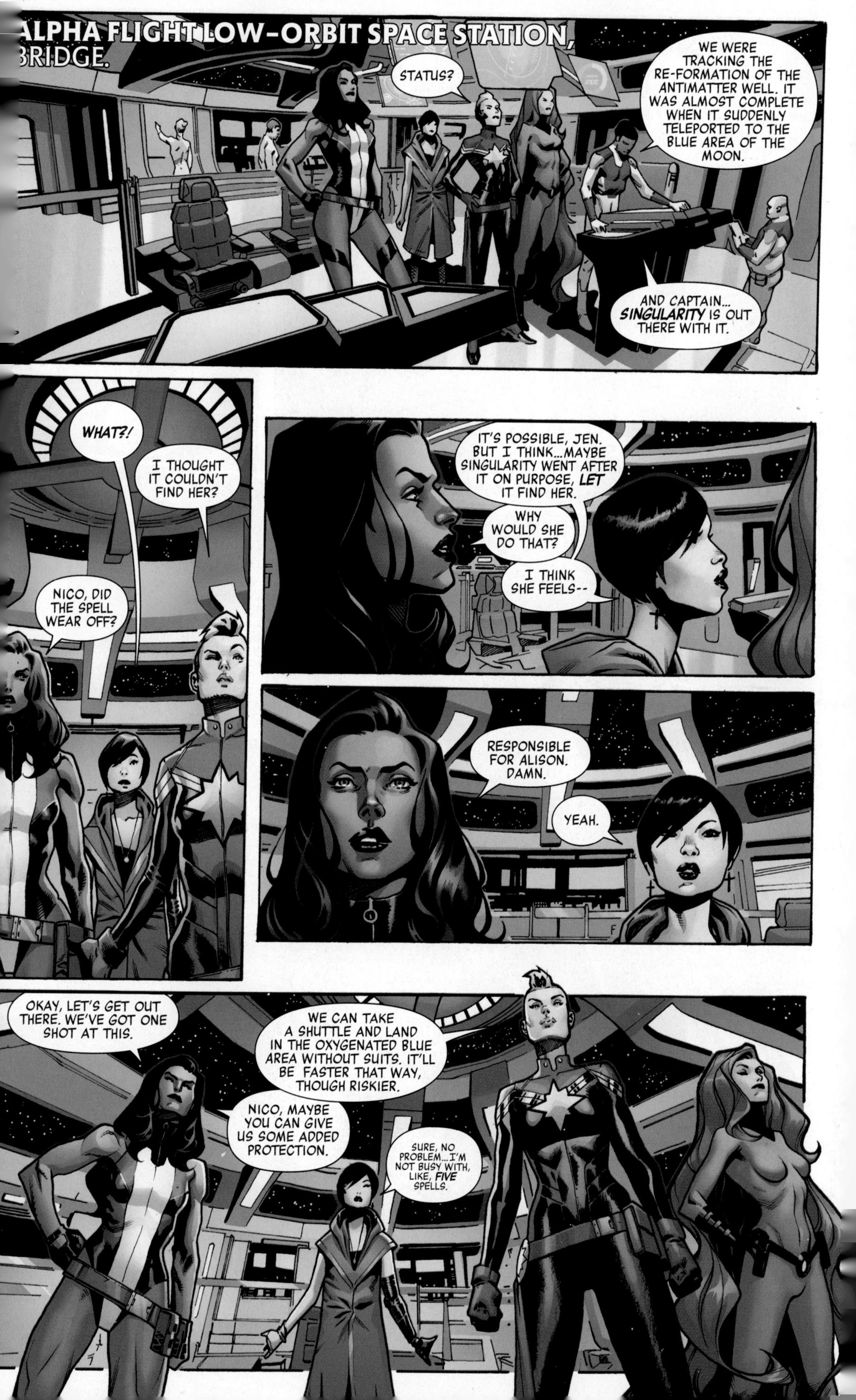
ALPHA FLIGHT LOW-ORBIT SPACE STATION, BRIDGE.
STATUS?
WE WERE TRACKING THE RE-FORMATION OF THE ANTIMATTER WELL. IT WAS ALMOST COMPLETE WHEN IT SUDDENLY TELEPORTED TO THE BLUE AREA OF THE MOON.
AND CAPTAIN... SINGULARITY IS OUT THERE WITH IT.
WHAT?!
I THOUGHT IT COULDN'T FIND HER?
NICO, DID THE SPELL WEAR OFF?
IT'S POSSIBLE, JEN. BUT I THINK...MAYBE SINGULARITY WENT AFTER IT ON PURPOSE, LET IT FIND HER.
WHY WOULD SHE DO THAT?
I THINK SHE FEELS--
RESPONSIBLE FOR ALISON. DAMN.
YEAH.
OKAY, LET'S GET OUT THERE. WE'VE GOT ONE SHOT AT THIS.
WE CAN TAKE A SHUTTLE AND LAND IN THE OXYGENATED BLUE AREA WITHOUT SUITS. IT'LL BE FASTER THAT WAY, THOUGH RISKIER.
NICO, MAYBE YOU CAN GIVE US SOME ADDED PROTECTION.
SURE, NO PROBLEM...I'M NOT BUSY WITH, LIKE, FIVE SPELLS.

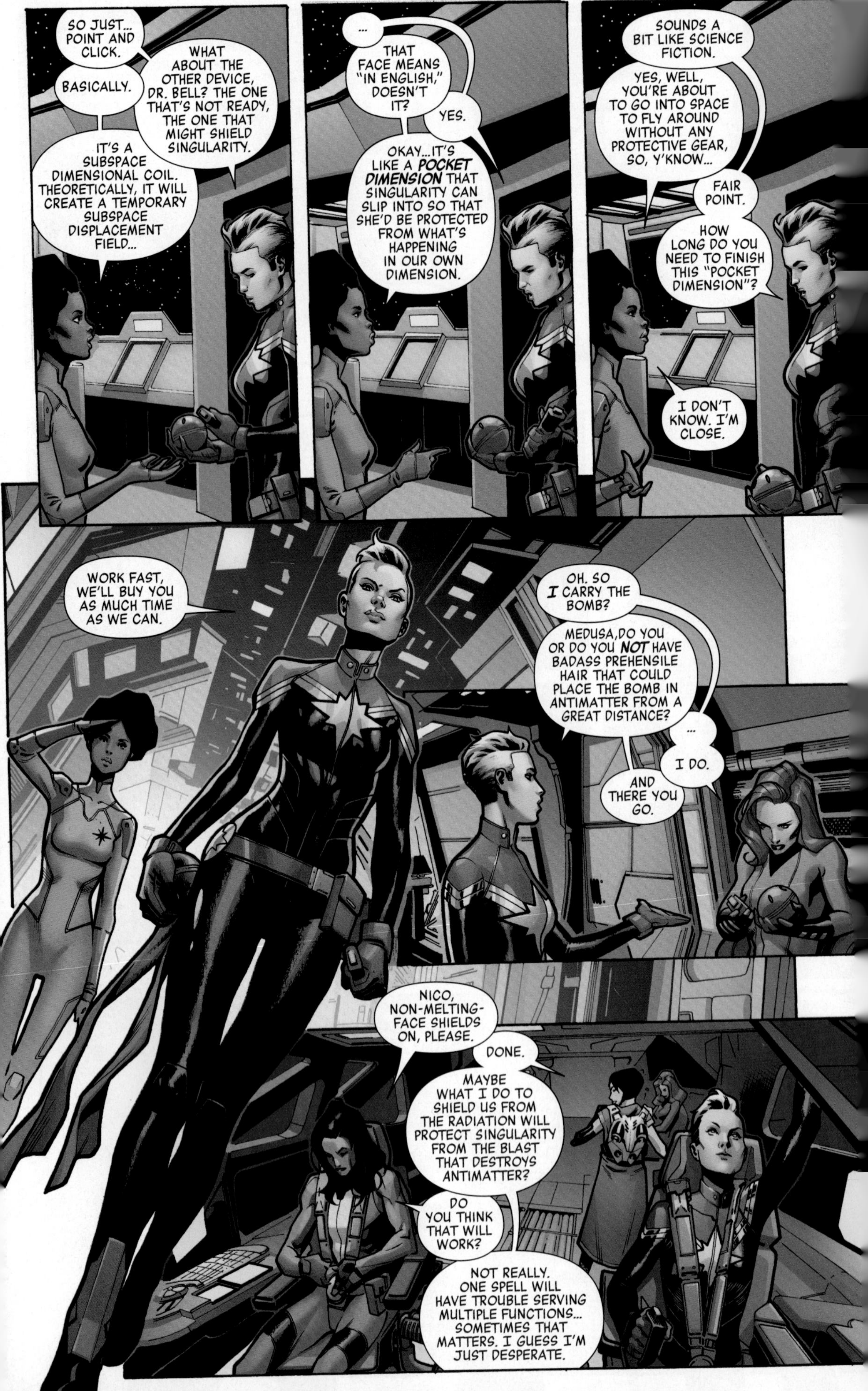
SO JUST... POINT AND CLICK.
BASICALLY.
WHAT ABOUT THE OTHER DEVICE, DR. BELL? THE ONE THAT'S NOT READY, THE ONE THAT MIGHT SHIELD SINGULARITY.
IT'S A SUBSPACE DIMENSIONAL COIL. THEORETICALLY, IT WILL CREATE A TEMPORARY SUBSPACE DISPLACEMENT FIELD...
...
THAT FACE MEANS "IN ENGLISH," DOESN'T IT?
YES.
OKAY...IT'S LIKE A POCKET DIMENSION THAT SINGULARITY CAN SLIP INTO SO THAT SHE'D BE PROTECTED FROM WHAT'S HAPPENING IN OUR OWN DIMENSION.
SOUNDS A BIT LIKE SCIENCE FICTION.
YES, WELL, YOU'RE ABOUT TO GO INTO SPACE TO FLY AROUND WITHOUT ANY PROTECTIVE GEAR, SO, Y'KNOW...
FAIR POINT.
HOW LONG DO YOU NEED TO FINISH THIS "POCKET DIMENSION"?
I DON'T KNOW. I'M CLOSE.
WORK FAST, WE'LL BUY YOU AS MUCH TIME AS WE CAN.
OH. SO I CARRY THE BOMB?
MEDUSA,DO YOU OR DO YOU NOT HAVE BADASS PREHENSILE HAIR THAT COULD PLACE THE BOMB IN ANTIMATTER FROM A GREAT DISTANCE?
...
I DO.
AND THERE YOU GO.
NICO, NON-MELTING-FACE SHIELDS ON, PLEASE.
DONE.
MAYBE WHAT I DO TO SHIELD US FROM THE RADIATION WILL PROTECT SINGULARITY FROM THE BLAST THAT DESTROYS ANTIMATTER?
DO YOU THINK THAT WILL WORK?
NOT REALLY. ONE SPELL WILL HAVE TROUBLE SERVING MULTIPLE FUNCTIONS... SOMETIMES THAT MATTERS. I GUESS I'M JUST DESPERATE.

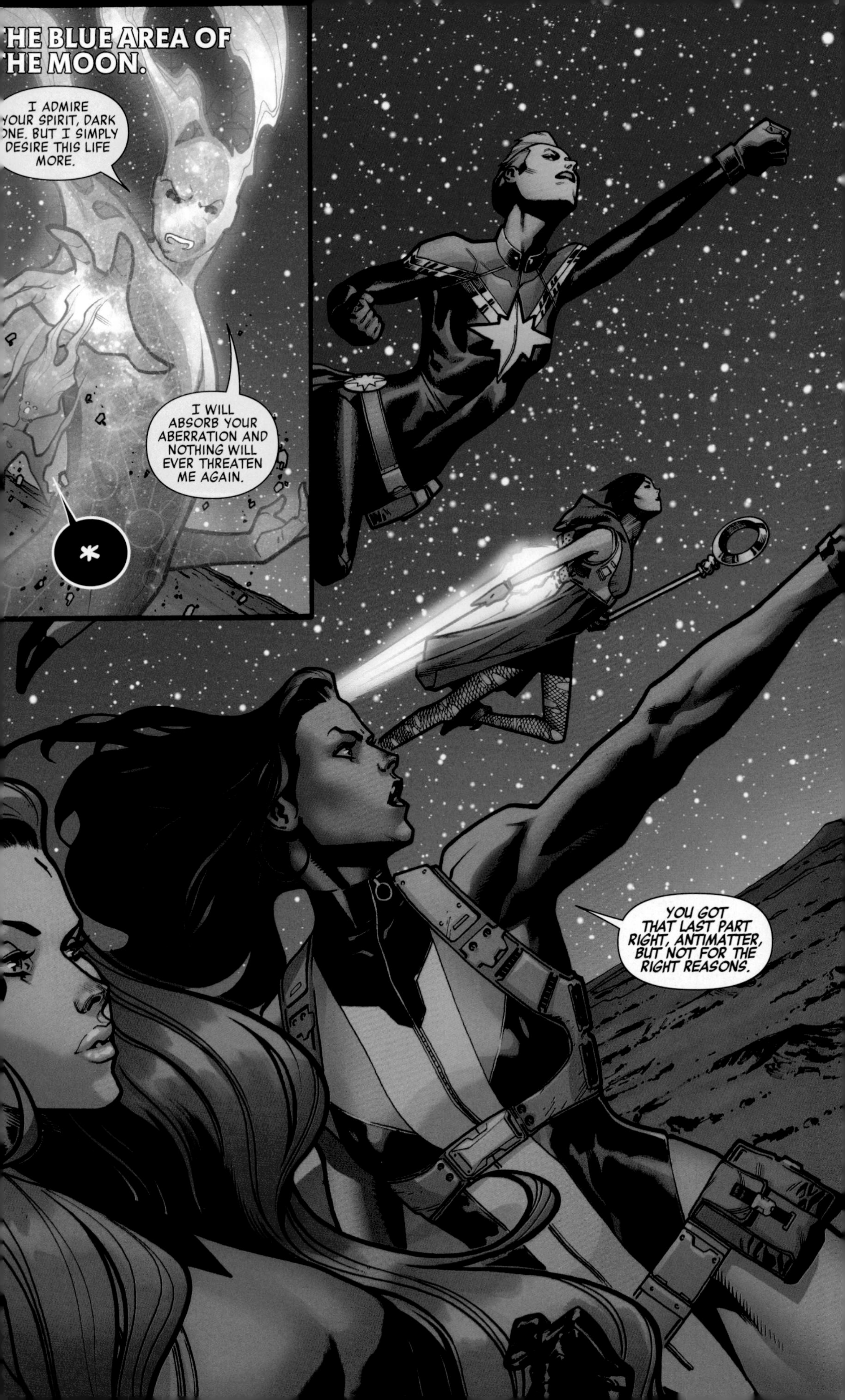
HE BLUE AREA OF
HE MOON.
I ADMIRE YOUR SPIRIT, DARK ONE. BUT I SIMPLY DESIRE THIS LIFE MORE.
I WILL ABSORB YOUR ABERRATION AND NOTHING WILL EVER THREATEN ME AGAIN.
*
YOU GOT THAT LAST PART RIGHT, ANTIMATTER, BUT NOT FOR THE RIGHT REASONS.

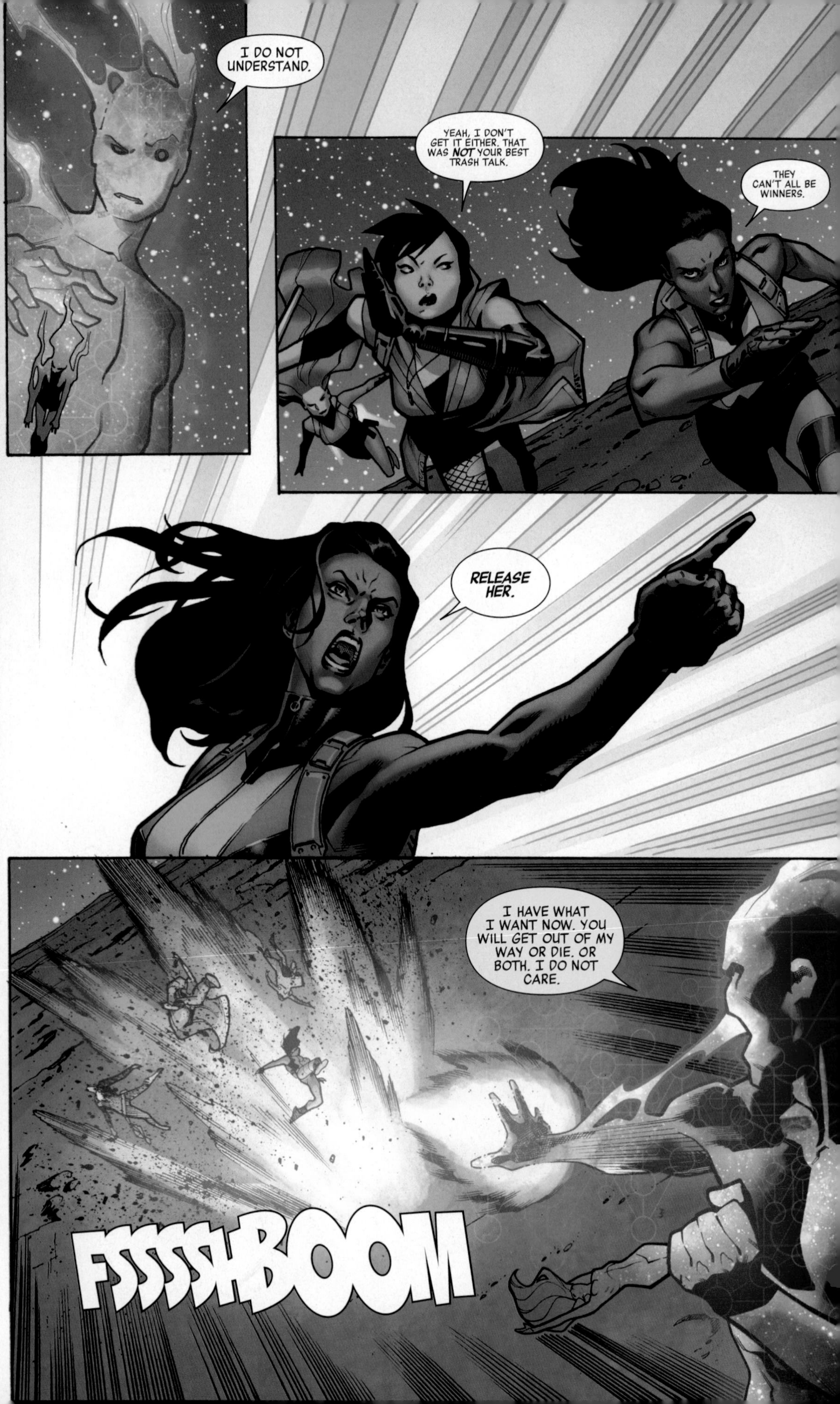
I DO NOT UNDERSTAND.
YEAH, I DON'T GET IT EITHER. THAT WAS *NOT* YOUR BEST TRASH TALK.
THEY CAN'T ALL BE WINNERS.
RELEASE HER.
I HAVE WHAT I WANT NOW. YOU WILL GET OUT OF MY WAY OR DIE. OR BOTH. I DO NOT CARE.
FSSSSHBOOM

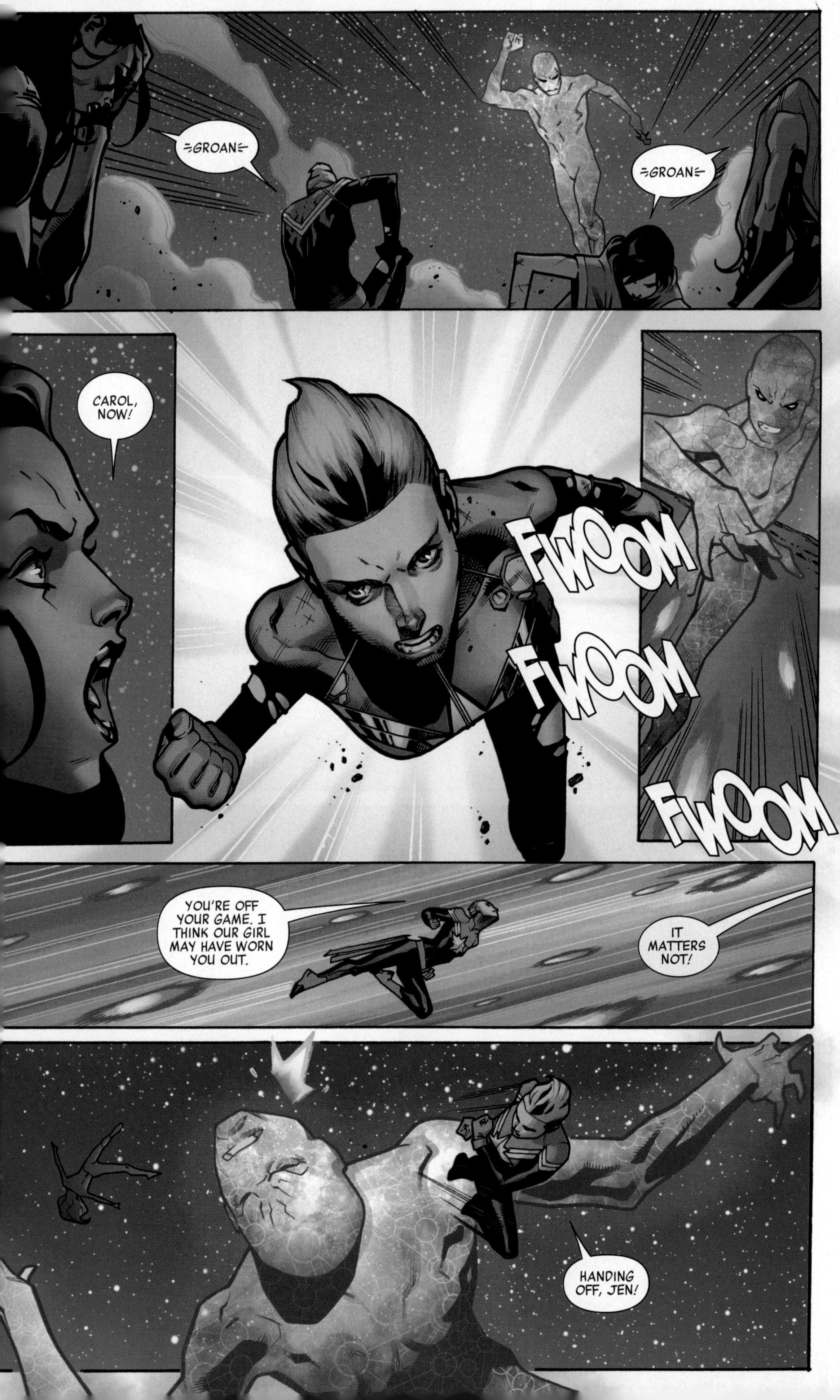

=GROAN=
=GROAN=
CAROL, NOW!
FWOOM
FWOOM
FWOOM
YOU'RE OFF YOUR GAME. I THINK OUR GIRL MAY HAVE WORN YOU OUT.
IT MATTERS NOT!
HANDING OFF, JEN!

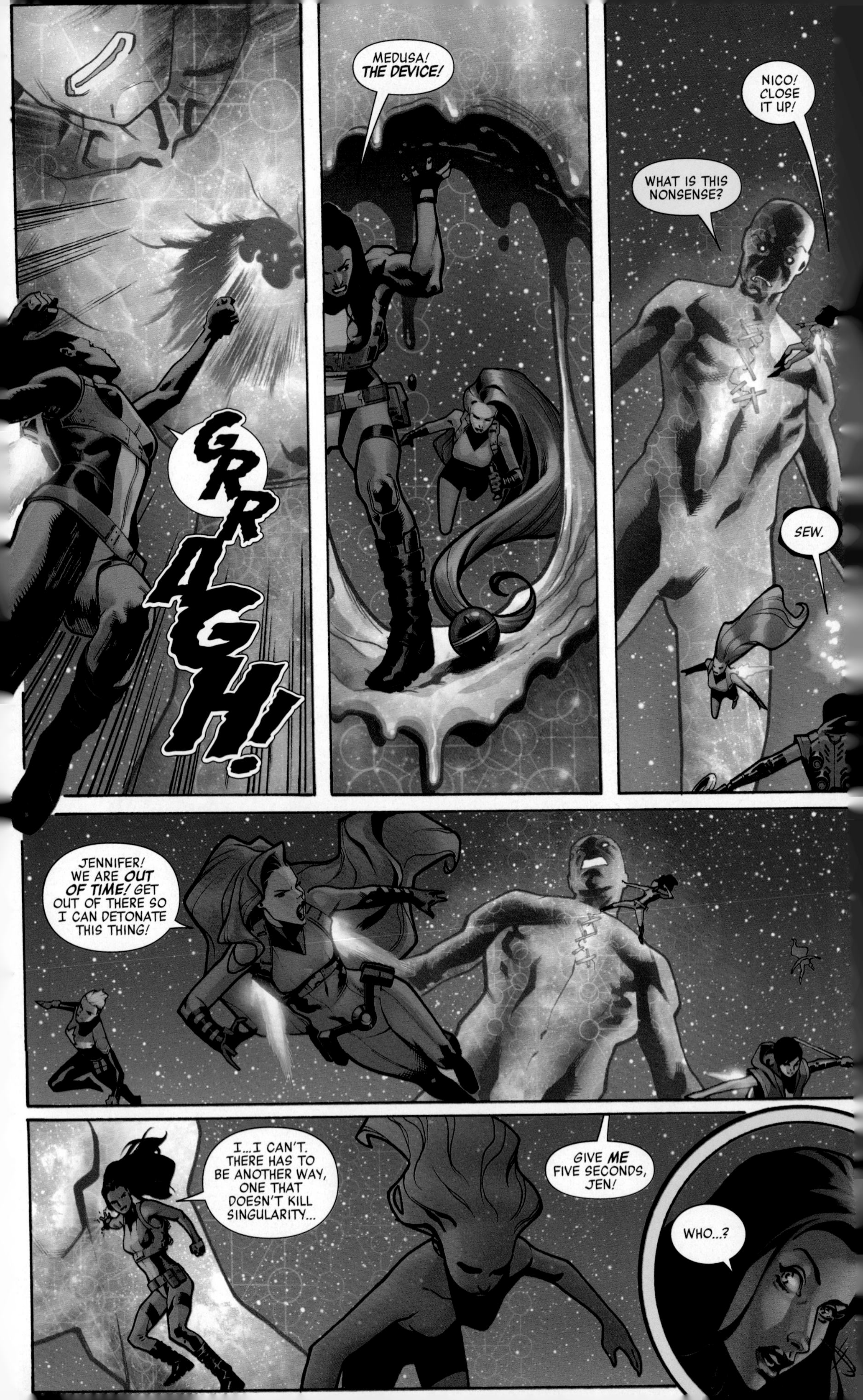
GRRAGH!
MEDUSA! THE DEVICE!
NICO! CLOSE IT UP!
WHAT IS THIS NONSENSE?
SEW.
JENNIFER! WE ARE OUT OF TIME! GET OUT OF THERE SO I CAN DETONATE THIS THING!
I...I CAN'T. THERE HAS TO BE ANOTHER WAY, ONE THAT DOESN'T KILL SINGULARITY...
GIVE ME FIVE SECONDS, JEN!
WHO...?

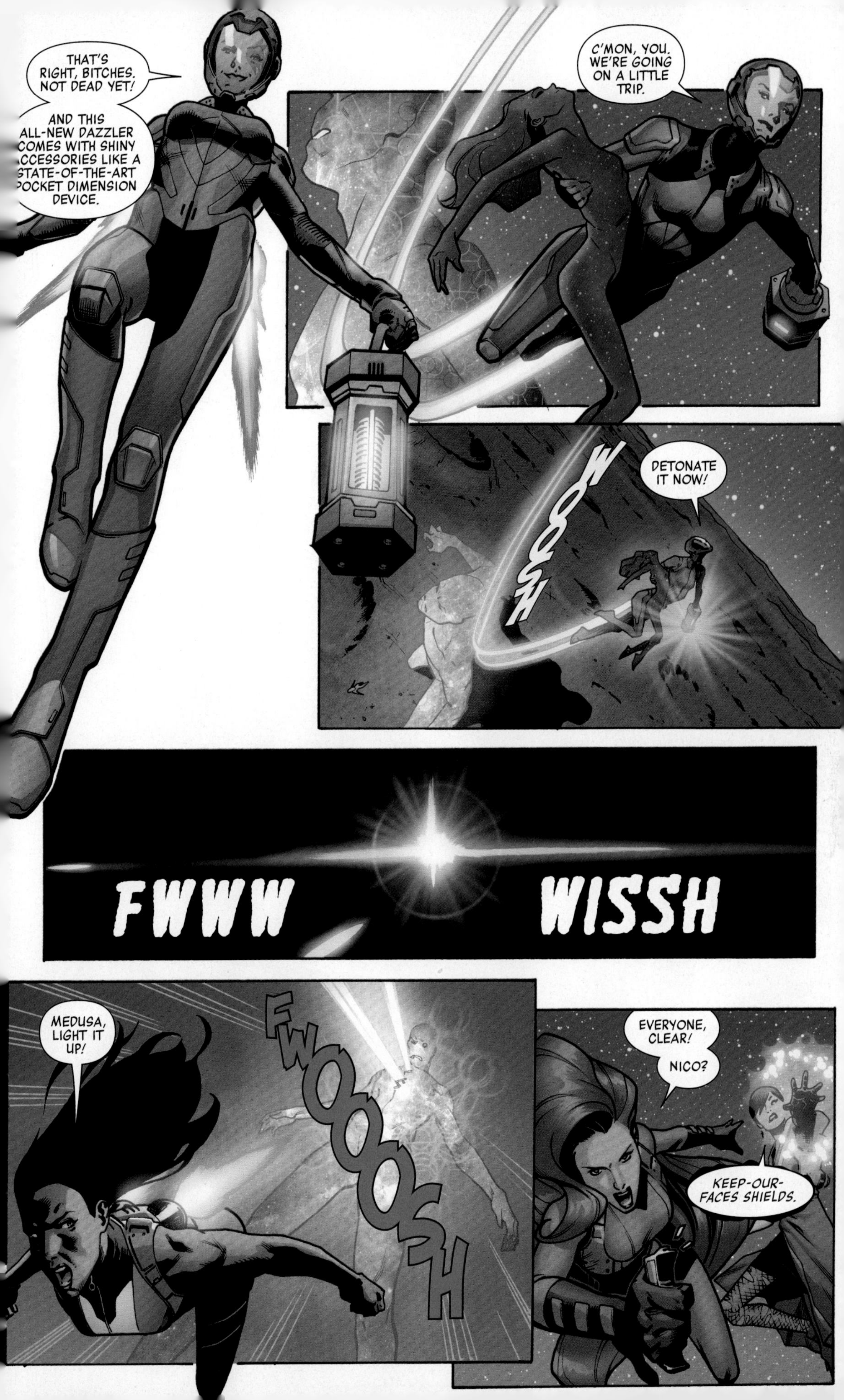
THAT'S RIGHT, BITCHES. NOT DEAD YET!
AND THIS ALL-NEW DAZZLER COMES WITH SHINY ACCESSORIES LIKE A STATE-OF-THE-ART POCKET DIMENSION DEVICE.
C'MON, YOU. WE'RE GOING ON A LITTLE TRIP.
WOOSH
DETONATE IT NOW!
FWWW
WISSH
MEDUSA, LIGHT IT UP!
FWOOOOSH
EVERYONE, CLEAR!
NICO?
KEEP-OUR-FACES SHIELDS.

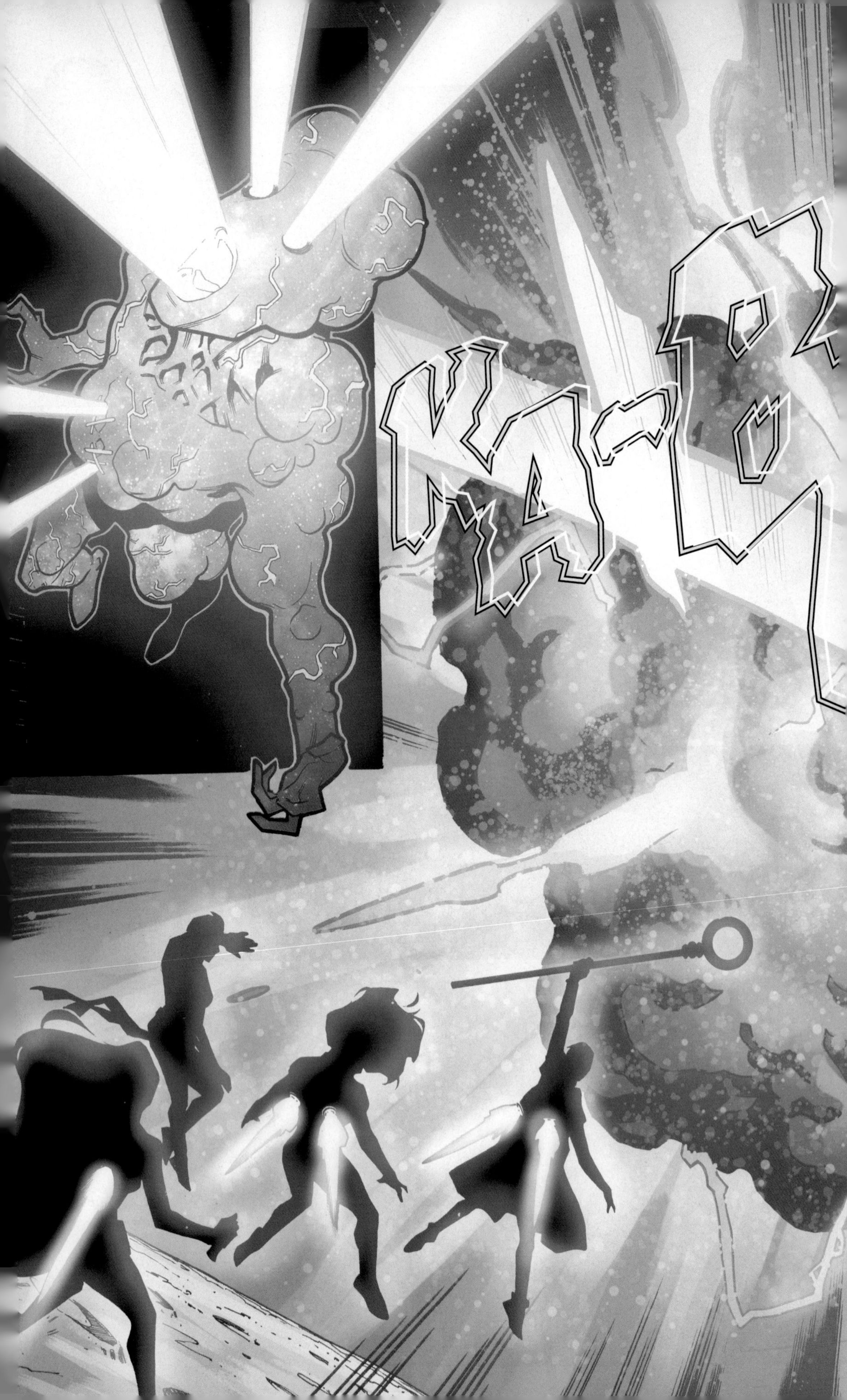
KA-B

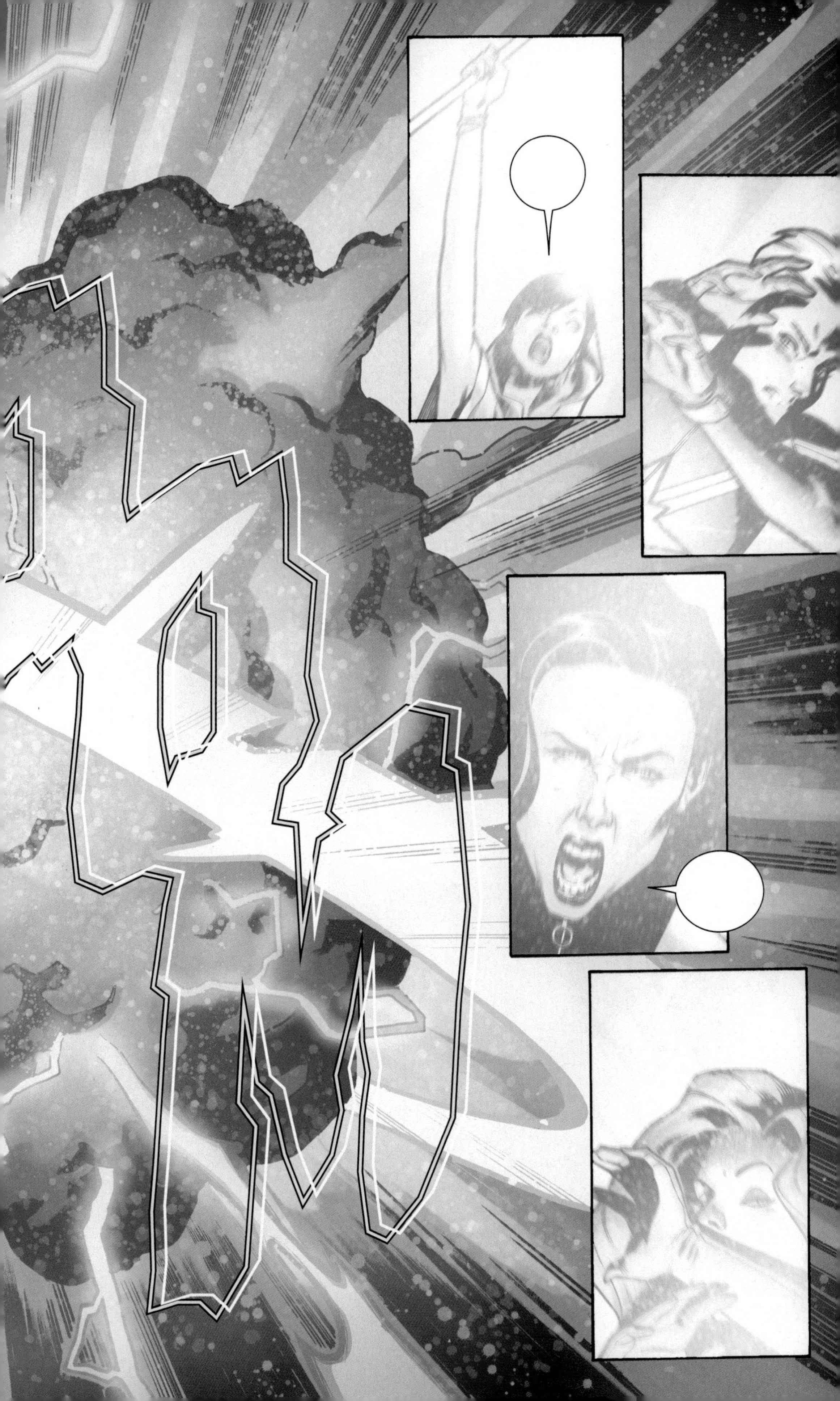

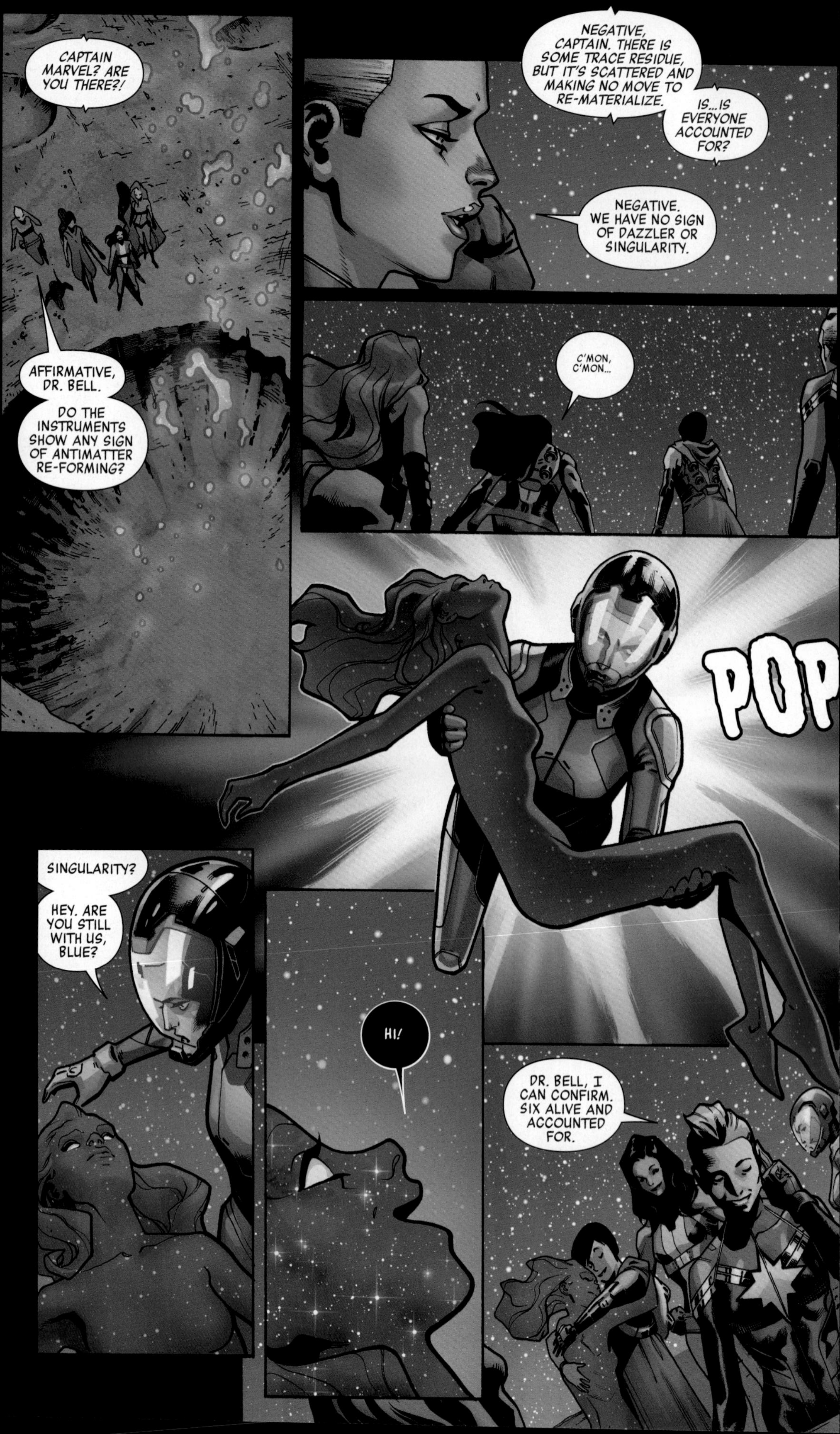
CAPTAIN MARVEL? ARE YOU THERE?!
NEGATIVE, CAPTAIN. THERE IS SOME TRACE RESIDUE, BUT IT'S SCATTERED AND MAKING NO MOVE TO RE-MATERIALIZE.
IS...IS EVERYONE ACCOUNTED FOR?
NEGATIVE. WE HAVE NO SIGN OF DAZZLER OR SINGULARITY.
AFFIRMATIVE, DR. BELL.
DO THE INSTRUMENTS SHOW ANY SIGN OF ANTIMATTER RE-FORMING?
C'MON, C'MON...
POP
SINGULARITY?
HEY. ARE YOU STILL WITH US, BLUE?
HI!
DR. BELL, I CAN CONFIRM. SIX ALIVE AND ACCOUNTED FOR.

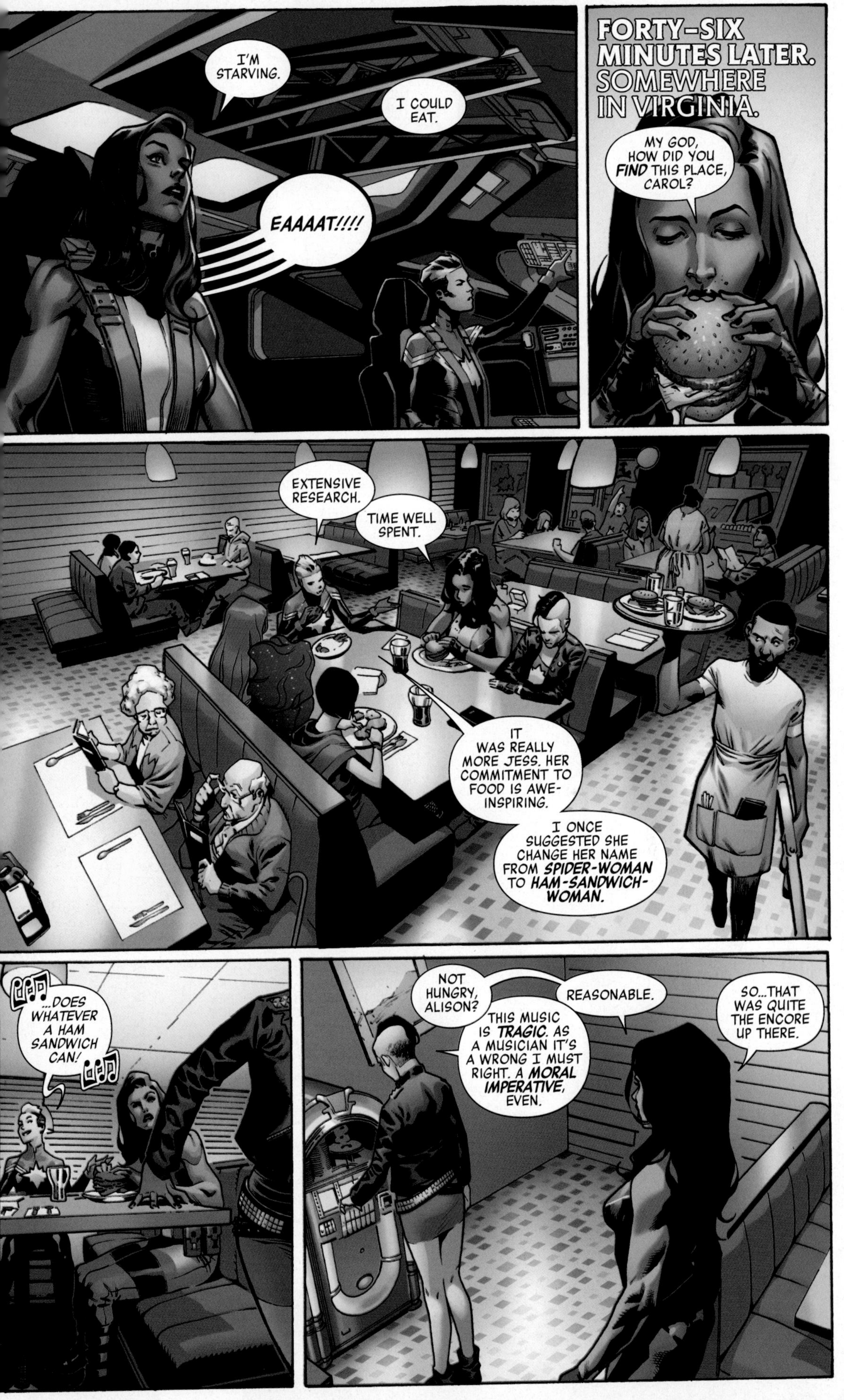
I'M STARVING.
I COULD EAT.
EAAAAT!!!!
FORTY-SIX MINUTES LATER. SOMEWHERE IN VIRGINIA.
MY GOD, HOW DID YOU FIND THIS PLACE, CAROL?
EXTENSIVE RESEARCH.
TIME WELL SPENT.
IT WAS REALLY MORE JESS. HER COMMITMENT TO FOOD IS AWE-INSPIRING.
I ONCE SUGGESTED SHE CHANGE HER NAME FROM SPIDER-WOMAN TO HAM-SANDWICH-WOMAN.
...DOES WHATEVER A HAM SANDWICH CAN!
NOT HUNGRY, ALISON?
REASONABLE.
THIS MUSIC IS TRAGIC. AS A MUSICIAN IT'S A WRONG I MUST RIGHT. A MORAL IMPERATIVE, EVEN.
SO...THAT WAS QUITE THE ENCORE UP THERE.

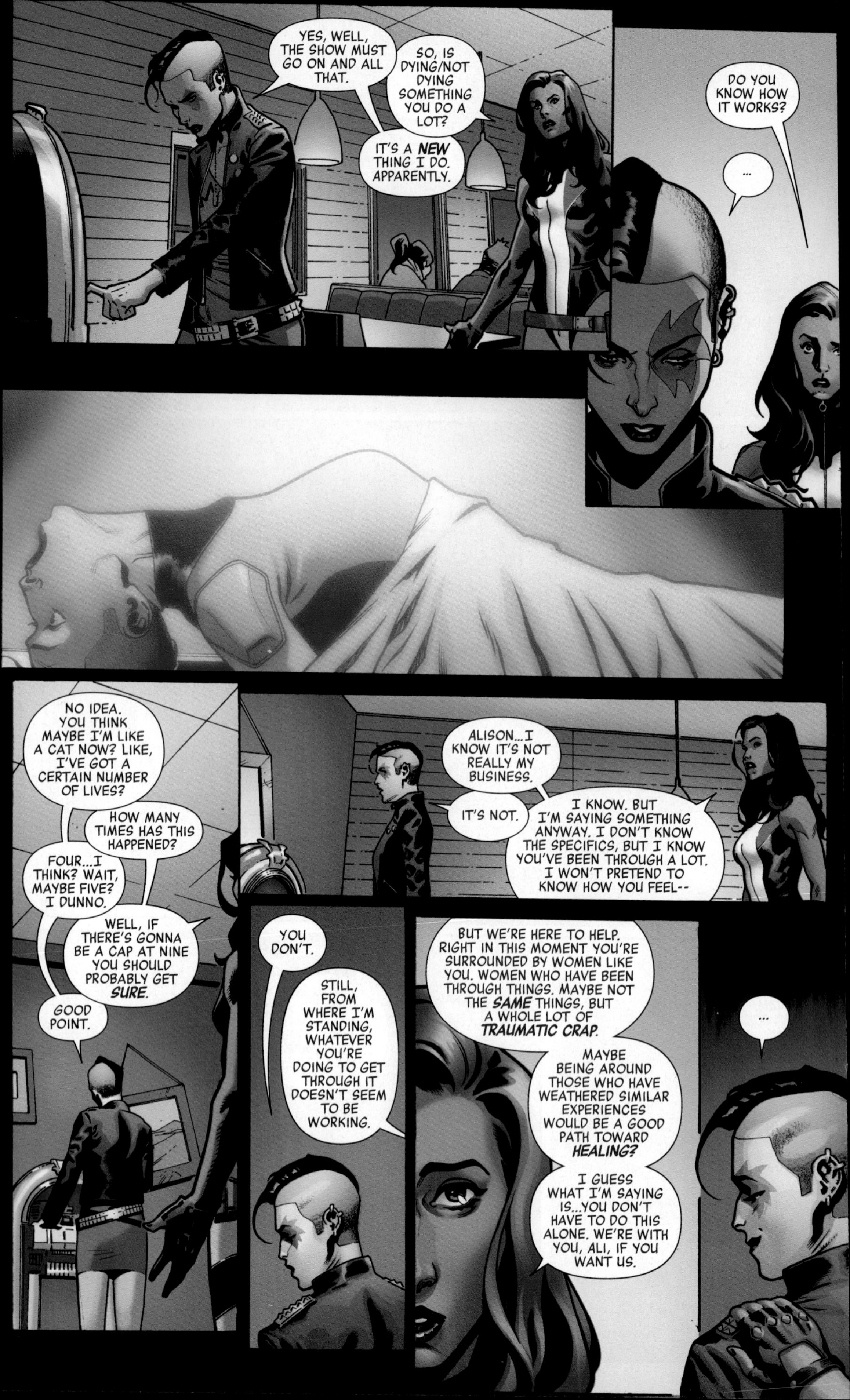
YES, WELL, THE SHOW MUST GO ON AND ALL THAT.
SO, IS DYING/NOT DYING SOMETHING YOU DO A LOT?
IT'S A NEW THING I DO. APPARENTLY.
DO YOU KNOW HOW IT WORKS?
...
NO IDEA. YOU THINK MAYBE I'M LIKE A CAT NOW? LIKE, I'VE GOT A CERTAIN NUMBER OF LIVES?
HOW MANY TIMES HAS THIS HAPPENED?
FOUR...I THINK? WAIT, MAYBE FIVE? I DUNNO.
WELL, IF THERE'S GONNA BE A CAP AT NINE YOU SHOULD PROBABLY GET SURE.
GOOD POINT.
ALISON...I KNOW IT'S NOT REALLY MY BUSINESS.
IT'S NOT.
I KNOW. BUT I'M SAYING SOMETHING ANYWAY. I DON'T KNOW THE SPECIFICS, BUT I KNOW YOU'VE BEEN THROUGH A LOT. I WON'T PRETEND TO KNOW HOW YOU FEEL--
YOU DON'T.
STILL, FROM WHERE I'M STANDING, WHATEVER YOU'RE DOING TO GET THROUGH IT DOESN'T SEEM TO BE WORKING.
BUT WE'RE HERE TO HELP. RIGHT IN THIS MOMENT YOU'RE SURROUNDED BY WOMEN LIKE YOU. WOMEN WHO HAVE BEEN THROUGH THINGS. MAYBE NOT THE SAME THINGS, BUT A WHOLE LOT OF TRAUMATIC CRAP.
MAYBE BEING AROUND THOSE WHO HAVE WEATHERED SIMILAR EXPERIENCES WOULD BE A GOOD PATH TOWARD HEALING?
I GUESS WHAT I'M SAYING IS...YOU DON'T HAVE TO DO THIS ALONE. WE'RE WITH YOU, ALI, IF YOU WANT US.
...

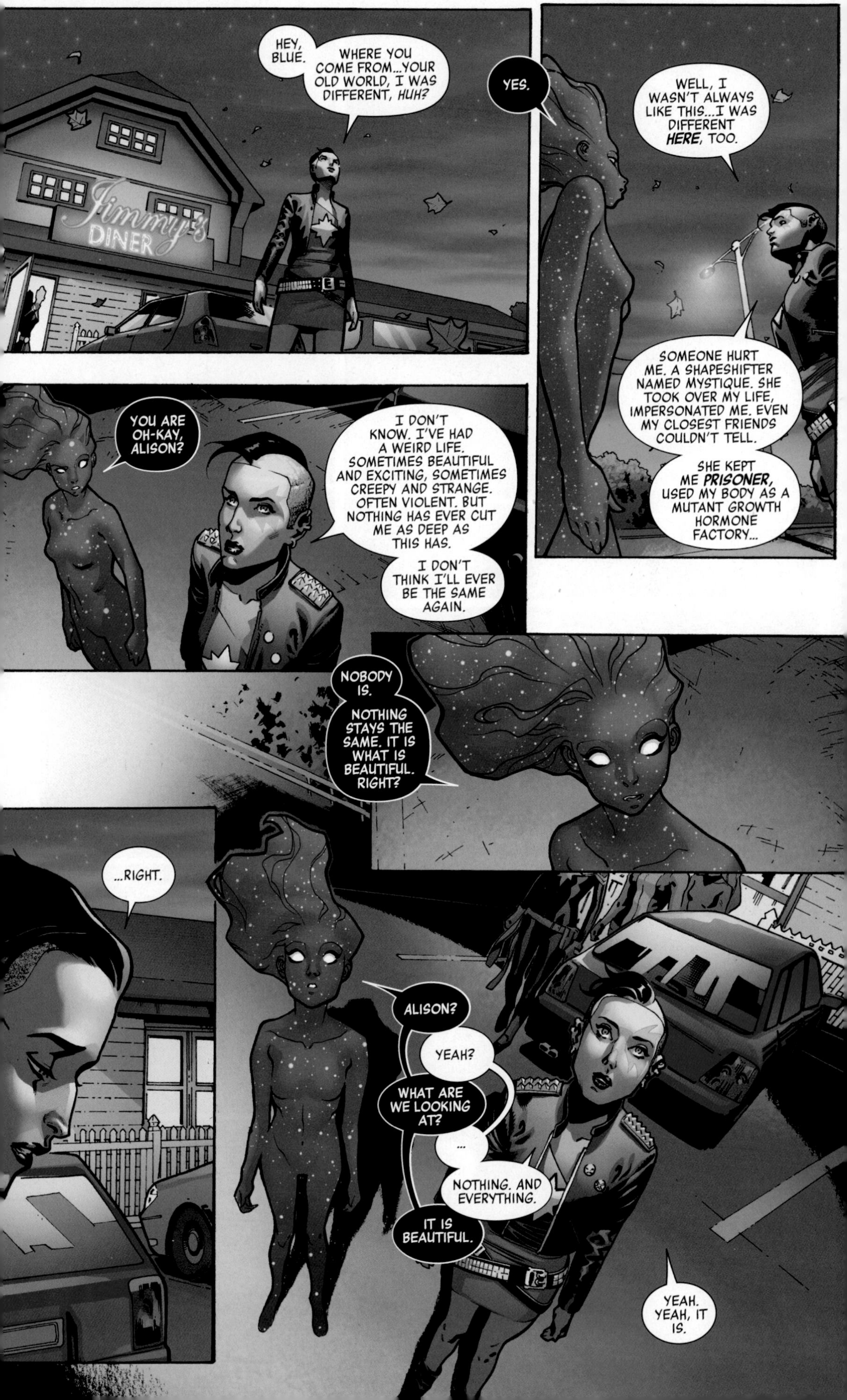
HEY, BLUE.
WHERE YOU COME FROM...YOUR OLD WORLD, I WAS DIFFERENT, HUH?
YES.
WELL, I WASN'T ALWAYS LIKE THIS...I WAS DIFFERENT HERE, TOO.
SOMEONE HURT ME. A SHAPESHIFTER NAMED MYSTIQUE. SHE TOOK OVER MY LIFE, IMPERSONATED ME. EVEN MY CLOSEST FRIENDS COULDN'T TELL.
SHE KEPT ME PRISONER, USED MY BODY AS A MUTANT GROWTH HORMONE FACTORY...
YOU ARE OH-KAY, ALISON?
I DON'T KNOW. I'VE HAD A WEIRD LIFE. SOMETIMES BEAUTIFUL AND EXCITING, SOMETIMES CREEPY AND STRANGE. OFTEN VIOLENT. BUT NOTHING HAS EVER CUT ME AS DEEP AS THIS HAS.
I DON'T THINK I'LL EVER BE THE SAME AGAIN.
NOBODY IS.
NOTHING STAYS THE SAME. IT IS WHAT IS BEAUTIFUL. RIGHT?
...RIGHT.
ALISON?
YEAH?
WHAT ARE WE LOOKING AT?
...
NOTHING. AND EVERYTHING.
IT IS BEAUTIFUL.
YEAH. YEAH, IT IS.

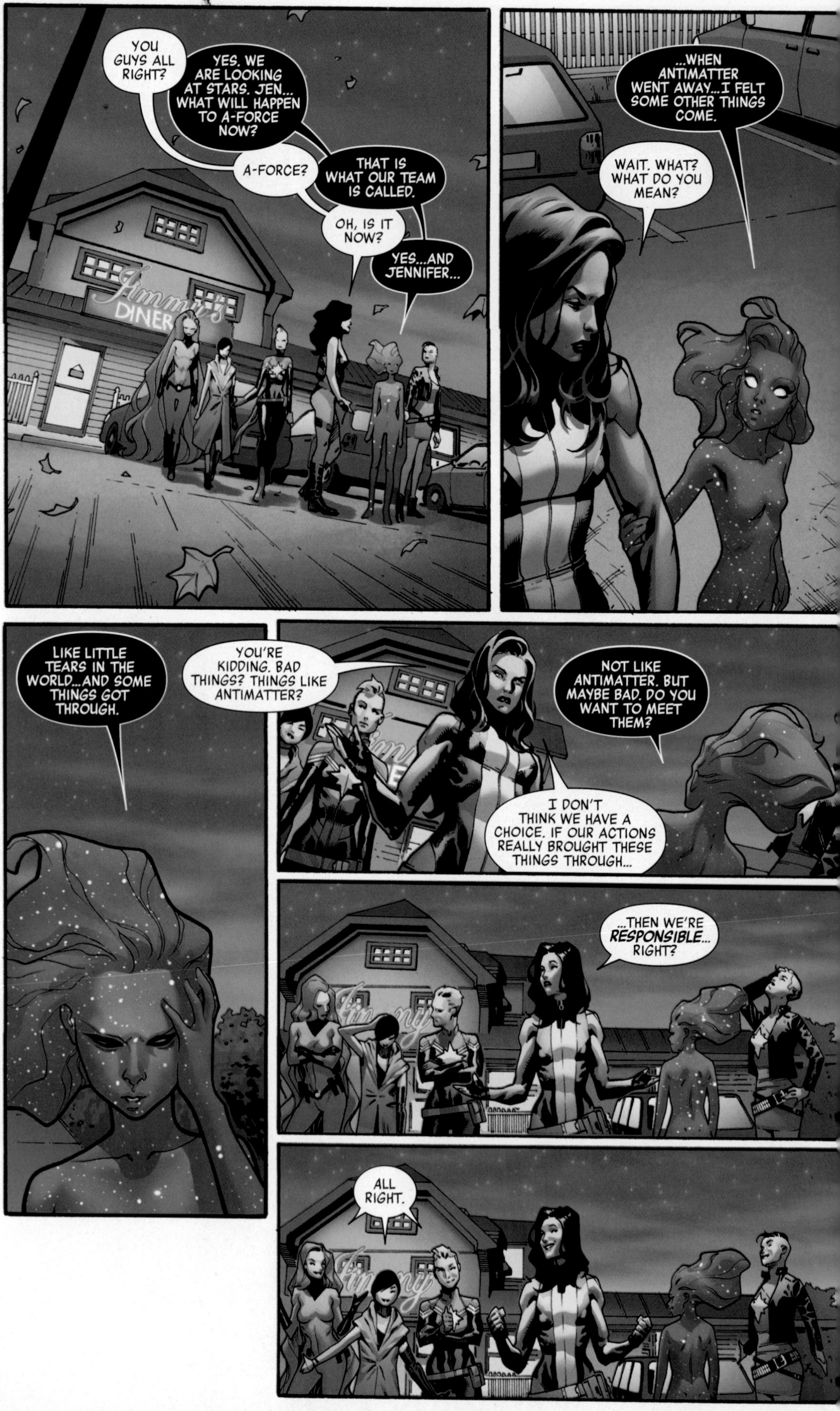
YOU GUYS ALL RIGHT?
YES. WE ARE LOOKING AT STARS. JEN... WHAT WILL HAPPEN TO A-FORCE NOW?
A-FORCE?
THAT IS WHAT OUR TEAM IS CALLED.
OH, IS IT NOW?
YES...AND JENNIFER...
Jimmy's DINER
...WHEN ANTIMATTER WENT AWAY...I FELT SOME OTHER THINGS COME.
WAIT. WHAT? WHAT DO YOU MEAN?
LIKE LITTLE TEARS IN THE WORLD...AND SOME THINGS GOT THROUGH.
YOU'RE KIDDING. BAD THINGS? THINGS LIKE ANTIMATTER?
NOT LIKE ANTIMATTER. BUT MAYBE BAD. DO YOU WANT TO MEET THEM?
I DON'T THINK WE HAVE A CHOICE. IF OUR ACTIONS REALLY BROUGHT THESE THINGS THROUGH...
...THEN WE'RE *RESPONSIBLE*... RIGHT?
ALL RIGHT.

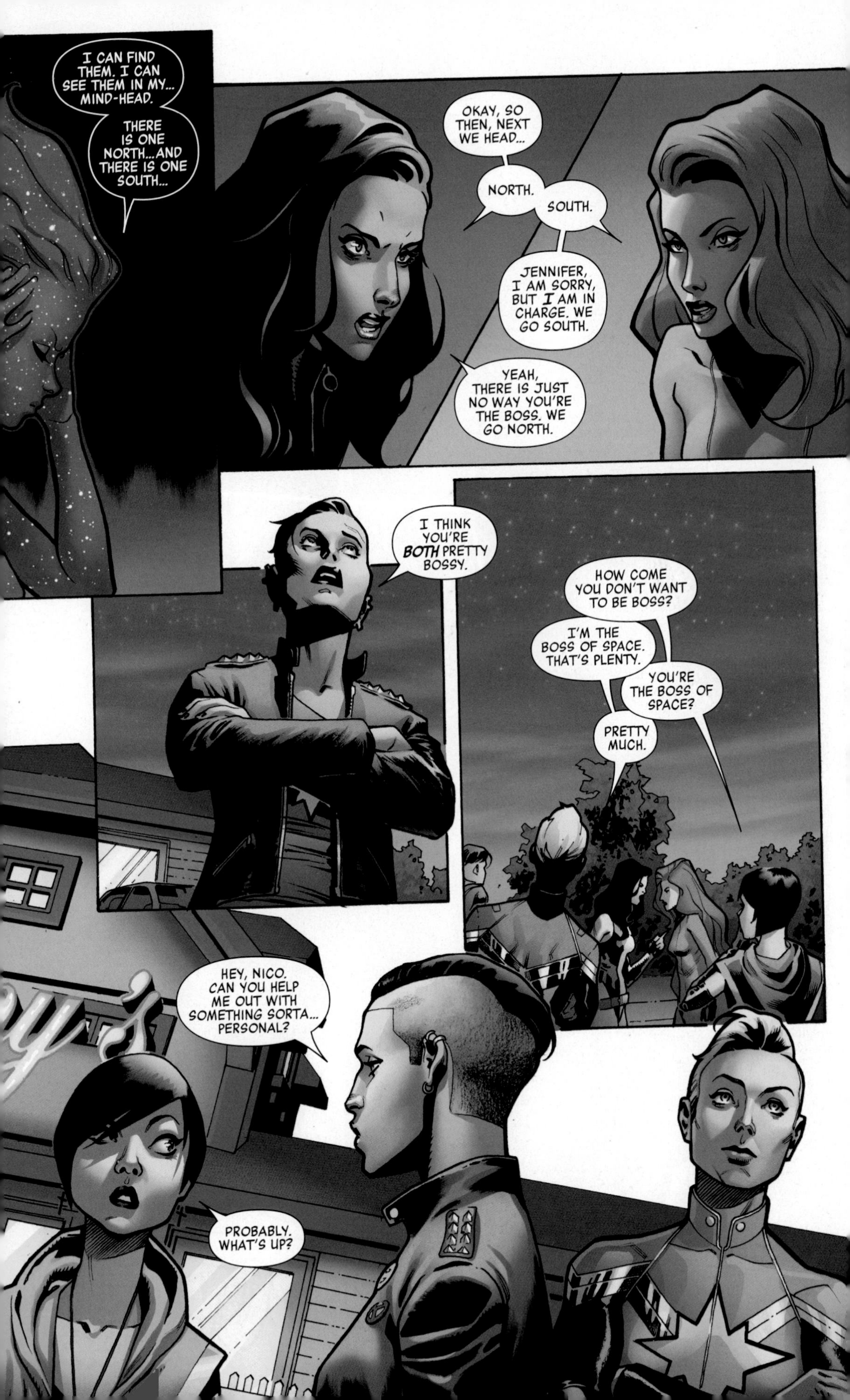
I CAN FIND THEM. I CAN SEE THEM IN MY... MIND-HEAD.
THERE IS ONE NORTH...AND THERE IS ONE SOUTH...
OKAY, SO THEN, NEXT WE HEAD...
NORTH.
SOUTH.
JENNIFER, I AM SORRY, BUT *I* AM IN CHARGE. WE GO SOUTH.
YEAH, THERE IS JUST NO WAY YOU'RE THE BOSS. WE GO NORTH.
I THINK YOU'RE *BOTH* PRETTY BOSSY.
HOW COME YOU DON'T WANT TO BE BOSS?
I'M THE BOSS OF SPACE. THAT'S PLENTY.
YOU'RE THE BOSS OF SPACE?
PRETTY MUCH.
HEY, NICO. CAN YOU HELP ME OUT WITH SOMETHING SORTA... PERSONAL?
PROBABLY. WHAT'S UP?

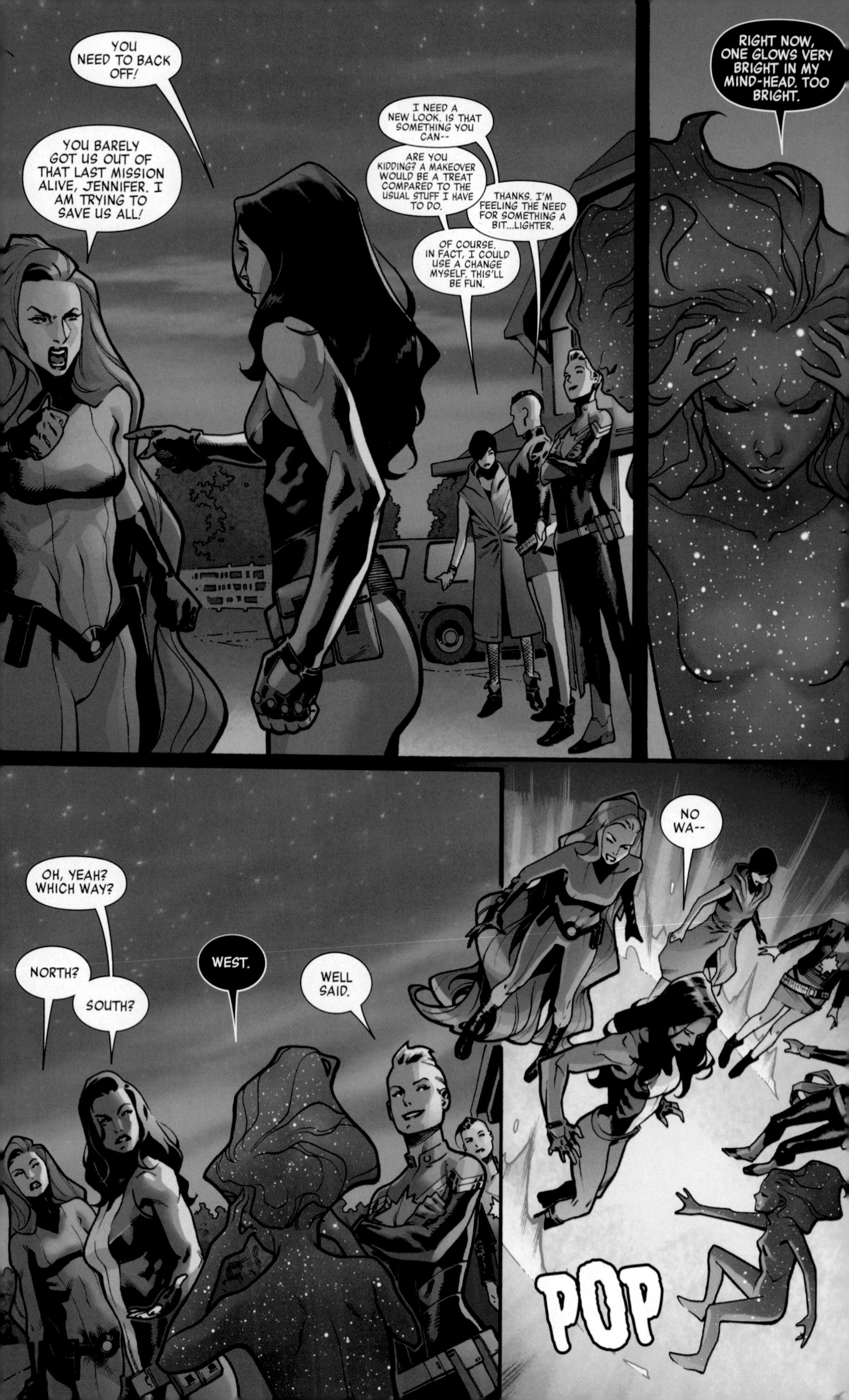
YOU NEED TO BACK OFF!
YOU BARELY GOT US OUT OF THAT LAST MISSION ALIVE, JENNIFER. I AM TRYING TO SAVE US ALL!
I NEED A NEW LOOK. IS THAT SOMETHING YOU CAN--
ARE YOU KIDDING? A MAKEOVER WOULD BE A TREAT COMPARED TO THE USUAL STUFF I HAVE TO DO.
THANKS. I'M FEELING THE NEED FOR SOMETHING A BIT...LIGHTER.
OF COURSE. IN FACT, I COULD USE A CHANGE MYSELF. THIS'LL BE FUN.
RIGHT NOW, ONE GLOWS VERY BRIGHT IN MY MIND-HEAD. TOO BRIGHT.
OH, YEAH? WHICH WAY?
NORTH?
SOUTH?
WEST.
WELL SAID.
NO WA--
POP

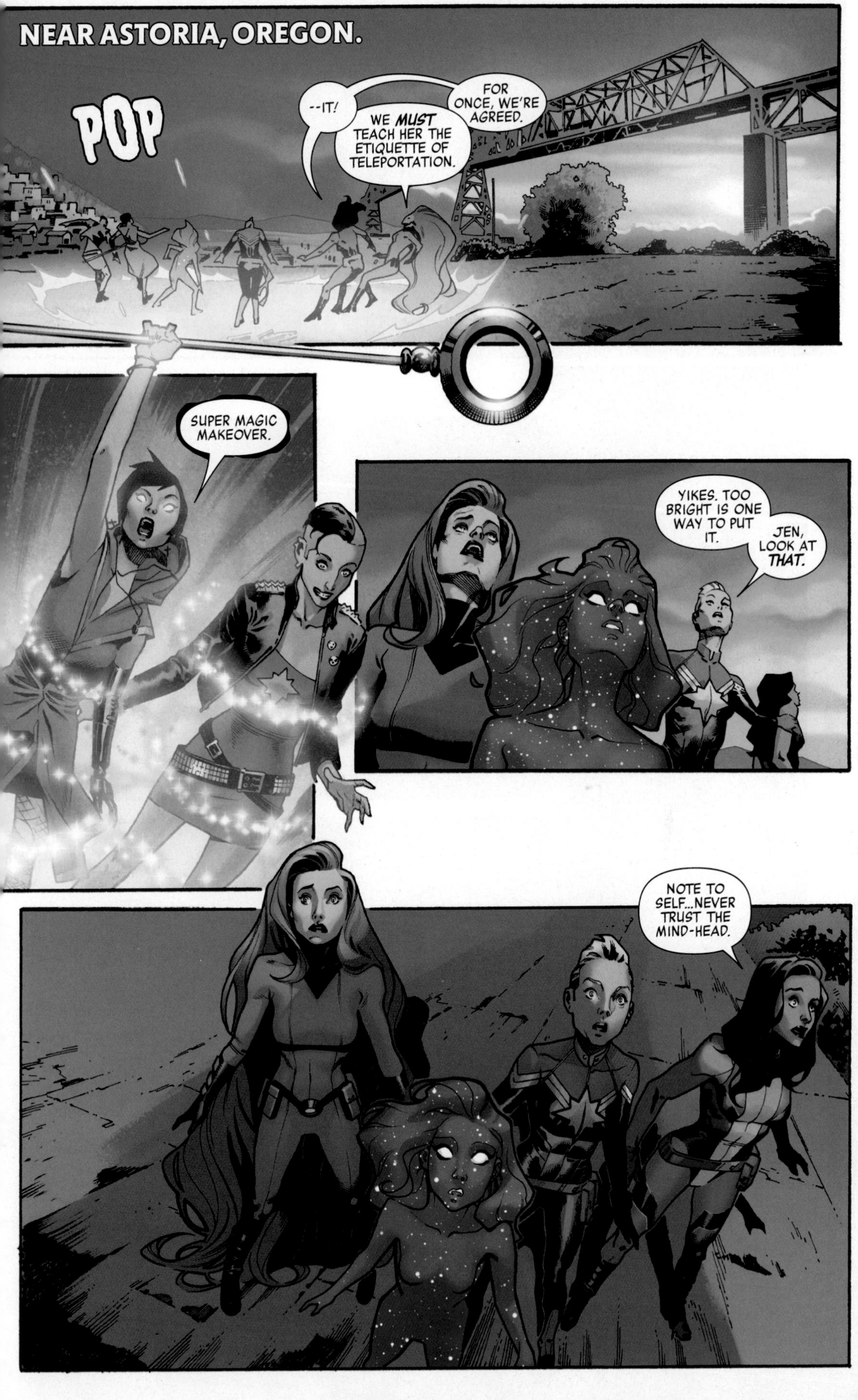
NEAR ASTORIA, OREGON.
POP
--IT!
WE MUST TEACH HER THE ETIQUETTE OF TELEPORTATION.
FOR ONCE, WE'RE AGREED.
SUPER MAGIC MAKEOVER.
YIKES. TOO BRIGHT IS ONE WAY TO PUT IT.
JEN, LOOK AT THAT.
NOTE TO SELF...NEVER TRUST THE MIND-HEAD.

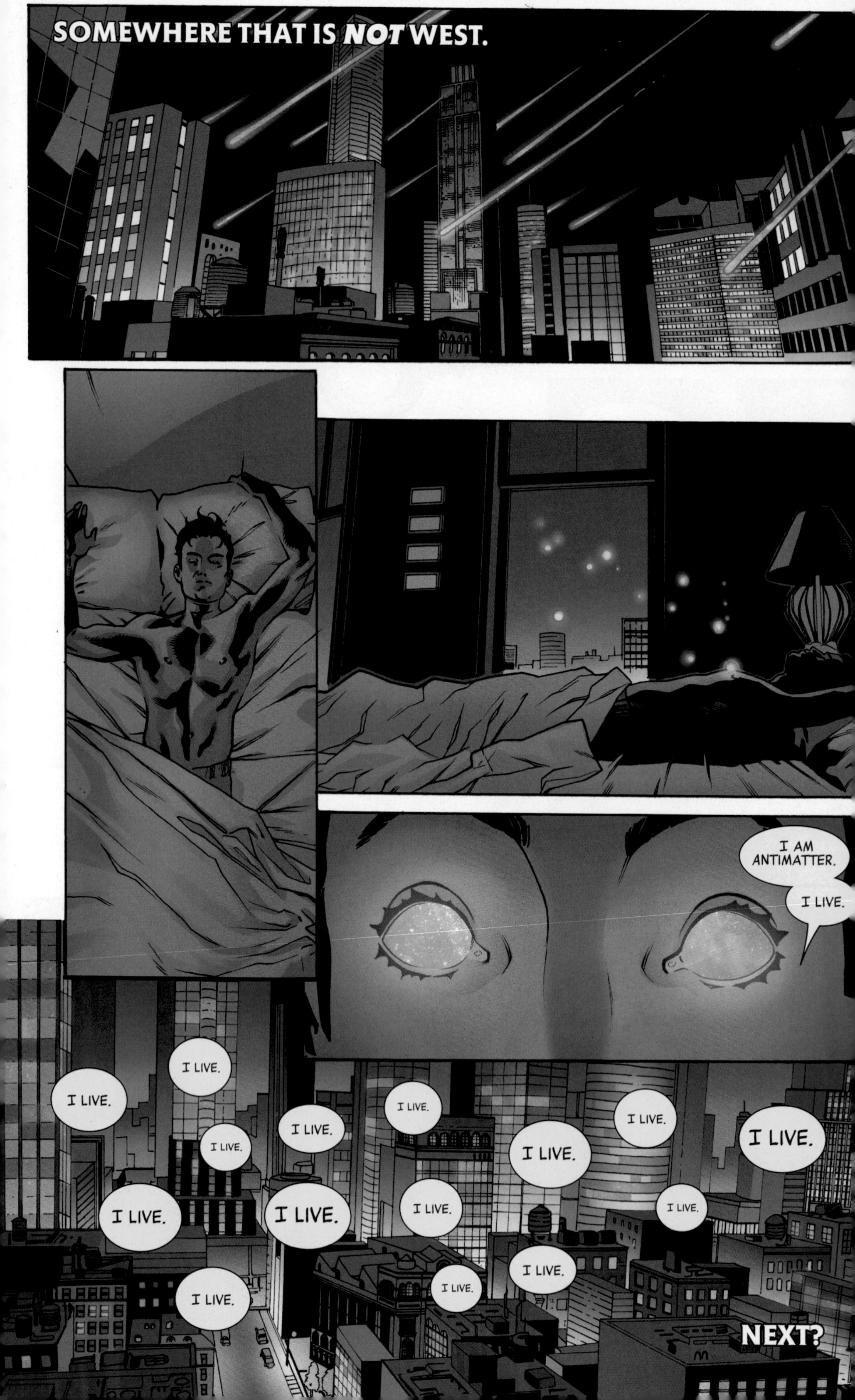
SOMEWHERE THAT IS NOT WEST.
I AM ANTIMATTER.
I LIVE.
I LIVE.
I LIVE.
I LIVE.
I LIVE.
I LIVE.
I LIVE.
I LIVE.
I LIVE.
I LIVE.
I LIVE.
I LIVE.
I LIVE.
I LIVE.
I LIVE.
I LIVE.
I LIVE.
NEXT?

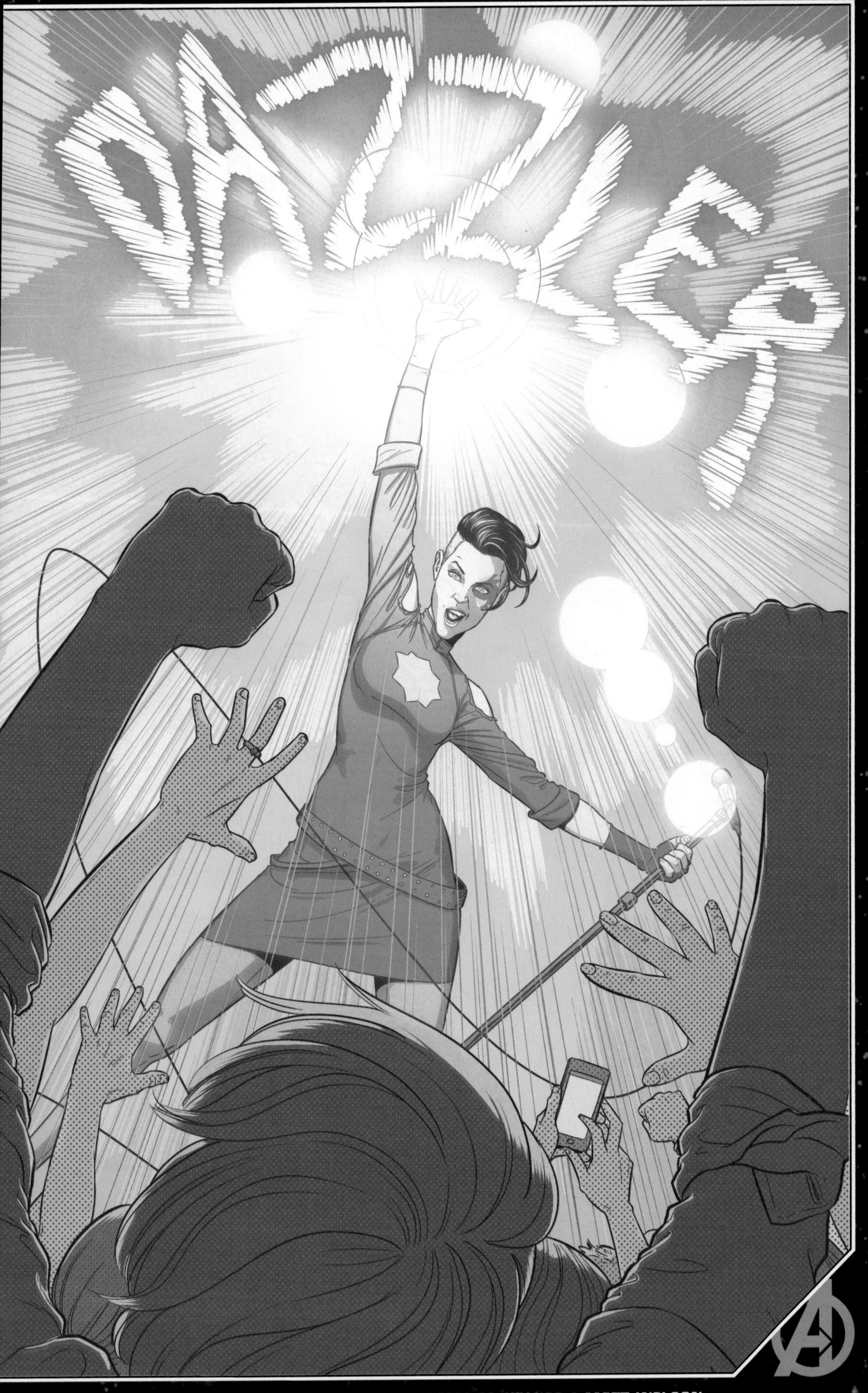
DAZZLER

#3 WOMEN OF POWER VARIANT BY **JAMIE McKELVIE** & **MATT WILSON**

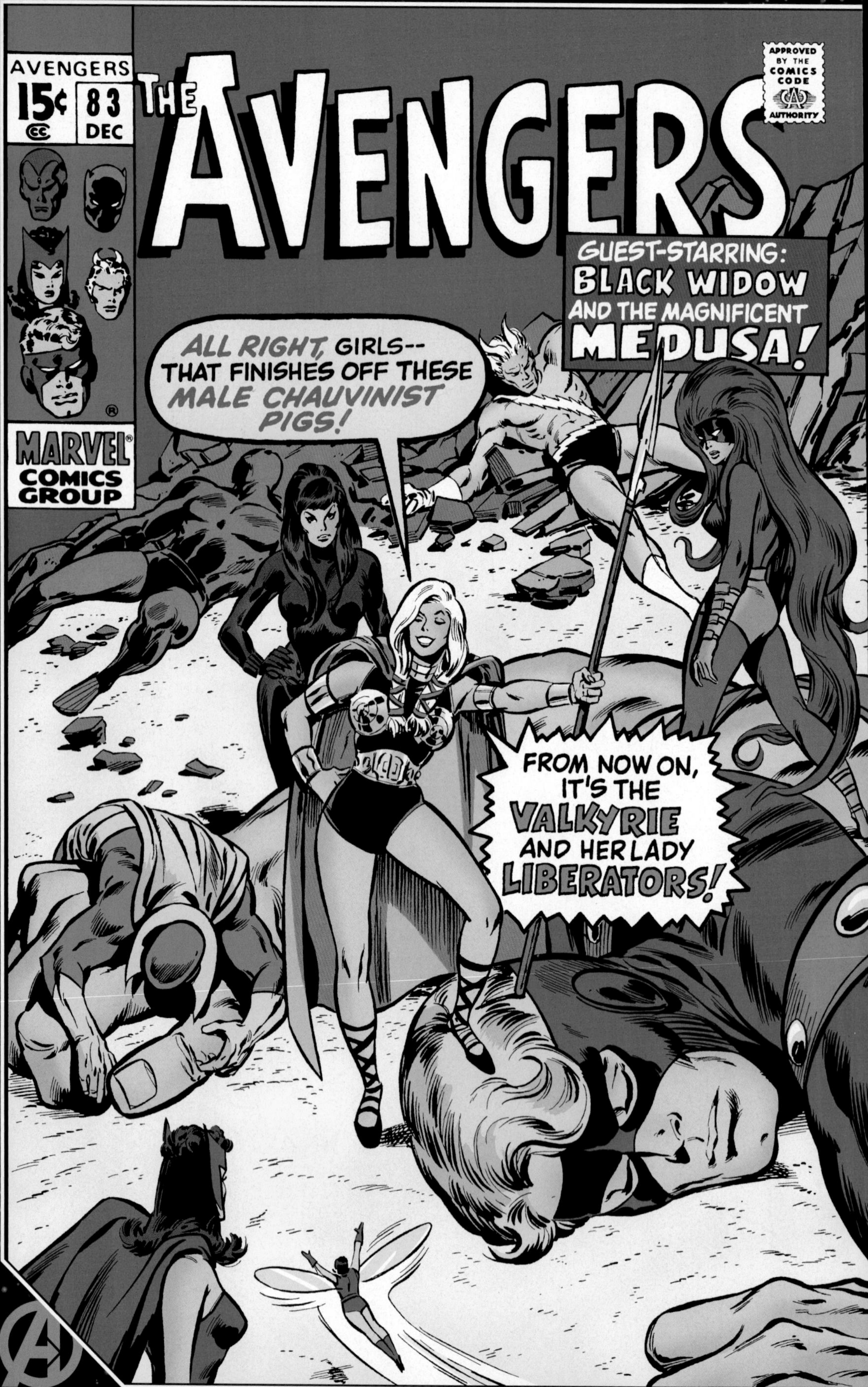
AVENGERS
15¢
CC
83
DEC
THE AVENGERS
APPROVED BY THE COMICS CODE AUTHORITY
MARVEL COMICS GROUP
GUEST-STARRING: BLACK WIDOW AND THE MAGNIFICENT MEDUSA!
ALL RIGHT, GIRLS-- THAT FINISHES OFF THESE MALE CHAUVINIST PIGS!
FROM NOW ON, IT'S THE VALKYRIE AND HER LADY LIBERATORS!

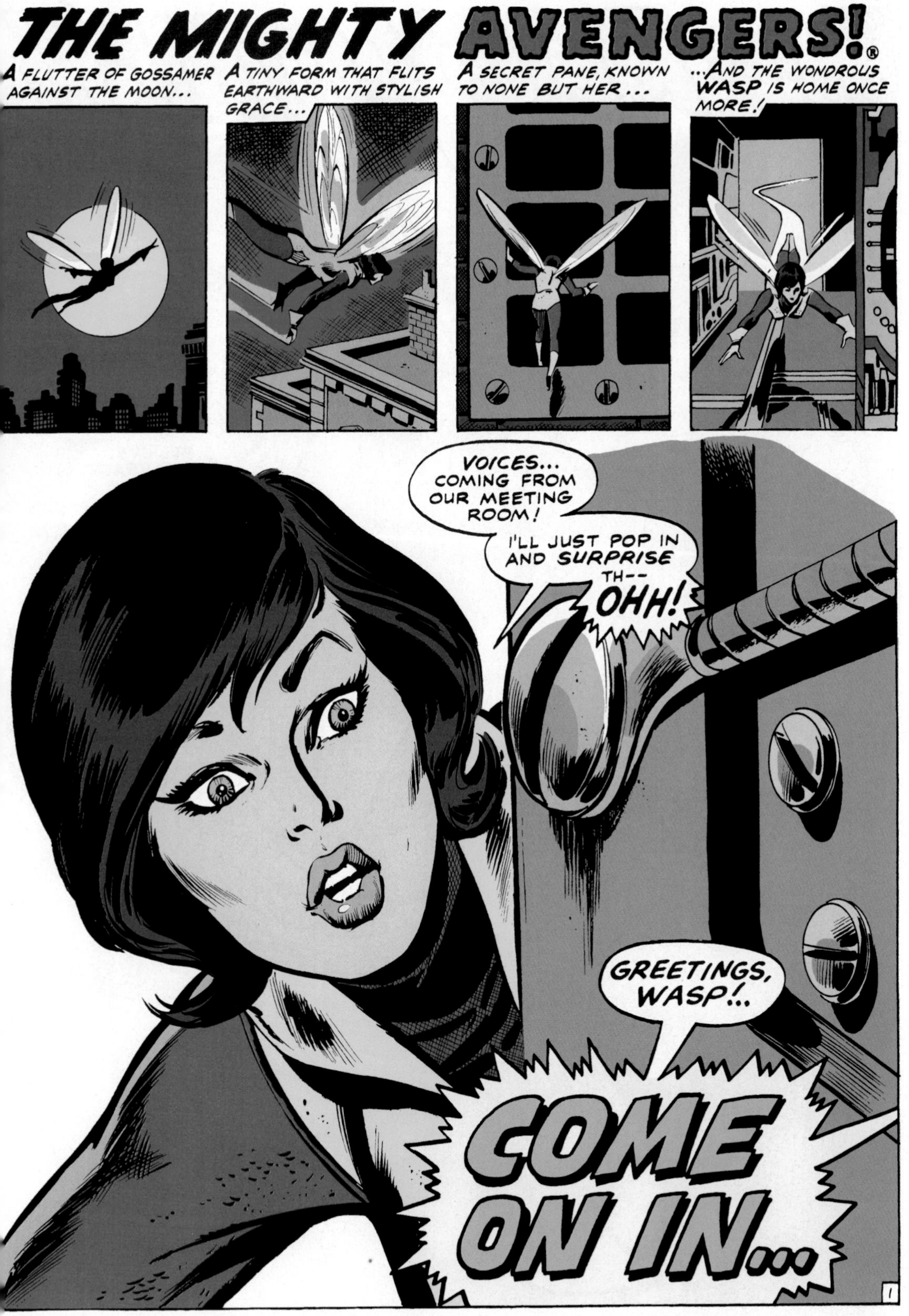
THE MIGHTY AVENGERS!®
A FLUTTER OF GOSSAMER AGAINST THE MOON...
A TINY FORM THAT FLITS EARTHWARD WITH STYLISH GRACE...
A SECRET PANE, KNOWN TO NONE BUT HER...
...AND THE WONDROUS WASP IS HOME ONCE MORE!
VOICES... COMING FROM OUR MEETING ROOM!
I'LL JUST POP IN AND SURPRISE TH--
OHH!
GREETINGS, WASP!..
COME ON IN...
1

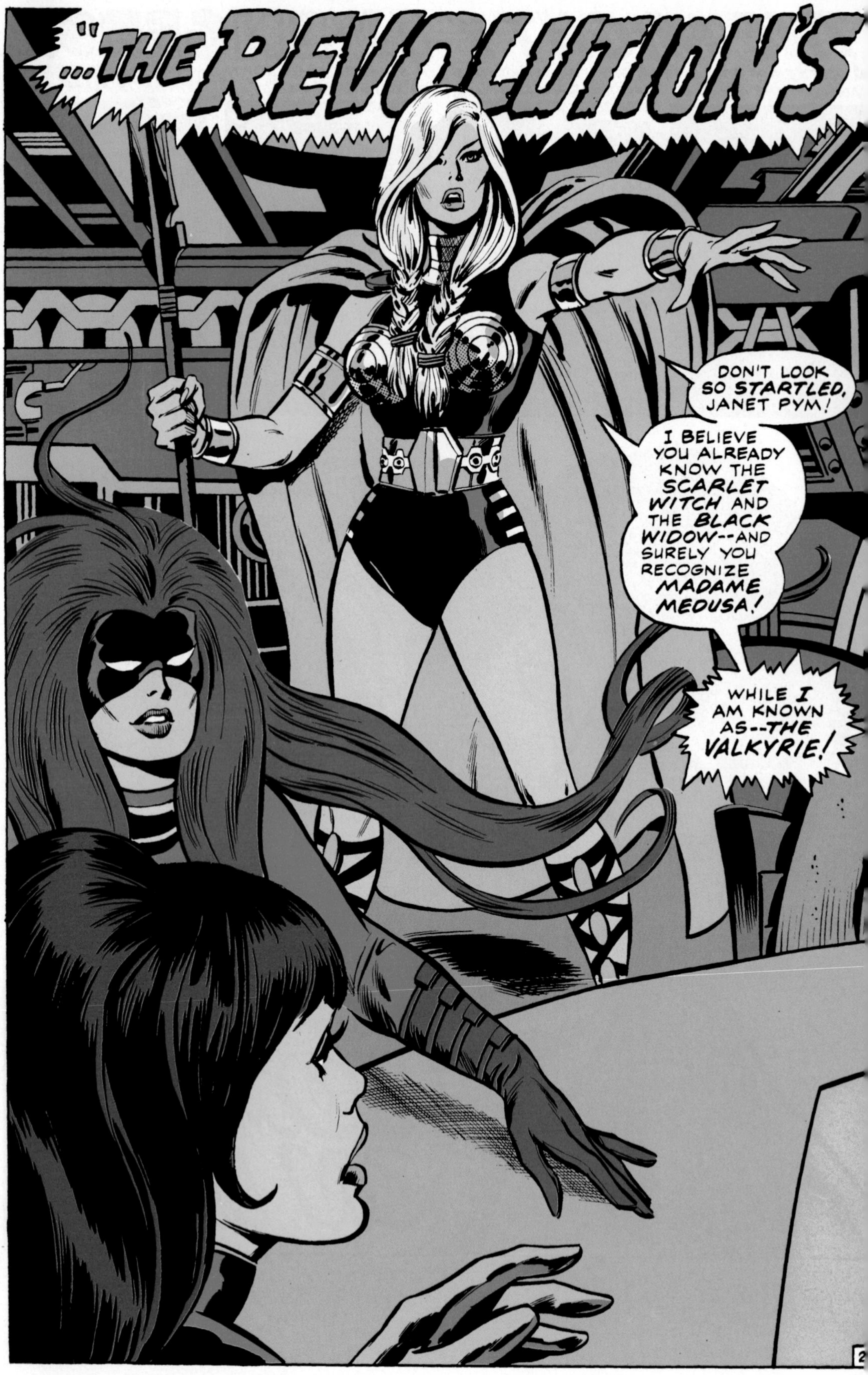

..."THE REVOLUTION'S
DON'T LOOK SO STARTLED, JANET PYM!
I BELIEVE YOU ALREADY KNOW THE SCARLET WITCH AND THE BLACK WIDOW--AND SURELY YOU RECOGNIZE MADAME MEDUSA!
WHILE I AM KNOWN AS--THE VALKYRIE!

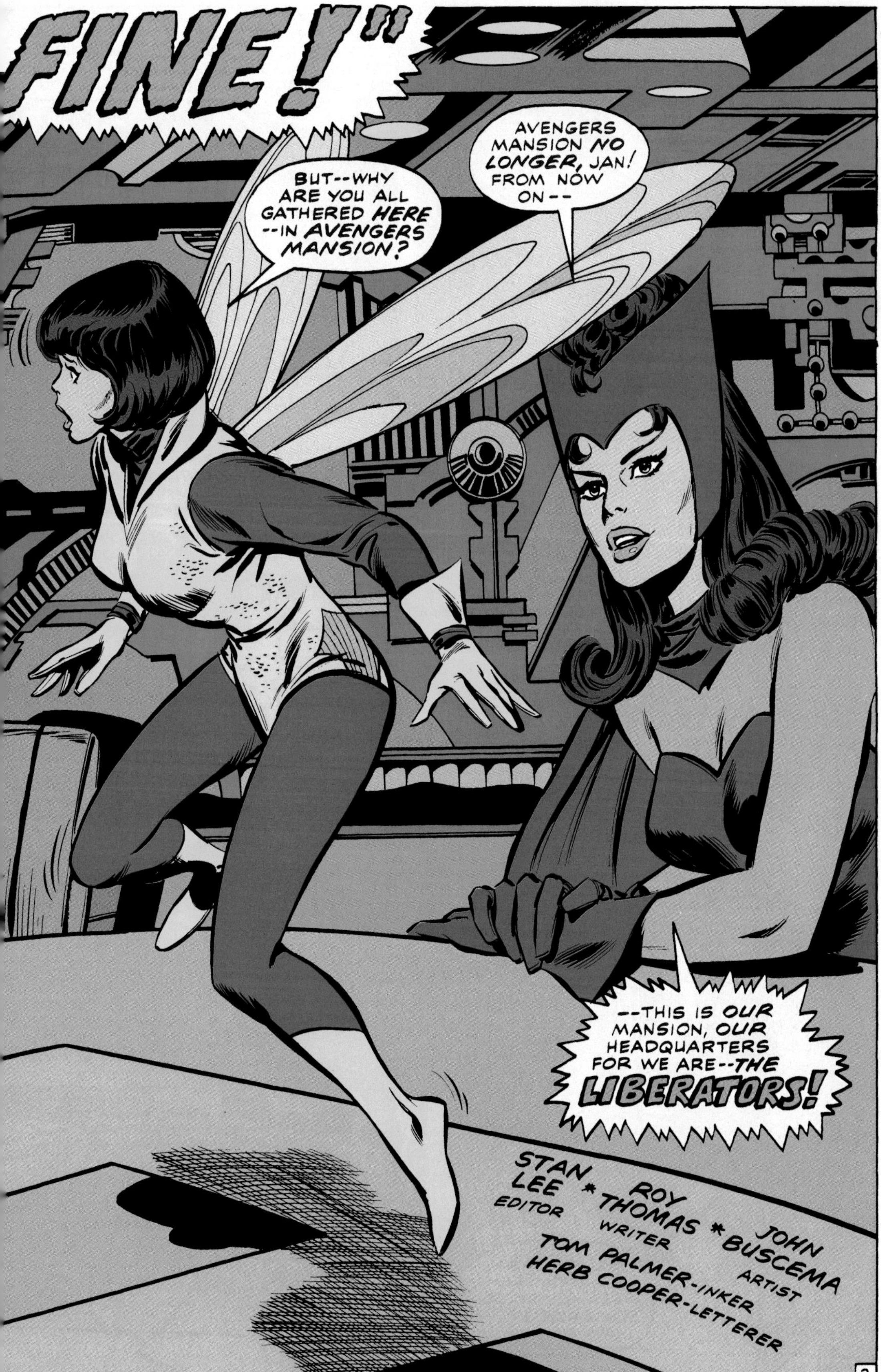
FINE!"
BUT--WHY ARE YOU ALL GATHERED HERE --IN AVENGERS MANSION?
AVENGERS MANSION NO LONGER, JAN! FROM NOW ON--
--THIS IS OUR MANSION, OUR HEADQUARTERS FOR WE ARE--THE LIBERATORS!
STAN LEE EDITOR * ROY THOMAS WRITER * JOHN BUSCEMA ARTIST
TOM PALMER-INKER
HERB COOPER-LETTERER
3

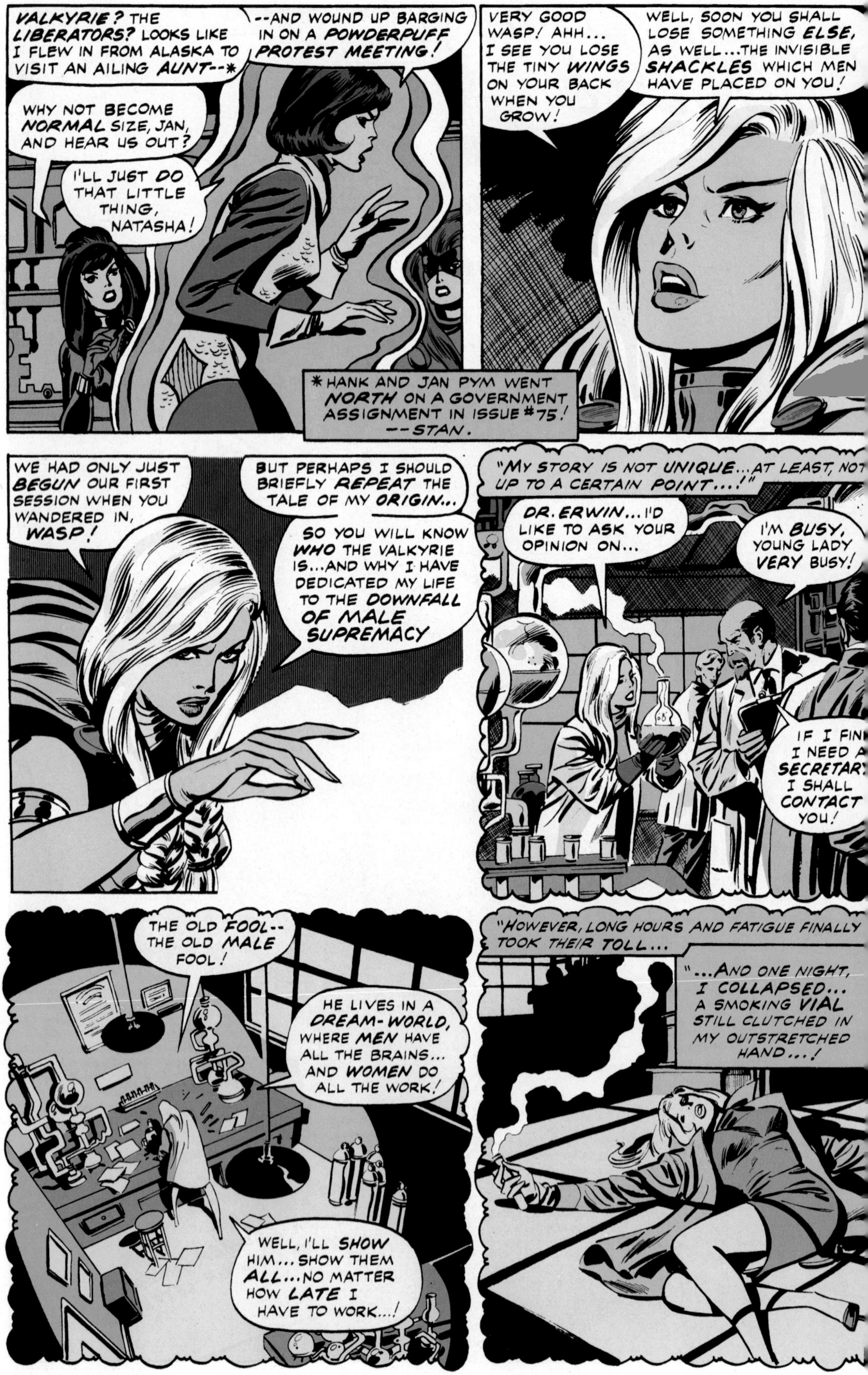
VALKYRIE? THE LIBERATORS? LOOKS LIKE I FLEW IN FROM ALASKA TO VISIT AN AILING AUNT--*
--AND WOUND UP BARGING IN ON A POWDERPUFF PROTEST MEETING!
WHY NOT BECOME NORMAL SIZE, JAN, AND HEAR US OUT?
I'LL JUST DO THAT LITTLE THING, NATASHA!
VERY GOOD WASP! AHH... I SEE YOU LOSE THE TINY WINGS ON YOUR BACK WHEN YOU GROW!
WELL, SOON YOU SHALL LOSE SOMETHING ELSE, AS WELL...THE INVISIBLE SHACKLES WHICH MEN HAVE PLACED ON YOU!
* HANK AND JAN PYM WENT NORTH ON A GOVERNMENT ASSIGNMENT IN ISSUE #75! --STAN.
WE HAD ONLY JUST BEGUN OUR FIRST SESSION WHEN YOU WANDERED IN, WASP!
BUT PERHAPS I SHOULD BRIEFLY REPEAT THE TALE OF MY ORIGIN...
SO YOU WILL KNOW WHO THE VALKYRIE IS...AND WHY I HAVE DEDICATED MY LIFE TO THE DOWNFALL OF MALE SUPREMACY
"MY STORY IS NOT UNIQUE...AT LEAST, NOT UP TO A CERTAIN POINT...!"
DR. ERWIN...I'D LIKE TO ASK YOUR OPINION ON...
I'M BUSY, YOUNG LADY VERY BUSY!
IF I FIN I NEED A SECRETAR I SHALL CONTACT YOU!
THE OLD FOOL-- THE OLD MALE FOOL!
HE LIVES IN A DREAM-WORLD, WHERE MEN HAVE ALL THE BRAINS... AND WOMEN DO ALL THE WORK!
WELL, I'LL SHOW HIM... SHOW THEM ALL...NO MATTER HOW LATE I HAVE TO WORK...!
"HOWEVER, LONG HOURS AND FATIGUE FINALLY TOOK THEIR TOLL...
"...AND ONE NIGHT, I COLLAPSED... A SMOKING VIAL STILL CLUTCHED IN MY OUTSTRETCHED HAND...!

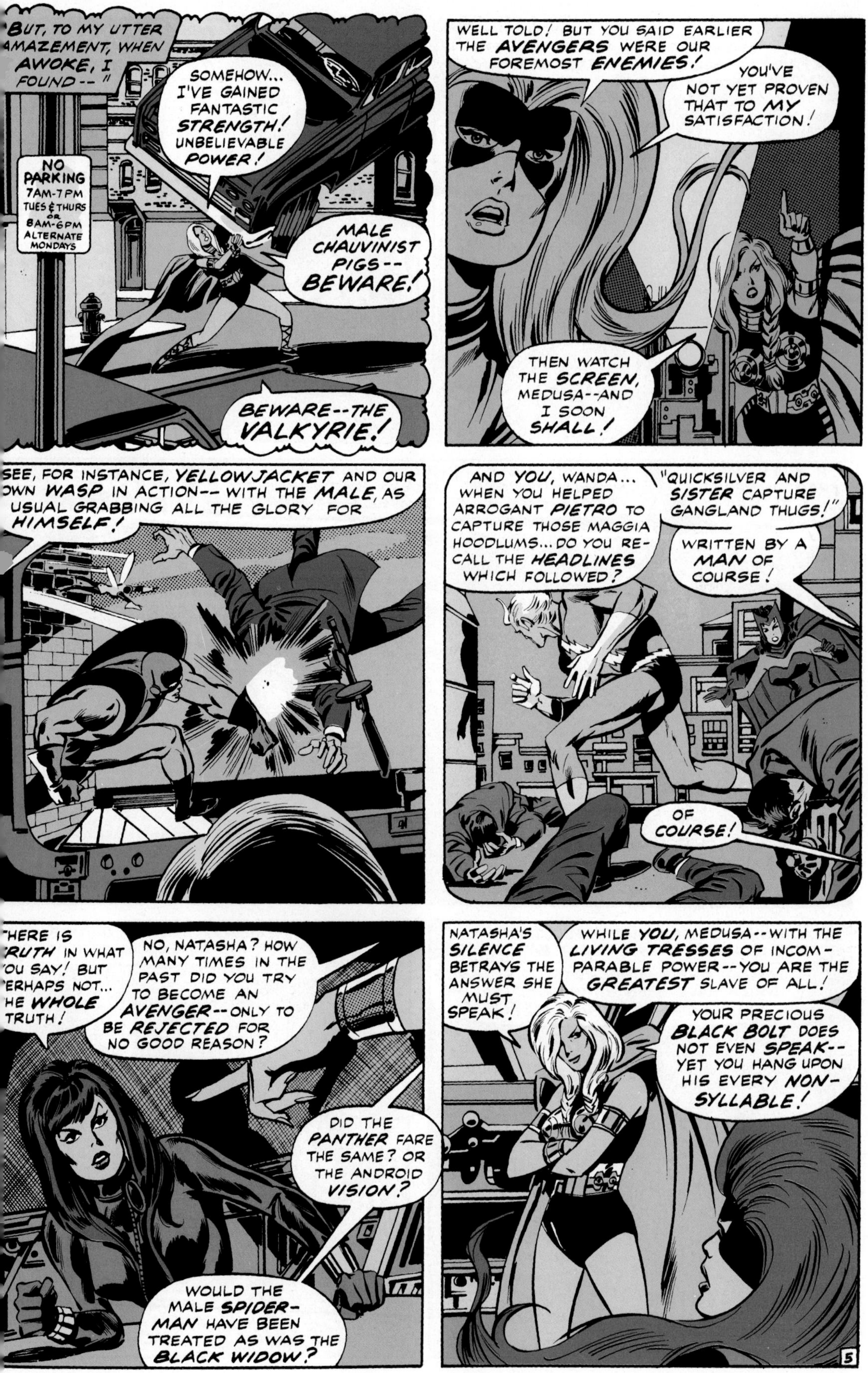
"BUT, TO MY UTTER AMAZEMENT, WHEN I AWOKE, I FOUND--"
SOMEHOW... I'VE GAINED FANTASTIC STRENGTH! UNBELIEVABLE POWER!
NO PARKING 7AM-7PM TUES & THURS OR 8AM-6PM ALTERNATE MONDAYS
MALE CHAUVINIST PIGS--BEWARE!
BEWARE--THE VALKYRIE!
WELL TOLD! BUT YOU SAID EARLIER THE AVENGERS WERE OUR FOREMOST ENEMIES!
YOU'VE NOT YET PROVEN THAT TO MY SATISFACTION!
THEN WATCH THE SCREEN, MEDUSA--AND I SOON SHALL!
SEE, FOR INSTANCE, YELLOWJACKET AND OUR OWN WASP IN ACTION-- WITH THE MALE, AS USUAL GRABBING ALL THE GLORY FOR HIMSELF!
AND YOU, WANDA... WHEN YOU HELPED ARROGANT PIETRO TO CAPTURE THOSE MAGGIA HOODLUMS... DO YOU RECALL THE HEADLINES WHICH FOLLOWED?
"QUICKSILVER AND SISTER CAPTURE GANGLAND THUGS!"
WRITTEN BY A MAN OF COURSE!
OF COURSE!
THERE IS TRUTH IN WHAT YOU SAY! BUT PERHAPS NOT... THE WHOLE TRUTH!
NO, NATASHA? HOW MANY TIMES IN THE PAST DID YOU TRY TO BECOME AN AVENGER--ONLY TO BE REJECTED FOR NO GOOD REASON?
DID THE PANTHER FARE THE SAME? OR THE ANDROID VISION?
WOULD THE MALE SPIDER-MAN HAVE BEEN TREATED AS WAS THE BLACK WIDOW?
NATASHA'S SILENCE BETRAYS THE ANSWER SHE MUST SPEAK!
WHILE YOU, MEDUSA--WITH THE LIVING TRESSES OF INCOMPARABLE POWER--YOU ARE THE GREATEST SLAVE OF ALL!
YOUR PRECIOUS BLACK BOLT DOES NOT EVEN SPEAK--YET YOU HANG UPON HIS EVERY NON-SYLLABLE!
5

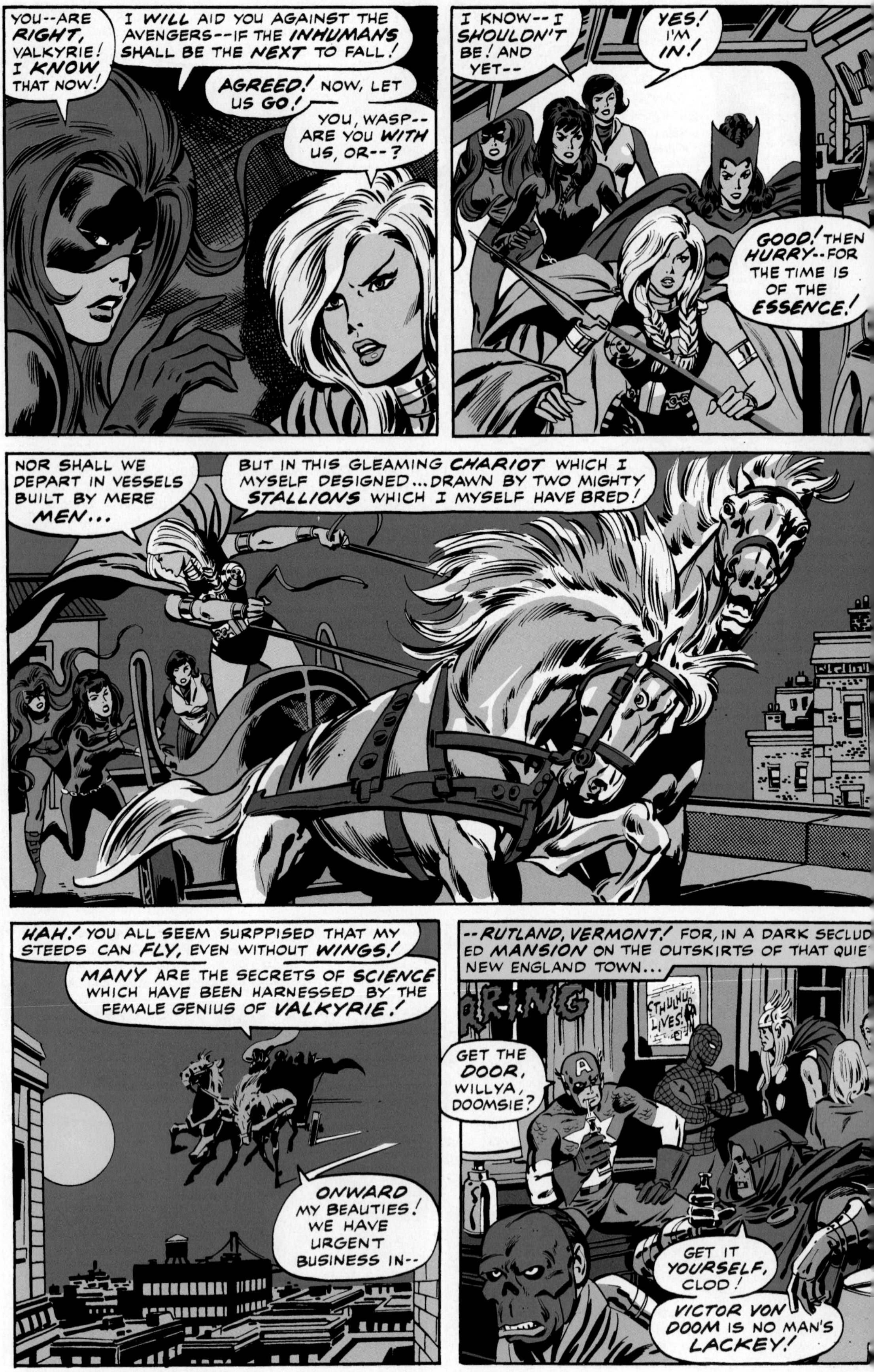
YOU--ARE RIGHT, VALKYRIE! I KNOW THAT NOW!
I WILL AID YOU AGAINST THE AVENGERS--IF THE INHUMANS SHALL BE THE NEXT TO FALL!
AGREED! NOW, LET US GO!
YOU, WASP--ARE YOU WITH US, OR--?
I KNOW--I SHOULDN'T BE! AND YET--
YES! I'M IN!
GOOD! THEN HURRY--FOR THE TIME IS OF THE ESSENCE!
NOR SHALL WE DEPART IN VESSELS BUILT BY MERE MEN...
BUT IN THIS GLEAMING CHARIOT WHICH I MYSELF DESIGNED...DRAWN BY TWO MIGHTY STALLIONS WHICH I MYSELF HAVE BRED!
HAH! YOU ALL SEEM SURPRISED THAT MY STEEDS CAN FLY, EVEN WITHOUT WINGS!
MANY ARE THE SECRETS OF SCIENCE WHICH HAVE BEEN HARNESSED BY THE FEMALE GENIUS OF VALKYRIE!
ONWARD MY BEAUTIES! WE HAVE URGENT BUSINESS IN--
--RUTLAND, VERMONT! FOR, IN A DARK SECLUD ED MANSION ON THE OUTSKIRTS OF THAT QUIE NEW ENGLAND TOWN...
BRING
GET THE DOOR, WILLYA, DOOMSIE?
GET IT YOURSELF, CLOD!
VICTOR VON DOOM IS NO MAN'S LACKEY!

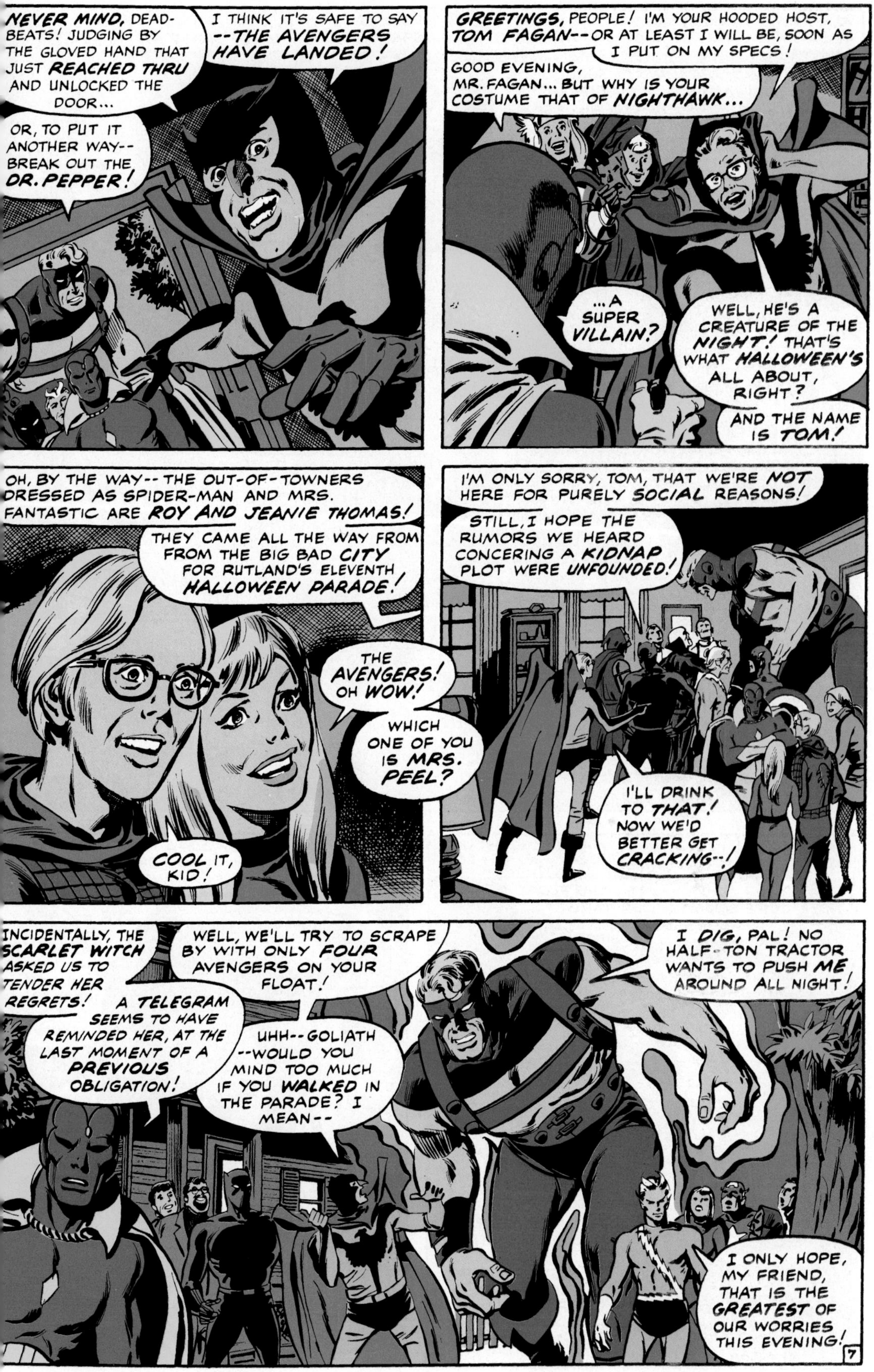
NEVER MIND, DEAD-BEATS! JUDGING BY THE GLOVED HAND THAT JUST REACHED THRU AND UNLOCKED THE DOOR...
I THINK IT'S SAFE TO SAY --THE AVENGERS HAVE LANDED!
OR, TO PUT IT ANOTHER WAY-- BREAK OUT THE DR. PEPPER!
GREETINGS, PEOPLE! I'M YOUR HOODED HOST, TOM FAGAN--OR AT LEAST I WILL BE, SOON AS I PUT ON MY SPECS!
GOOD EVENING, MR. FAGAN... BUT WHY IS YOUR COSTUME THAT OF NIGHTHAWK...
...A SUPER VILLAIN?
WELL, HE'S A CREATURE OF THE NIGHT! THAT'S WHAT HALLOWEEN'S ALL ABOUT, RIGHT?
AND THE NAME IS TOM!
OH, BY THE WAY--THE OUT-OF-TOWNERS DRESSED AS SPIDER-MAN AND MRS. FANTASTIC ARE ROY AND JEANIE THOMAS!
THEY CAME ALL THE WAY FROM FROM THE BIG BAD CITY FOR RUTLAND'S ELEVENTH HALLOWEEN PARADE!
THE AVENGERS! OH WOW!
WHICH ONE OF YOU IS MRS. PEEL?
COOL IT, KID!
I'M ONLY SORRY, TOM, THAT WE'RE NOT HERE FOR PURELY SOCIAL REASONS!
STILL, I HOPE THE RUMORS WE HEARD CONCERING A KIDNAP PLOT WERE UNFOUNDED!
I'LL DRINK TO THAT! NOW WE'D BETTER GET CRACKING--!
INCIDENTALLY, THE SCARLET WITCH ASKED US TO TENDER HER REGRETS!
A TELEGRAM SEEMS TO HAVE REMINDED HER, AT THE LAST MOMENT OF A PREVIOUS OBLIGATION!
WELL, WE'LL TRY TO SCRAPE BY WITH ONLY FOUR AVENGERS ON YOUR FLOAT!
UHH--GOLIATH --WOULD YOU MIND TOO MUCH IF YOU WALKED IN THE PARADE? I MEAN--
I DIG, PAL! NO HALF-TON TRACTOR WANTS TO PUSH ME AROUND ALL NIGHT!
I ONLY HOPE, MY FRIEND, THAT IS THE GREATEST OF OUR WORRIES THIS EVENING!
7

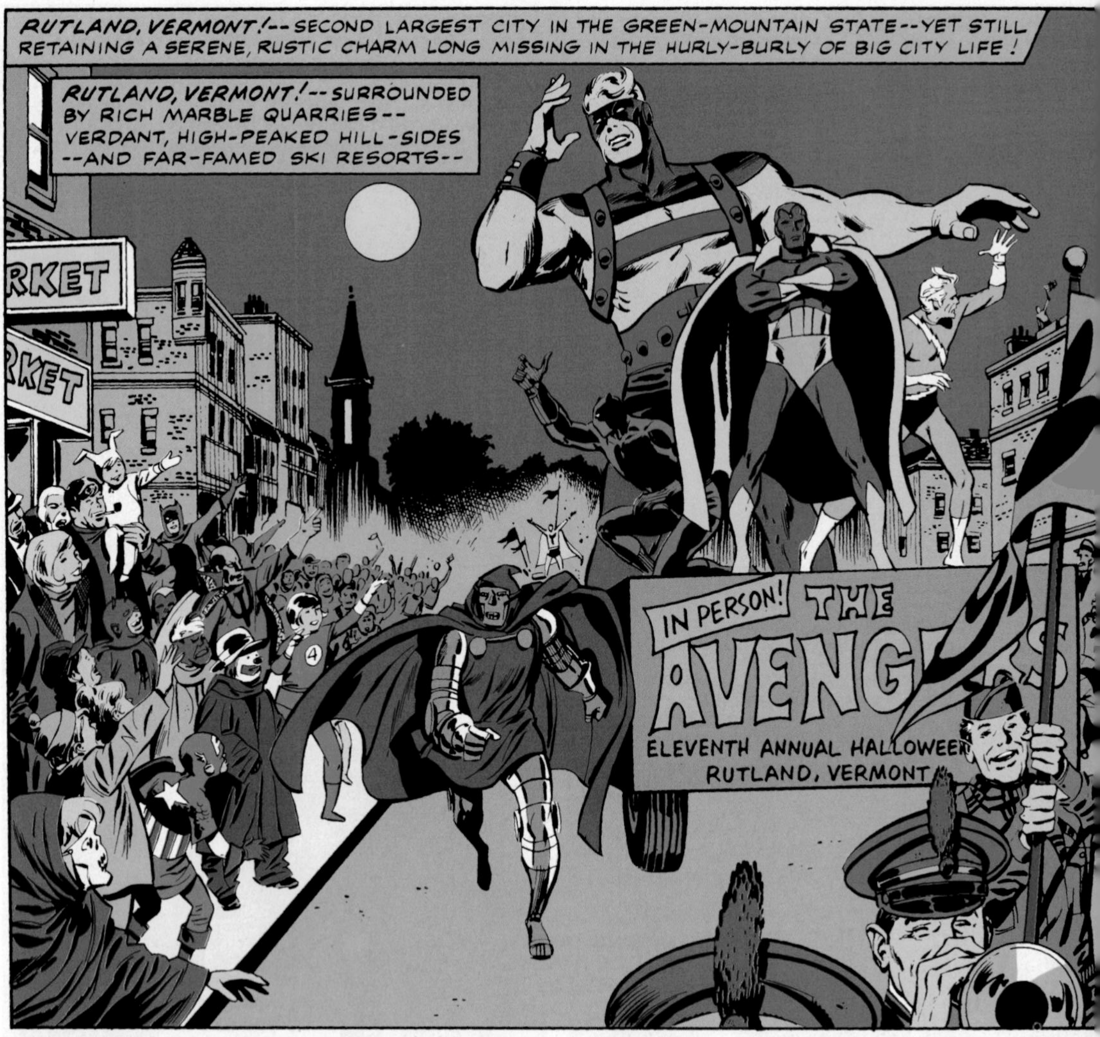
RUTLAND, VERMONT!--SECOND LARGEST CITY IN THE GREEN-MOUNTAIN STATE--YET STILL RETAINING A SERENE, RUSTIC CHARM LONG MISSING IN THE HURLY-BURLY OF BIG CITY LIFE!
RUTLAND, VERMONT!--SURROUNDED BY RICH MARBLE QUARRIES--VERDANT, HIGH-PEAKED HILL-SIDES--AND FAR-FAMED SKI RESORTS--
IN PERSON! THE AVENGERS
ELEVENTH ANNUAL HALLOWEEN
RUTLAND, VERMONT

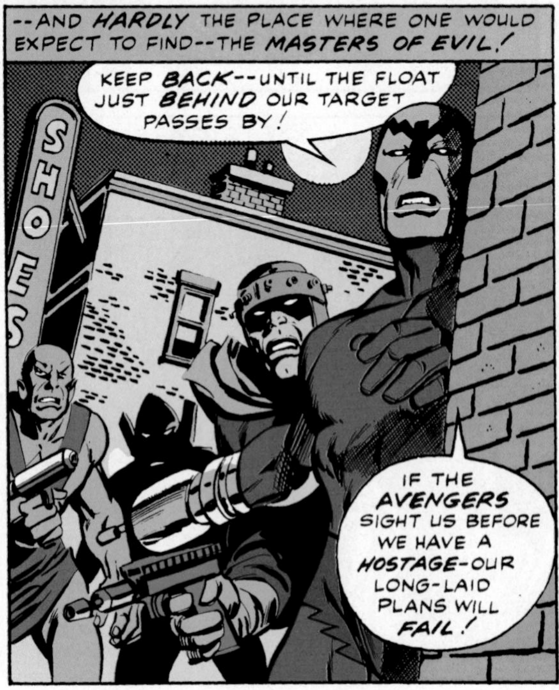
--AND HARDLY THE PLACE WHERE ONE WOULD EXPECT TO FIND--THE MASTERS OF EVIL!
KEEP BACK--UNTIL THE FLOAT JUST BEHIND OUR TARGET PASSES BY!
SHOES
IF THE AVENGERS SIGHT US BEFORE WE HAVE A HOSTAGE--OUR LONG-LAID PLANS WILL FAIL!

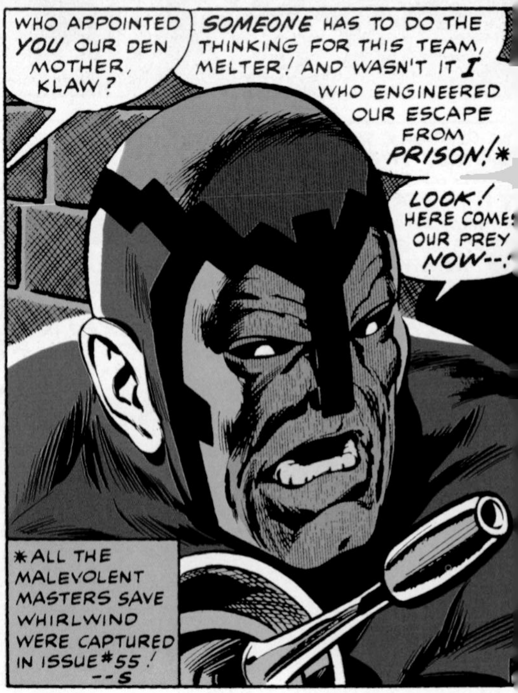
WHO APPOINTED YOU OUR DEN MOTHER, KLAW?
SOMEONE HAS TO DO THE THINKING FOR THIS TEAM, MELTER! AND WASN'T IT I WHO ENGINEERED OUR ESCAPE FROM PRISON!*
LOOK! HERE COMES OUR PREY NOW--
*ALL THE MALEVOLENT MASTERS SAVE WHIRLWIND WERE CAPTURED IN ISSUE #55! --S

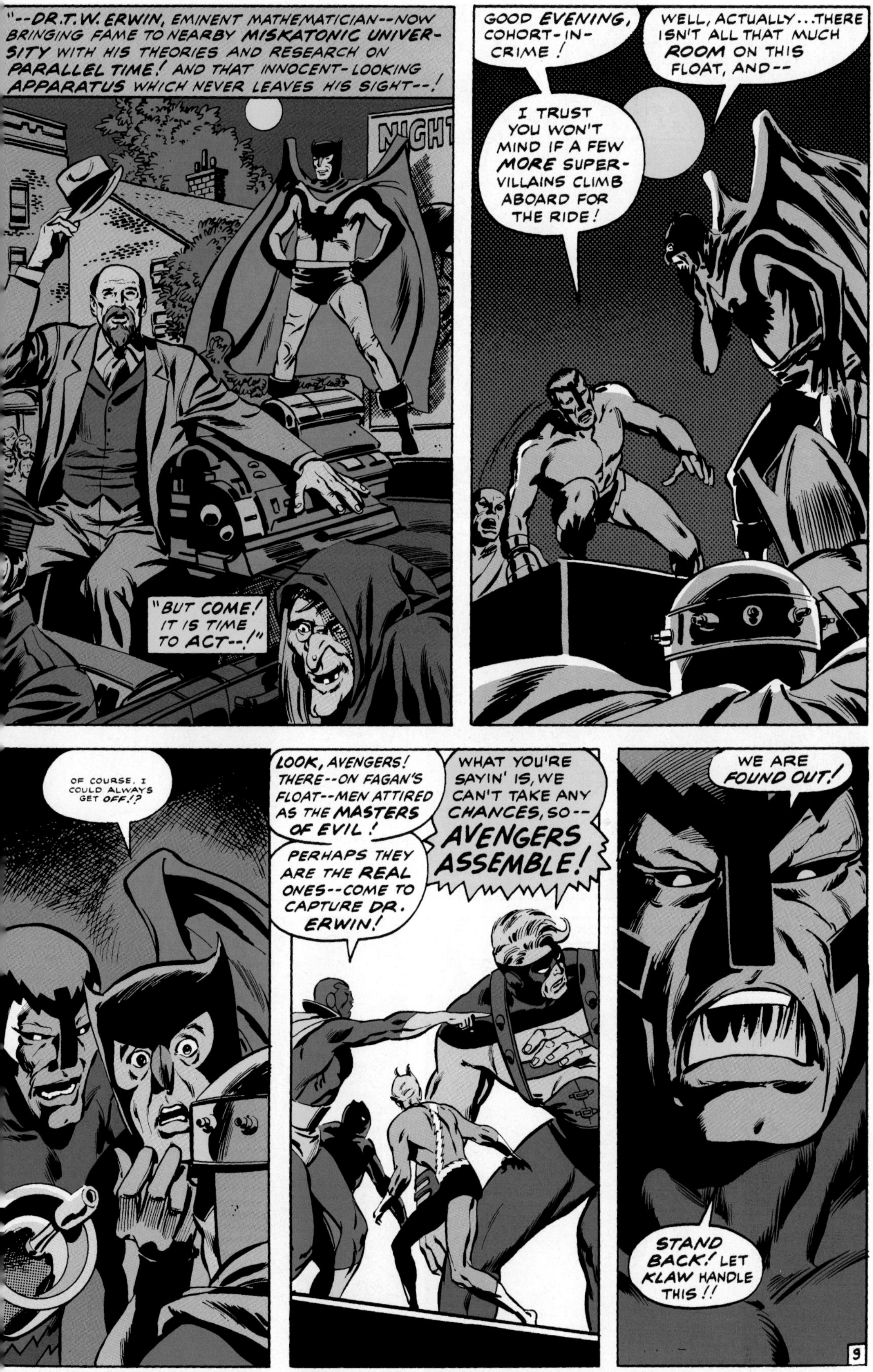
"--DR. T.W. ERWIN, EMINENT MATHEMATICIAN--NOW BRINGING FAME TO NEARBY MISKATONIC UNIVERSITY WITH HIS THEORIES AND RESEARCH ON PARALLEL TIME! AND THAT INNOCENT-LOOKING APPARATUS WHICH NEVER LEAVES HIS SIGHT--!
NIGHT
"BUT COME! IT IS TIME TO ACT--!"
GOOD EVENING, COHORT-IN-CRIME!
I TRUST YOU WON'T MIND IF A FEW MORE SUPER-VILLAINS CLIMB ABOARD FOR THE RIDE!
WELL, ACTUALLY...THERE ISN'T ALL THAT MUCH ROOM ON THIS FLOAT, AND--
OF COURSE, I COULD ALWAYS GET OFF!?
LOOK, AVENGERS! THERE--ON FAGAN'S FLOAT--MEN ATTIRED AS THE MASTERS OF EVIL!
PERHAPS THEY ARE THE REAL ONES--COME TO CAPTURE DR. ERWIN!
WHAT YOU'RE SAYIN' IS, WE CAN'T TAKE ANY CHANCES, SO--
AVENGERS ASSEMBLE!
WE ARE FOUND OUT!
STAND BACK! LET KLAW HANDLE THIS!!
9

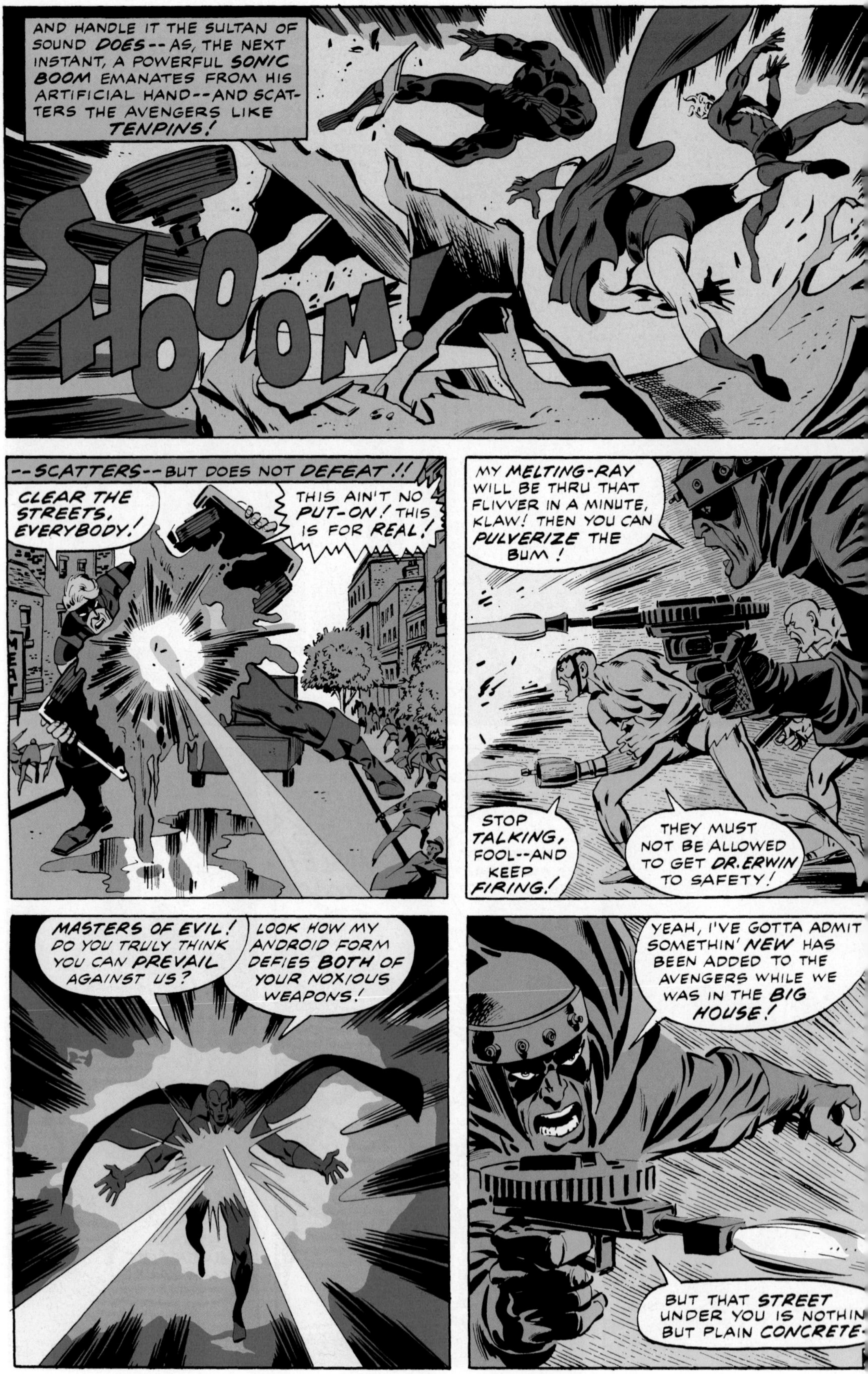

AND HANDLE IT THE SULTAN OF SOUND DOES--AS, THE NEXT INSTANT, A POWERFUL SONIC BOOM EMANATES FROM HIS ARTIFICIAL HAND--AND SCATTERS THE AVENGERS LIKE TENPINS!
SHOOOM!
--SCATTERS--BUT DOES NOT DEFEAT!!
CLEAR THE STREETS, EVERYBODY!
THIS AIN'T NO PUT-ON! THIS IS FOR REAL!
MY MELTING-RAY WILL BE THRU THAT FLIVVER IN A MINUTE, KLAW! THEN YOU CAN PULVERIZE THE BUM!
STOP TALKING, FOOL--AND KEEP FIRING!
THEY MUST NOT BE ALLOWED TO GET DR. ERWIN TO SAFETY!
MASTERS OF EVIL! DO YOU TRULY THINK YOU CAN PREVAIL AGAINST US?
LOOK HOW MY ANDROID FORM DEFIES BOTH OF YOUR NOXIOUS WEAPONS!
YEAH, I'VE GOTTA ADMIT SOMETHIN' NEW HAS BEEN ADDED TO THE AVENGERS WHILE WE WAS IN THE BIG HOUSE!
BUT THAT STREET UNDER YOU IS NOTHIN BUT PLAIN CONCRETE-

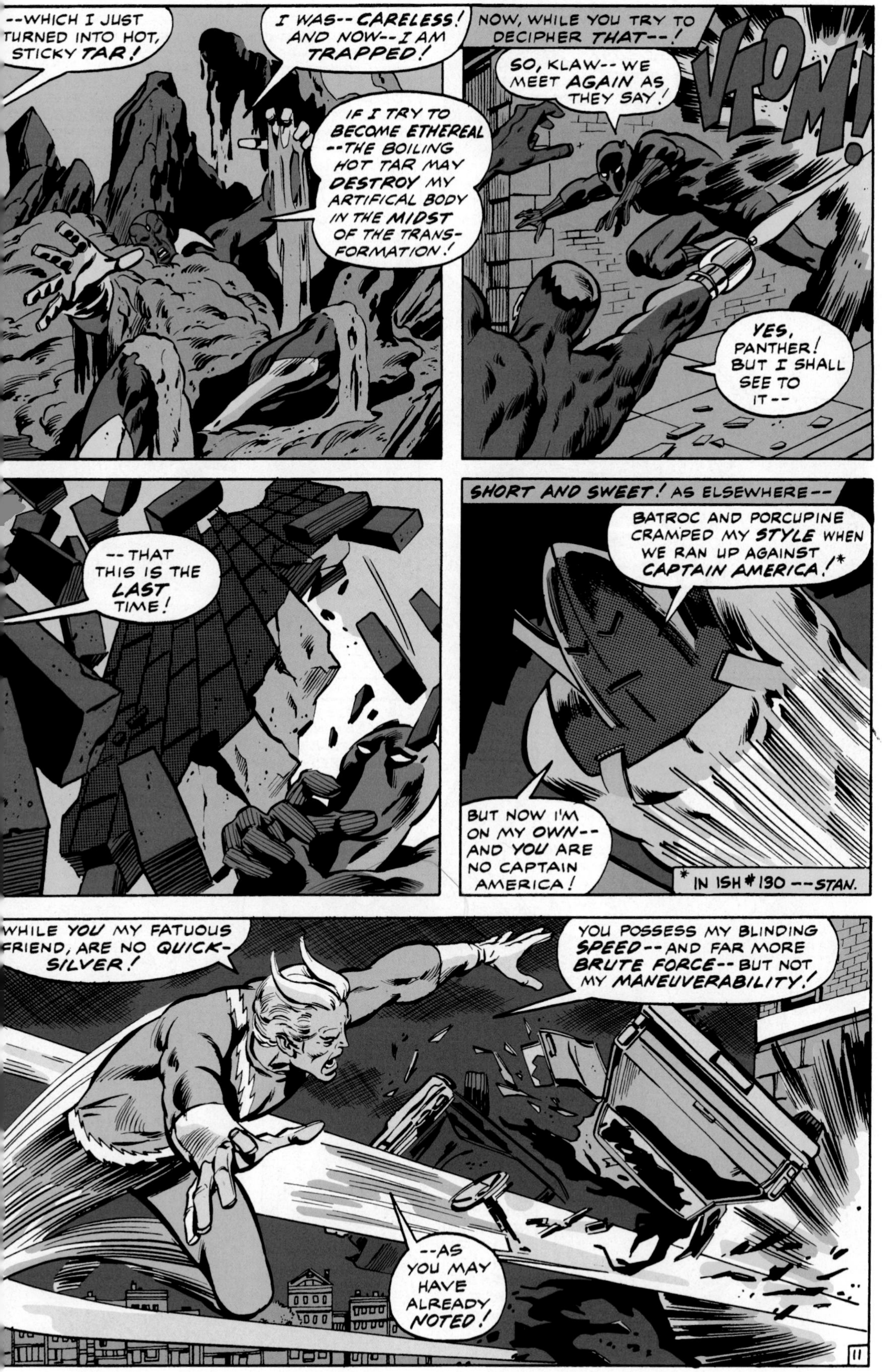
--WHICH I JUST TURNED INTO HOT, STICKY TAR!
I WAS--CARELESS! AND NOW--I AM TRAPPED!
IF I TRY TO BECOME ETHEREAL --THE BOILING HOT TAR MAY DESTROY MY ARTIFICAL BODY IN THE MIDST OF THE TRANS-FORMATION!
NOW, WHILE YOU TRY TO DECIPHER THAT--!
SO, KLAW--WE MEET AGAIN AS THEY SAY!
VTOM!
YES, PANTHER! BUT I SHALL SEE TO IT--
--THAT THIS IS THE LAST TIME!
SHORT AND SWEET! AS ELSEWHERE--
BATROC AND PORCUPINE CRAMPED MY STYLE WHEN WE RAN UP AGAINST CAPTAIN AMERICA!*
BUT NOW I'M ON MY OWN--AND YOU ARE NO CAPTAIN AMERICA!
* IN ISH #130 --STAN.
WHILE YOU MY FATUOUS FRIEND, ARE NO QUICK-SILVER!
YOU POSSESS MY BLINDING SPEED--AND FAR MORE BRUTE FORCE--BUT NOT MY MANEUVERABILITY!
--AS YOU MAY HAVE ALREADY NOTED!

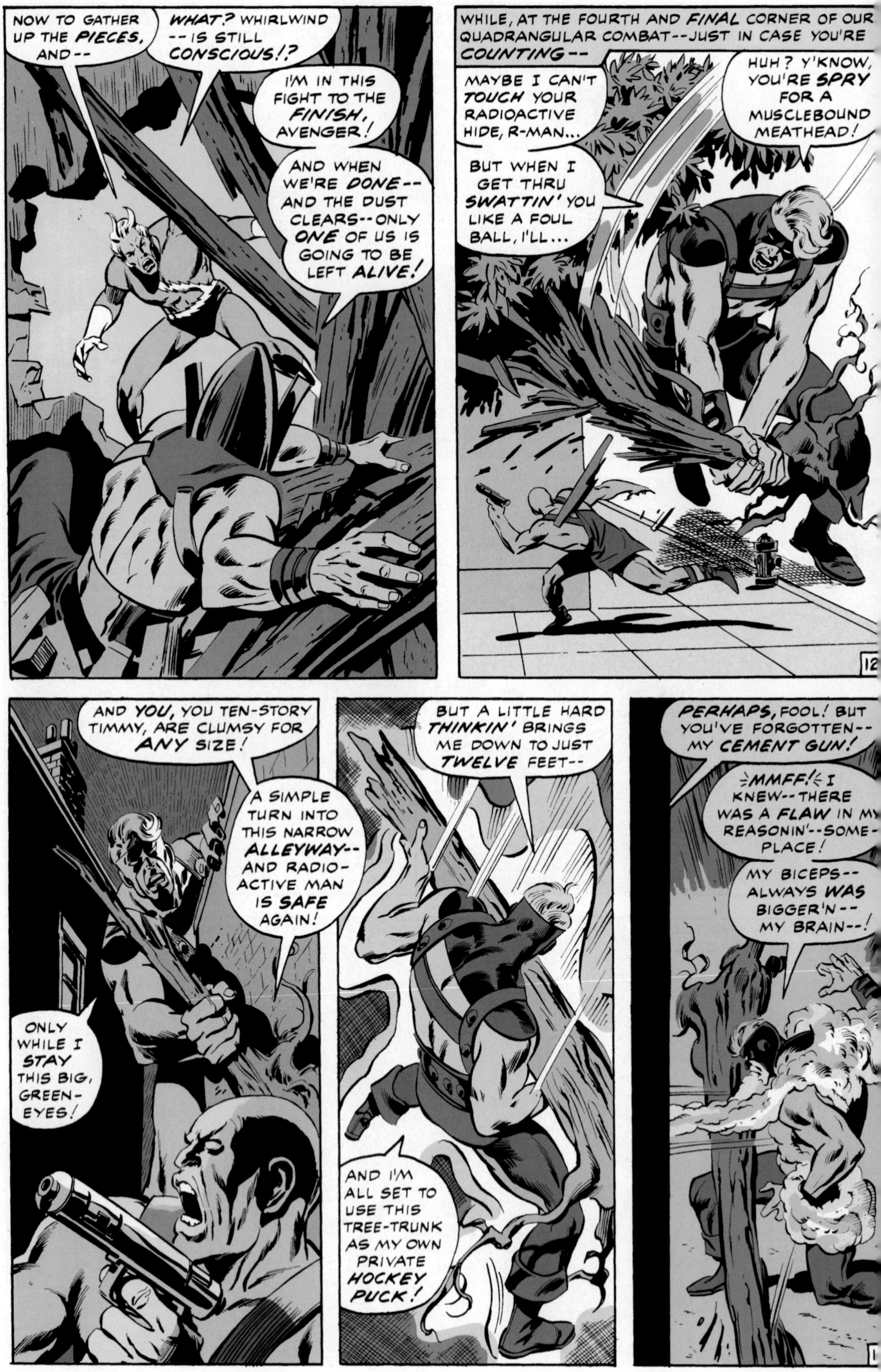
NOW TO GATHER UP THE PIECES, AND--
WHAT? WHIRLWIND --IS STILL CONSCIOUS!?
I'M IN THIS FIGHT TO THE FINISH, AVENGER!
AND WHEN WE'RE DONE-- AND THE DUST CLEARS--ONLY ONE OF US IS GOING TO BE LEFT ALIVE!
WHILE, AT THE FOURTH AND FINAL CORNER OF OUR QUADRANGULAR COMBAT--JUST IN CASE YOU'RE COUNTING--
MAYBE I CAN'T TOUCH YOUR RADIOACTIVE HIDE, R-MAN...
BUT WHEN I GET THRU SWATTIN' YOU LIKE A FOUL BALL, I'LL...
HUH? Y'KNOW, YOU'RE SPRY FOR A MUSCLEBOUND MEATHEAD!
12
AND YOU, YOU TEN-STORY TIMMY, ARE CLUMSY FOR ANY SIZE!
A SIMPLE TURN INTO THIS NARROW ALLEYWAY-- AND RADIO-ACTIVE MAN IS SAFE AGAIN!
ONLY WHILE I STAY THIS BIG, GREEN-EYES!
BUT A LITTLE HARD THINKIN' BRINGS ME DOWN TO JUST TWELVE FEET--
AND I'M ALL SET TO USE THIS TREE-TRUNK AS MY OWN PRIVATE HOCKEY PUCK!
PERHAPS, FOOL! BUT YOU'VE FORGOTTEN-- MY CEMENT GUN!
MMFF! I KNEW--THERE WAS A FLAW IN MY REASONIN'--SOME-PLACE!
MY BICEPS-- ALWAYS WAS BIGGER'N-- MY BRAIN--!

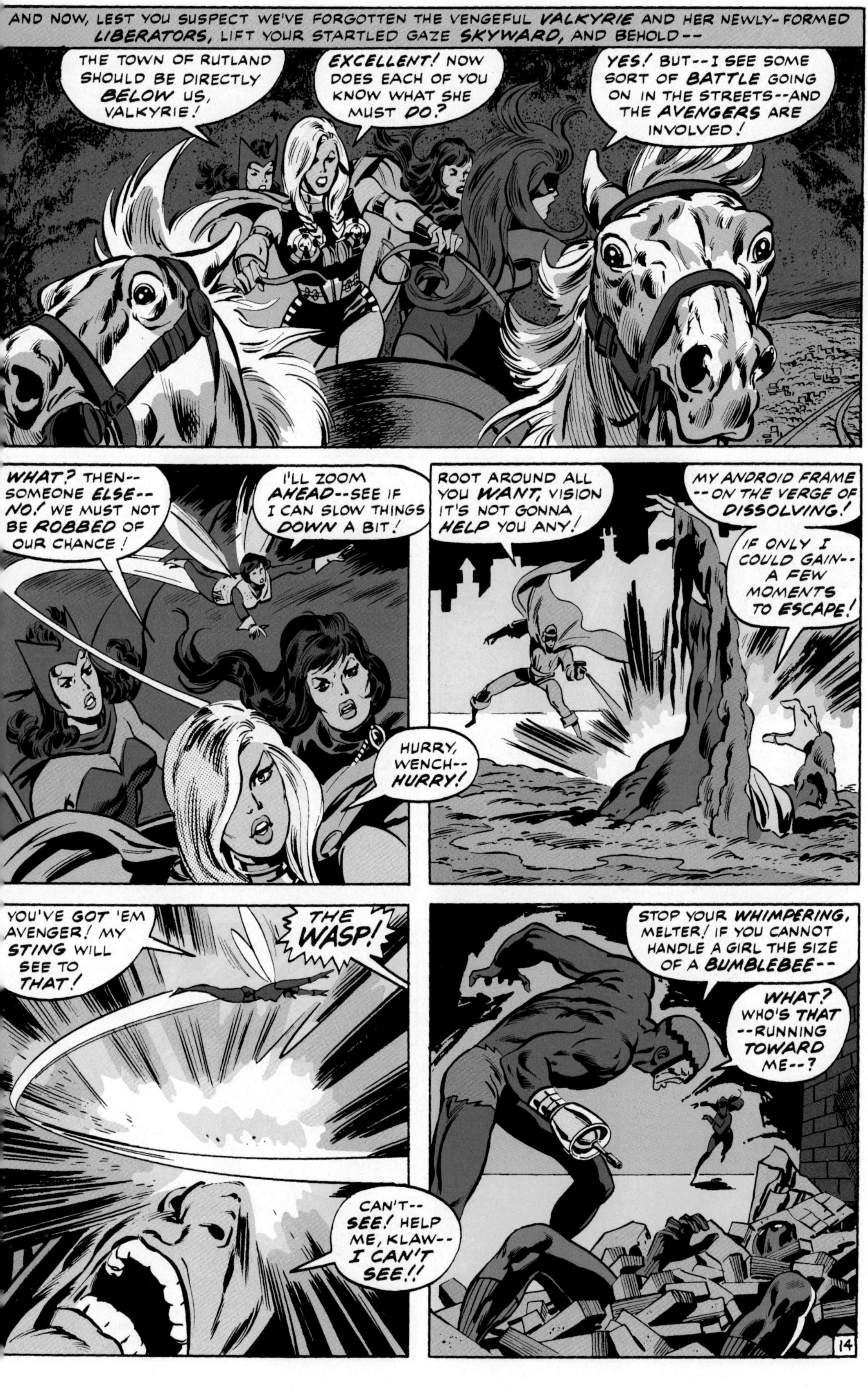

AND NOW, LEST YOU SUSPECT WE'VE FORGOTTEN THE VENGEFUL VALKYRIE AND HER NEWLY-FORMED LIBERATORS, LIFT YOUR STARTLED GAZE SKYWARD, AND BEHOLD--
THE TOWN OF RUTLAND SHOULD BE DIRECTLY BELOW US, VALKYRIE!
EXCELLENT! NOW DOES EACH OF YOU KNOW WHAT SHE MUST DO?
YES! BUT--I SEE SOME SORT OF BATTLE GOING ON IN THE STREETS--AND THE AVENGERS ARE INVOLVED!
WHAT? THEN-- SOMEONE ELSE-- NO! WE MUST NOT BE ROBBED OF OUR CHANCE!
I'LL ZOOM AHEAD--SEE IF I CAN SLOW THINGS DOWN A BIT!
HURRY, WENCH-- HURRY!
ROOT AROUND ALL YOU WANT, VISION IT'S NOT GONNA HELP YOU ANY!
MY ANDROID FRAME --ON THE VERGE OF DISSOLVING!
IF ONLY I COULD GAIN-- A FEW MOMENTS TO ESCAPE!
YOU'VE GOT 'EM AVENGER! MY STING WILL SEE TO THAT!
THE WASP!
CAN'T-- SEE! HELP ME, KLAW-- I CAN'T SEE!!
STOP YOUR WHIMPERING, MELTER! IF YOU CANNOT HANDLE A GIRL THE SIZE OF A BUMBLEBEE--
WHAT? WHO'S THAT --RUNNING TOWARD ME--?

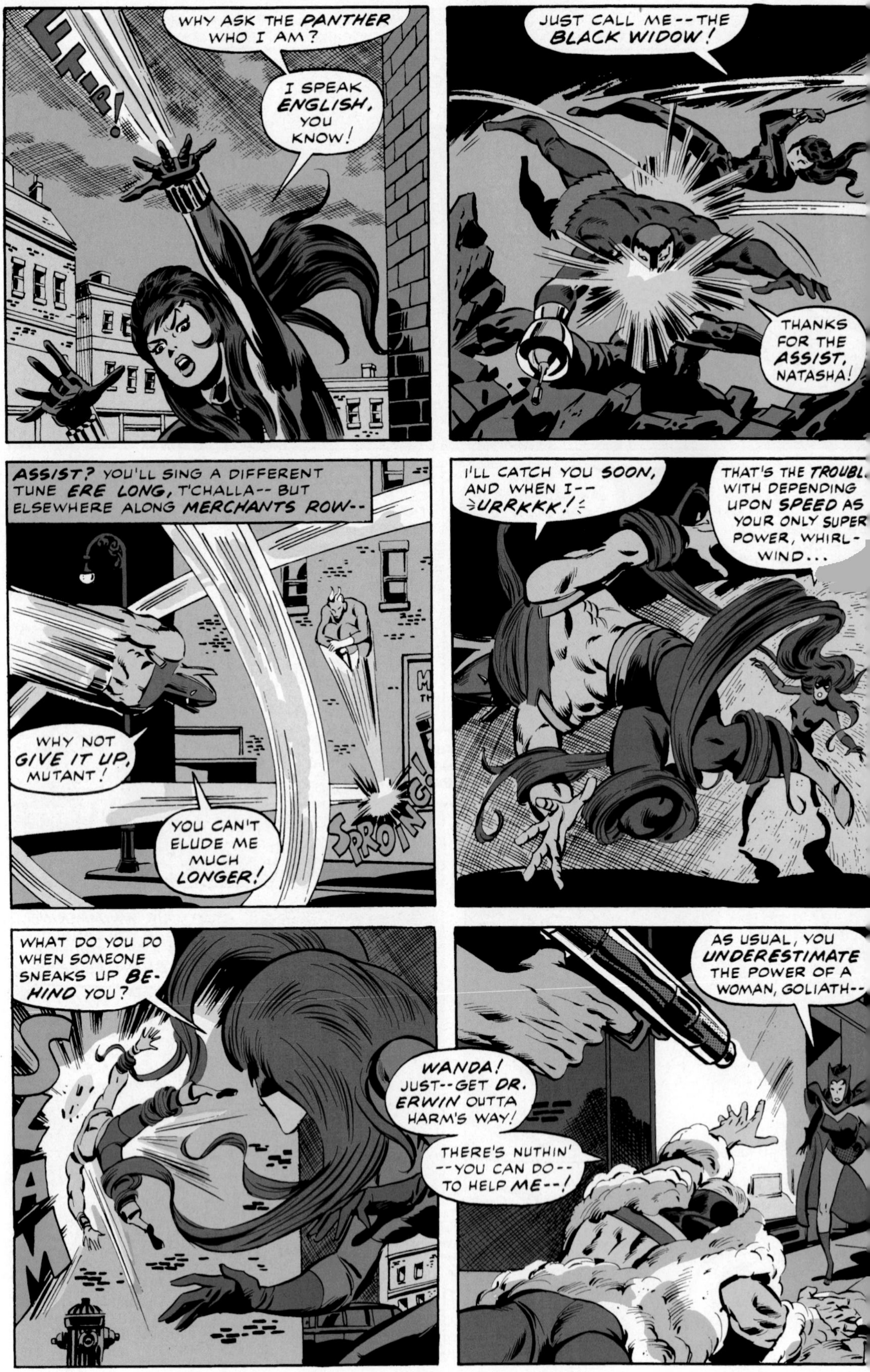
WHY ASK THE PANTHER WHO I AM?
I SPEAK ENGLISH, YOU KNOW!
JUST CALL ME--THE BLACK WIDOW!
THANKS FOR THE ASSIST, NATASHA!
ASSIST? YOU'LL SING A DIFFERENT TUNE ERE LONG, T'CHALLA-- BUT ELSEWHERE ALONG MERCHANTS ROW--
WHY NOT GIVE IT UP, MUTANT!
YOU CAN'T ELUDE ME MUCH LONGER!
SPROING!
I'LL CATCH YOU SOON, AND WHEN I-- URRKKK!
THAT'S THE TROUBL WITH DEPENDING UPON SPEED AS YOUR ONLY SUPER POWER, WHIRL-WIND...
WHAT DO YOU DO WHEN SOMEONE SNEAKS UP BE-HIND YOU?
AS USUAL, YOU UNDERESTIMATE THE POWER OF A WOMAN, GOLIATH--
WANDA! JUST--GET DR. ERWIN OUTTA HARM'S WAY!
THERE'S NUTHIN' --YOU CAN DO-- TO HELP ME--!

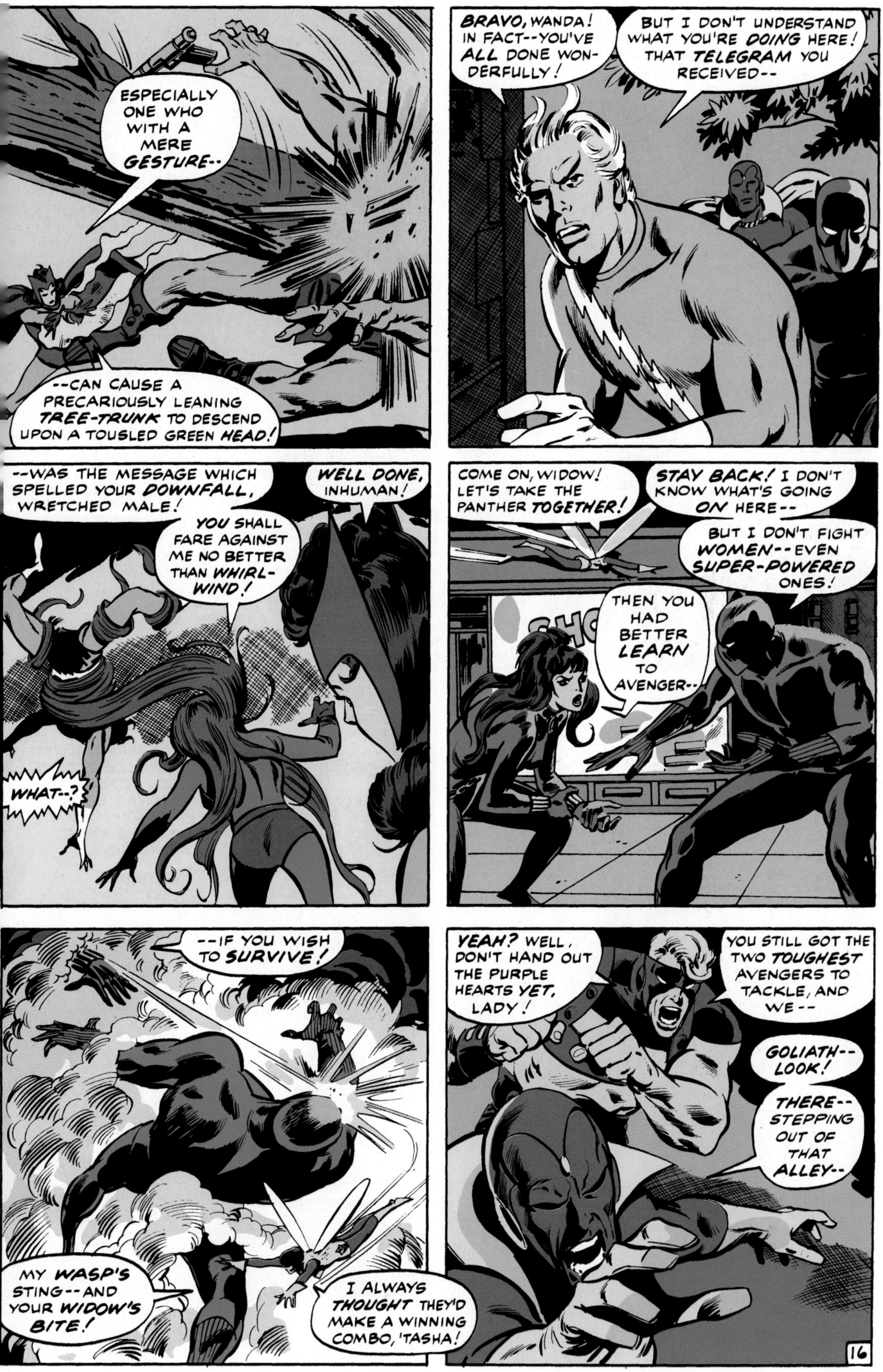
ESPECIALLY ONE WHO WITH A MERE GESTURE--
--CAN CAUSE A PRECARIOUSLY LEANING TREE-TRUNK TO DESCEND UPON A TOUSLED GREEN HEAD!
BRAVO, WANDA! IN FACT--YOU'VE ALL DONE WONDERFULLY!
BUT I DON'T UNDERSTAND WHAT YOU'RE DOING HERE! THAT TELEGRAM YOU RECEIVED--
--WAS THE MESSAGE WHICH SPELLED YOUR DOWNFALL, WRETCHED MALE!
WELL DONE, INHUMAN!
YOU SHALL FARE AGAINST ME NO BETTER THAN WHIRLWIND!
WHAT--?
COME ON, WIDOW! LET'S TAKE THE PANTHER TOGETHER!
STAY BACK! I DON'T KNOW WHAT'S GOING ON HERE--
BUT I DON'T FIGHT WOMEN--EVEN SUPER-POWERED ONES!
THEN YOU HAD BETTER LEARN TO AVENGER--
--IF YOU WISH TO SURVIVE!
MY WASP'S STING--AND YOUR WIDOW'S BITE!
I ALWAYS THOUGHT THEY'D MAKE A WINNING COMBO, 'TASHA!
YEAH? WELL, DON'T HAND OUT THE PURPLE HEARTS YET, LADY!
YOU STILL GOT THE TWO TOUGHEST AVENGERS TO TACKLE, AND WE--
GOLIATH--LOOK!
THERE--STEPPING OUT OF THAT ALLEY--
16

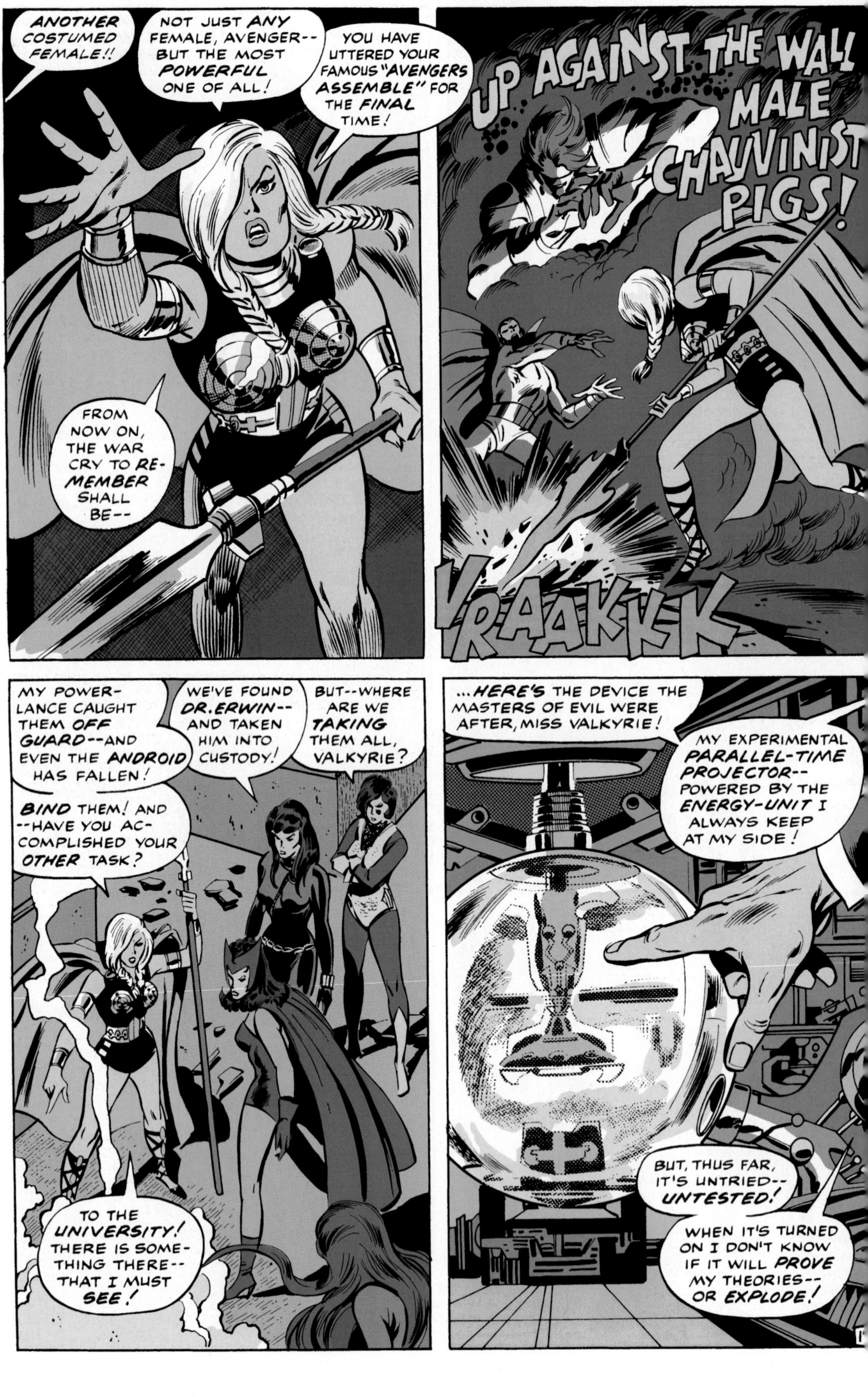

ANOTHER COSTUMED FEMALE!!
NOT JUST ANY FEMALE, AVENGER-- BUT THE MOST POWERFUL ONE OF ALL!
YOU HAVE UTTERED YOUR FAMOUS "AVENGERS ASSEMBLE" FOR THE FINAL TIME!
FROM NOW ON, THE WAR CRY TO RE-MEMBER SHALL BE--
UP AGAINST THE WALL MALE CHAUVINIST PIGS!
VRAAKKK
MY POWER-LANCE CAUGHT THEM OFF GUARD--AND EVEN THE ANDROID HAS FALLEN!
WE'VE FOUND DR. ERWIN-- AND TAKEN HIM INTO CUSTODY!
BUT--WHERE ARE WE TAKING THEM ALL, VALKYRIE?
BIND THEM! AND --HAVE YOU AC-COMPLISHED YOUR OTHER TASK?
TO THE UNIVERSITY! THERE IS SOME-THING THERE-- THAT I MUST SEE!
...HERE'S THE DEVICE THE MASTERS OF EVIL WERE AFTER, MISS VALKYRIE!
MY EXPERIMENTAL PARALLEL-TIME PROJECTOR-- POWERED BY THE ENERGY-UNIT I ALWAYS KEEP AT MY SIDE!
BUT, THUS FAR, IT'S UNTRIED-- UNTESTED!
WHEN IT'S TURNED ON I DON'T KNOW IF IT WILL PROVE MY THEORIES-- OR EXPLODE!

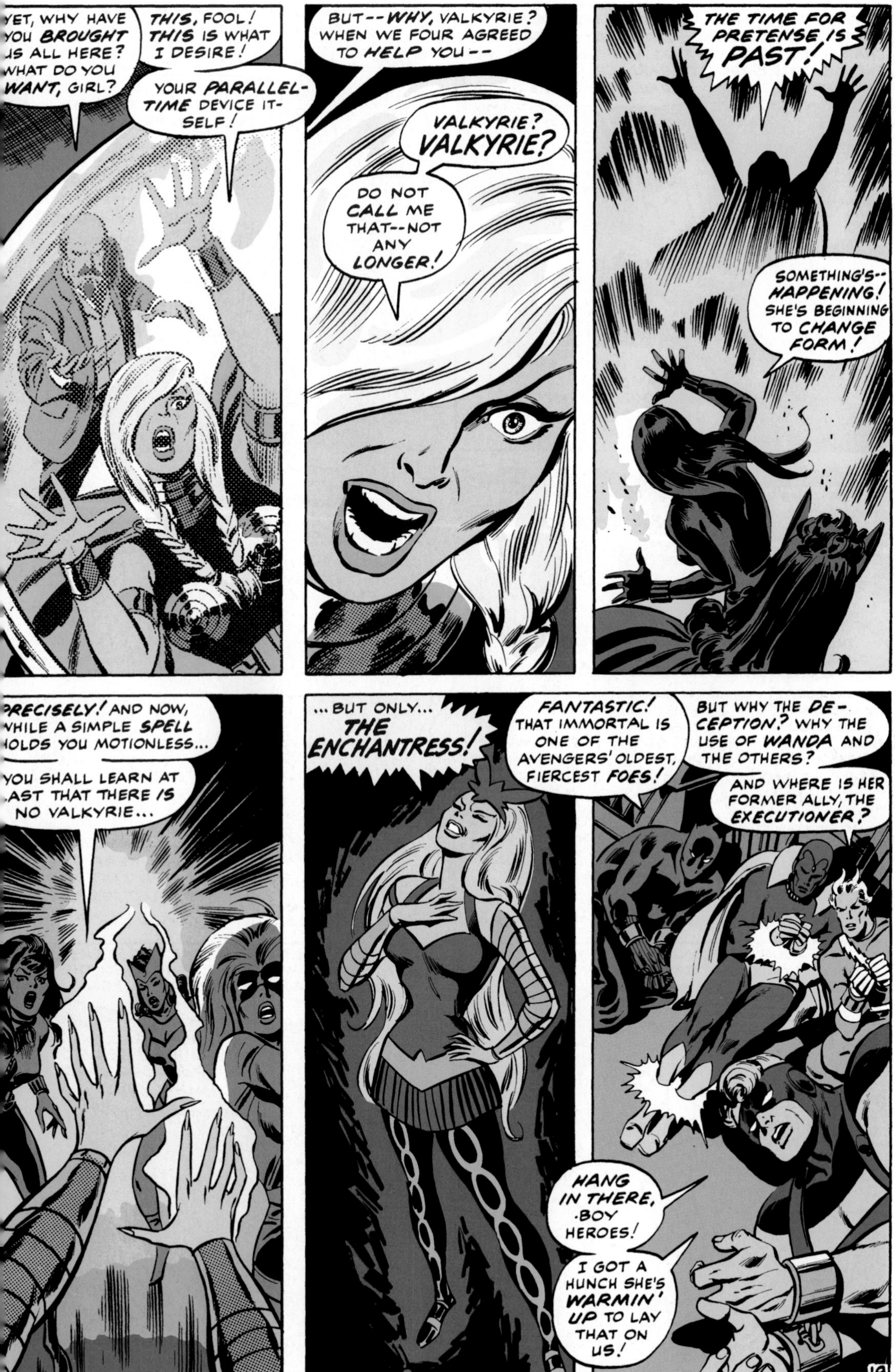
YET, WHY HAVE YOU BROUGHT US ALL HERE? WHAT DO YOU WANT, GIRL?
THIS, FOOL! THIS IS WHAT I DESIRE!
YOUR PARALLEL-TIME DEVICE IT-SELF!
BUT--WHY, VALKYRIE? WHEN WE FOUR AGREED TO HELP YOU--
VALKYRIE? VALKYRIE?
DO NOT CALL ME THAT--NOT ANY LONGER!
THE TIME FOR PRETENSE IS PAST!
SOMETHING'S--HAPPENING! SHE'S BEGINNING TO CHANGE FORM!
PRECISELY! AND NOW, WHILE A SIMPLE SPELL HOLDS YOU MOTIONLESS...
YOU SHALL LEARN AT LAST THAT THERE IS NO VALKYRIE...
... BUT ONLY... THE ENCHANTRESS!
FANTASTIC! THAT IMMORTAL IS ONE OF THE AVENGERS' OLDEST, FIERCEST FOES!
BUT WHY THE DE-CEPTION? WHY THE USE OF WANDA AND THE OTHERS?
AND WHERE IS HER FORMER ALLY, THE EXECUTIONER?
HANG IN THERE, BOY HEROES!
I GOT A HUNCH SHE'S WARMIN' UP TO LAY THAT ON US!

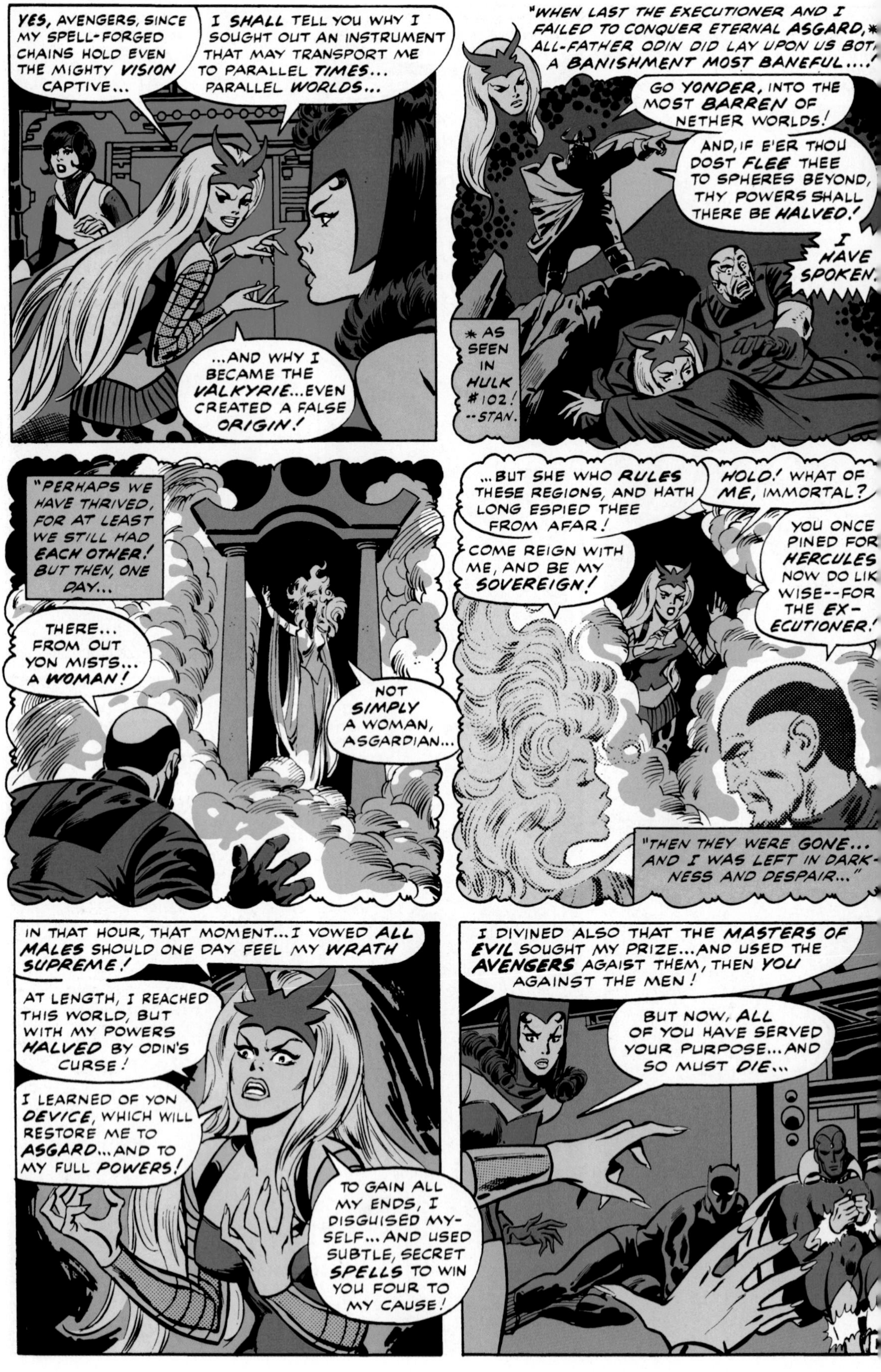

YES, AVENGERS, SINCE MY SPELL-FORGED CHAINS HOLD EVEN THE MIGHTY VISION CAPTIVE...
I SHALL TELL YOU WHY I SOUGHT OUT AN INSTRUMENT THAT MAY TRANSPORT ME TO PARALLEL TIMES... PARALLEL WORLDS...
...AND WHY I BECAME THE VALKYRIE...EVEN CREATED A FALSE ORIGIN!
"WHEN LAST THE EXECUTIONER AND I FAILED TO CONQUER ETERNAL ASGARD,* ALL-FATHER ODIN DID LAY UPON US BOT A BANISHMENT MOST BANEFUL...!
GO YONDER, INTO THE MOST BARREN OF NETHER WORLDS!
AND, IF E'ER THOU DOST FLEE THEE TO SPHERES BEYOND, THY POWERS SHALL THERE BE HALVED!
I HAVE SPOKEN
*AS SEEN IN HULK #102! --STAN.
"PERHAPS WE HAVE THRIVED, FOR AT LEAST WE STILL HAD EACH OTHER! BUT THEN, ONE DAY...
THERE... FROM OUT YON MISTS... A WOMAN!
NOT SIMPLY A WOMAN, ASGARDIAN...
...BUT SHE WHO RULES THESE REGIONS, AND HATH LONG ESPIED THEE FROM AFAR!
COME REIGN WITH ME, AND BE MY SOVEREIGN!
HOLD! WHAT OF ME, IMMORTAL?
YOU ONCE PINED FOR HERCULES NOW DO LIK WISE--FOR THE EX-ECUTIONER!
"THEN THEY WERE GONE... AND I WAS LEFT IN DARK-NESS AND DESPAIR..."
IN THAT HOUR, THAT MOMENT...I VOWED ALL MALES SHOULD ONE DAY FEEL MY WRATH SUPREME!
AT LENGTH, I REACHED THIS WORLD, BUT WITH MY POWERS HALVED BY ODIN'S CURSE!
I LEARNED OF YON DEVICE, WHICH WILL RESTORE ME TO ASGARD...AND TO MY FULL POWERS!
TO GAIN ALL MY ENDS, I DISGUISED MY-SELF...AND USED SUBTLE, SECRET SPELLS TO WIN YOU FOUR TO MY CAUSE!
I DIVINED ALSO THAT THE MASTERS OF EVIL SOUGHT MY PRIZE...AND USED THE AVENGERS AGAIST THEM, THEN YOU AGAINST THE MEN!
BUT NOW, ALL OF YOU HAVE SERVED YOUR PURPOSE...AND SO MUST DIE...

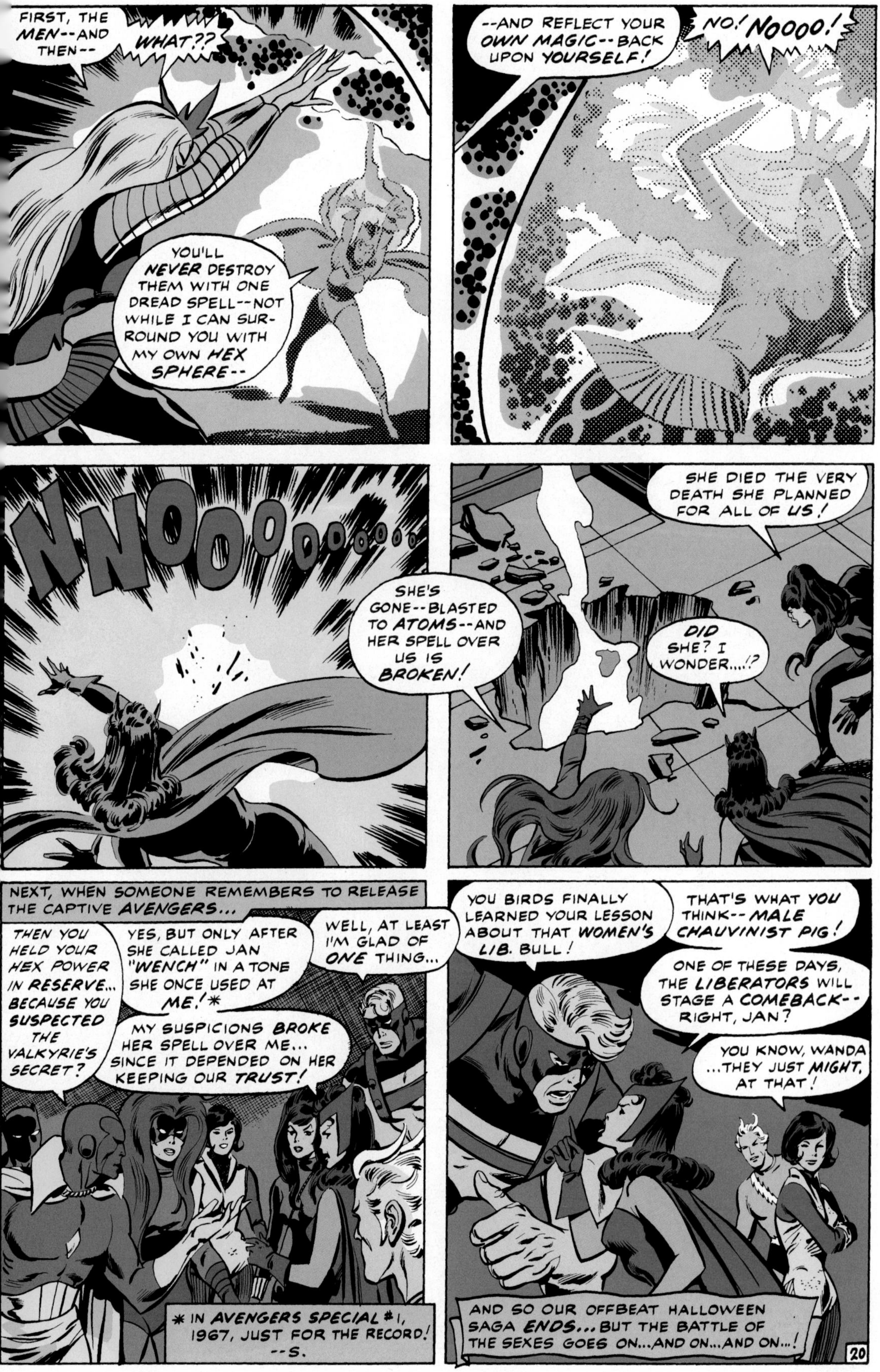

FIRST, THE MEN--AND THEN--
WHAT??
YOU'LL NEVER DESTROY THEM WITH ONE DREAD SPELL--NOT WHILE I CAN SURROUND YOU WITH MY OWN HEX SPHERE--
--AND REFLECT YOUR OWN MAGIC--BACK UPON YOURSELF!
NO! NOOOO!
NNOOOOOoooo...
SHE'S GONE--BLASTED TO ATOMS--AND HER SPELL OVER US IS BROKEN!
SHE DIED THE VERY DEATH SHE PLANNED FOR ALL OF US!
DID SHE? I WONDER....!?
NEXT, WHEN SOMEONE REMEMBERS TO RELEASE THE CAPTIVE AVENGERS...
THEN YOU HELD YOUR HEX POWER IN RESERVE... BECAUSE YOU SUSPECTED THE VALKYRIE'S SECRET?
YES, BUT ONLY AFTER SHE CALLED JAN "WENCH" IN A TONE SHE ONCE USED AT ME!*
WELL, AT LEAST I'M GLAD OF ONE THING...
MY SUSPICIONS BROKE HER SPELL OVER ME... SINCE IT DEPENDED ON HER KEEPING OUR TRUST!
* IN AVENGERS SPECIAL #1, 1967, JUST FOR THE RECORD! --S.
YOU BIRDS FINALLY LEARNED YOUR LESSON ABOUT THAT WOMEN'S LIB. BULL!
THAT'S WHAT YOU THINK--MALE CHAUVINIST PIG!
ONE OF THESE DAYS, THE LIBERATORS WILL STAGE A COMEBACK--RIGHT, JAN?
YOU KNOW, WANDA ...THEY JUST MIGHT, AT THAT!
AND SO OUR OFFBEAT HALLOWEEN SAGA ENDS... BUT THE BATTLE OF THE SEXES GOES ON...AND ON...AND ON...!
20

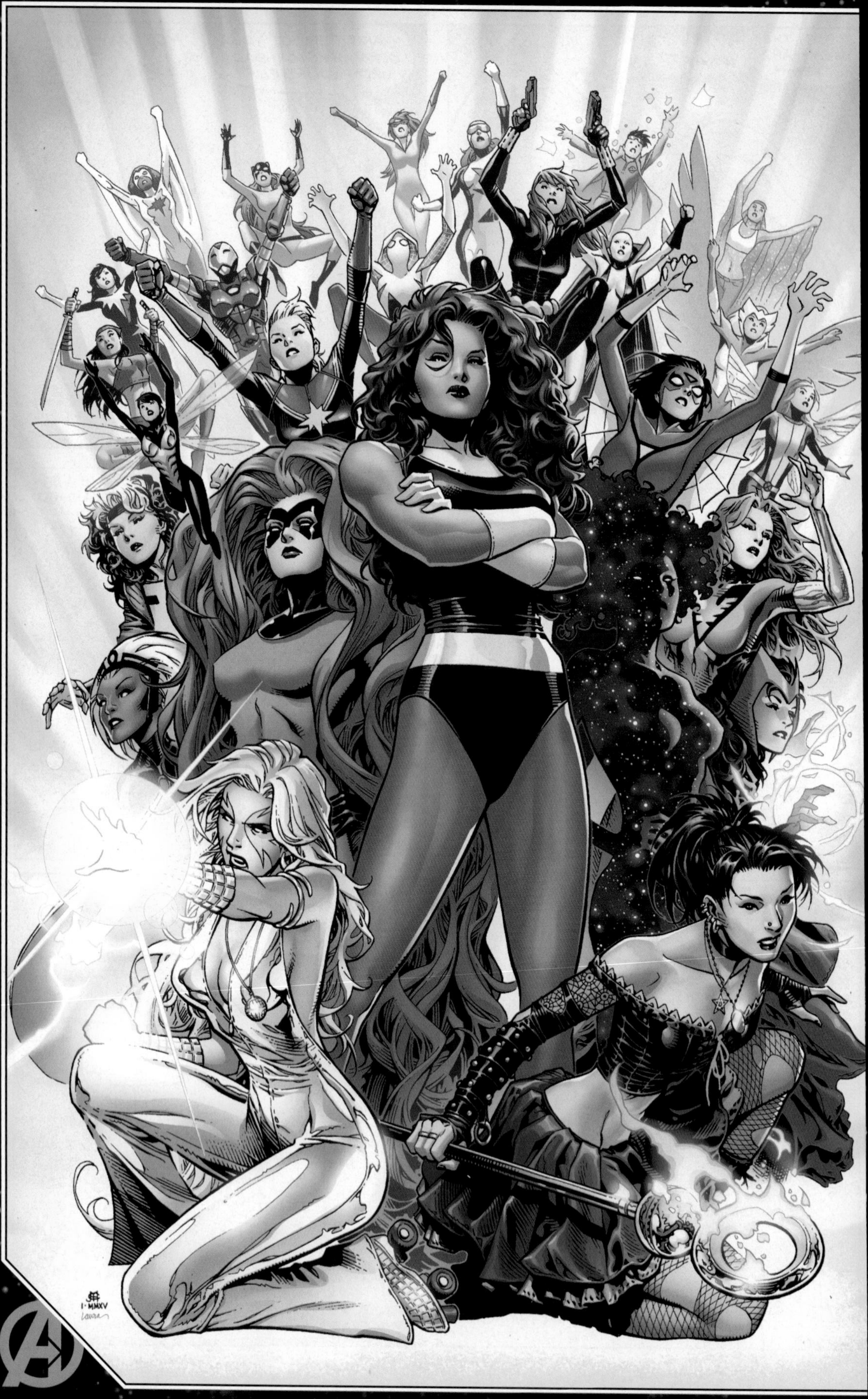

A-FORCE (2015) #1

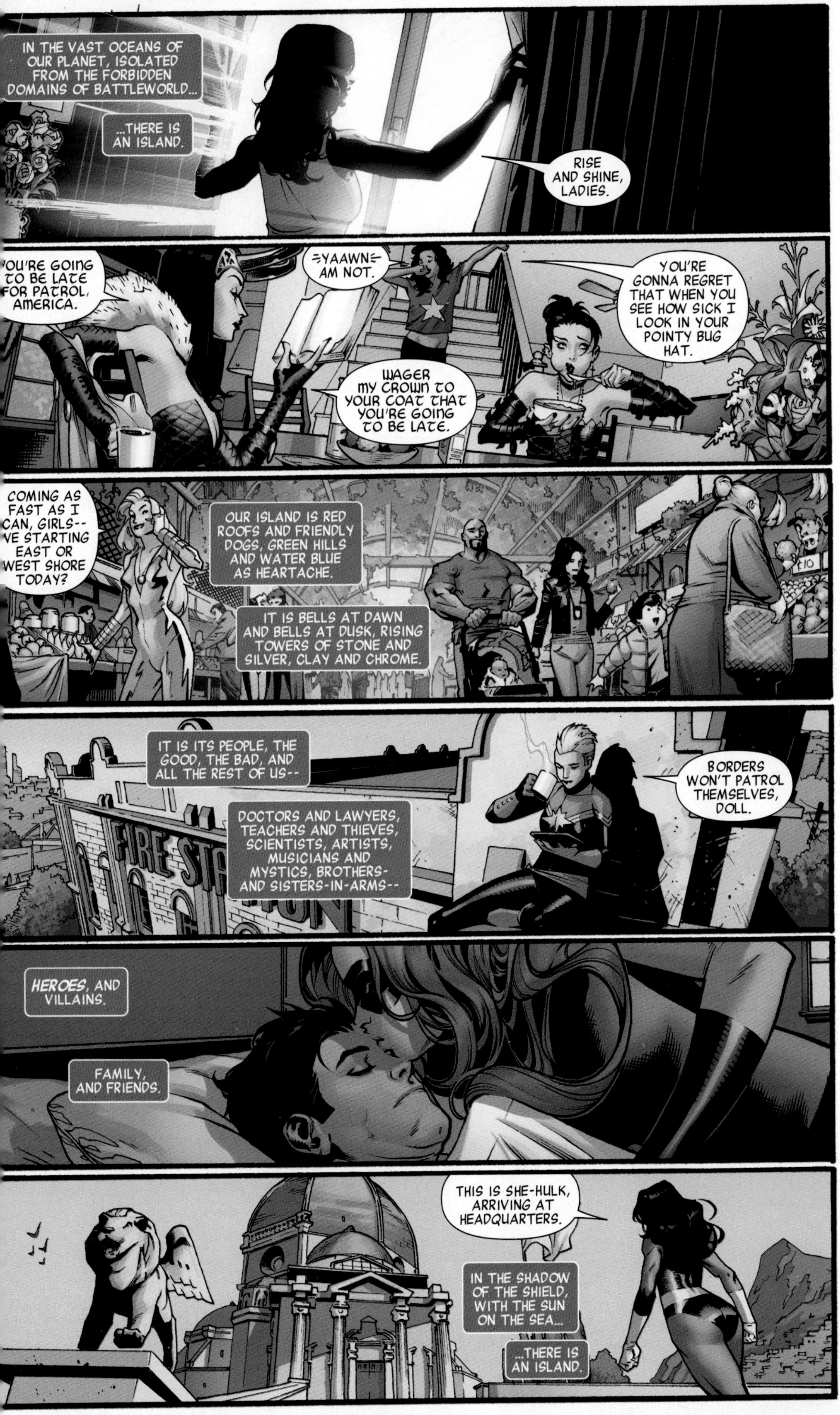
IN THE VAST OCEANS OF OUR PLANET, ISOLATED FROM THE FORBIDDEN DOMAINS OF BATTLEWORLD...
...THERE IS AN ISLAND.
RISE AND SHINE, LADIES.
YOU'RE GOING TO BE LATE FOR PATROL, AMERICA.
=YAAWN= AM NOT.
YOU'RE GONNA REGRET THAT WHEN YOU SEE HOW SICK I LOOK IN YOUR POINTY BUG HAT.
WAGER MY CROWN TO YOUR COAT THAT YOU'RE GOING TO BE LATE.
COMING AS FAST AS I CAN, GIRLS-- WE STARTING EAST OR WEST SHORE TODAY?
OUR ISLAND IS RED ROOFS AND FRIENDLY DOGS, GREEN HILLS AND WATER BLUE AS HEARTACHE.
IT IS BELLS AT DAWN AND BELLS AT DUSK, RISING TOWERS OF STONE AND SILVER, CLAY AND CHROME.
IT IS ITS PEOPLE, THE GOOD, THE BAD, AND ALL THE REST OF US--
DOCTORS AND LAWYERS, TEACHERS AND THIEVES, SCIENTISTS, ARTISTS, MUSICIANS AND MYSTICS, BROTHERS- AND SISTERS-IN-ARMS--
BORDERS WON'T PATROL THEMSELVES, DOLL.
HEROES, AND VILLAINS.
FAMILY, AND FRIENDS.
THIS IS SHE-HULK, ARRIVING AT HEADQUARTERS.
IN THE SHADOW OF THE SHIELD, WITH THE SUN ON THE SEA...
...THERE IS AN ISLAND.

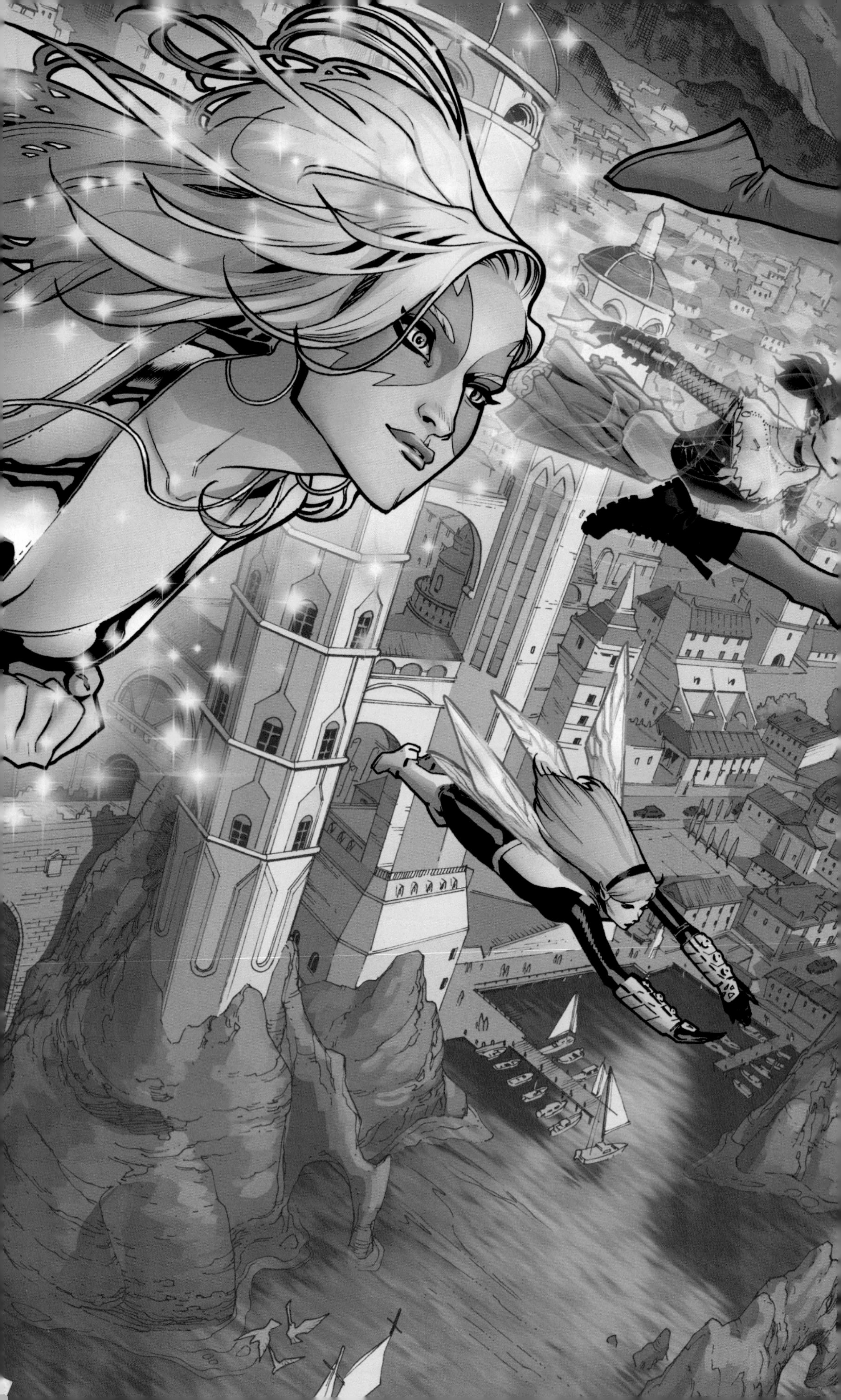

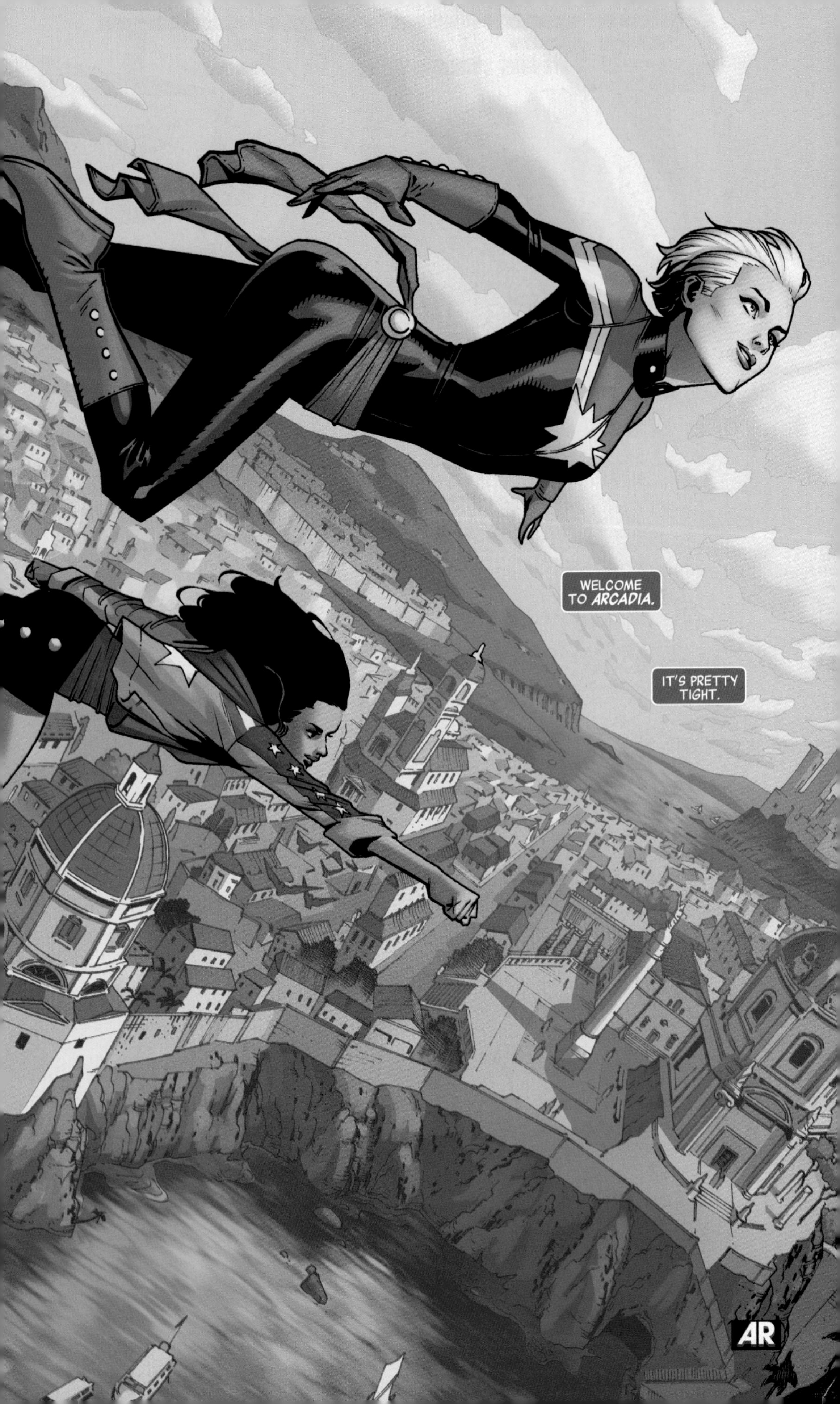
WELCOME TO ARCADIA.
IT'S PRETTY TIGHT.
AR

SECRET WARS

THE MULTIVERSE WAS DESTROYED!

THE HEROES OF EARTH-616 AND EARTH-1610
WERE POWERLESS TO SAVE IT!

NOW, ALL THAT REMAINS...IS **BATTLEWORLD!**

A MASSIVE, PATCHWORK PLANET COMPOSED OF THE FRAGMENTS OF
WORLDS THAT NO LONGER EXIST, MAINTAINED BY THE IRON WILL OF ITS
GOD AND MASTER, VICTOR VON DOOM!

EACH REGION IS A DOMAIN UNTO ITSELF!

THIS IS THE STORY OF...

A-FORCE

WRITERS:
MARGUERITE BENNETT
G. WILLOW WILSON

PENCILER:
JORGE MOLINA

INKERS:
JORGE MOLINA
CRAIG YEUNG

COLORISTS:
LAURA MARTIN
MATT MILLA

LETTERER:
VC'S CORY PE

COVER:
JIM CHEUNG
LAURA MARTIN

VARIANT COVERS:
Skottie Young; Russell Dauterman & Matt Wilson; Shane Davis & Jesus Aburtov;
Sia Oum; Stephanie Hans; Adam Hughes; Jorge Molina; Sara Pichelli & Edgar Delga

ASSISTANT EDITOR:
ALANNA SMITH

EDITOR:
DANIEL KETCHUM

EDITOR IN CHIEF:
AXEL ALONSO

CHIEF CREATIVE OFFICER:
JOE QUESADA

PUBLISHER:
DAN BUCKLEY

EXEC. PRODU
ALAN FINE

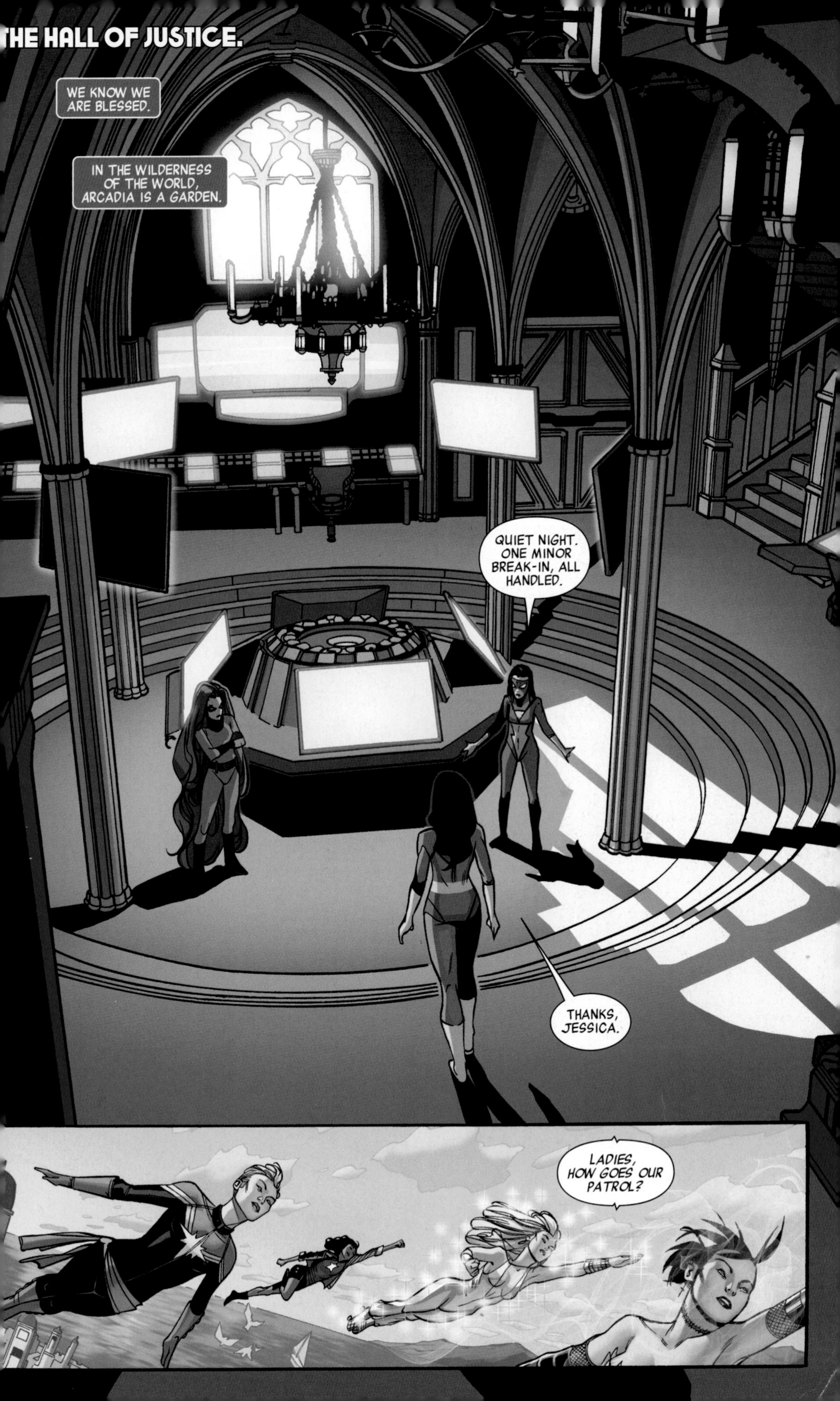
THE HALL OF JUSTICE.
WE KNOW WE ARE BLESSED.
IN THE WILDERNESS OF THE WORLD, ARCADIA IS A GARDEN.
QUIET NIGHT. ONE MINOR BREAK-IN, ALL HANDLED.
THANKS, JESSICA.
LADIES, HOW GOES OUR PATROL?

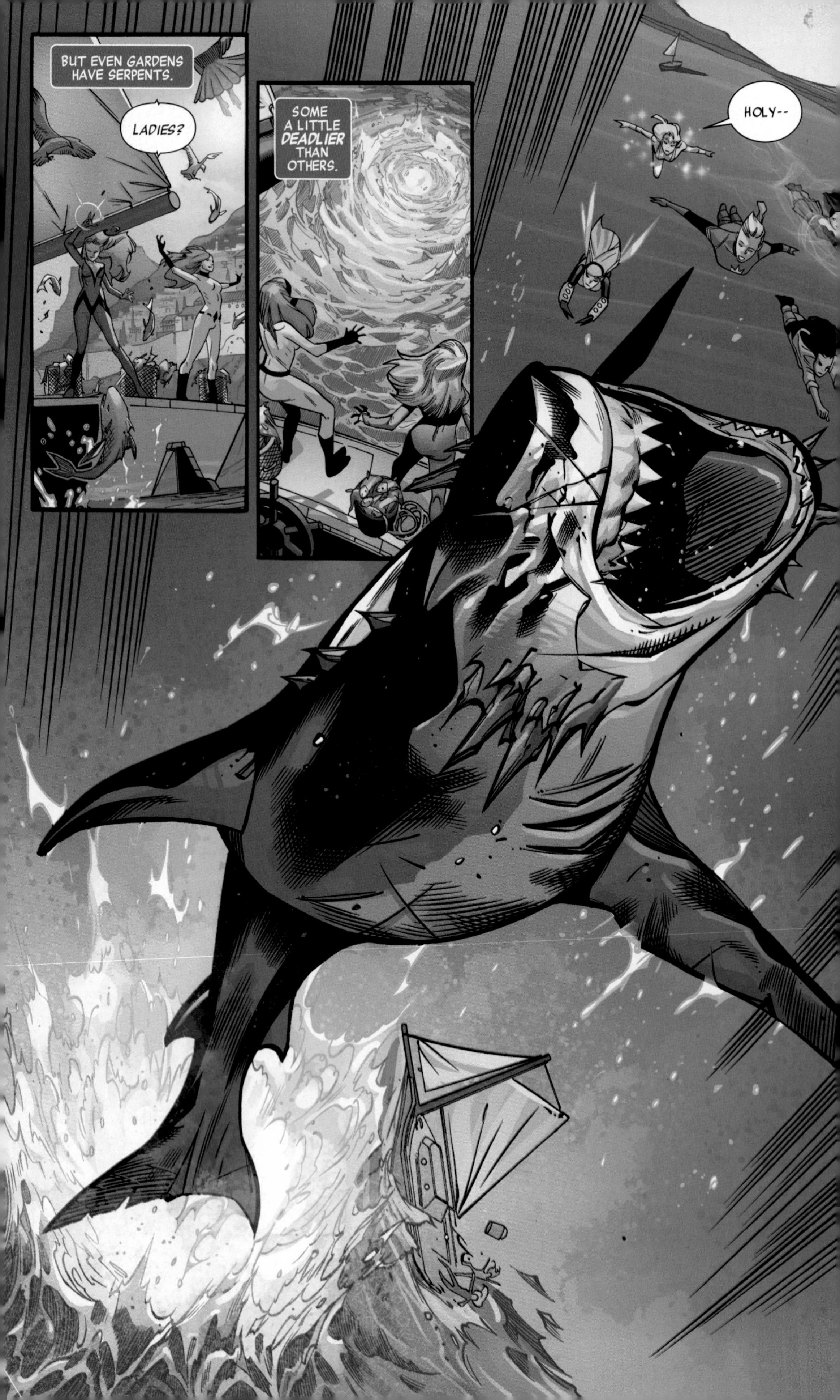

BUT EVEN GARDENS HAVE SERPENTS.
LADIES?
SOME A LITTLE DEADLIER THAN OTHERS.
HOLY--

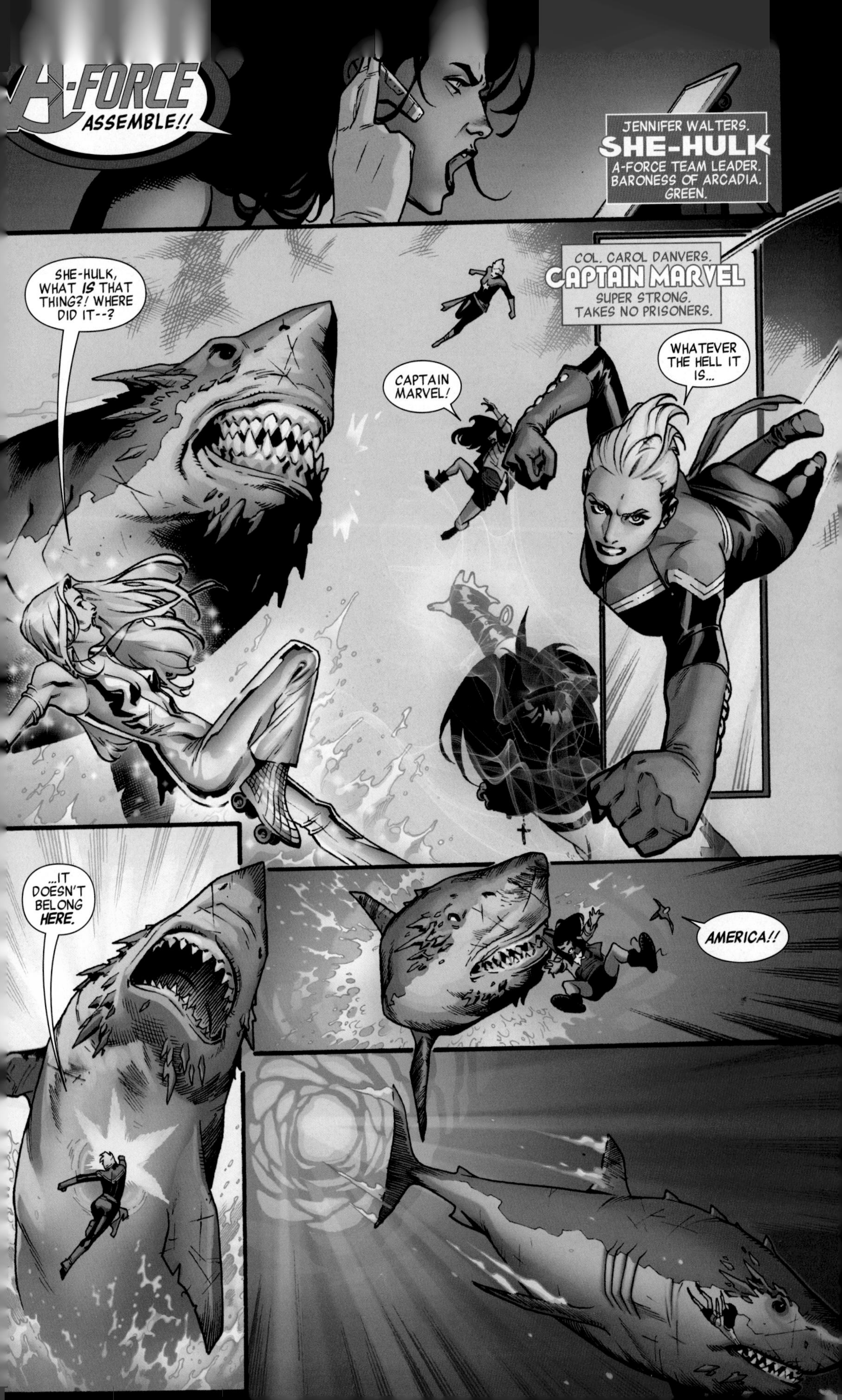
A-FORCE ASSEMBLE!!
JENNIFER WALTERS.
SHE-HULK
A-FORCE TEAM LEADER.
BARONESS OF ARCADIA.
GREEN.
SHE-HULK, WHAT IS THAT THING?! WHERE DID IT--?
COL. CAROL DANVERS.
CAPTAIN MARVEL
SUPER STRONG.
TAKES NO PRISONERS.
CAPTAIN MARVEL!
WHATEVER THE HELL IT IS...
...IT DOESN'T BELONG HERE.
AMERICA!!

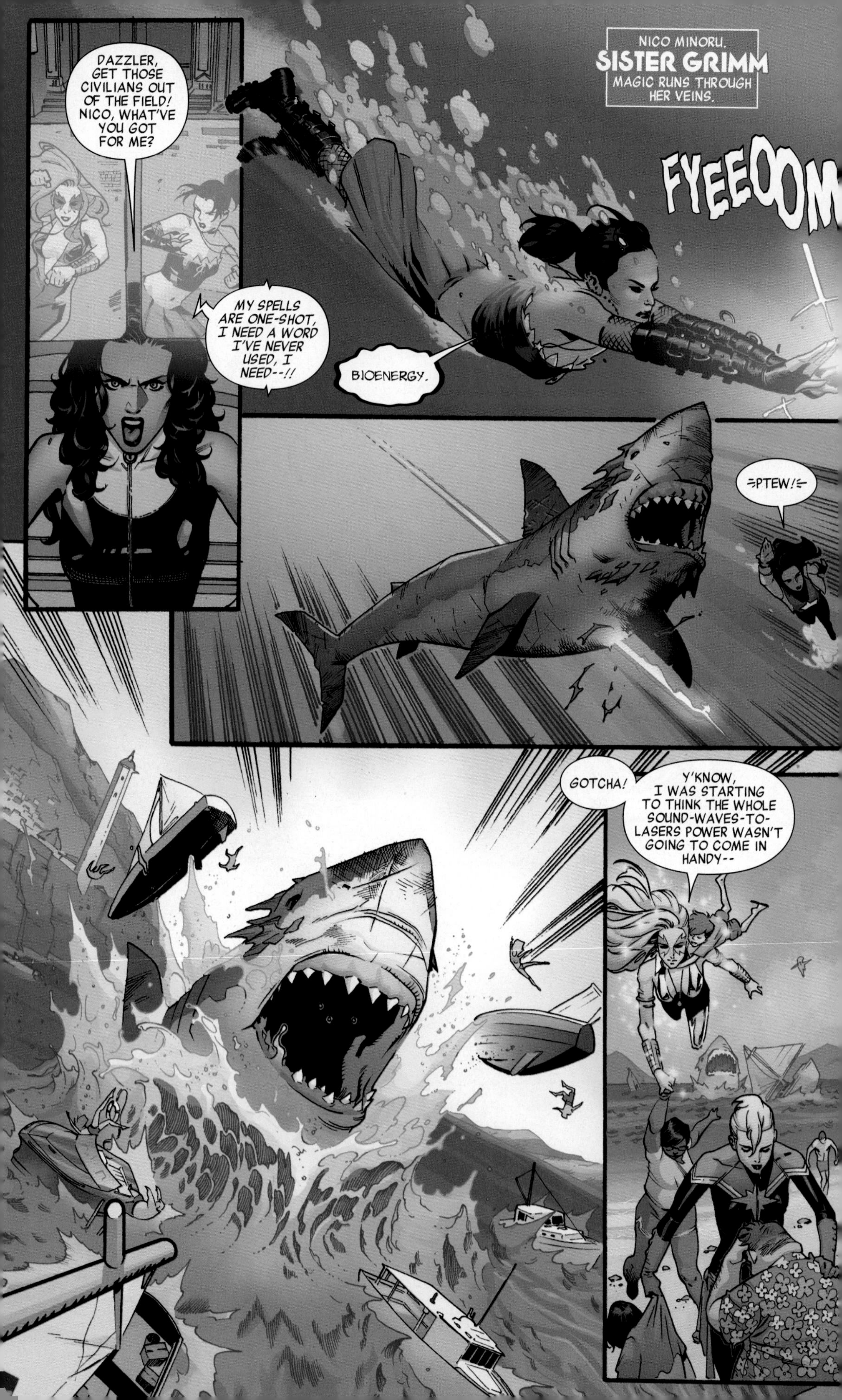
DAZZLER, GET THOSE CIVILIANS OUT OF THE FIELD! NICO, WHAT'VE YOU GOT FOR ME?
MY SPELLS ARE ONE-SHOT, I NEED A WORD I'VE NEVER USED, I NEED--!!
NICO MINORU. SISTER GRIMM MAGIC RUNS THROUGH HER VEINS.
FYEEOOM
BIOENERGY.
=PTEW!=
GOTCHA!
Y'KNOW, I WAS STARTING TO THINK THE WHOLE SOUND-WAVES-TO-LASERS POWER WASN'T GOING TO COME IN HANDY--

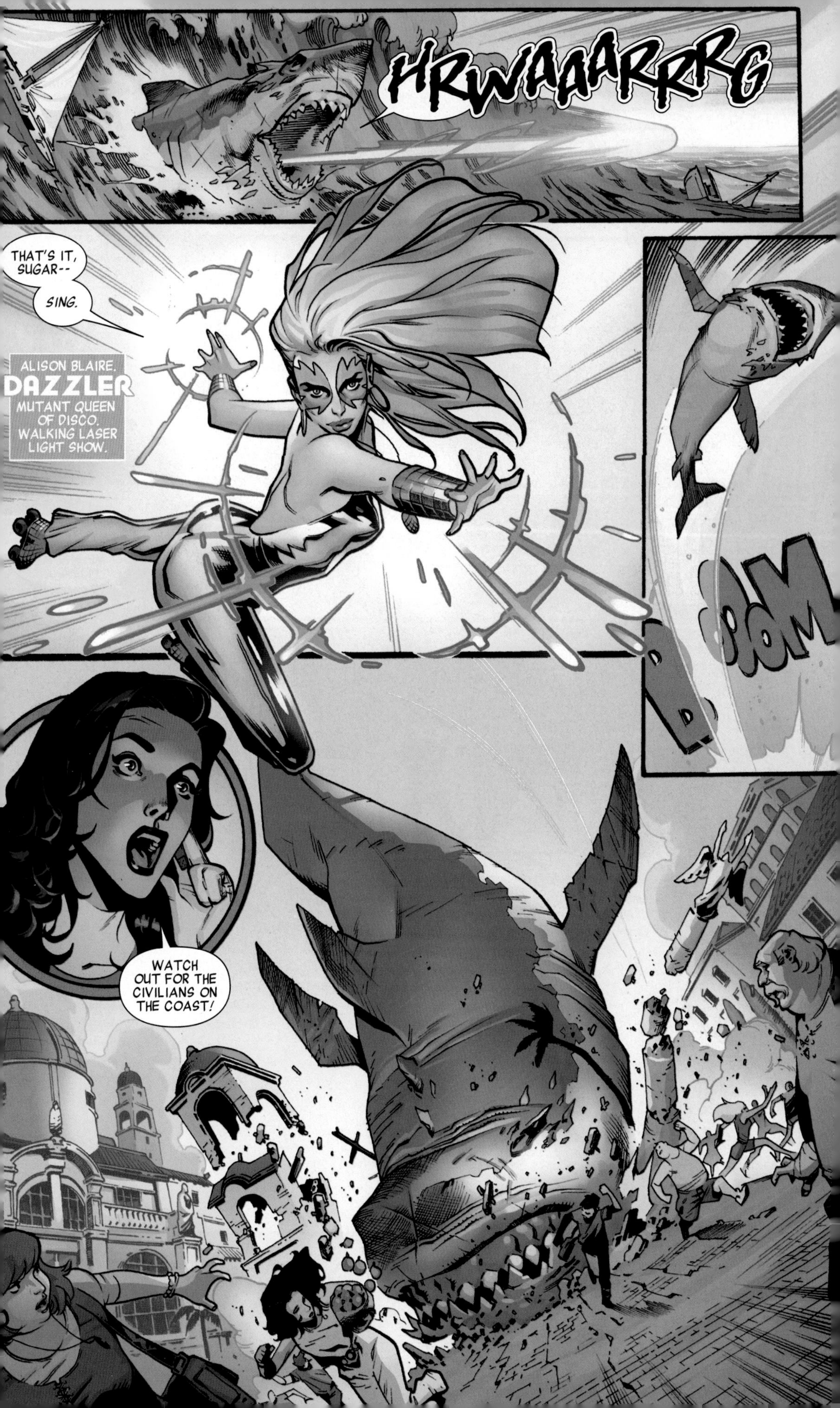
HRWAAARRRG
THAT'S IT, SUGAR--
SING.
ALISON BLAIRE.
DAZZLER
MUTANT QUEEN OF DISCO. WALKING LASER LIGHT SHOW.
BOOM
WATCH OUT FOR THE CIVILIANS ON THE COAST!

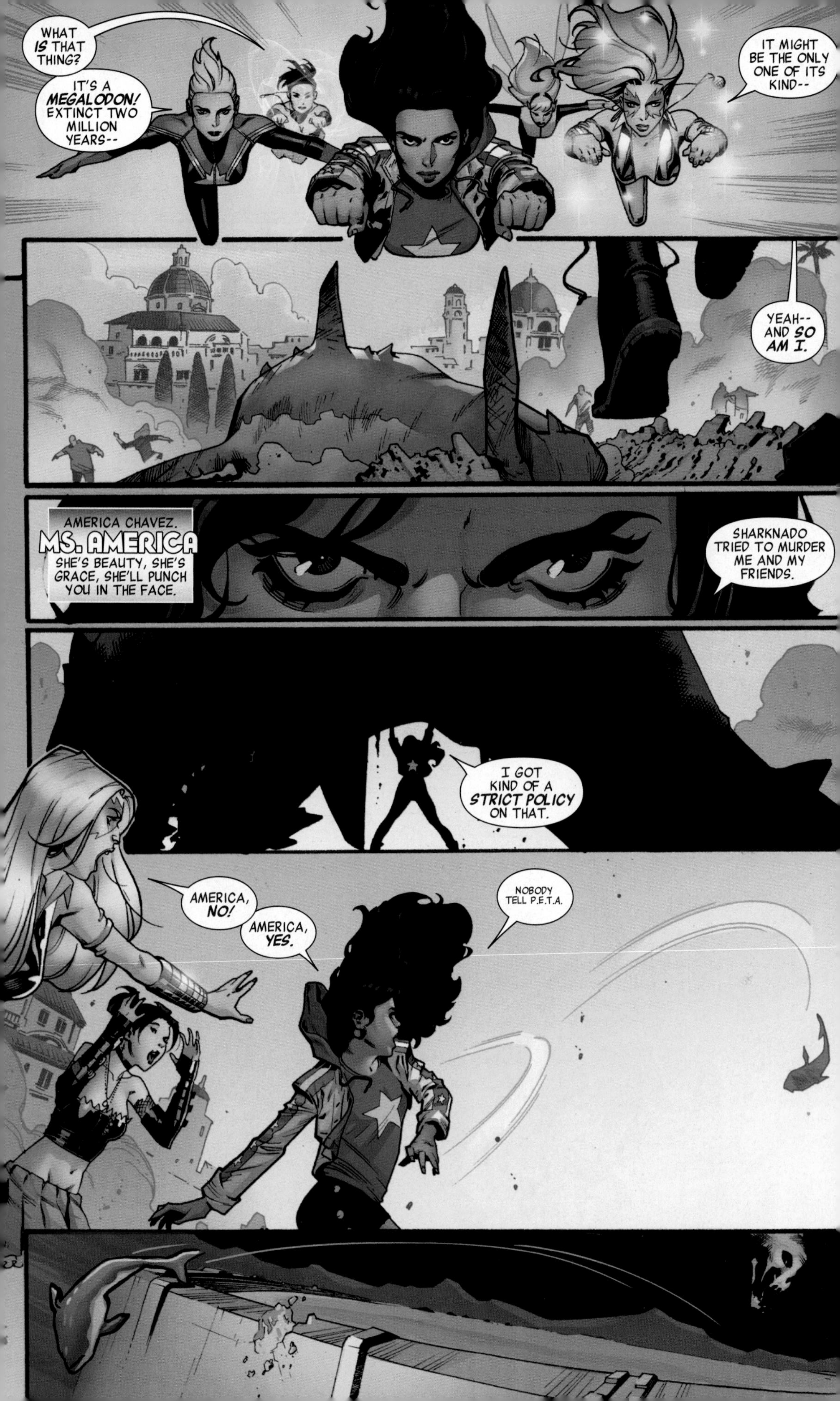

WHAT IS THAT THING?
IT'S A MEGALODON! EXTINCT TWO MILLION YEARS--
IT MIGHT BE THE ONLY ONE OF ITS KIND--
YEAH-- AND SO AM I.
AMERICA CHAVEZ.
MS. AMERICA
SHE'S BEAUTY, SHE'S GRACE, SHE'LL PUNCH YOU IN THE FACE.
SHARKNADO TRIED TO MURDER ME AND MY FRIENDS.
I GOT KIND OF A STRICT POLICY ON THAT.
AMERICA, NO!
AMERICA, YES.
NOBODY TELL P.E.T.A.

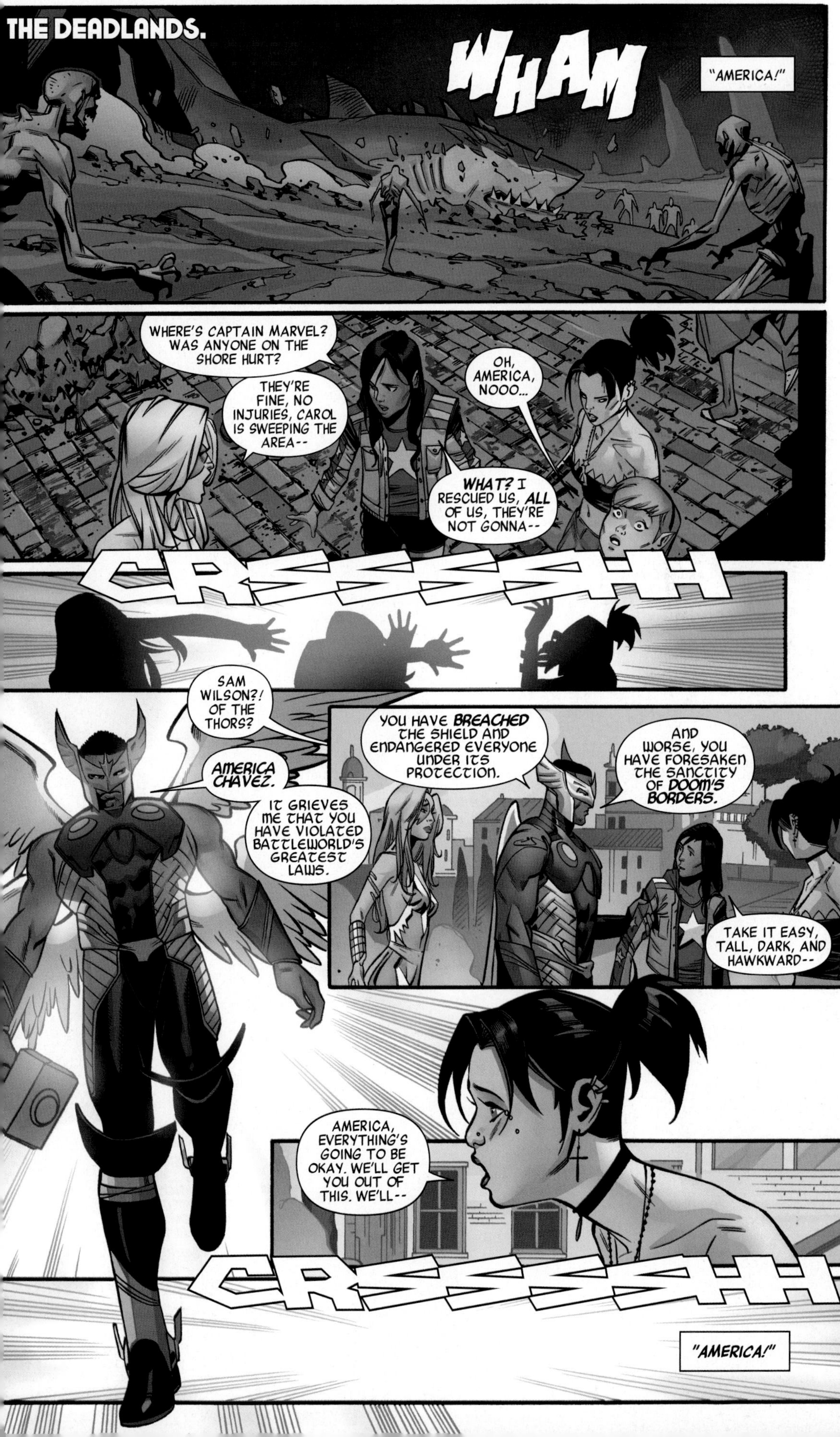
THE DEADLANDS.
WHAM
"AMERICA!"
WHERE'S CAPTAIN MARVEL? WAS ANYONE ON THE SHORE HURT?
THEY'RE FINE, NO INJURIES, CAROL IS SWEEPING THE AREA--
OH, AMERICA, NOOO...
WHAT? I RESCUED US, ALL OF US, THEY'RE NOT GONNA--
CRSSSSHH
SAM WILSON?! OF THE THORS?
AMERICA CHAVEZ.
IT GRIEVES ME THAT YOU HAVE VIOLATED BATTLEWORLD'S GREATEST LAWS.
YOU HAVE BREACHED THE SHIELD AND ENDANGERED EVERYONE UNDER ITS PROTECTION.
AND WORSE, YOU HAVE FORESAKEN THE SANCTITY OF DOOM'S BORDERS.
TAKE IT EASY, TALL, DARK, AND HAWKWARD--
AMERICA, EVERYTHING'S GOING TO BE OKAY. WE'LL GET YOU OUT OF THIS. WE'LL--
CRSSSSHH
"AMERICA!"

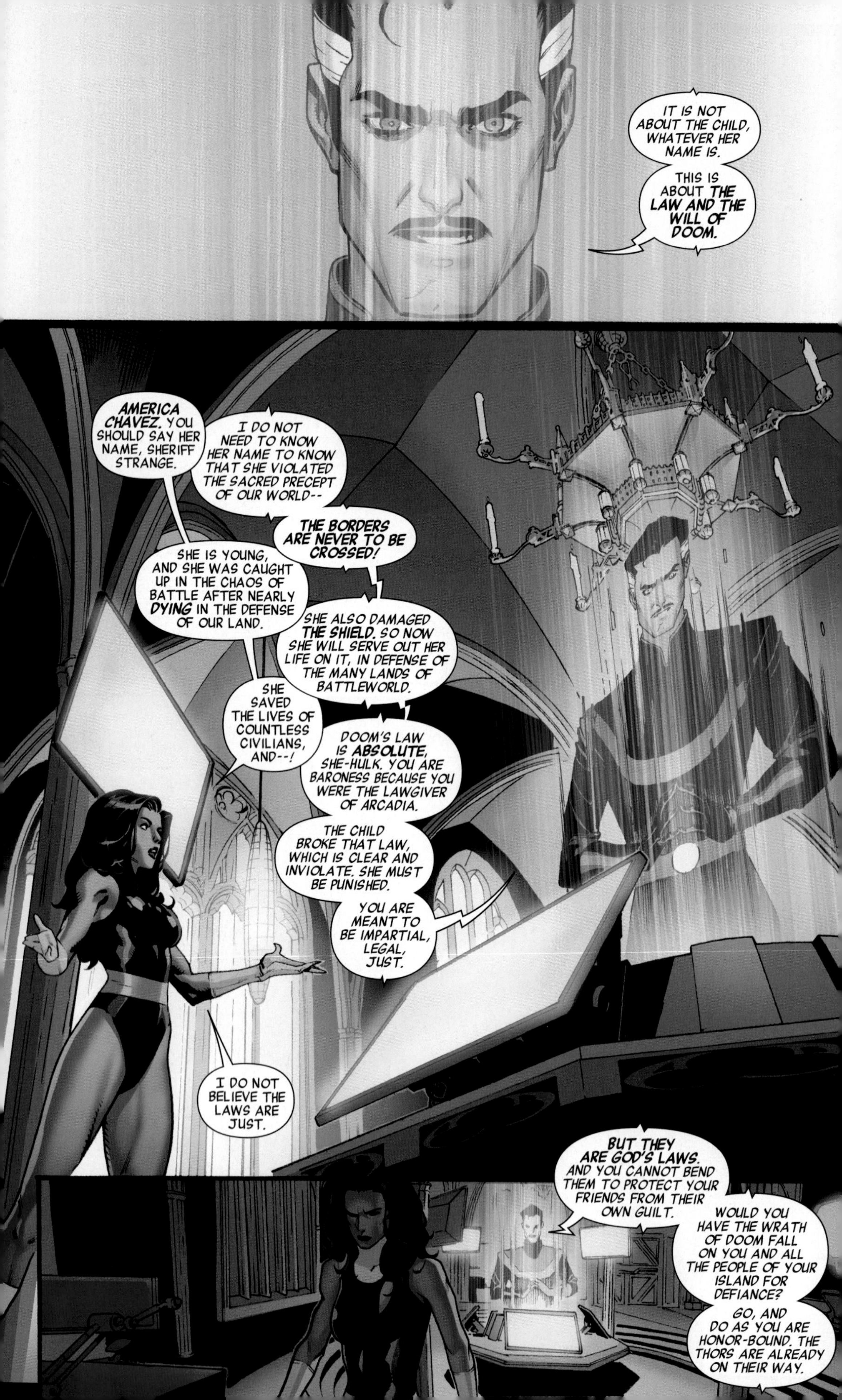
IT IS NOT ABOUT THE CHILD, WHATEVER HER NAME IS.
THIS IS ABOUT THE LAW AND THE WILL OF DOOM.
AMERICA CHAVEZ. YOU SHOULD SAY HER NAME, SHERIFF STRANGE.
I DO NOT NEED TO KNOW HER NAME TO KNOW THAT SHE VIOLATED THE SACRED PRECEPT OF OUR WORLD--
THE BORDERS ARE NEVER TO BE CROSSED!
SHE IS YOUNG, AND SHE WAS CAUGHT UP IN THE CHAOS OF BATTLE AFTER NEARLY DYING IN THE DEFENSE OF OUR LAND.
SHE ALSO DAMAGED THE SHIELD. SO NOW SHE WILL SERVE OUT HER LIFE ON IT, IN DEFENSE OF THE MANY LANDS OF BATTLEWORLD.
SHE SAVED THE LIVES OF COUNTLESS CIVILIANS, AND--!
DOOM'S LAW IS ABSOLUTE, SHE-HULK. YOU ARE BARONESS BECAUSE YOU WERE THE LAWGIVER OF ARCADIA.
THE CHILD BROKE THAT LAW, WHICH IS CLEAR AND INVIOLATE. SHE MUST BE PUNISHED.
YOU ARE MEANT TO BE IMPARTIAL, LEGAL, JUST.
I DO NOT BELIEVE THE LAWS ARE JUST.
BUT THEY ARE GOD'S LAWS. AND YOU CANNOT BEND THEM TO PROTECT YOUR FRIENDS FROM THEIR OWN GUILT.
WOULD YOU HAVE THE WRATH OF DOOM FALL ON YOU AND ALL THE PEOPLE OF YOUR ISLAND FOR DEFIANCE?
GO, AND DO AS YOU ARE HONOR-BOUND. THE THORS ARE ALREADY ON THEIR WAY.

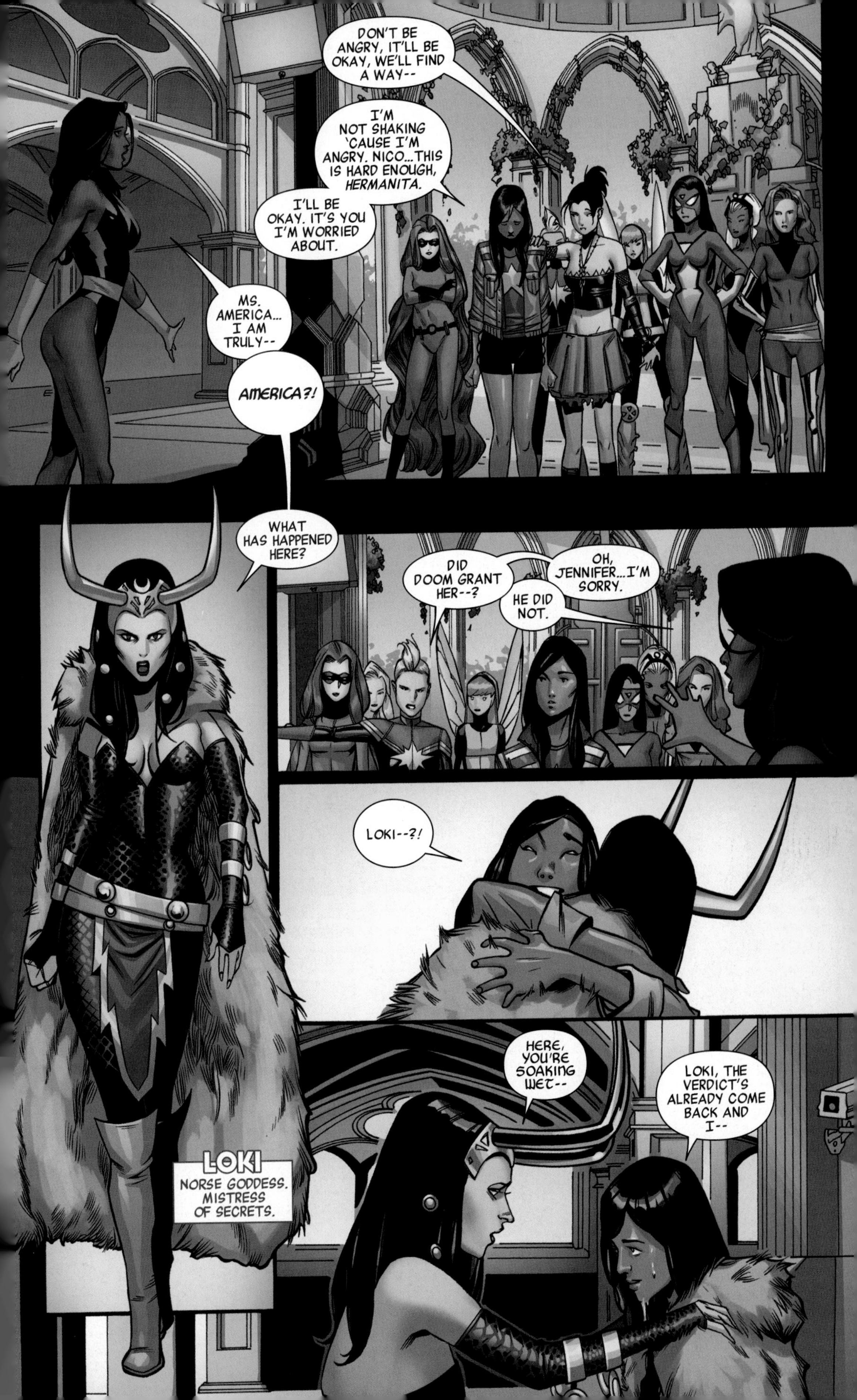

DON'T BE ANGRY, IT'LL BE OKAY, WE'LL FIND A WAY--
I'M NOT SHAKING 'CAUSE I'M ANGRY. NICO...THIS IS HARD ENOUGH, *HERMANITA.*
I'LL BE OKAY. IT'S YOU I'M WORRIED ABOUT.
MS. AMERICA... I AM TRULY--
AMERICA?!
WHAT HAS HAPPENED HERE?
DID DOOM GRANT HER--?
OH, JENNIFER...I'M SORRY.
HE DID NOT.
LOKI--?!
LOKI
NORSE GODDESS. MISTRESS OF SECRETS.
HERE, YOU'RE SOAKING WET--
LOKI, THE VERDICT'S ALREADY COME BACK AND I--

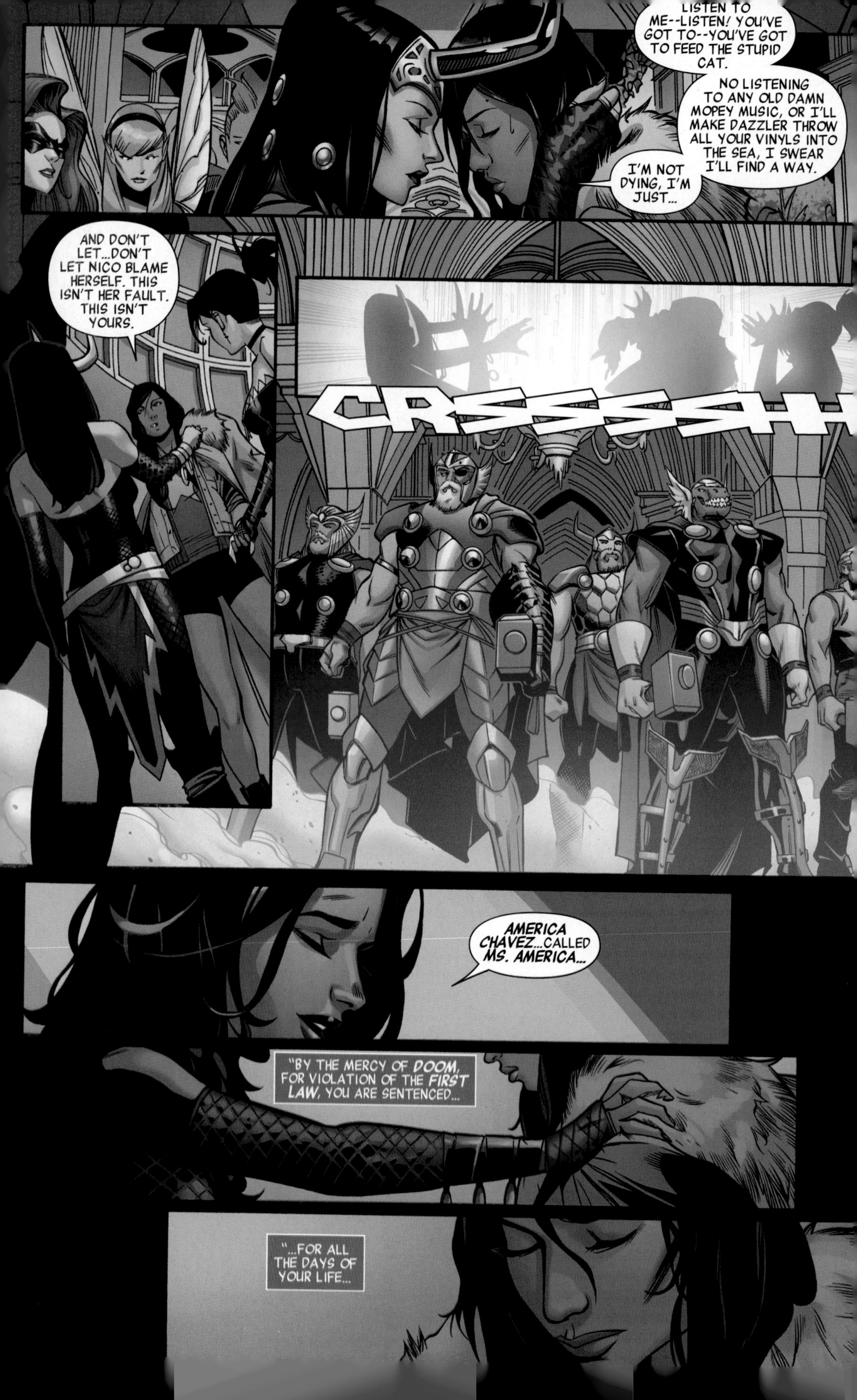

LISTEN TO ME--LISTEN! YOU'VE GOT TO--YOU'VE GOT TO FEED THE STUPID CAT.
NO LISTENING TO ANY OLD DAMN MOPEY MUSIC, OR I'LL MAKE DAZZLER THROW ALL YOUR VINYLS INTO THE SEA, I SWEAR I'LL FIND A WAY.
I'M NOT DYING, I'M JUST...
AND DON'T LET...DON'T LET NICO BLAME HERSELF. THIS ISN'T HER FAULT. THIS ISN'T YOURS.
CRSSSSHH
AMERICA CHAVEZ...CALLED MS. AMERICA...
"BY THE MERCY OF DOOM, FOR VIOLATION OF THE FIRST LAW, YOU ARE SENTENCED...
"...FOR ALL THE DAYS OF YOUR LIFE...

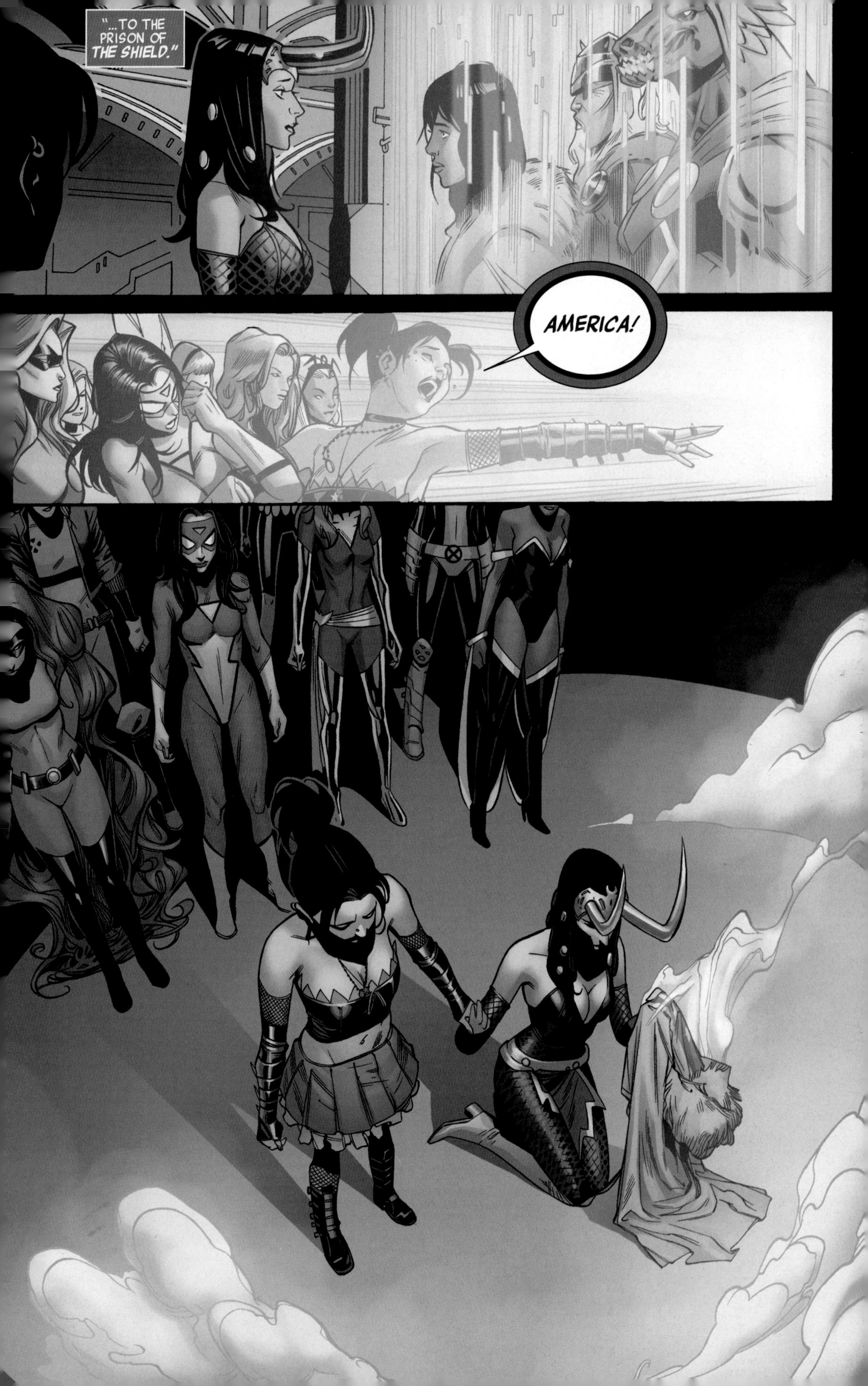
"...TO THE PRISON OF THE SHIELD."
AMERICA!

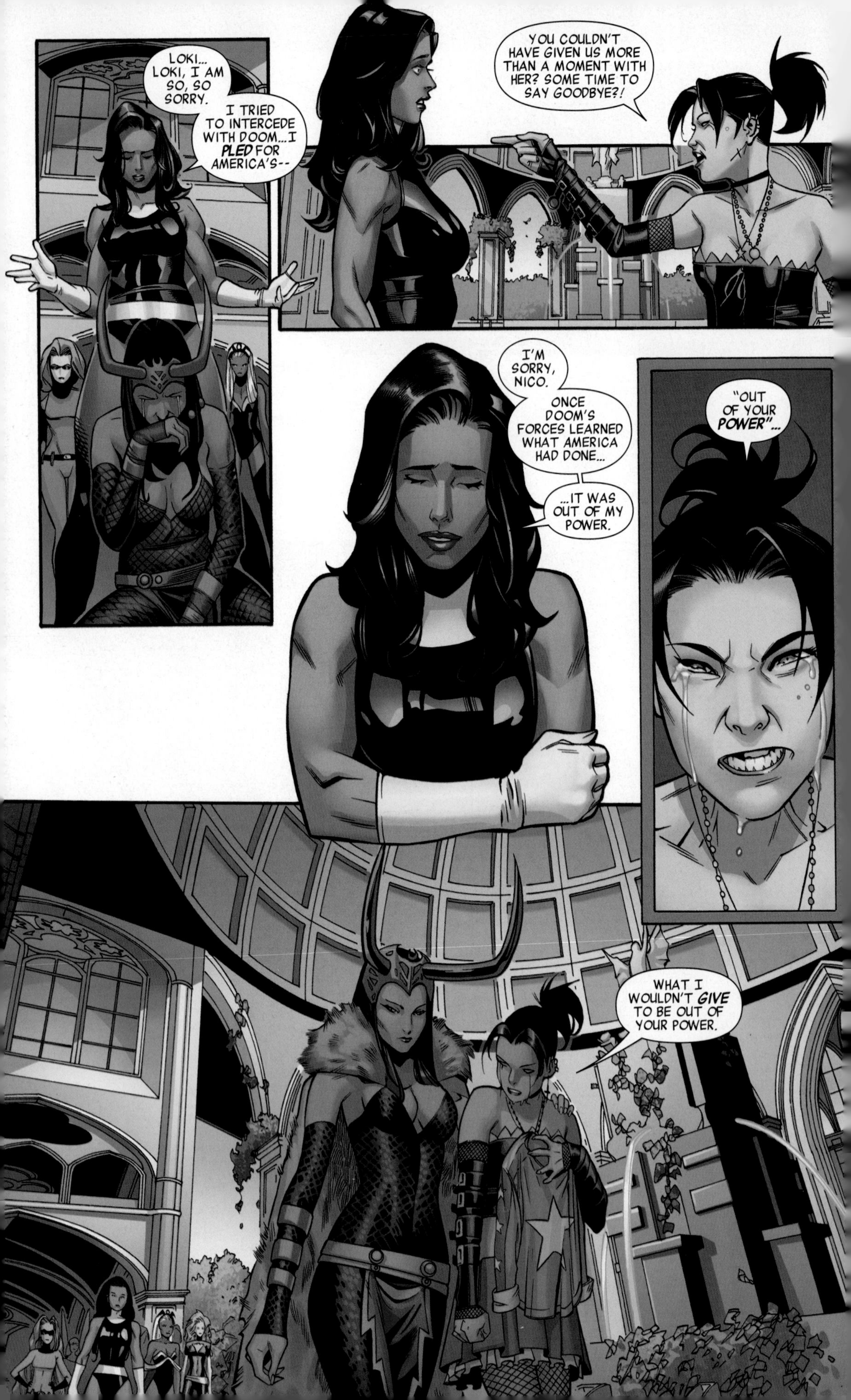
LOKI... LOKI, I AM SO, SO SORRY.
I TRIED TO INTERCEDE WITH DOOM...I PLED FOR AMERICA'S--
YOU COULDN'T HAVE GIVEN US MORE THAN A MOMENT WITH HER? SOME TIME TO SAY GOODBYE?!
I'M SORRY, NICO.
ONCE DOOM'S FORCES LEARNED WHAT AMERICA HAD DONE...
...IT WAS OUT OF MY POWER.
"OUT OF YOUR POWER"...
WHAT I WOULDN'T GIVE TO BE OUT OF YOUR POWER.

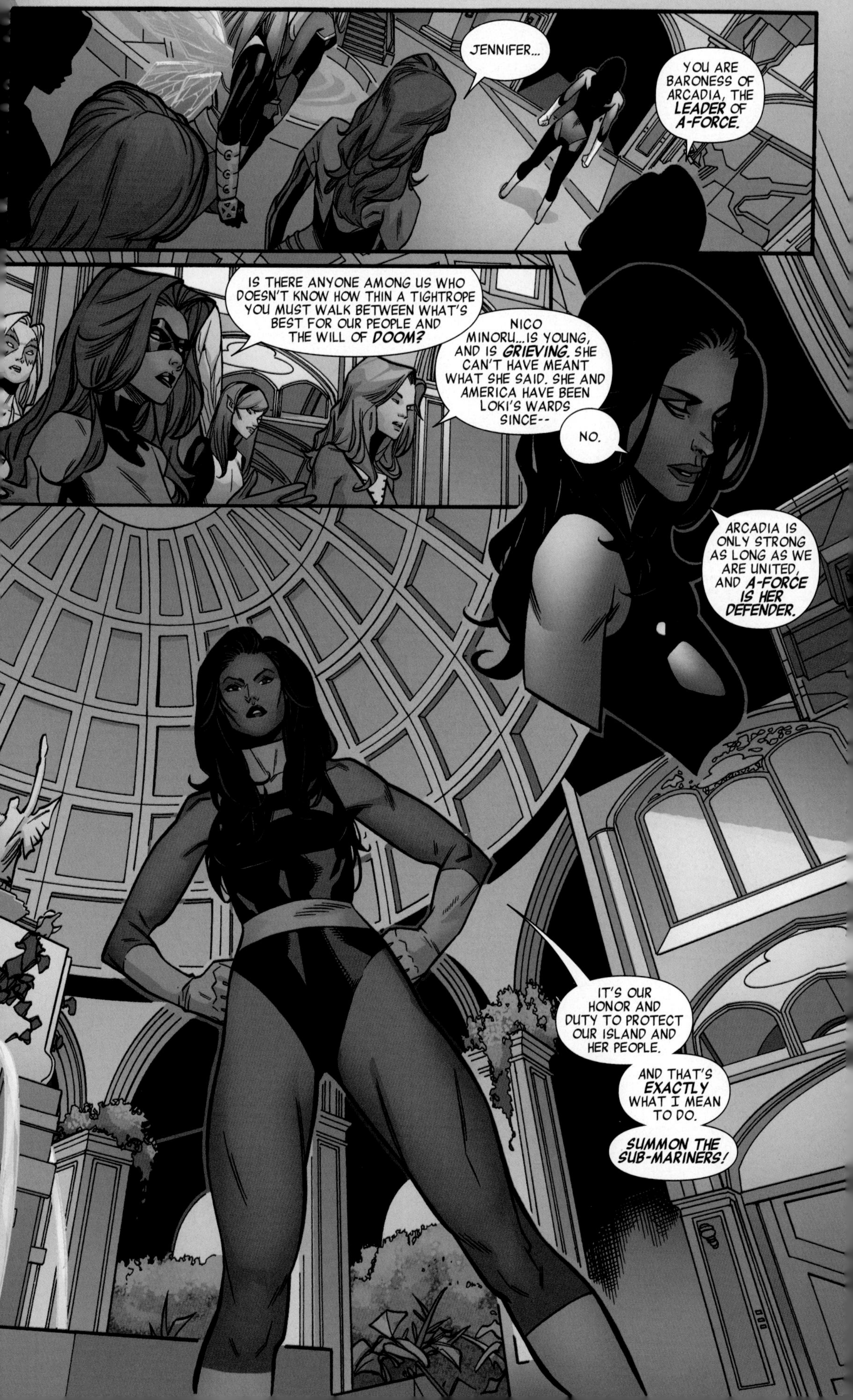
JENNIFER...
YOU ARE BARONESS OF ARCADIA, THE LEADER OF A-FORCE.
IS THERE ANYONE AMONG US WHO DOESN'T KNOW HOW THIN A TIGHTROPE YOU MUST WALK BETWEEN WHAT'S BEST FOR OUR PEOPLE AND THE WILL OF DOOM?
NICO MINORU...IS YOUNG, AND IS GRIEVING. SHE CAN'T HAVE MEANT WHAT SHE SAID. SHE AND AMERICA HAVE BEEN LOKI'S WARDS SINCE--
NO.
ARCADIA IS ONLY STRONG AS LONG AS WE ARE UNITED, AND A-FORCE IS HER DEFENDER.
IT'S OUR HONOR AND DUTY TO PROTECT OUR ISLAND AND HER PEOPLE.
AND THAT'S EXACTLY WHAT I MEAN TO DO.
SUMMON THE SUB-MARINERS!

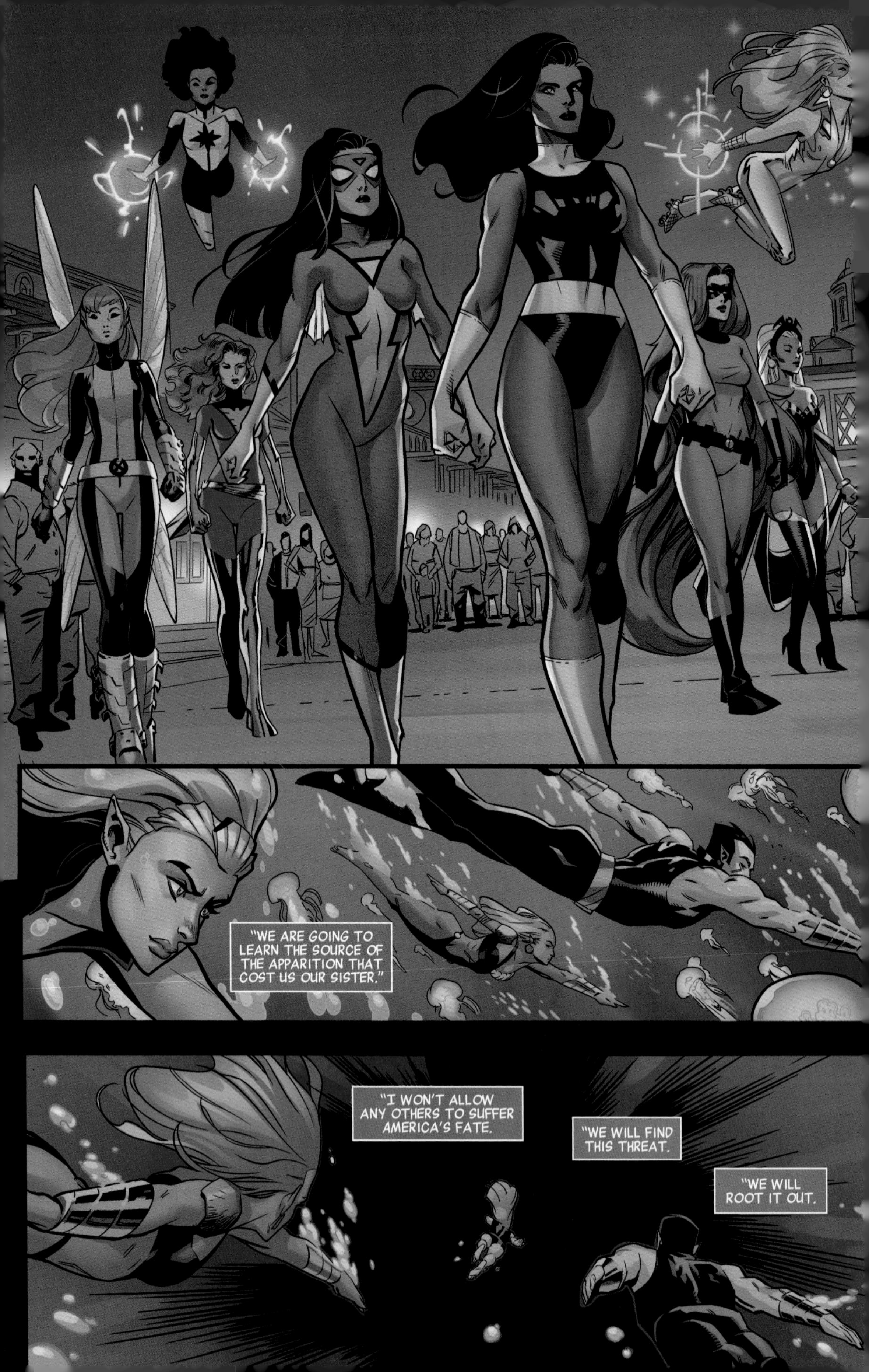
"WE ARE GOING TO LEARN THE SOURCE OF THE APPARITION THAT COST US OUR SISTER."
"I WON'T ALLOW ANY OTHERS TO SUFFER AMERICA'S FATE.
"WE WILL FIND THIS THREAT.
"WE WILL ROOT IT OUT.

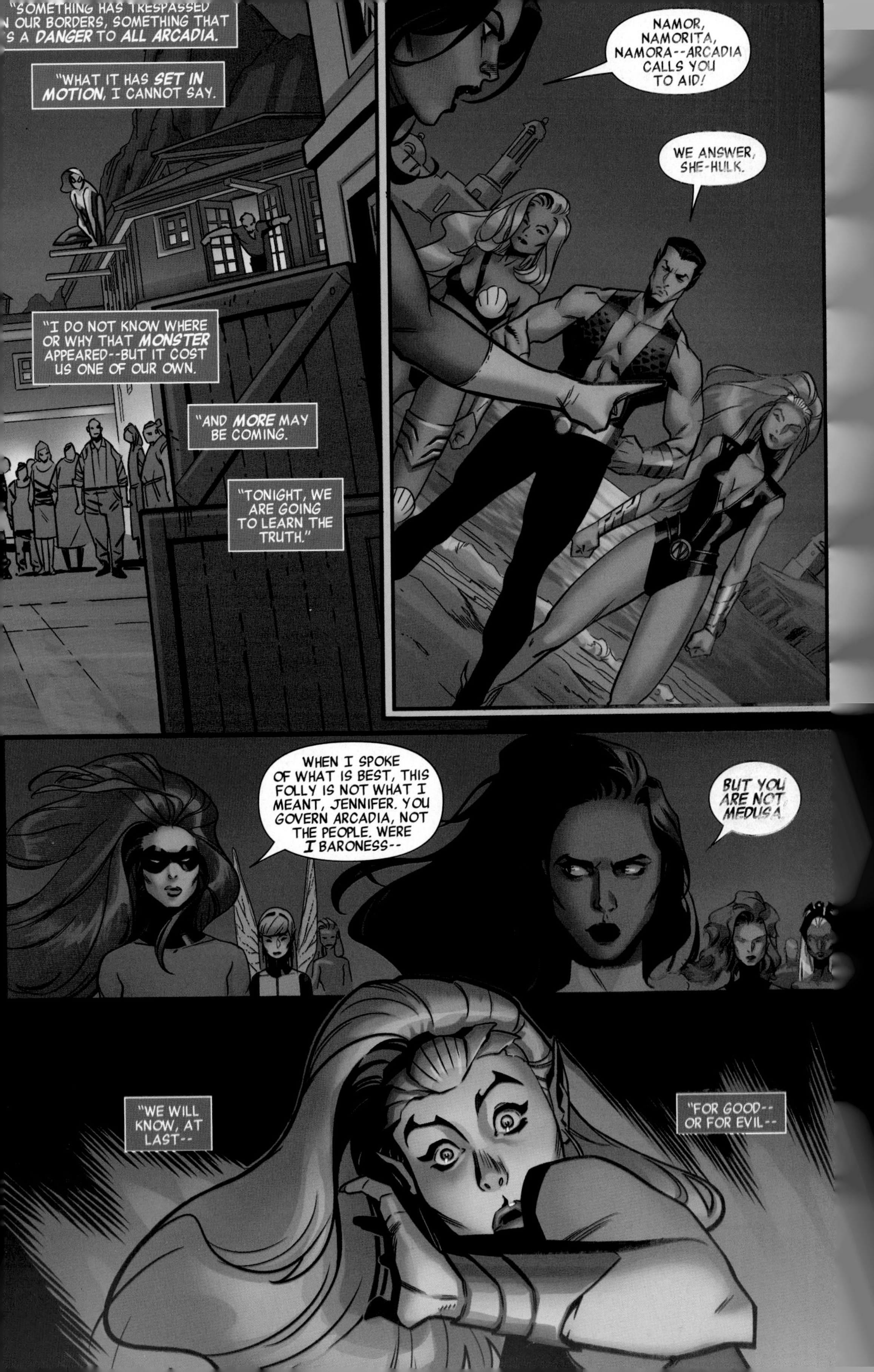
"SOMETHING HAS TRESPASSED ON OUR BORDERS, SOMETHING THAT IS A DANGER TO ALL ARCADIA.
"WHAT IT HAS SET IN MOTION, I CANNOT SAY.
"I DO NOT KNOW WHERE OR WHY THAT MONSTER APPEARED--BUT IT COST US ONE OF OUR OWN.
"AND MORE MAY BE COMING.
"TONIGHT, WE ARE GOING TO LEARN THE TRUTH."
NAMOR, NAMORITA, NAMORA--ARCADIA CALLS YOU TO AID!
WE ANSWER, SHE-HULK.
WHEN I SPOKE OF WHAT IS BEST, THIS FOLLY IS NOT WHAT I MEANT, JENNIFER. YOU GOVERN ARCADIA, NOT THE PEOPLE. WERE I BARONESS--
BUT YOU ARE NOT MEDUSA.
"WE WILL KNOW, AT LAST--
"FOR GOOD-- OR FOR EVIL--

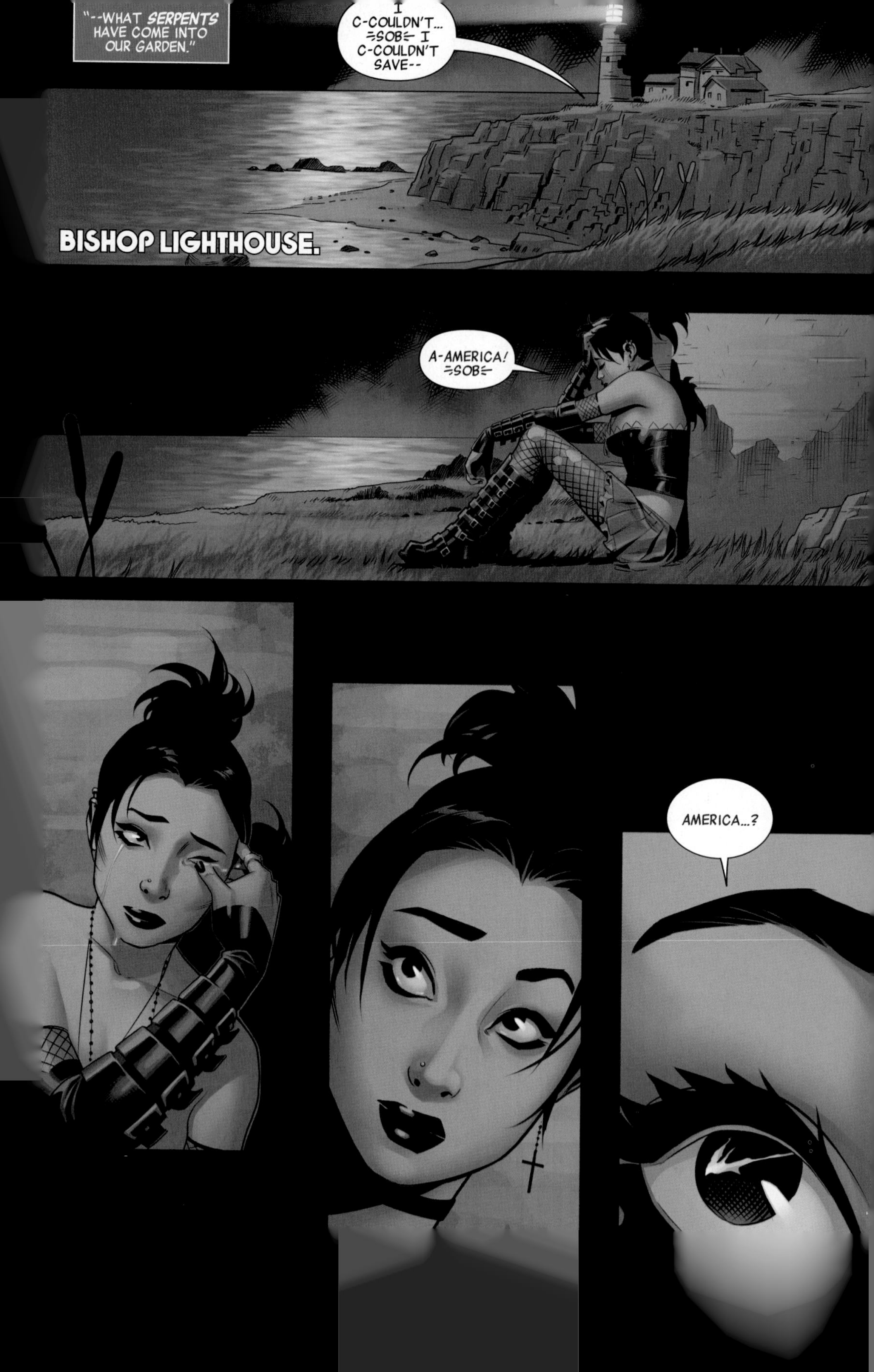
"--WHAT SERPENTS HAVE COME INTO OUR GARDEN."
I C-COULDN'T... =SOB= I C-COULDN'T SAVE--
BISHOP LIGHTHOUSE.
A-AMERICA! =SOB=
AMERICA...?

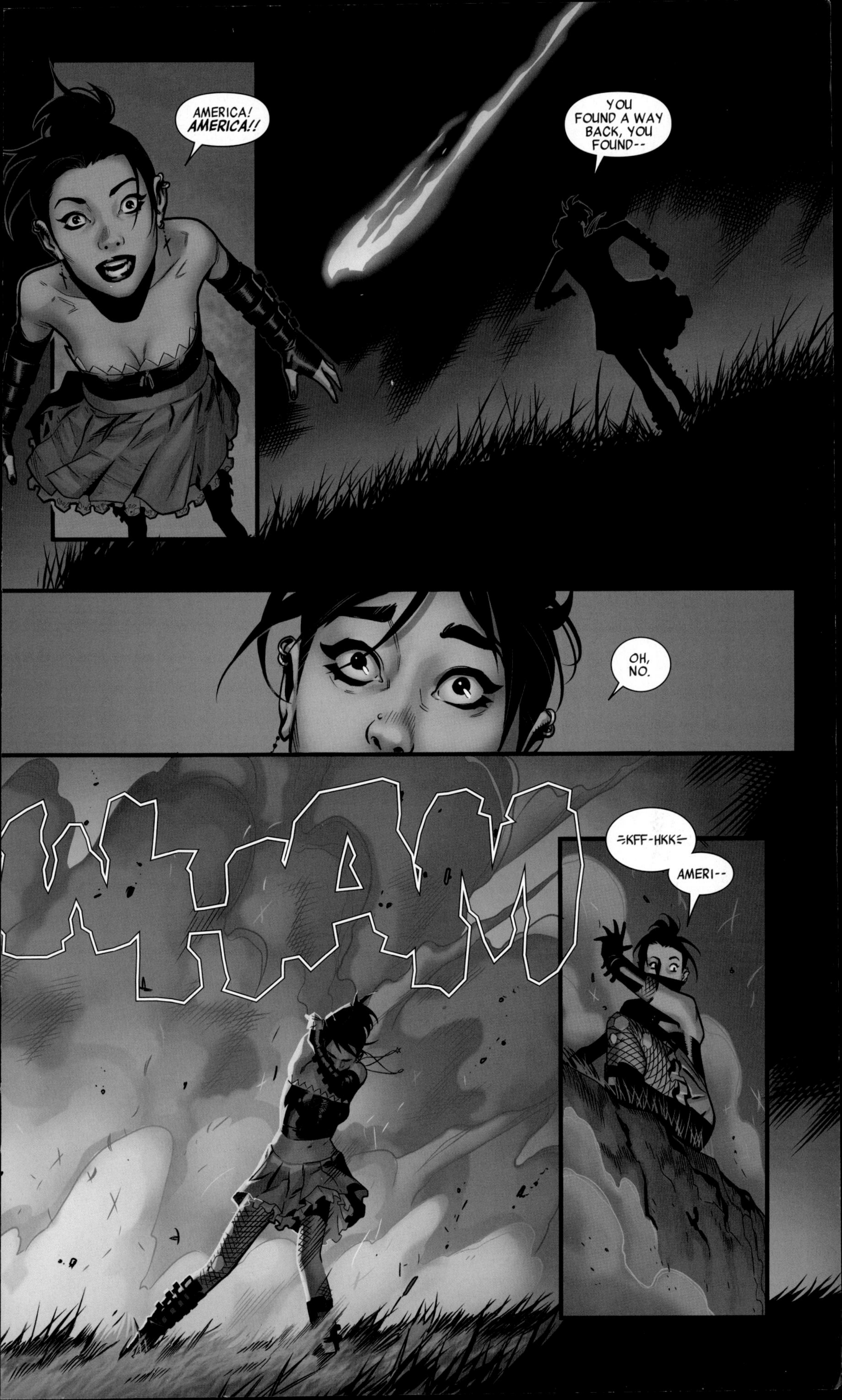
AMERICA! AMERICA!!
YOU FOUND A WAY BACK, YOU FOUND--
OH, NO.
WHAM
=KFF-HKK=
AMERI--

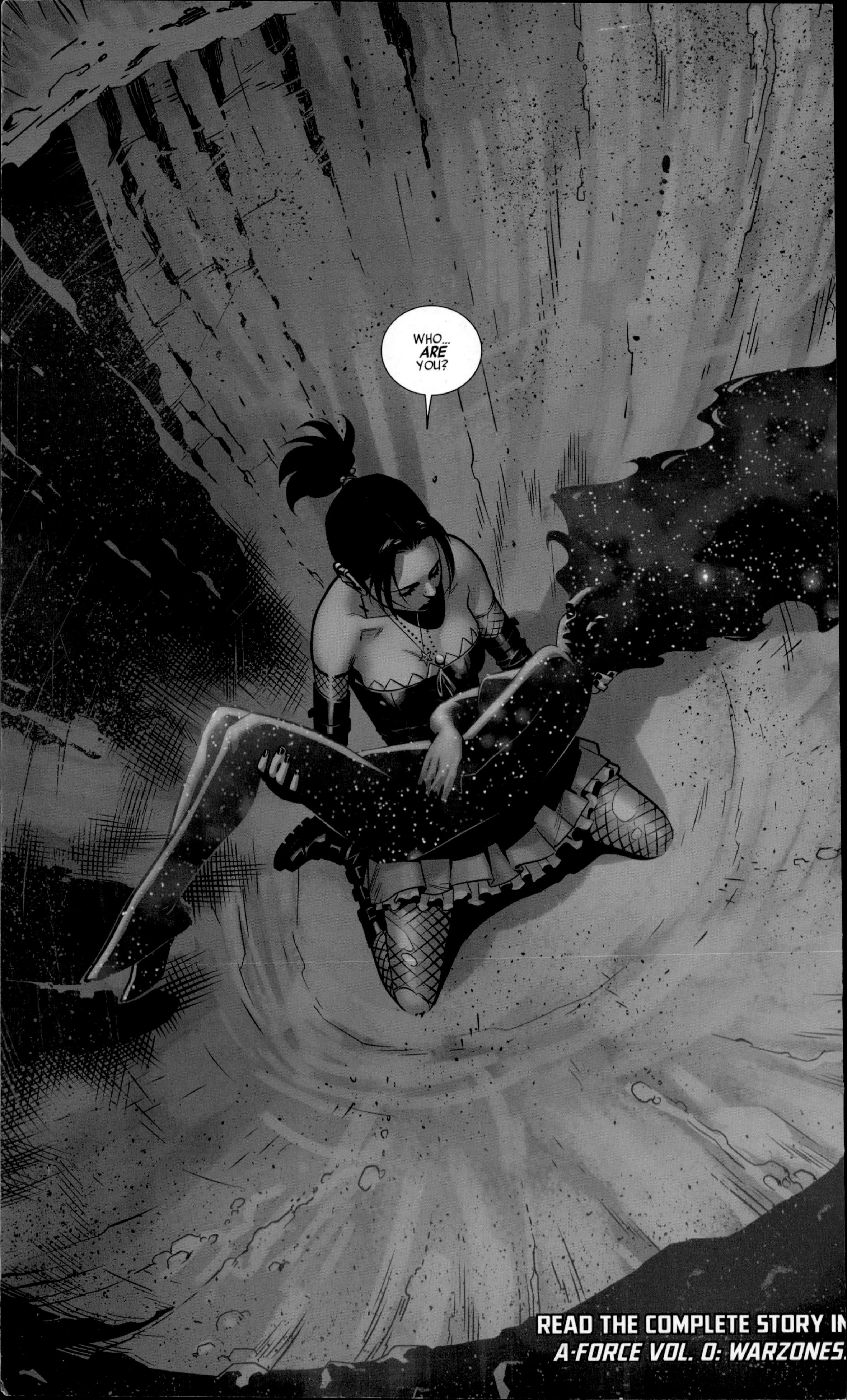
WHO... ARE YOU?
READ THE COMPLETE STORY IN
A-FORCE VOL. 0: WARZONES!

#1 HIP-HOP VARIANT BY **ADAM HUGHES**

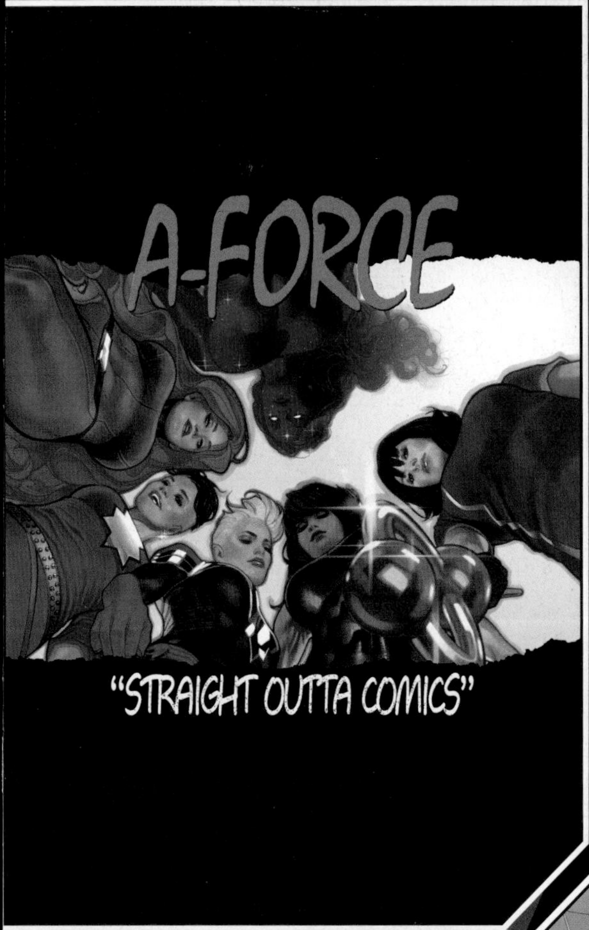
A-FORCE
"STRAIGHT OUTTA COMICS"

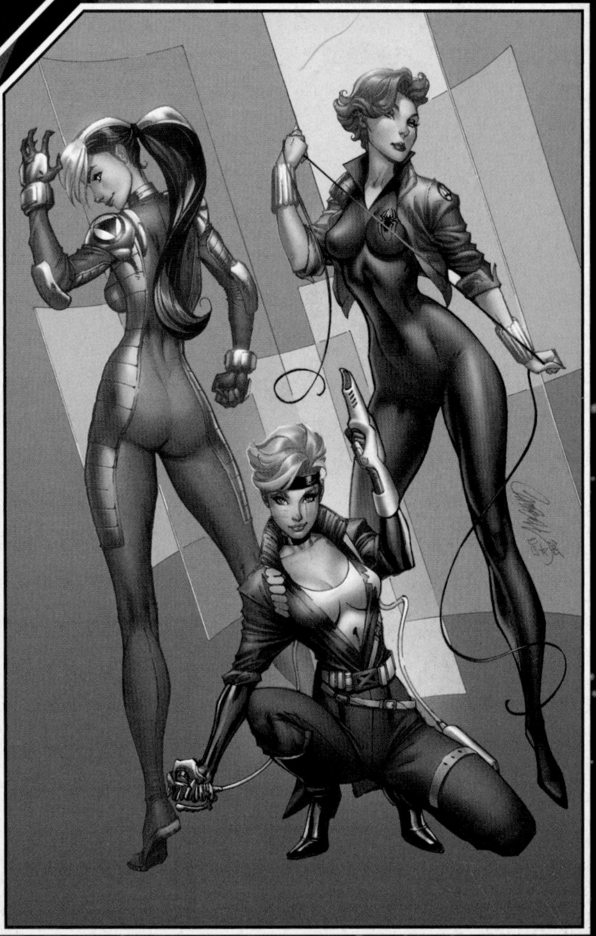

#1 MARVEL '92 VARIANT
BY **J. SCOTT CAMPBELL** & **NEI RUFFINO**

#3 VARIANT BY **MARK BROOKS**

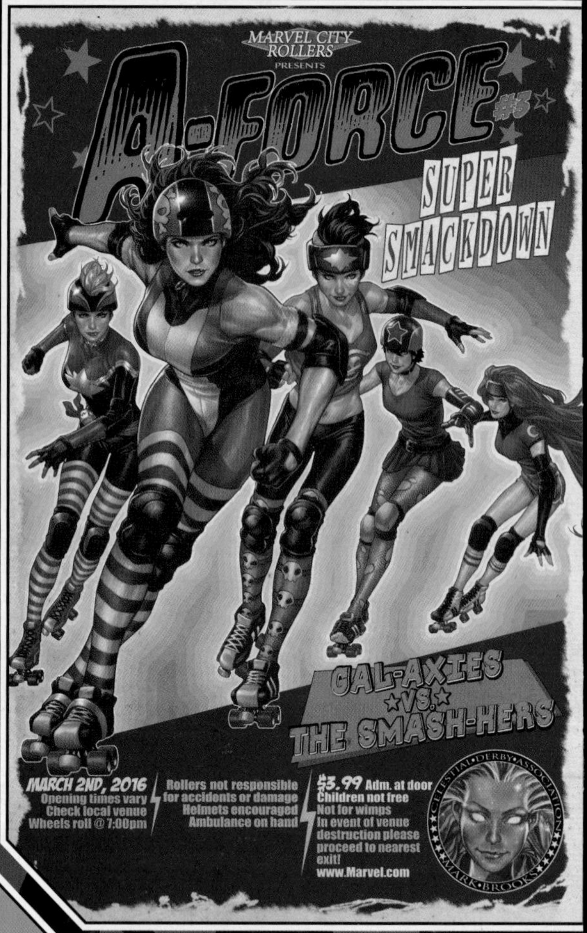
MARVEL CITY ROLLERS
PRESENTS
A-FORCE #3
SUPER SMACKDOWN
GAL-AXIES ★VS.★ THE SMASH-HERS
MARCH 2ND, 2016
Opening times vary
Check local venue
Wheels roll @ 7:00pm
Rollers not responsible
for accidents or damage
Helmets encouraged
Ambulance on hand
$3.99 Adm. at door
Children not free
Not for wimps
In event of venue
destruction please
proceed to nearest
exit!
www.Marvel.com
CELESTIAL•DERBY•ASSOCIATION
MARK•BROOKS

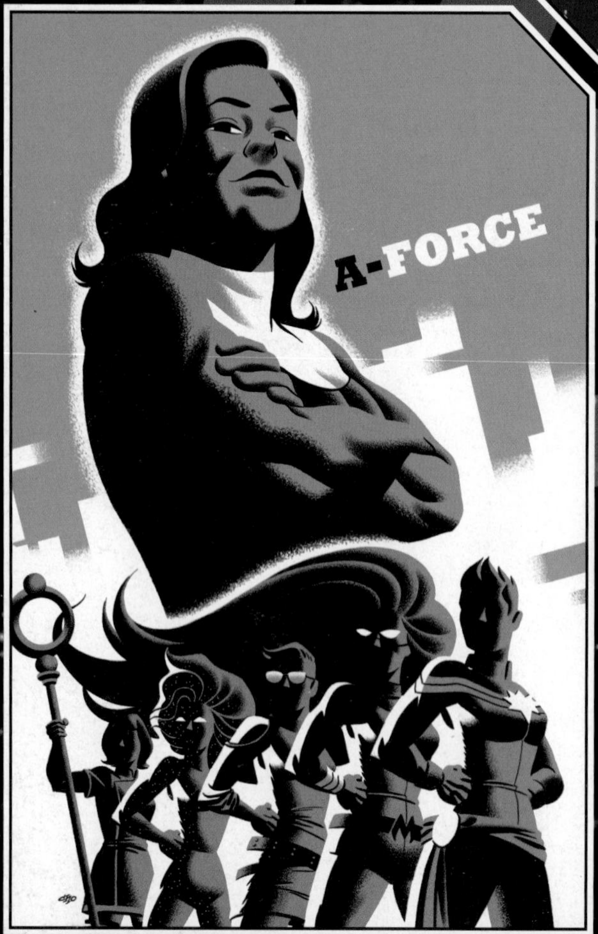
A-FORCE

#3 VARIANT BY **MICHAEL CHO**

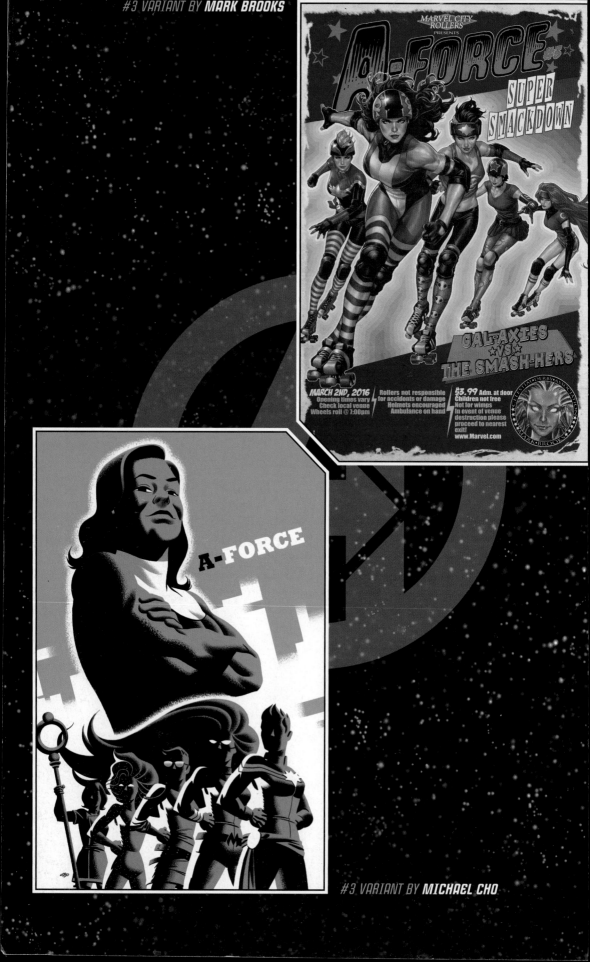